The Modern
War Machine

PUTNAM'S HISTORY OF AIRCRAFT

The Modern War Machine

Military Aviation since 1945

Series Editor: Philip Jarrett

PUTNAM

Title page photograph: In 1958 the USAF's 335th Tactical Fighter Squadron of the 4th Tactical Fighter Wing, Tactical Air Command, based at Eglin Air Force Base, became the world's first combat squadron to be equipped with Mach 2 strike aircraft when it took delivery of Republic F-105B Thunderchiefs. First to arrive was F-105B-6RE Thunderchief 54-0111, the sole example of the 'Bravo Six' variant, which arrived in the spring of the year and is seen here with its four-petal speed brake open.

The Modern War Machine

Series Editor: Philip Jarrett

Philip Jarrett is a freelance author, editor, sub-editor and consultant specialising in aviation. He began writing on aviation history in 1967, and in 1971 became assistant editor of *Aerospace*, the Royal Aeronautical Society's newspaper. He was assistant editor of *Aeroplane Monthly* from 1973 to 1980, and production editor of *Flight International* from 1980 to 1989.

Dr David Baker

David Baker has worked for NASA and the US Department of Defense for thirty years. He was involved with mission planning on projects such as Apollo and the Shuttle, before working in aerospace business development. He serves on several advisory boards and runs the consulting firm Sigma Aerospace. He has written more than sixty books and is currently the editor of *Jane's Aircraft Upgrades* and *Aerospace Review*.

Keith Chapman

Group Captain Keith Chapman served in the RAF from 1960 to 1994, a career that culminated in command of a Hercules squadron. His other appointments included tours as RAF member of the directing staff at the British Army Staff College; Deputy Director of Air Transport Operations in the Ministry of Defence; and Chief of NATO's International Airlift Control Element.

Norman Friedman

Norman Friedman works as a naval analyst at the Hudson Institute in New York and lectures around the world. Described as 'America's leading naval writer', he is the author of numerous articles and more than twenty books, including *British Carrier Aviation* and *Naval Institute Guide to World Naval Weapons Systems*.

Robert Jackson

A former pilot and navigation instructor, and a squadron leader in the Royal Air Force Volunteer Reserve, Robert Jackson is now a full-time writer and lecturer, and defence correspondent for several national newspapers. He has written more than sixty factual works on aviation and military subjects, as well as regular popular science features. He is also the author of over twenty novels, mostly set in the Second World War.

Air Vice-Marshal R A Mason, CB, CBE, MA, DSc

Tony Mason is Director of the Centre for Studies in Security and Diplomacy at the University of Birmingham. He retired from the RAF in 1989. For more than twenty years he has written and spoken internationally on air warfare, defence policy and international security. His most recent publications include *Air Power: A Centennial Appraisal* and *The Aerospace Revolution*.

Elfan ap Rees

Elfan ap Rees has been involved with helicopters for more than thirty years, owning and publishing the journals *Helicopter International* and *Helidata News*, and, from 1969, building up a collection of historic rotorcraft that today forms the nucleus of the International Helicopter Museum. He also represents the helicopter industry on several national and international bodies.

Jeremy C Scutts

Jerry Scutts has been a freelance aviation author since 1970 and to date has published more than forty books, some of which have included his own profile and perspective artwork. A journalist and editor for over twenty years, he was a press officer with the UK Civil Aviation Authority in the early 1980s, before publishing his own aviation magazine. He specialises in combat aircraft operations and markings, with an emphasis on the US air forces and the Luftwaffe.

Mike Spick

Mike Spick is a full-time aviation writer and commentator, with almost forty books to his name. An associate of the Royal Aeronautical Society, he is also a consultant to *AirForces Monthly*, the Swiss-based Project Atlas and, more recently, Microsoft Corporation.

© Putnam Aeronautical Books 2000

First published in Great Britain in 2000 by Putnam Aeronautical Books, a division of Chrysalis Books Ltd
9 Blenheim Court, Brewery Road
London N7 9NT
Telephone: 020 7700 7611
Fax: 020 7700 4552
Web: www.putnamaeronautical.com

A member of the Chrysalis Group plc

A CIP catalogue record for this book is available from the British Library.

ISBN 0 85177 880 1

Printed and bound in Spain
Printed and bound in Spain by Bookprint, S.L, Barcelona

Contents

Introduction
Philip Jarrett

At the end of the Second World War the aeroplane was undergoing changes more fundamental than those affecting any other transport vehicle. The piston-engined aeroplane was reaching the limits of its performance. Pilots were encountering compressibility in high-speed dives, which caused violent buffeting and loss of control as supersonic shockwaves affected some areas of the their machines. Moreover, the engines were approaching the limits of development, and the tips of their propellers were going supersonic even earlier than the affected areas of the airframe, and generating more noise than thrust. Aircraft particularly affected by this problem were the Hawker Typhoon, Lockheed P-38 Lightning and Republic P-47 Thunderbolt. Late-war designs such as the Hawker Sea Fury and de Havilland Hornet represented the ultimate generation of high-speed piston-engined aircraft.

Seemingly on cue, in Germany and Great Britain, the jet engine reached a state of development at which it could be put into service in military aircraft, and an entirely different means of propulsion was available to take the aeroplane through the 'sound barrier'. However, the new regimes of transonic and supersonic flight demanded increased research into supersonic aerodynamics, a subject that had been somewhat neglected by the Allies, but to which the Germans had devoted a great deal of attention. That early wartime work formed the foundation of postwar research in the Allied nations. In parallel, structures, flying controls, instrumentation and avionics were also the subject of rapid development. Many lessons were learnt, often at the cost of brave test pilots' lives, aircraft capabilities were expanded and developed, and new operational techniques perfected. Aviation was entering yet another new and exciting era, but it was also an era full of ominous threats to the world peace that so many had hoped for after six years of war.

The great divide that opened up between the Western powers and the Eastern Bloc nations brought global insecurity and a Cold War, with the new and formidable threat of a nuclear conflict in which there would ultimately be no winners. By maintaining a delicate balance of deadly weaponry between the opposing forces, those in power averted Armageddon, though a continuous series of major confrontations centred on national, political or religious differences has kept the world in a state of permanent unrest. Armageddon has not gone; it is on

hold. Since the disappearance of the Iron Curtain, in fact, global imbalances and unrest have become even more destabilising. World peace, it seems, is only a dream for the common man. Ruthless, self-seeking governments, dictators and religious leaders continue to inflict pain and misery on millions in efforts to achieve their own ends.

In all of these conflicts aircraft have played significant and contrary roles, both as deliverers of aggression and bringers of mercy. It can be argued that aircraft have made war more terrifying than it could otherwise have been and increased the cost in human lives, but equally it might also be claimed that they have forestalled escalation and saved countless lives. After all, the aeroplane is only a man-made machine, and it is man who decides whether his creations are used wisely or otherwise. An inanimate object is simply the tool of man's destructive nature. The hard truth is that deterrent forces will be needed as long as there are seekers of ultimate power.

On the positive side, the constant demand for development and improvement has fed across into civil aviation, where spin-offs from military research have benefited mankind in many ways. New materials, advanced avionics and powerplant developments have made commercial aviation safer and both mechanically and financially more efficient.

In this volume leading aviation authors survey the development of military aircraft over the last half-century, and what an extraordinary half-century it has been. If the growth of aviation in the first five decades of powered flight seemed rapid, its advance in the succeeding fifty years has been truly phenomenal. As a simple example, aeroplane speeds rose from 30mph in 1903 to around the 700mph mark in 1953, but by 1967 a man had flown at well over 3,000mph, and flights at Mach 3 became routine for pilots of Lockheed's amazing SR-71 shortly thereafter.

Air Vice-Marshal Tony Mason sets the scene with an overview of significant developments and events that have shaped and reshaped 'The Air Warfare Requirement' over the years. He shows that sustaining strategic nuclear deterrence inhibited full identification of air warfare requirements, but that the ending of the Cold War has enabled those requirements to be recognised and met as the new century dawns.

The weaponry of air warfare forms the subject of Jerry Scutts's chapter, wherein the survival and predominance of conventional weapons is evident. While there was a threat of nuclear attack by long-range bombers, interceptors had to have the means of countering them before they could deliver their deadly cargoes, and progress from simple unguided rockets to complex and expensive missiles with their own guidance systems was inevitable and rapid. Guns, on the other hand, developed more slowly, but both defensive and offensive weapons of awesome firepower are now in common use, either integral with the aircraft or carried in pods. The advent of the gunship, with its formidable battery of multi-barrelled guns, is also recorded. As far as bombs are concerned, armouries can now include everything from conventional 'dumb' bombs to the ultimate weapon, the cruise missile, which can be launched against its target from a great distance.

In his second chapter, Jerry Scutts surveys the evolution of the heart of the combat aeroplane, the jet engine, and looks at the wide and varied applications, successful and otherwise. Britain's sad failure to exploit the Rolls-Royce Nene in its own combat aircraft was compounded by its speedy adoption in the USSR, where, as the author records, it 'formed the basis of the entire Soviet powerplant manufacturing programme'. Persistent and significant developments in technology and materials have resulted in engines of outstanding reliability and extraordinary power, but the powerplants of the military aircraft of the new century will put even these masterpieces of the engineer's craft into the shade.

Powerful engines are useless without suitable airframes, and Dr David Baker examines the advances in aerodynamics and structures which have enabled barriers that once seemed insurmountable to be pushed aside. Swept wings, area rule, variable geometry and high-speed aerofoils were developed, while sophisticated alloys and composites, and new structural techniques, overcame the problems of stress and strain that were beyond the tolerance of traditional materials. The 'brute force' approach, in which individual engineering teams competed to preserve their own elements in a design, has given way to a new engineering attitude, in which every element is integrated into a total system to evolve the optimum design. Finally, the author looks at the latest advances in manoeuvrability and stealth.

Norman Friedman's following chapter covers the enormous strides made in military avionics: the radar, weapon-aiming, missile-guidance and targeting systems that have made a deadly game far more deadly, and the electronic devices and systems that track, interpret and deceive. He also charts the relatively recent but drastic changes to the pilot's workplace, which have seen the traditional instrument panel with its mass of analogue instruments replaced by the multifunctional screens of the digital-avionics era.

In 'Offensive Aircraft in a New Age', Robert Jackson begins with a study the greatest strategic bomber of the post-Second World War era, the Boeing B-52 Stratofortress, still in service after more than forty years, albeit with essential periodic updates and modifications. Its participation in the Vietnam War and its adaptation to carry air-launched cruise missiles is covered. Its successors, the B-1B and stealthy B-2, and its Soviet counterparts, including the Tupolev Tu-16 and Tu-22, are also discussed. The author then turns his attention on the interdictors, spotlighting the F-111, F-15, Panavia Tornado and F-117, and finally looks at aircraft designed to fulfil the battlefield-support role.

As Elfan ap Rees points out, it has taken a long time for the attack helicopter to achieve dominance on the battlefield. His chapter tells the story of that development, which has resulted in machines far removed from the original attack helicopters of the 1950s and 1960s, 'arguably the most sophisticated weapons systems available on the battlefield' in the author's opinion. Whereas those first attack helicopters were relatively crude adaptations of standard models, the latest are purpose-designed for the mission, heavily armed and armoured.

As well as tracing the evolution of the modern defensive fighter, with its high manoeuvrability and the capability to engage an opponent either at close range or beyond visual range, in the next chapter Robert Jackson describes some of the manoeuvres that have stood the test of time and war. While one, the simple break, dates back to the First World War, others have been devised to meet the demands of jet-age encounters. Strategic interceptors, electronic support and air-combat training are also covered here, and a double-page spread is devoted to the classic period cutaway drawing of the revolutionary Lockheed F-104 Starfighter by that master of the genre, Frank Munger.

Airlift operations are an essential part of military actions in distant theatres or remote locations, and Keith Chapman examines their increasing importance since 1945, highlighting specific examples of successful and unsuccessful operations. The need to move men, equipment and essential support supplies over intercontinental distances at short notice resulted in the establishment of substantial airlift capabilities by the world's major air arms, and the principal aircraft currently used are described, including logistic helicopters.

Another essential role is tactical support, which embraces such duties as photographic and electronic reconnaissance, electronic countermeasures, and maritime and battlefield reconnaissance. As Mike Spick recounts, these tasks have been undertaken both by variants of standard aircraft and aircraft designed specifically for particular roles. Undoubtedly the outstanding examples of the latter are the extraordinary Lockheed U-2 and SR-71 high-altitude reconnaissance aircraft, which have allowed the USA to gain vital intelligence information with impunity.

A glimpse into the future is provided by Robert Jackson, who describes the development of next-generation aircraft including Eurofighter, the Dassault Rafale and the Lockheed F-22. He also spotlights the growing use of remotely piloted vehicles in the reconnaissance role, which has undoubtedly saved many pilots' lives and costly manned aircraft, and the advent of smart bullets, which will be able to follow the evolutions of the target aircraft as its pilot endeavours to avoid being hit. Until relatively recently such weapons were the subjects of science fiction; they are now on the verge of practical application.

Finally, Norman Friedman surveys the development of naval aviation. The adaptation of jet aircraft for carrier operation, and, conversely, the adaptation of the carrier for jet aircraft, was accomplished with great success. Nonetheless, this prime means of force projection went through some very difficult times, in the face of both military and political opposition. The author describes the advent of the commando carrier and the small carrier, made possible by the unique capabilities of the Sea Harrier, and also traces developments in antisubmarine warfare. The aircraft carrier has certainly proved its worth in recent years, in the troubled Middle East for instance, and the indications are that, despite their enormous cost, carriers will continue to be built into the foreseeable future, probably operating a smaller assortment of multirole aircraft.

The advent of pilotless combat aircraft has been predicted repeatedly over the postwar decades, but it seems that their time may at last be approaching. Freedom from the limitations of human physiology would certainly endow such aircraft with unprecedented performance and manoeuvrability, but there is always the nagging thought that, sometimes, a human being is needed to make those vital judgements and decisions that are based on more than plain data.

Philip Jarrett

1
The Air Warfare Requirement
Air Vice-Marshal Tony Mason

The end of the Second World War followed closely upon the dropping of two atomic bombs by United States Army Air Force (USAAF) Boeing B-29s on Hiroshima and Nagasaki in August 1945. During the war air warfare had played an increasingly prominent role in every theatre. It had powered German *blitzkreig* into Western Europe and to the gates of Moscow; it had denied Hitler the opportunity to invade Britain in 1940; close air and surface co-operation had been forged in North Africa, northwestern Europe, in the Pacific and in the Atlantic; in 1944 the Allied air forces prepared the way for the successful Normandy invasion; and the combined bomber offensive had forced large proportions of German war industry to give priority to home defence, severely constrained production and finally starved German armed forces of fuel and oils.

By the war's end there were few doubts about the overall contribution of air power. For USAAF General Carl Spaatz strategic air power was:

> ... the most powerful instrument of war thus far known, because of its ability to concentrate force from widely dispersed parts on to specific targets, because it could penetrate deeply to destroy vital targets beyond the reach of armies and navies and because it could be economical in the force required to concentrate on a limited number of vital target systems; in sum, strategic bombing was the first war instrument of history capable of stopping the heart mechanism of a great industrialised country.

General Bradley of the US Army observed:

> Granting the axiomatic and supreme importance of air superiority ... a proper conception of the term regards it as securing control of the air in order to ensure the unrestricted use of that element in carrying out offensive operations against the enemy, not only in the air but on land and sea.

British Admiral of the Fleet Hill Norton subsequently wrote: 'One lesson [of the war] was that no naval commander could hope to survive long without air power while his fleet was within range of enemy air power.'

During the war, the impact on air power of radar, jet engines, rocket technology, electronic warfare and, above all, of the atomic weapon, was dramatic. Comprehensive analysis of that impact did not, however, immediately take place. Unfortunately, the shadow of further conflict

between the victorious allies quickly arose, and consequently the 'lessons' that were drawn and projected into the new confrontation were based on personal experience, perception and incomplete evidence. For the foreseeable future, 'air warfare requirements' would be largely determined by a 'cold war' which would not occur.

In 1945 three countries possessed powerful air forces. Each would perceive different future cold warfare requirements, but only two would be able to allocate adequate resources to meet them.

Britain
The Gloster Meteor Mark I entered RAF service in July 1944, and the Mark III in August 1945. It was the only allied jet fighter to see combat. After the war more than 3,000 Meteors of different marks were built, several hundred being exported. Britain, however, was economically exhausted, and immediately cut back its military strength and aircraft production. Within eighteen months the RAF was reduced from 9,000 combat aircraft to 1,000. Re-equipment of fighter squadrons was slowed down and the entry into service of a jet bomber postponed until 1951. No long-term postwar planning had taken place, and the Air Staff gave priority in operational requirements to fighters that would climb swiftly to high-altitude combat height, and to medium- and long-range bombers that would, similarly, operate at high level, i.e. above 40,000ft (12,000m). The Air Staff appear to have had no doubts about the need to develop an atomic weapon carrier, but were very cautious about jet bomber development, being prepared, for the time being, to rely upon existing later-war-period aircraft such as the Avro Lincoln.

Consequently, while Britain secured a strong position in the contemporary international combat aircraft market, there was little British military postwar impetus to maintain that leadership with a successor generation. Sadly, with the exception of the revolutionary Harrier, Britain has not had a major influence on the evolution of combat aircraft since 1945.

Soviet Union
By 1945 the Soviet Union was able to produce 42,000 aircraft in one year, compared with British production of 26,000, and 93,000 in the USA. The majority, however, had single piston engines and were timber framed. In that year, however, probably four-fifths of German aircraft production fell into Soviet hands. Large numbers

Flown for the first time in 1947, the Soviet MiG-15 proved a formidable foe in the Korean War. These are Polish Air Force aircraft.

of complete aircraft, designers, engineers, chemists and fuel specialists were transported to the USSR.

Stalin gave priority to air defence, beginning the construction of early-warning radars and jet fighters. The swept-wing MiG-15 flew for the first time in December 1947. Earlier in the same year Soviet bomber deployment had begun with the Tupolev Tu-4, a reverse-engineered B-29. In 1949 the Soviet Union exploded its own atomic weapon, well ahead of the schedule expected in the West. When Soviet bomber development continued with the Myasishchyev M-4 and Tu-20 (95), concurrently with the construction of a number of bomber bases in Soviet Arctic territories, the scene was set for long-range, nuclear-capable East–West air force confrontation.

As the Cold War hardened, perception of Soviet capabilities came to dominate Western combat aircraft procurement. In Britain it reinforced the requirement for swift-climbing, high-altitude interceptors and penetrating bombers. In the USA it fostered the strategic concepts and ambitions of the USAF, which achieved its independence from the US Army in 1947.

The USSR equipped its allies, friends and sympathisers worldwide with fighters and light bombers. Soviet military aviation thus had a strong and sustained indirect influence on the evolution of postwar Western air power.

United States domination

In 1943, plans for an independent USAF were being prepared in Washington. By 1945 a large and politically influential group of aerospace industries had been established and a coherent military doctrine of 'strategic' air power was being formulated, based on the long-range bomber and the nuclear weapon. Alone of the victorious allies, the USA possessed the industrial strength, the economic resources, the political will and the military inclination to exploit the technological innovations of the Second World War. Since 1945, aircraft, weapons and systems procured for the USAF have dominated air warfare. For much of that time the USAF itself was dominated by concepts formulated immediately after the war. On some occasions the concepts were found wanting, with unwelcome results.

The nuclear priority

In November 1944 General H H (Hap) Arnold, Commanding General, USAAF, invited Dr Theodore Von Karman of the California Institute of Technology to prepare a blueprint for the postwar direction of US air

The first Soviet nuclear weapon carrier was the Tupolev Tu-4, a reverse-engineered Boeing B-29 which first appeared in 1947.

A Soviet Air Force miscellany on display at Moscow's Domodedovo Airfield in July 1967. The Myasischyev 3M, nearest, posed an intercontinental nuclear threat to the USA. Behind it are a Tupolev Tu-16 bomber and a Yakovlev Yak-28P interceptor.

power. In his memorandum the General set out the USAAF's central concepts. 'Strategic action against the enemy's economic resources' and 'tactical action against his armed forces' were the main concern. Major wars would continue, but global war 'must be contemplated'. 'Offensive, not defensive, weapons win wars. Counter-measures are of secondary importance'. Personnel casualties would 'continue to be distasteful' and the USA would 'continue to fight mechanical rather than man-power wars'. Requirements included 'more potent explosives, supersonic speed, greater mass offensive efficiency, increased weapon flexibility and control'.

Nine months later, immediately after the end of the war, Von Karman submitted a first report on *Long Range Research Problems of the AIR FORCES with a Review of German Plans and Development*. In his introduction he identified eight 'new aspects of warfare ... to be considered as fundamental realities' which should shape the future of US planning for research and development. He identified many of the major features of air power in the ensuing fifty years: manned and unmanned aircraft would move at speeds far beyond the velocity of sound; unmanned devices would strike targets at several thousand metres' range; small amounts of explosive would cause widespread destruction; air defences would rely heavily on surface-to-air missiles; very high speed would be necessary to penetrate such defences; all-weather navigation, communication and target-acquisition systems would arise, and long-range airborne forces would be supplied by air.

In the body of his report Von Karman called for analysis of long-range offensive operations to determine how far the manned bomber could be replaced by missiles. He emphasised the dividends that would accrue from overcoming the limitations of night and bad weather, and went on to specify the importance of what would be known as airborne warning and control systems (AWACS):

Tremendous improvement in the control and marshalling of air forces appears possible through the medium of airborne radar. Control of air operations includes military functions, involving radar surveillance of movements of friendly and enemy aircraft and the guidance of our own planes on their missions.

In December 1945 Von Karman submitted a second report to General Arnold on behalf of the Army Air Forces Scientific Advisory Group, entitled *Towards New Horizons*. In it, Von Karman defined the postwar requirements and rationale of the USAAF. The tone was set in the opening paragraphs: 'Until recently, it was not generally recognized that destruction from the air is the most efficient method for defeating an enemy'. Because international control of atomic energy was unlikely to be achieved, atomic weapons would be used in future wars. An opponent's atomic capacity would be the first target of war to be attacked by air forces. Target locations would lie deep in enemy territory anywhere on the globe. A powerful air force was, therefore, required *inter alia*, capable of 'reaching remote targets swiftly and hitting them with great destructive power'. Hence, two basic requirements were long range and high speed.

Despite emphasising the likelihood of atomic or 'total' warfare, Von Karman counselled against total dependence upon nuclear weapons:

> In many cases of future warfare, we shall not be willing to use means of utter destruction … Economic and political reasons may suggest the use of conventional explosives as an alternative to atomic explosives…. Warfare is directed primarily to securing the safety of our nation and not to the indiscriminate destruction of others.

According to him, bomber effectiveness in the face of enemy air defences should be enhanced by increased speed, height and manoeuvrability rather than by 'reliance on complex and necessarily heavy defensive armament'. Conversely, interceptors should be procured with high rates of climb capable of intercepting 'the fastest and most manoeuvrable enemy bombers, reaching equal or higher altitudes than the enemy'. Overall, however, 'the best defence is adequate preparation for a strong offence'.

Although Arnold had invited Von Karman's Scientific Advisory Group to address both 'strategic' and 'tactical' actions, the study did not identify the problems of providing firepower support to friendly ground forces or of interdicting hostile formations, or their solutions.

The struggle for air superiority was conceived as taking place between interceptor and high-altitude bomber. No lessons were drawn from any of the Second World War theatres beyond the bombing campaigns against Germany and Japan, with the added destructive power of the atomic weapon. Problems of targeting, destruction, communications, electronic countermeasures, navigation and air defence were examined in careful and imaginative detail, but all were set in the context of strategic bombardment.

Von Karman's qualifications on the use of atomic weapons and the need to include ballistic missiles in the offensive equation were not echoed in official USAAF statements. In November 1945, in his *Third Report to the Secretary of War*, Arnold identified eight 'considerations'

associated with the 'future of aerial warfare', expressed in language almost identical to Von Karman's eight 'new aspects of warfare', but then proceeded to place unqualified emphasis on nuclear weapons. 'The influence of atomic energy can be stated very simply,' he wrote. 'It has made air power all important. Air power provides not only the best present means of striking an enemy with atomic bombs, but also the best available protection against the misuse of atomic explosives.' He continued by explaining the cost-effectiveness of atomic weapons delivered by long-range bombers. In future, when anti-aircraft defences should improve, the bomber could be replaced by the ballistic missile. Meanwhile, however, missile accuracy was poor, with a projected average error of 60 miles (95km) over a 3,000-mile (4,800km) range, and cost-effective improvements remained well in the future.

The Berlin Airlift

Arguably the most important contribution made by air power to the outcome of the Cold War occurred despite US preoccupation with strategic bombardment. Between June 1948 and September 1949 British, American and French transport aircraft broke the Soviet blockade on Berlin, escorted by fighters and supported by deployments of nuclear-capable B-29s to bases in Europe. President Truman overruled a USAF preference to retain the transports to carry unassembled nuclear bombs and supporting equipment for heavy-bomber deployments elsewhere.

The alternatives to the airlift were capitulation to Soviet pressure or the outbreak of a land war for which the West was ill-prepared. In the event, 2,325,808 tons of supplies were flown into the beleaguered city. Instead of marking a tightening of the Soviet grip on central Europe, Berlin was sustained, to become a symbol of Western determination and the irritant whose toppling walls ultimately became the symbol of the collapse of communism itself.

During the airlift the Western allies were transformed from occupying forces to protectors, and West Germany was enabled to adopt a new democratic constitution. The USA had demonstrated a new commitment to the freedom of Europe, while additional impetus was given to the creation of the North Atlantic Treaty Organisation (NATO) in April 1949. The Berlin Airlift, the first decisive battle in the Cold War, was won by the unfashionable, unglamorous transport arm. No weapons were discharged, but fifty-four British, American and German lives were given in the victory.

Strategic reconnaissance

Like all warfare, the Cold War stimulated a requirement for reconnaissance. The USSR covered an area of 8,649,500 square miles (22,393,500km^2). It was a closed society, and the only maps available to the newly established Strategic Air Command (SAC) in 1949 were based on Luftwaffe photographs largely restricted to territory west of the Urals, supplemented by some czarist regional maps and a 1912 Baedeker railway timetable. Without targeting information, concepts and capability for strategic bombing were valueless. Initially, reconnaissance missions were flown along the periphery of the Soviet Union, relying on slant-range radar and cameras. Boeing RB-29s and other aircraft flew electronic intelligence (ELINT) sorties to glean information about Soviet air defences. In 1952 and 1954 RAF crews flew North American RB-45s deep into Soviet airspace, and between 1946 and 1960 at least thirteen US aircraft and ninety airmen were lost on reconnaissance missions around or over Soviet territory.

In 1956 the Lockheed U-2 made its first overflight of the USSR, and the impact on US intelligence gathering was immediate. From an unassailable height of 70,000ft (21,000m), the U-2's Hycon B camera covered a swathe 150 miles (240km) wide with high resolution and 750 miles (1,200km) wide for general reconnaissance. Its ELINT collection systems acquired invaluable data on Soviet communications and air defences. Soviet bomber and missile production, location and capacity were revealed. Weapon test sites were monitored, and the whole of the SAC's target list was revised and expanded from 3 to 20,000 locations.

In 1962 information provided by U-2s formed the basis for US identification and management of the Cuban missile crisis, allowing both sides to step back from mutual destruction. Despite the loss of Gary Powers' U-2 to an SA-2 missile over the USSR in 1960, the aircraft has been progressively modified, and continued to provide valuable data on Iraq's installations and movements in the recurring crises of the 1990s.

Lockheed's U-2 has been a major contributor to Western intelligence-gathering since 1956. This U-2D came to the UK in 1967 to investigate clear-air turbulence at altitudes of six miles and above.

In 1966 the Lockheed SR-71 joined the U-2 in USAF reconnaissance duties. The 'Blackbird' was the first operational aircraft to evince the stealth characteristics of aerodynamic design, surfaces and colour. Its speed, in excess of Mach 3 at heights over 85,000ft (26,000m), kept it invulnerable to interception. Its contribution to the gathering of intelligence deep into the heart of the Soviet Union and other potentially hostile territories was ended in 1990, when the advent of satellites and unmanned air-breathing vehicles (UAVs) were believed to have rendered its contribution superfluous. Since then, however, shortcomings in satellite cover have been exposed and UAV development has proceeded more slowly than expected. As a result, two SR-71s were reactivated in 1995 and continued in service in 1998.

Strictly speaking, neither transport nor reconnaissance aircraft are 'war machines', but their contribution to warfare, especially to cold warfare, has been inestimable since 1945. In 1950, however, longer-term focus was distracted by unexpected events on the Pacific Rim.

The impact of the Korean War

The emphasis in the USA on strategic bombing was increased in 1948 when Tactical Air Command (TAC) was abolished and its functions, along with those of air defence and training of reserves, were reallocated to a new Continental Air Command. It was argued that an air force capable of achieving strategic success in the first decisive phase of a conflict would be equally capable of tactical operations in the follow-up phase. Retention of a specialised tactical air arm was, therefore, rendered unnecessary.

Consequently, the outbreak and events of the Korean War, from 1950 to 1954, were a severe shock to the USAF. Lessons from the tactical air forces of the Second World War had to be relearned. The rapid southward advance of North Korean forces into South Korea, the lack of large-scale targets and the strong reservations of the USA's UN coalition partners precluded the use of atomic weapons. Air power was called upon to reprise the campaigns of the Second World War in northwest Europe, rather than the raids on Hiroshima or Nagasaki.

In 1950 the UN Command order of battle in Korea included B-29s, B-26s, F-80 and F-84 fighter-bombers, F-51 Mustangs, F-86 air-superiority fighters, F4U Marine Corsairs and US Navy F7F, F9F and AD-1 Skyraiders, supported by the air wing from HMS *Triumph* and two Mustang squadrons from the Royal Australian and South African air forces.

Air superiority was contested and won by F-86s against MiG-15s. Interdiction and close air support played a crucial part in checking the North Korean drive on Pusan in July 1950 and disrupting the Chinese offensive later in the year. The Mustangs replaced F-80s temporarily in 1950 because of their ability to carry bombs

United Nations' air superiority in the Korean War was secured primarily by the North American F-86F Sabre.

and napalm from primitive airstrips in the close-support role. However, when the jets were fitted with bomb pylons and wing tanks the F-80C and more capable F-84E could provide twice the number of sorties with lower maintenance time, higher readiness rates and reduced vulnerability to ground fire. Although B-29s were employed against industrial targets in the north, they were constrained by Chinese AA fire to bomb from above 18,000ft (5,000m), with consequent loss of accuracy.

Fortunately for the UN coalition there was considerable experience to draw upon, but the overwhelming air superiority enjoyed by the USAF and its partners could not be fully exploited, partly because of the mismatch between preparation, concepts and circumstances and partly because 'What had been remembered from the Second World War had not been written down or, if written down, had not been disseminated or, if disseminated, had not been read or understood'. The events of the Korean War were so far removed from the forecasts of Arnold and Von Karman that it might have been expected that the conflict would redefine the requirements for combat aircraft. In fact, with the exception of the US Navy's procurement of the Vought F-8 Crusader and the McDonnell Douglas F-4 Phantom, designed, respectively, to contest close-in and beyond-visual-range (BVR) air superiority, the concepts of 1945–50 were not abandoned but actually reinforced after 1954. There were several reasons.

The Eisenhower administration was committed to reducing defence expenditure, and to seeking 'more bang for the buck over the long haul' by increasing dependence on nuclear weapons. There was widespread military agreement that, in any event, the Korean War had been an aberration. The contemporary US Secretary of the Air

McDonnell's F-4 Phantom 2 was arguably the best combat aircraft of its era. This is a US Marine Corps aircraft.

Although it was designed to deliver nuclear weapons, the massive Republic F-105 Thunderchief all-weather fighter-bomber bore the brunt of attacks against targets in North Vietnam. These F-105Ds with external fuel tanks were photographed in 1961.

Force observed that the war had been '... a special case, and air power can learn little from there about its future role in United States foreign policy in the East'. The FEAF end-of-war report was unequivocal: 'Any attempt to build an air force from the model of the Korean requirements could be fatal to the United States'. Even reluctant measures taken during the war to impose close air support were abandoned by the USA, and the US Army began to look to its own helicopters to provide it.

Others believed that, had SAC been fully operational in 1950, the war would not have occurred in the

The F-100C Super Sabre, a genuine multi-role fighter-bomber, was also adapted for the nuclear strike role.

first place. All 'lessons' led to the same conclusion: 'No more Koreas!'

By the middle of the 1950s the 'century' series of USAF 'fighters' had flown. Of them, the F-102, F-106 and F-104 were configured as bomber interceptors, while the F-101A/C, F-104C and F-105 were nuclear-strike 'fighters'. The need for a highly agile, high-performance fighter to contest air superiority with the MiG family, disclosed in Korea, was lost in the production of the F-104, which combined Mach 2 speed, a very high rate of climb and a ceiling of 58,000ft (17,600m): excellent attributes for an interceptor of bombers but insufficient for an air-superiority fighter.

The F-100 Super Sabre was the only genuine multi-role fighter bomber of its generation, but it also became adapted for nuclear attack of area targets. So much so that the Pacific Air Forces' F-100 training manual in 1961 specified: 'Nuclear training will, in every instance, take precedence over non-nuclear familiarisation and qualification. It is emphasized that conventional training will not be accomplished at the expense of the higher priority nuclear training required by this Manual.'

The NATO influence

Meanwhile, in Europe, the members of the Atlantic Alliance were failing to meet the conventional force goals that had been set at Lisbon in 1952. By 1950 a nuclear weapon small enough to be carried by a fighter had been developed. Even while the Korean War continued, the USAF continued to focus on the central confrontation against the USSR, and began to modify its jet fighters to carry nuclear weapons. The F-84G and F-100 were modified, and by the mid-1950s were mounting nuclear-alert states in several regions. There was a convenient convergence between the opportunity to replace alliance manpower shortfalls by 'tactical' nuclear weapons, the opportunity for TAC to compete more effectively with SAC for funding and the Eisenhower administration's objective of reducing the defence budget.

In 1960, however, the installation of the government of President Kennedy coincided with a reconsideration of the US and NATO strategy of massive retaliation based on nuclear weapons. The new concept of flexible response emphasised readiness to meet a full range of combat possibilities. In 1962 Secretary of Defense Mac-Namara instigated an examination of land warfare and aviation support. However, there was little meeting of minds between the US Army and Air Force. The Army had doubled its inventory of helicopters and light air-craft between 1955 and 1959, believing, with some jus-tification, that the USAF gave low priority to close air support. Meanwhile, the USAF's view continued to be

that high-performance tactical fighter-bombers could perform multiple roles, ranging from nuclear strikes in general war to close air support of ground forces. Fur-ther disagreement arose, the army wanting dedicated custom-built aircraft under army control and allocating multi-role aircraft, as required, to air superiority, inter-diction or close air support.

South Vietnam

Not surprisingly with such disagreements, US forces drifted into the war in Southeast Asia with no agreed doctrine, concepts, command and control, communica-tions or procedures for air-to-ground co-operation.

Before 1965 the USAF was not allowed to employ jet aircraft in Vietnam for attack missions. Initially, obsolete B-26s and T-28s were used until in 1964 their wings lit-erally began to fall off and the remainder were with-drawn from operations. In 1965 air strikes in South Vietnam began to be delivered by Martin B-57s, F-100s and F-4s. Although the jets could achieve much quicker response times to provide close air support, their high speed in the target area made the acquisition of small targets in featureless terrain, masked by dense jungle canopies, very difficult. They could not loiter and, at low

The B-57, a variant of the English Electric Canberra produced by Martin in the USA, was deployed in South Vietnam. This is a B-57B, first flown in June 1954, which introduced a rotary bomb door with the stores carried on the door itself, and underwing pylons for rockets or bombs.

Entering service in 1967, the Cessna O-2A, a military variant of the Type 337 Skymaster, supplemented the same manufacturer's O-1 Bird Dog in the forward air controller role in Vietnam.

North American's OV-10A Bronco purpose-designed counterinsurgency aircraft made a major contribution to the provision of close air support for US ground forces in Vietnam, as a forward air controller.

level, fuel consumption rose considerably. One solution was the adaptation of C-47, C-119 and C-130 transports as gunships. They could be vulnerable to ground fire but could apply very heavy concentrated firepower at night or in bad weather to relieve isolated ground forces. Increasingly, close-air-support missions were controlled by Forward Air Controllers flying O-1, O-2 and OV-10 piston-engined light aircraft.

More unexpected was the use of Boeing B-52s to attack targets in South Vietnam, foreshadowing their use in Operation 'Desert Storm' a generation later. A modified B-52 could drop more than seventeen tons of bombs and, while a large proportion fell on uninhabited jungle, their psychological impact on the Vietnamese opposition, according to prisoner-of-war reports, was considerable. It was very difficult to assess the practical impact of such bombing because of the nature of guerrilla warfare in South Vietnam, which precluded measurement by subsequent territorial gain, and because of perpetual bad weather and universal ground cover.

The one notable exception was the defence of Khe Sanh in 1968. There, 6,000 US Marines and South Vietnamese Rangers were besieged by 20,000 North Vietnamese troops for 78 days. The garrison was sustained totally by air, even though its airstrip was under continuous fire. Tactical aircraft flew more than 24,000 sorties, dropping more than 95,000 tons of ordnance on the besieging forces. B-52s contributed 2,548 of the sorties and 53,162 tons of the bombs. As Khe Sanh was isolated near the Laotian border, the siege was not prominently covered by the media but, had the outpost fallen, the impact on subsequent events would undoubtedly have matched that of the loss of Dien Bien Phu in the French colonial campaign fourteen years previously.

Meanwhile, the US Army had continued to increase its employment of combat helicopters. Between 1960 and 1965 their numbers doubled to more than 5,000. In the entire war in Southeast Asia 4,869 were lost, but their contribution stimulated the development that culminated in the AH-64 Apaches of the Gulf War.

North Vietnam

Air attacks on targets in North Vietnam started in 1964 and ended in 1973. In 1968 the first phase was halted by President Johnson after attacks had failed either to block North Vietnamese supply and reinforcement routes or to coerce the Hanoi government to the conference table. North Vietnam took advantage of the pause to rebuild bridges, restore damaged routes and to reinforce air defences. After 1968, however, the US was committed to a gradual withdrawal, and placed greater emphasis on air-delivered firepower to support the remaining US ground forces and their South Vietnamese allies.

North Vietnamese troop concentrations, supply routes and air defences were repeatedly struck. A large-scale invasion by fourteen North Vietnamese divisions and 600 tanks in the spring of 1972 was checked by air attack. In May 1972 President Nixon initiated Operation 'Linebacker', which included the mining of Haiphong and other North Vietnamese harbours, and strikes on many previously prohibited targets close to Hanoi. With its ground forces severely weakened and its homeland under heavy air attack, the North Vietnamese government expressed interest in peace negotiations, and Operation 'Linebacker' was therefore suspended in October 1972.

When the negotiations broke down, Nixon authorised Operation 'Linebacker II', an eleven-day attack in December 1972 on North Vietnamese targets in the

Hanoi and Haiphong area. In 729 sorties B-52s dropped 15,237 tons of bombs for the loss of fifteen aircraft. A further 5,000 tons of ordnance were dropped in 1,216 sorties by other USAF and USN aircraft, including the newly deployed General Dynamics F-111. Targets included SAM sites, airfields, fuel storage areas, power plants, rail yards, railways and other supply routes. Meanwhile, air attacks on the North Vietnamese army below the 20th parallel were increased from thirty-five a day to fifty. Battered at home, and with its armies dwindling daily, North Vietnam agreed to end the conflict in January 1973.

The impact on air power

A great deal about the Vietnam War remains controversial, but it was a watershed for the evolution of air power in the second half of the century. This time the USA could not ignore the lessons. American crews flew more than 1,248,000 fixed-wing and more than 37,000,000 helicopter sorties between 1965 and 1973. For them the war lasted more than twice as long as the Second World War. Eight million tons of ordnance were dropped on Southeast Asia, twice the tonnage dropped by all participants in the Second World War. Fixed-wing losses to all causes were 3,720; 58,000 Americans were killed, 300,000 were wounded and only half of the aircrew shot down were ever recovered.

The impact of air power during the conflict was weakened by poor command and control, restrictions on target selection, political uncertainty, weaknesses in concepts and doctrine and, by no means least, equipment limitations which quickly became apparent. For example, the F-105 bore the brunt of attacks against the North, but its radar bombing system was designed for nuclear release, with an acceptable error of 1,500–2,000ft (450–600m). It was, therefore, ineffective against point targets, caused considerable collateral damage and prompted targets to be selected for ease of location rather than military significance. Early attempts to increase the F-105's accuracy by using EB-66s as pathfinders were of little help because of the dependence on release points for the bombers being called for in unison from the pathfinder.

Furthermore, the F-105 was not designed to sustain battle damage. Of 833 F-105s built, 383 were lost in combat in Vietnam. Its vulnerability was increased because of its lack of manoeuvrability in close encounters with MiG-17s and MiG-21s. Even the F-4 had been designed as a bomber interceptor, depending on air-to-air missiles for kills, and it too, while on a par with the MiG-21, could be outmanoeuvred by the MiG-17. US rules of engagement over Vietnam demanded visual identification, which precluded the F-4 taking 'first shot' advantage with its BVR AIM-7 missiles. Because of defensive manoeuvring, F-4 aircrews could not maintain radar illumination of their target, causing the AIM-7 to break lock. Between 1965 and 1968 224 AIM-7s were fired for to achieve twenty kills: an 8.9 per cent kill rate. In the same period 175 AIM-9B Sidewinders achieved twenty-five kills, a rate of 16 per cent. The overall American air-to-air kill ratio during the war was 2.4:1, compared with 13.9:1 in the last two years of the Korean War.

The highly agile, widely exported MiG-21 remained immune to US counter air operations on its bases in North Vietnam. This one carries an AA-22 infrared-homing air-to-air missile on its starboard pylon and an ECM jammer pod on the port pylon.

Originally deployed to extend the range of Strategic Air Command bombers, Boeing KC-135 jet tankers became the force multiplier for many of air power's roles. These are aircraft of the 93rd Bomb Wing at Castle Air Force Base, Merced, California.

Gradually the equipment problems were addressed, either during the war or after it. The precursor of the Boeing E-3 AWACS, the EC-121 Rivet Top airborne radar system, entered service in 1965. It was unable to detect airborne targets at low level and could not control intercepts or provide early warning of MiG attacks, but did co-ordinate strike packages, combat search and rescue, and tanker hook-ups.

The extensive North Vietnamese air defences prompted a variety of defence-suppression measures. In 1965 a number of two-seat F-100s were equipped with a compact radar frequency/receiver direction finder and given a new role of locating and destroying SAM sites. They were soon replaced by F-105s armed with Shrike anti-radiation missiles and the role was named 'Wild Weasel'. For much of the war the Wild Weasels were constrained by rules of engagement which restricted their attacks to sites directly threatening USAF formations, but the concept was firmly rooted and the role was inherited by F-4Gs in 1978 and successfully applied against Iraq's air defences in 1991.

Belatedly, other electronic lessons from earlier conflicts were recalled and new jamming pods were installed on all strike aircraft. Chaff corridors were laid to decoy SAM and AAA radars on exactly the same principle employed by RAF Lancasters dropping 'window' tinfoil strips over Germany in the Second World War. After Vietnam the provision of electronic countermeasures and counter-countermeasures (ECM and ECCM) systems became essential for all modern combat aircraft.

During the war, reconnaissance frequently revealed the ineffectiveness of traditional bombing against targets such as bridges and other strongly defended targets. An early attack on the Than Hoa bridge by forty-six F-105s, including sixteen carrying visually tracked air-to-ground Bullpup missiles, failed to inflict any discernible damage. The need for powerful precision-guided munitions (PGMs) was first met by the US Walleye electro-optically guided glide bomb with a 1,000lb (450kg) warhead, which destroyed the Than Hoa bridge in 1968. Of sixty-eight Walleye drops, sixty-five scored direct hits.

During 1972 Paveway laser-guided bombs with 2,000lb (900kg) warheads began to be used against bridges and targets where collateral damage was unacceptable. One example was a hydroelectric power station only 50ft (15m) away from a dam, and PGMs were also used against individual tanks in the defence of Hue against the North Vietnamese offensive. In this period, air-launched PGMs accounted for more than 70 per cent of enemy tanks destroyed or damaged. These events were the first in the sequence that was to lead to PGM attacks in 'Desert Storm' in 1991 and 'Deliberate Force' in Bosnia in 1995.

Two other innovations were the CBU-24 cluster submunition weapon for use against AAA sites and deployed ground troops, and the Snake-eye folding-fin retarding attachment to the standard Mark 82 general-purpose bomb, to allow low-altitude, lay-down attacks.

Less obtrusively, flight refuelling tankers made a major contribution to attacks on North Vietnam. In 'Linebacker II' about 750 refuellings a day were made by a fleet of more than 200 KC-135s. Hitherto, USAF flight refuelling had been primarily dedicated to SAC support. In future it was to become indispensable to conventional theatre operations and would make a major contribution to 'Desert Storm'.

Convergence

Such was the impact of Vietnam on the USAF that the shortcomings that had been revealed, and the innovations that had succeeded, would probably have given impetus to equipment programmes designed to meet the new requirements. Meanwhile, however, other factors had converged to ensure that there could not be any repeat of the post Korean War reversion to outdated concepts and preferences.

NATO evolution

The deployment by NATO of 'tactical' nuclear weapons after the failure of the Alliance to meet the Lisbon conventional force goals of 1952 was not immediately influenced by the Soviet detonation of a thermonuclear weapon in 1953. But by 1957 the USSR had also begun to deploy short-range surface-to-surface nuclear missiles in Europe, and the launch of Sputnik seemed to indicate an ability to strike in a similar manner against the USA. Consequently, the subsequent change in emphasis by the Kennedy administration noted above, away from a strategy of 'massive retaliation' towards a more 'flexible response', was reluctantly and finally adopted by NATO in 1967.

The eclipse of the strategic bomber

In the same period, the dominance of the long-range bomber in a predominantly nuclear strategy was challenged by two other developments. The first was the shooting down of Gary Powers' U-2 over Sverdlovsk in 1960 by a Soviet SA-2. At a stroke, the high-level immunity enjoyed by the B-52 and the RAF's V-bomber Force was removed. The first antidote, of dropping to low-level penetration, reduced both range and airframe life. In the same period the submarine-launched intercontinental ballistic missile (SSBM) and the mobile land-based ICBM became operational, offering unstoppable reach and destructive power with, in the case of the SSBM, well nigh invulnerable launching platforms.

The cumulative impact was an eclipse of the long-range strategic bomber until its re-emergence in the stealthy form of the B-2 in the 1990s. In 1967 the North American XB-70 programme was ended. Production of the Convair B-58 Hustler, designed in 1949 in the 'higher and faster' period, was curtailed in 1962, and Secretary MacNamara directed its withdrawal from service in 1970. One beneficiary of the changed environment was the F-111, which, with long range at very low altitude, became the most powerful potential deep penetrator of Warsaw Pact air defences.

In 1969 the new Nixon administration did encourage the development of a new-generation strategic bomber, the Rockwell B-1, designed to cruise at high altitude at above Mach 2 and to penetrate enemy air defences at low level at high subsonic speeds. It incorporated stealth

For many years the deep-penetrating, low-level, all-weather General Dynamics FB-111A was the most potent combat aircraft available to NATO's Supreme Allied Commander Europe. This one was the first of the type.

technology in its blended wing and aerodynamic shape, which were designed to reduce radar cross-section. Originally, 244 B-1s were expected to replace the B-52s, but during the 1970s cost overruns placed the programme in jeopardy. At the same time, the addition of the air-launched cruise missile to the B-52's inventory offered a cost-effective alternative and the B-2 programme was begun. In 1977 President Carter cancelled the B-1 programme. It was reactivated in 1981 as the B-1B Lancer, with potential numbers reduced to 100, and entered USAF service in 1985, but development continued to be slow and it did not participate in the Gulf War in 1991. By 1998 it had been equipped to carry, as part of a 'force package', a wide range of concentrated munitions, but had not seen combat.

Soviet Air Force modernisation

Throughout the period of NATO–Warsaw Pact confrontation, perception of the Soviet threat remained the strongest influence on Western combat aircraft programmes. Unfortunately, just as the NATO alliance elected to move to a more flexible strategy in 1967, the USSR disclosed a new generation of its own combat aircraft, admirably suited to prosecuting a conventional campaign.

In the mid-1950s, bombers and long-range missiles had competed for procurement priority but, throughout the decade, Soviet military doctrine had emphasised the need for combined arms conventional operations even when deep nuclear strikes were taking place. In the 1960s, Soviet concentration turned to multi-role combat aircraft for deployment by Frontal Aviation. In 1967, at an air display in Moscow, a number of new aircraft were revealed, including the MiG-23/27 series, the Su-17 and uprated MiG-21. They were followed into service in the 1970s by the Su-24 and MiG-25. All were accompanied by new generations of air-to-air heat-seeking and radar-guided missiles. Consequently, the need for Western air superiority, implicit in the strategy of 'Flexible Response' and laid bare in Vietnam, became even more urgent.

The US response

The US Navy led the way with the F-14A Tomcat, which first flew in 1970. USAF research and development in the same period produced the F-15, specifically designed to replace the F-4 but far more manoeuvrable with light-weight, high-thrust afterburning turbofan engines, electronic stability-augmentation systems, advanced radars and armed with both cannon and missiles. The lighter, multi-role F-16, with computer-controlled inherent aerodynamic instability, followed in 1974, and the F/A-18 Hornet in 1978. The procurement priority given to this 'sixth' generation of combat aircraft marked the abandonment of the nuclear preoccupation. They incorporated the new technology of the computer age into avionics, cockpit design, target-acquisition and weapon-delivery. Collectively, the F-14, F-15, F-16 and F/A-18 established Western air supremacy, which remained unchallenged at the end of the century.

Combat proven

In June 1982 the Israeli Air Force (IAF) inflicted a catastrophic defeat on the Syrian Air Force, destroying at least eighty aircraft for the loss of, possibly, one Israeli fighter. The damage was done largely by F-15s and F-16s. Not for the first time since 1945, the Arab–Israeli conflict had produced a significant milestone in the evolution of modern air power.

In the Six Day War of 1967 the IAF destroyed 500 Arab aircraft in one day, for the loss of 20 Israeli; 75 per cent of Egypt's combat strength was destroyed on the ground. The IAF achieved total surprise, attacking below early-warning radars and high-level SA-2s. Total air supremacy was achieved within twenty-four hours and exploited during the following five days to wreak havoc on Egyptian and Syrian ground forces and to secure territory in Sinai, on the West Bank and on the Golan Heights. The war prompted immediate construction programmes in NATO and the Warsaw Pact of hardened aircraft shelters (HASs), additional runways and taxiways and, where possible, aircraft dispersals.

The Rockwell B-1, seen refuelling from a KC-135, survived a number of setbacks in development to become a powerful conventional-weapon carrier in the post-Cold War world.

In October 1973 Israel, in turn, was taken by surprise, and suffered heavy losses to well co-ordinated SAM and AAA fire when using aircraft to halt simultaneous ground offensives from Egypt and Syria. Only when Egyptian ground forces advanced beyond their co-ordinated air defence cover and counterattacking Israeli ground forces overran some of the air-defence segments could the IAF bring its full firepower to bear. The IAF had trained to replay the Six Day War, and had forgotten the essential details of closely co-ordinated land/air operations. The Egyptians, on the other hand, pursued a strategy which, had it been sustained and not modified after initial success, could, to a very great extent, have neutralised the IAF's advantages.

Again the world watched and learned a lesson: this time the essential need to neutralise hostile air defences before attempting other air operations and, as far as possible, to restrict exposure to low-level combinations of AA guns and SAMs.

Beka'a, 1982

Nine years later the cumulative lessons learned in Vietnam and in previous Middle Eastern episodes were applied using the aircraft, weapons and systems produced in the intervening period. In June 1982, as part of a retributive Israeli campaign against the Palestine Liberation Organisation in Lebanon, the IAF sought to neutralise any Syrian units which might interfere. Before the attack, Syrian air defences had been watched and

monitored by IAF surveillance aircraft and remotely piloted vehicles (RPVs). First, other RPVs were flown into the Syrian air defences to trigger the SA-6 engagement radars, which were then struck by F-4s and F-16s, delivering anti-radiation missiles and other PGMs, as well as by long-range artillery and battlefield missiles. Other reconnaissance RPVs relayed battle damage reports back to the Israeli force commander. Seventeen of nineteen SA-6 sites, as well as several others, were destroyed in a matter of minutes.

When the Syrian Air Force scrambled a large number of fighters to engage the attacking aircraft, they were observed by an Israeli E-2C Hawkeye AWACS which vectored F-15s and F-16s from combat air patrols towards intercept. Syrian control and airborne radars, surface-to-air communications and missiles were jammed or decoyed by chaff and flares. Twenty-three Syrian fighters were shot down in the first engagement, and the rest followed in the subsequent days. Israeli technical advantages were reinforced by superior concepts, leadership, training and flexibility.

The Beka'a confrontation coincided with the well-publicised fight between Britain and Argentina over the Falkland Islands. There, the Argentinian Air Force inflicted heavy casualties on a Royal Navy bereft of AEW and with only light and spasmodic air cover. RAF Harriers provided close air support to British ground forces and one Vulcan, sustained by thirteen Victor tankers, attacked Port Stanley airfield from its base on

The McDonnell Douglas F/A-18 Hornet followed the Grumman F-14 Tomcat into US Navy service to restore air superiority after the experiences of Vietnam.

Disproportionate impact: in 1982, attacks by RAF Avro Vulcans on targets in the Falkland Islands, more than 4,000 miles (6,440km) from their base – Wideawake Airfield on Ascension Island, where they are seen here – prompted the Argentinian Air Force to divert interceptors to protect targets on the Argentine mainland.

Ascension Island, 4,000 miles (6,400km) away. Other Vulcan attacks were made on Argentinian radar and other installations. While the damage inflicted by the Vulcans was slight, it prompted the Argentinian Air Force to move a squadron of Mirage interceptors north to provide cover for Buenos Aires, thereby denying their aircraft attacking the Falklands any opportunity to win air superiority. The British victory in the Falklands was an astonishing achievement over such distances, but in the evolution of modern air power it was, compared with events over the Beka'a Valley, an anachronism. The IAF engagements on the other hand, with a combination of ELINT, RPVs, defence suppression, PGMs, contemporary air-to-air missiles and fighters, all operating in a dense electronic warfare environment, foreshadowed the environment of the air war in the Persian Gulf nine years later.

The Soviet response
At first the USSR relied on propaganda to minimise the impact of the annihilation, in the Beka'a debacle, of Soviet equipment widely deployed in the Warsaw Pact. Within two years selective lessons were being extracted, and probably gave impetus to the USSR's own next-generation air-superiority fighters, missiles and systems

associated with the MiG-29 and Su-27. The collapse, first of the Warsaw Pact and then of the Soviet Union itself, denied the Soviet Air Force any opportunity to show how well the Beka'a lessons had been learned. Instead, in the last great air battle of the twentieth century, another beneficiary of Soviet equipment, organisation, concepts and training met disaster at the hands of the reformed, re-equipped and revitalised USAF and coalition partners.

The Gulf War
The neutralisation of Iraq's air force and air defence within forty-eight hours in January 1991 revealed, for the first time, the impact on air power of late twentieth-century technology when harnessed to imaginative concepts and delivered by highly skilled professionals. The Iraqi Air Force (IQAF) had more than 700 combat aircraft, including a number of MiG-23s, MiG-25s, MiG-29s, Su-24s and French Mirage F.1s. In addition, air defences included 11,000 missiles and 8,500 AA guns, with a density protecting Baghdad twice that of any NATO target in Eastern Europe.

The Coalition Air Forces, however, had a number of advantages. They outnumbered the IQAF by five to one, with 3,380 aircraft, and Coalition leadership, training, concepts and skill were far superior. Most of the Coalition combat aircraft were also superior to all but a handful of IQAF MiG-29s. In total combat technology the Coalition was a generation ahead.

The devastation of Iraq's air defences was achieved by Apache helicopters, F-117 stealth fighter bombers, F-4Gs, F-15Es, F-111s, RAF Tornadoes and Tomahawk sea-launched cruise missiles. Defence radars were stimulated by air-launched decoys and struck by anti-radiation guided missiles. Other radars and communications were jammed by EF-111s, EA-6Bs and EC-130s. Specialist aircraft, such as RC-135 Rivet Joint, continuously monitored Iraq's military and political frequencies, while E-8 Joint Stars provided the theatre commander with an unprecedented view of Iraqi ground force deployment and movement. Almost 2,500 coalition sorties each day were co-ordinated by E-3 and E-2C AWACS. Almost 60 per cent of sorties flown by receiver equipped aircraft required in-flight refuelling, prompting an average of 275 tanker sorties per day.

The combination of laser-guided bomb (LGB) and F-117 was particularly deadly. The F-117 fighter-bomber flew only 2 per cent of Coalition attacks but struck 40 per cent of strategic targets without loss to the forty-two aircraft involved. The F-117 was never invisible, but its reduced radar, optical and infrared signatures, coupled with accurate intelligence on Iraqi ground radar locations and ranges, enabled it consistently to reach even the most heavily defended target unimpeded. Consequently, control of the LGB during its delivery was much less hazardous. Elsewhere, when air superiority had been established above the reach of low-level defences, the LGB became the weapon of choice on many targets, ultimately including HASs and individual armoured vehicles. More than 17,000 PGMs were used, including 9,342 LGBs. In addition, 210,000 unguided bombs were dropped, mainly on Iraqi ground forces deployed in and around Kuwait.

The devastation of Iraq's ground forces was hastened by the contribution of B-52s bombing the stranded troops from high altitude and by F-16s, A-10s, US Marine Corps Harriers, RAF Jaguars and US Army Apache helicopters. Above, combat air patrols were sustained by RAF Tornado F.3s and RSAF and USAF F-15s against the remote possibility of IQAF interference.

Iraq was believed to have deployed 336,000 troops into the Kuwait theatre, and Saddam had promised the Coalition 'the mother of all battles'. Instead, after forty days and nights of incessant air attack the Iraqi army capitulated. The Coalition had prepared 18,000 hospital beds in the war zone, plus a further 25,000 in Europe and the USA. In the 100-hour land engagement the Coalition suffered 340 combat deaths and 776 injuries, and 25 per cent of the deaths and 10 per cent of the injuries were the result of 'friendly fire'.

From the arrival in theatre of Coalition aircraft in August 1990 to the ceasefire on 28 February 1991, air power had shaped the environment. The swift arrival of US and British combat aircraft immediately after Iraq's invasion of Kuwait presented an additional complication to any plan Saddam Hussein may have had to move south on to the Saudi Arabian oilfields. Thereafter, the Coalition force build-up took place secure beneath Coalition combat air patrols. In the conflict, total Coalition air supremacy denied Iraq both knowledge of, and opportunity to interfere with, General Schwarzkopf's plans for encirclement. Information dominance, airborne control and in-flight refuelling were maintained without IQAF challenge. This, in addition to the destruction of Iraq's air defences and the decimation and demoralisation of the ground forces, was the total contribution of air power to the Gulf War.

The PGM impact

The use of PGMs in the Gulf War was not an innovation. The LGB was constrained by cloud, fog or smoke. The need for the designating aircraft to loiter within sight of the target until weapon detonation would have been hazardous without stealth technology or air superiority. Nonetheless, it is the widespread availability and employment of the PGM which, more than any other single advance in technology, has transformed the cost-effectiveness of air power in the last decade of the century. In the Second World War the bombing accuracy probability for a B-17 was 3,300ft (1,000m). In 'Desert Storm' the F-117 consistently achieved an accuracy of less than 10ft (3m).

Quite apart from reduced risks of inadvertent damage and casualties in the target area, increased accuracy can be directly translated into reduced requirements to achieve a given effect: fewer weapons, aircraft, aircrew, ground crew, fuel, logistics, air bases, training, headquarters; reductions in all areas of air force structure and support. As the world moves into an age of limited conflicts and UN operations where costs, casualties and collateral damage are all very sensitive considerations, the cost-effectiveness and political attraction of PGMs are of considerable significance.

In Bosnia in 1995, in Operation 'Deliberate Force', almost all air attacks on Serbian installations were made by PGM. In circumstances far removed from those in the Gulf War, the effect was the same. An opponent, on this occasion a peace breaker, was denied the opportunity to pursue a strategy of his choice, the numbers of ground forces required to complete the task were considerably reduced and opposition was speedily terminated.

Requirements and options

At the turn of the century, air warfare requirements are clearly defined. They range from the least likely but most demanding major conflict to the most likely but least demanding low-intensity or peacekeeping scenarios. Differences, however, are likely to be in scale rather than in complexity and sophistication. Air superiority, defence suppression, precision attack, information gathering and distribution will be needed in many conflicts. At all levels, contemporary aircraft, weapons and air defences may be encountered. They may have been bought in a highly competitive international market, or handed down from ex-Cold War reductions, or inherited from a dispossessed regime, or nationally produced. Most environments will be complicated by electronic warfare.

Debates are more likely to be about how to meet the requirements, rather than defining the requirements themselves. Already UAVs are making a major contribution to information gathering and communications. Combat UAVs are still some distance away, with considerable problems of situation awareness and communications vulnerability still to be resolved. Yet, with the B-2 Spirit stealth bomber costing up to $2 billion a unit, and with sophisticated reconnaissance aircraft such as E-8 Joint STARS requiring twenty or more crew members, incentives to increase reliance on UAVs are certain to continue.

Overhead, satellites already contribute irreplaceably to information gathering, communication, navigation and weather forecasting; essential features in meeting the requirements of modern air warfare.

The last decade of the century is, in some respects, akin to that of the post-Second World War period. Then, as now, air warfare had undergone revolutionary changes. Then, as now, one country was pre-eminent in air warfare. Then, however, one interpretation of the requirements of air warfare dominated all others: strategic nuclear bombardment. That interpretation, sustaining nuclear deterrence, undoubtedly enhanced East–West stability and inhibited the Cold War from exploding into a third world war. It also, however, inhibited the full identification of the requirements of air warfare in many different scenarios, at great cost to the USAF in particular. Now, all the requirements may be both identified and met.

Bibliography

Arnold, Gen H H, 'Memorandum for Dr Von Karman', HQ Army Air Forces, Washington DC, 7 November 1944. Reproduced in Daso, R, *Architects of American Air Supremacy* (Air University Press, Maxwell AFB, Alabama, 1997).

'Third Report to the Secretary of War by the Commanding General of the Army Air Forces', 12 November 1945, reproduced in Emme, *The Impact of Air Power* (Van Nostrand, Princeton, 1959).

BBC Timewatch television programme 'Spies in the Sky', broadcast 27 May 1994.

Bradley, Gen O, 'Effects of Air Power on Military Operations: Western Europe', report from 12 Army Group, 15 July 1945. Excerpts in Emme, *Impact of Air Power* (Van Nostrand, Princeton, 1959).

Edmonds, M, 'The Development of British Combat Military Aircraft 194570', in *Perspectives in British Defence Policy 1945–70* (Department of Adult Education, University of Southampton, 1978).

Far East Air Force, 'Report on the Korean War', 26 March 1954.

Finletter, T K, 'Air Power and World Strategy, Especially in the Far East', *The Annals*, May 1955.

Freedman, L, *The Evolution of Military Strategy* (Macmillan, IISS London, 1981).

Gowing, M, *Independence and Deterrence*, Vol 1 (Macmillan, London, 1974).

Hallion, R, *Storm over Iraq* (Smithsonian Institution Press, Washington DC, 1992).

Lambeth, B S, *The Maturation of American Air Power* (Rand, Santa Monica, 1998).

'Moscow's Lessons from the 1982 Lebanon Air War', in Mason, R A (ed), *War in the Third Dimension* (Brassey's, London, 1985).

Lashmar, P, 'Shootdowns', *Aeroplane Monthly*, August 1994.

Lord Hill Norton, Admiral of the Fleet, *Sea Power* (Faber & Faber, London, 1982).

MacIsaac, D, 'The Evolution of Air Power since 1945', in Mason, R A (ed), ibid.

Mason, R A and Taylor, J W R, *The Soviet Air Force* (Jane's Information Group, London, 1986).

Mason, R A, *The Aerospace Revolution* (Brassey's, London, 1998).

Sokolovsky, V D, *Military Strategy, Soviet Doctrine and Concepts* (Pall Mall, London, 1963).

Spaatz, Gen C, 'Strategic Airpower: Fulfilment of a Concept', *Foreign Affairs*, April 1946.

Telford, E J, *Set up: What the Air Force did in Vietnam and Why* (Air University Press, Maxwell AFB, Alabama, 1991).

United States Air Force, *Gulf War Summary*, April 1993.

Project 'Corona Harvest' papers, quoted in *Close Air Support* (Office of Air Force History, Washington DC, 1990).

United States Department of Defense, *Conduct of the Persian Gulf War, Final Report to Congress* (Washington DC, April 1992).

Von Karman, T, 'Where We Stand', 22 August 1945, Section II, 'The Art of Radar', reproduced in Daso, R, ibid.

'Towards New Horizons', Washington, DC, 15 December 1945, Section 1.4, reproduced in Daso, R, ibid.

Yost, G, *Spy Technology* (Harrap, London, 1975).

2
From Nuclear Bomb to Cruise Missile
Jerry Scutts

By the end of the Second World War air power had influenced international conflict to such a degree that it was abundantly clear that any country wishing to defend its homeland adequately and project prestige abroad had to maintain an air force. While there was mass demobilisation of personnel and scrapping of combat aircraft on a huge scale, not all of the swords were turned into ploughshares.

The advent of the atomic bomb and its operational use against Japan in 1945 guaranteed the USA a position as the most powerful nation on Earth. This dominance was not to last much longer than a decade; Britain, as a significant technical contributor to the Manhattan Project that produced the atomic bomb, had its own operational air-launched bomb by 1955.

By combining the overt sharing of data with espionage, the Soviet Union obtained the means to develop an embryonic atomic arsenal earlier than it might otherwise have done. The first Soviet atomic weapon was apparently detonated on 4 April 1949, the year that NATO was formed. France and China followed as members of an increasingly less exclusive nuclear 'club'.

The possession of weapons of mass destruction by what came to be termed the 'superpowers' put a select few nations at the top of the tree, but the ordnance that had largely been developed between 1939 and 1945 was efficient enough for the conflicts of succeeding decades. War, of the 'conventional' kind, was raging in some parts of the world even as the Allies terminated global conflict on the deck of the USS *Missouri* on 2 September 1945.

In the first months of peace the victorious powers were able to examine the vast strides in aeronautics made by Germany. With evidence that rockets, guided missiles, turbojets and swept wings were practical propositions, it was clear that the future had already arrived. Aircraft on European and American drawing boards as the war ended were not highly advanced. German data was used to modify some of them to incorporate new features, preferably without putting development programmes too far behind schedule. Others that could not be readily adapted were dropped to make way for aircraft that would find an enduring place in the new 'jet age'.

In embarking upon new weapons programmes for this fresh generation of military aircraft, engineers faced a huge challenge, for what they created had inevitably to be hypothetical in terms of deployment. Service chiefs faced a similar dilemma in agreeing specifications for new weapons in most categories; few even had a clear idea of the type of aircraft required. The seeming inevitability of a third world war as East–West suspicion plumbed new depths only clouded the issue. Incidents such as the blockade of Berlin by the Russians in 1948, the brutal suppression of the uprising in Hungary in 1956 and the Cuban missile crisis of 1962 did nothing to dispel the uneasy feeling that international peace was fragile at best. Fortunately, none of these and other flashpoints sparked off conflict between the power blocs.

The 'bomber interception' years

This crossroads for military aircraft design encompassed the weapons that might be needed if a future war did not actually 'go nuclear'. Many diverse aerial guns, missiles and bombs were consequently tested during the 1950s and early 1960s. Aircraft were beginning to be designed around specific armament as 'weapons systems'. The idea that the Russians would sooner or later attack the West with long-range bombers took hold, and a similar possibility occurred to governments in the East, and so began a lengthy period of designing for such an eventuality. New jet fighters were given the primary mission of intercepting high-flying bombers, and destroying them with guns or missiles.

Although fleets of bombers would fail to materialise in anyone's airspace, service chiefs could hardly know that and the strategic response took precedence, to some detriment of the modern needs of air-to-air fighter combat and ground attack. Not all democratic governments agreed that the Russians would be the ones to start the next war. France refused to take this stance, and made plans to initiate its own response, wherever the attack might come from.

Initially there was a widespread belief in the West that tactical air power had had its day, and there was even some evidence of a return to the 1930s' maxim that 'the bomber would always get through'. In the late 1940s the prospect of that bomber carrying nuclear weapons concentrated minds as never before.

Moving quickly to establish a modern long-range bomber force, the USA formed SAC on 21 March 1946. Equipped initially with obsolete Boeing B-17s and B-29s marginally uprated in performance over the Superfortresses that had devastated Japan, SAC had a heavy responsibility. The B-29, reclassified as a medium rather than heavy bomber with the advent of the Convair B-36, gave way to the improved but similar B-50, which entered service in 1948.

Preceding the B-50 was the six-engined B-36, first delivered to SAC in August 1947. This monster, then the world's largest bomber with a wingspan of 230ft (70.10m) and length of 162ft 1in (49.37m), was for a time the cornerstone of US bombing strategy. It became the focal point of inter-Service rivalry, with the US Navy making a convincing case for sharing the nuclear strike role. 'The bomb' could equally well be delivered from a carrier-borne aircraft as from a hugely expensive ($US6.25 million each) and, as many admirals thought, vulnerable bomber capable of cruising at only just over 200mph (173.68km/h) or 381mph (330.86km/h) flat out. The Navy had to be nuclear-capable if its far-too-vulnerable carriers (as USAF chiefs believed) were to be retained as the core of a modern fleet. By the end of 1949 the USN was able to test nuclear strike capability with its largest shipborne aircraft to date, the mixed-propulsion North American AJ-1/2 Savage. Having formed the first AJ-1 squadron that September, the USN came to terms with handling big twin-engined aircraft aboard carriers. The Savage spanned 75ft 2in (22.92m) over its wingtip tanks and was 63ft 10in (19.23m) long, and it provided valuable experience in anticipation of the Navy's first twin jet with a swept-wing configuration, the Douglas A3D Skywarrior. Even larger than the AJ and also nuclear-capable, the A3D-1 would appear in 1956. In the meantime a handful of land-based Lockheed P2V-3 Neptunes were adapted for one-way carrier launch with a single nuclear weapon, just in case.

The bomber-versus-carrier row became very bitter indeed, but the USN made a good case for retaining the means to launch a retaliatory nuclear strike and successfully lobbied for funding its own nuclear bomb programme. With very capable new aircraft under test, the flexibility rather than vulnerability of carriers was emphasised and accepted.

Building the bomb

While the B-36 could lift a maximum of 72,000lb (32,660kg) of conventional bombs, it was seen as the spearhead of SAC's nuclear strike force, although atomic bomb production was initially modest. Only one example of the bomb dropped on Hiroshima, the Mk I 'Little Boy', was ever produced. Weighing 9,700lb (4,400kg), it was followed by the Mk II 'Fat Man'. After devastating Nagasaki this rotund 10,000lb (4,535kg) bomb, detonated by a radar proximity fuse, was chosen as the 'production' design. On 16 July 1945 an implosion detonation of this bomb represented the world's first nuclear weapons test.

The early US nuclear bombs were followed by the Mks 4 and 5, the latter being considerably lighter than its predecessors at 3,175lb (1,440kg) and the first model intended for mass production from 1948. It was also the first to be integrated as an aerial weapons system. Tested

The neatly enclosed tail gun of the Convair B-58 Hustler reflected a general US policy in retaining a minimum gun defence for strategic jet bombers. In the Hustler's case the weapon was a single radar-sighted six-barrel GE M61 cannon.

at Eniwetok Atoll in the spring of 1951, the Mk 5 weapon could also be carried by the smaller US bombers, including the North American B-45 Tornado. The first four-jet bomber to enter service (in 1948), the B-45 was destined for lengthy service, as was the Mk 5 nuclear bomb it might have had to drop in anger. The bomb remained in service until 1956, the same year that the Douglas B-66 Destroyer entered service to replace the B-45.

With tried and tested atomic bombs in production, the USA had the confidence that its first all-jet strategic bombers, the Boeing B-47 Stratojet and B-52 Stratofortress, were among the most effective air weapons anywhere. The B-47 entered service in mid-1951, and the first SAC Wing became operational with the B-52B in 1955. A year later the remarkable Convair B-58 Hustler, the first production US bomber capable of supersonic speeds, flew for the first time.

Britain's 'V' force

On the other side of the Atlantic the British planned a trio of new strategic bombers, primarily to counter anything the Russians might deploy in a similar role. After a protracted development period to bring the 1-kiloton-yield Blue Danube bomb to operational status, the first Vickers Valiant unit was formed early in 1955. This, No 138 Squadron at Gaydon, Warwickshire, thus had the awesome responsibility of spearheading the retaliation in the event of a nuclear strike on Britain.

In 1956 No 49 Squadron's Valiants were detached to the test range at Maralinga, South Australia, to drop a British thermonuclear bomb for the first time, a milestone reached on 11 October. In 1958 Yellow Sun, the first production-class bomb, was available to the RAF. This gave Bomber Command's V-force, which was gradually built up throughout this period, the capability to devastate any target within range.

The Valiant had a life of only ten years before metal fatigue caused the entire fleet to be withdrawn and scrapped in 1965. By that time the first Avro Vulcans had been delivered to the RAF for conversion training to forestall any dangerous gap in strategic capability. The Vulcan entered service in July 1957 with No 83 Squadron at Waddington, and was followed by the last of the V-force trio, the Handley Page Victor, which made its operational debut with No 10 Squadron at Cottesmore, Rutland, in April 1958. In the meantime the first British hydrogen bomb had appeared, and once again a Valiant of No 49 Squadron carried out the test drop, the H-bomb detonating over Christmas Island in the Pacific on 15 May 1957.

French independent force

The French Air Force formed its own nuclear strike force, the Force Nucléaire Stratégique (FNS), built around one aircraft type, the Dassault Mirage IVA. Flown for the first time on 17 June 1959, the prototype Mirage IV-01 attained a speed of Mach 1.9. A modification programme, including the installation of a dummy free-fall nuclear store, semi-recessed beneath the fuselage, had little detrimental effect on the aircraft's top speed, Mach 2.0 being attained on the thirty-third test flight. The first Mirage IVAs were delivered to the Armée de l'Air in 1964, a nuclear strike department having been established on 1 January that year. It was some eighteen months before a Mirage IVA crew gained practical experience of the aircraft's capabilities. In July 1966 an FNS

aircraft released an 18-kiloton free-fall bomb over Mururoa Atoll, 800 miles (1,287km) from Tahiti. By then France had had a fully independent nuclear air strike force for four months, President Charles de Gaulle having taken his country out of NATO on 10 March.

Later adapting its indigenous nuclear weapons to be used by tactical aircraft, France retained such capability with the AN 52, a bomb that could be carried by the Mirage IIIE and other types. By 1972 these Mirage fighters were fully nuclear-capable, typically representing a backup force to the FNS. Modified throughout what might be termed the 'tactical nuclear strike phase' of the 1970s and 1980s, the Mirage IV fleet of sixty-two production aircraft was gradually reduced to a current nineteen. As the Mirage IVP these machines have modern avionics and retain nuclear capability with the Aérospatiale ASMP stand-off missile.

Russian advances since 1945

Little of the West's progress in military aeronautics in postwar decades was lost on the Russians, whose designers soon found themselves embarking on projects to counter specific aircraft with which they might have had to contend in a war. Largely existing in dangerous ignorance not only of Soviet political ambitions but of exactly what the Soviet aviation design bureaux were currently achieving, Western nations took no chances and armed themselves to the teeth. They forged ahead with weapons which they confidently believed could win an East–West nuclear confrontation. By all accounts they might have had a very hard time of it.

Unlike other Western nations, France built its nuclear deterrent force around one type, the Mirage IVA. These potent machines served through the various changes in Armée de l'Air strike doctrine and ended up in tactical camouflage for the low-level strike role in vogue from the 1970s.

Having acquired examples of USAAF B-29s during the war, the Russians painstakingly dismantled and rebuilt the Superfortresses to provide the basis for series production as the Tupolev Tu-4. Being able to work with the actual B-29 systems, which included pressurisation and remotely controlled guns, saved the Russians months, if not years, of development work. Significant amounts of German research data, near-complete airframes and skilled personnel also facilitated the build-up of the Soviet air arm, the Voenno-Vozdushnye Sily (VVS). Like the West, Russia spent the next forty years or so testing a range of nuclear weapons and consolidating a potent 'power projection' air fleet.

As the world was subsequently to learn, even after the death of Stalin in 1953 an enduring Russian military hierarchy continued to fear much the same type of preemptive strike as the West envisaged coming from behind the Iron Curtain. Consequently, the enormous expenditure and effort necessary to keep ahead technically (which ultimately ruined the communist regimes in the East) rolled on. This process was already well advanced when Russia announced that it possessed the hydrogen bomb on 8 August 1953.

The Americans were then en route to perfecting a similar bomb, the 42,000lb (19,050kg) Mk 17 with a yield of 10–25 megatons, equivalent to up to 25 million tons of TNT. This bomb, air-dropped and detonated for the first time over Bikini Atoll on 1 May 1956, soon gave way to a smaller, more manageable (the Mk 17 was near-

ly 25ft (7.62m) long) series of nuclear bombs, the most widely used being the Mk 28. Not all of the intervening numbers were allocated to production bombs, although the much smaller and lighter Mks 12, 15 and 27 (the latter the result of a USN-funded programme) were intended for use by tactical fighters and medium bombers.

To deliver the H-bomb, the VVS was kept supplied with capable aircraft that paralleled the products of Western manufacturers. Despite having little historical experience of operating long-range bombers, the force soon had such aircraft, which also unwittingly provided the excuse for continued defence spending in the West. From the Tu-4, Tupolev's design bureau created the Tu-80 and Tu-85, technically advancing along the road to the Tu-95, which first flew on 16 February 1955. Carrying a 26,455lb (12,000kg) warload including nuclear bombs, this remarkable turboprop-powered aircraft was destined to remain in production for thirty-eight years, its numerous sub-variants reflecting revised operational needs over that period. Under current arms reduction agreements, savage cuts in the number of such aircraft kept operational by the Aviatsiya Voyska Strategischeskovo, which currently provides the airborne component of Russia's nuclear forces, have had to be made. Some ninety Tu-95s remain in service.

A similar extended Service life to that of the Tu-95 was found to be possible with the first Russian long-range turbojet bomber, the Tu-16. Entering production in late 1953, the Tu-16 made its Service debut the following year and was undoubtedly the most capable bomber of its day.

Carried under the fuselage of the Handley Page Victor B.2, but fitting a little more snugly than was possible with the Vulcan, Blue Steel was Britain's singular operational stand-off bomb. Powered by a Stentor rocket motor, it attained a speed of Mach 2 to deliver a warhead in the one-megaton range.

Designed to carry five classes of nuclear bomb, KS-1 anti-ship cruise missiles and conventional stores, the Tu-16 (*Badger* in the Air Standards Co-ordinating Committee (ASCC) reporting system) passed through many models during its production life, with conversions to tankers, electronic intelligence and electronic counter-measures aircraft reflecting the gradually diminishing nuclear strike requirement. China has produced this air-craft (as the Xian H-6) and other Russian types under licence to extend their service to the present decade.

In parallel with other air forces, over the years the VVS operated a range of twin-engined bombers in the medium-range category, the Ilyushin Il-28 and Yakovlev Yak-25 and Yak-27 being among the most important. Liberally supplied to Warsaw Pact countries, these were not seen to pose as much of a threat to the West as each new long-range type. Although these aircraft were scrutinised via satellite surveillance and other intelligence means, Western observers did not always judge the situation correctly, and what sometimes appeared to be the latest Russian bomber threat was in reality one of a substantial number of test vehicles. The notorious Tu-22 'Blinder' fell into this category. A variable-geometry version of the Tu-22K, the Tu-22M first flew on 30 August 1964. It took Western intelligence agencies five years to identify this important new aircraft, but by September 1969 the type was still three years from production start-up.

The proposition that modern bombers exemplified by the Tu-22 could well be an insurance against trouble a little closer to home was more or less confirmed during the autumn of 1964. China, Russia's unpredictable neighbour, exploded its first A-bomb on 16 October.

Shortly before the Soviet Union broke up, the variable-geometry Tu-160 became the most potent bomber the VVS had ever operated. It was no accident that it bore a marked resemblance to the North American B-1, for it was intended as a direct Soviet counter to the American type. Although the Tu-160 turned out to be more capable but very expensive and a little late, it still represented a great aeronautical achievement. Making its maiden flight on 19 December 1980, the aircraft was fitted with four of the most powerful engines in the world. A coating radar-absorbing material (RAM) gave it a level of stealth protection to deliver up to six Kh-55MS air-launched cruise missiles (ALCMs) at a maximum speed exceeding Mach 2.05 over a range of 7,650 miles (12,308km).

Funding for future military projects all but ran out as Russia's economy underwent a massive upheaval, and the Tu-160 was one of the victims. With the Soviet Union no longer existing, various Russian states inherited the air bases within their borders, among them the Ukraine. In May 1998 the government there decided that twenty-five Tu-95Ms and nineteen Tu-160s were too costly to maintain, and forty of these bombers are being scrapped, with the USA footing the bill. As only forty Tu-160s were built, current international arms-reduction agreements have relegated an important aircraft to little more than a footnote in history.

Change of delivery

Improved defence against the strategic bomber brought about a rethink of operational plans in the event of war. For a bomber to fly over, or indeed approach anywhere near the target, to release weapons of such destructive power carried an unacceptable risk. The 'other side' would understandably deploy any means to destroy the aircraft, and countries perceived to be under such a threat acquired improved radars and surface-to-air missiles to defend their most important cities and industrial targets.

The development of stand-off weapons such as Britain's Blue Steel helped keep the V-force viable under a revised operational plan. A 1-megaton-yield bomb with a range of 100 miles (320km), Blue Steel entered service in mid-1962, equipping the Vulcan B.2 and Victor. Each unit maintained one aircraft and crew on a quick reaction alert of fifteen minutes' notice, around the clock. Airfields were subject to maximum security and contingency plans were drawn up to disperse the aircraft should Britain come under attack. To maintain offensive capability, land-based missiles with nuclear warheads were purchased to back up bomber forces, which retained a theoretical independent effectiveness for a few years. But the nuclear attack submarine sidelined the intercontinental bomber as the main deterrent. Britain bought Polaris in 1962, and to fill any gap until a missile submarine force became operational, the RAF trained for a low-altitude nuclear delivery role designed to allow aircraft to penetrate hostile territory below radar-detection height using stand-off weapons. This was made possible by the WE-177 'lay-down' bomb, which saw operational service from 1966.

Placed on display at RAF Marham soon after it was withdrawn from service in mid-1998, the WE-177 tactical nuclear bomb was last intended for use by the Tornado. The breakup of the Soviet Union removed the need for RAF aircraft to carry such weapons, and the substantial stockpile was eliminated.

American developments

More muscle was added to SAC with the delivery of the first B-58A to the 43rd Bomb Wing at Carswell Air Force Base, Texas, on 15 March 1960. It was followed by a second Hustler Wing, the 305th at Bunker Hill, Indiana. Significantly different in configuration from other aircraft in the US inventory, the B-58, alias weapons system WS102A, carried its nuclear weapons in a ventral pod also containing fuel which would be burned off *en route* to the target, the pod being jettisoned after completion of the attack.

Nuclear delivery posed a considerable challenge in preserving a degree of safety for the crew. One novel approach by North American was followed through to USN service by the North American A3J (later A-5) Vigilante programme of 1956. Designed to deliver nuclear weapons, the A-5 had among other advanced features a linear bomb bay set between the engine tailpipes. A free-fall nuclear store was the primary armament, and this was to be ejected aft as the aircraft went into a high-speed climb. Two fuel tanks attached to the bomb were designed to stabilise it as it fell away, the fuel by then having been used up. Before this demanding role was perfected, USN policy changed and the Vigilante became the RA-5C reconnaissance aircraft.

The USA backed up its SAC bombers with a powerful nuclear-armed navy and a substantial land-based force of intercontinental ballistic missiles. Russia's forces were organised on similar lines. On a much smaller scale in terms of the number of warheads it could deploy, Britain followed a similar policy, maintaining a firm partnership with the USA via the NATO alliance. Although Royal Navy submarines officially assumed full responsibility for the UK strategic deterrent on 30 June 1969, the RAF retained nuclear strike capability, the emphasis by then having shifted almost entirely to tactical or 'sub-strategic' delivery. This brought smaller aircraft such as the Canberra into the picture to back up the remaining elements of the V-force, which was gradually wound down.

In subsequent years Hawker Siddeley Buccaneers, Sepecat Jaguars and McDonnell Douglas Phantoms were all nuclear-capable on an 'as required' basis, as was the Panavia Tornado. When the last Buccaneer squadron with such capability was disbanded in 1994, the Tornado GR.1 was the only RAF aircraft able to deliver WE-177 series munitions in a variety of weights, configurations and yields without special modifications having to be made.

The easing of East–West tension in the late 1980s led to a reduction of Britain's stockpiles of several hundred air-launched nuclear weapons and the relinquishing of an RAF role in delivery of the nuclear deterrent on 31 March 1998. If such a move seems rash, it is worth remembering that it is now perfectly feasible for a small but devastatingly powerful nuclear device to be packed into a suitcase.

Last of the bombers?

Despite SAC being stood down on 31 May 1992 under the biggest force-restructuring the USAF has had in recent times, the end of the Cold War did not see cancellation of the most expensive bomber in history. This, the Northrop B-2 Spirit, ran straight into *glasnost* arms-reduction agreements and a consequent review of the requirement, and it remains to be seen just how many the USAF will finally receive. First flown on 17 July 1989, the Spirit has an impressive capability: its variable weapons load can include up to sixteen B-83 free-fall nuclear bombs or eighty Mk 82 1,000lb (453kg) bombs. Costing about $US1 billion per unit, the B-2 has surely bought 'power projection' as far as it will probably ever need to go in this form. Stealth technology has enabled an even safer low-level role to be undertaken by the B-2. By reducing its radar signature through dramatically different airframe design and special materials, Northrop ensured that the aircraft appears as a much smaller, seemingly insignificant radar image than would otherwise be presented by its 172ft (52.43m) span and 69ft (21.03m) length. Currently the B-2 has been delivered only to the ominously numbered 509th Bomb Wing at Whiteman Air Force Base, Missouri (it was the specially formed 509th Composite Wing that dropped the atomic bombs on Japan). The US Congress has fought shy of funding more than twenty aircraft, although the USAF has announced a requirement for 133.

Stealth-type protection is not so easy with an older design. While the B-52 force adopted a low-level penetration mission profile in the 1970s, the bomber appears to be vulnerable to SAMs and interceptors. Yet B-52 crews have faced both with minimal losses, so vulnerability is relative; only really quantifiable in combat.

What might be termed an interim stealth solution to this problem of a strategic bomber surviving a modern defence was achieved by the Rockwell B-1 Lancer. Originally designed to replace the B-52, the cancelled B-1A of 1974 was followed by the resurrected B-1B in 1981. Given RAM coatings and engine-ducting masking, the Lancer carries a variable weapons load including B-61 and B-83 bombs, making it the USAF's primary nuclear bomber. The B-1B, 100 of which were delivered, continues to fly alongside its venerable Boeing stablemate as part of the current combined strike force or 'Super Wing' concept followed by the USAF's Air Combat Command.

The undisputed capability of current US bombers confirms the fact that, while the Strategic Arms Limitation Treaty (SALT) negotiations have led to significant reductions in stockpiles of nuclear-warhead weapons held by the superpowers, it has not been possible to stop them spreading. The nuclear club gained another member when India exploded a nuclear device on 18 May 1974. In mid-1998 India, along with Pakistan, appeared bent on a renewed arms race, and there remains the sobering prospect of less-responsible regimes, indifferent to world opinion, resorting to actual use – but few people should now believe that they also need a B-52 to do so!

Guns versus rockets

Aerial machine-guns had been so thoroughly refined during the Second World War that some postwar usage, in virtually identical form, was assured. The American Colt Browning M-2 and M-3 0.50in (12.7mm) gun, used in fixed and moveable mountings in most first-line fighters and bombers, became one of the outstanding aerial weapons of all time; its economy, reliability, ease of manufacture and maintenance gave a commonality that was appreciated by front-line units. Coupled with the APG-30 gunsight, the M-3 had a useful range and accuracy plus a high percentage of strikes from a firing rate of 1,000 rounds per minute (rpm).

In Russia this concept was followed by an even more efficient machine-gun, the Beresin UB. This, too, was a 12.7mm weapon, mass-produced in vast quantities, and continued to be used by the older front-line aircraft remaining in service during the immediate postwar period. However, cannon soon became the required fixed armament for jet fighters.

Russia's policy of building numerous prototypes and test vehicles resolved most technical problems, including those concerning gunnery, before new aircraft entered service. Proving that it is nevertheless impossible to solve every hitch, engine air starvation caused by gun gas occurred on the first Soviet jet fighter to enter service, the MiG-9. In that case, repositioning the three cannon – two NS-23s and one N-37 – higher on the fuselage sides overcame the drawback, also experienced in other parts of the world as fighter speeds increased.

International preference

Britain's designers had historically tended to favour the greater destructive power of cannon, and there was a general adherence to the 20mm Hispano for the early RAF and RN jet fighters. Weighing just 106lb (48kg), the wartime short-barrelled Mk V Hispano with a firing rate of 650–750rpm was eminently adaptable to the first-generation jets. The desirability of doubling the rate of fire with the acceptable penalty of heavier rounds eventually led to adoption of the 30mm gun. A revolver-action weapon, the Aden (Armament Development ENfield) cannon was chosen for volume production. At 200lb (90kg) the Aden gun was double the weight of the Hispano, but that was not the main problem facing designers of British fighters. What caused some headaches was safe disposal of spent rounds and, more importantly, the lightweight metal belt links for each round. Highly explosive firing gases also built up in gun

After many years of reliance on the 20mm Hispano, Britain finally developed the 30mm Aden cannon which was to serve the RAF equally well. A removable pack incorporating the breeches and ammunition feed for four guns was installed on most Hawker Hunters, represented here by an aircraft of No 74 Squadron.

bays, and this, added to the known factor of rapid pressure changes around engine intakes, could cause the links to be ingested, causing flame-out. This was similar to the problems experienced by the Russians, who had also found that discharging the MiG-9's guns above 24,600ft (7,500m) caused engine surge and flameout. This was cured, as mentioned earlier, by the redesign of the forward fuselage and repositioning of the guns.

Aden cannon were first used by the Supermarine Swift F.1s which entered service with No 56 Squadron in February 1954. The Hunter F.1 appeared in July that year, the aircraft issued to No 43 Squadron having four Adens in a belly pack which could be completely removed for servicing and rearming. Similarly armed was the Gloster Javelin FAW.1, which became operational with No 56 Squadron in February 1956. Later versions of the Javelin, the FAW.7 and 8, carried only two Aden cannon, their fixed armament being complemented by four Firestreak air-to-air missiles (AAMs) on wing launchers.

In June 1958 the Supermarine Scimitar, the only British naval fighter then having the 30mm Aden cannon as a fixed gun, was delivered to No 803 Squadron, Fleet Air Arm. Subsequently the Aden was used by FAA Phantoms and the Sea Harrier, the latter carrying two cannon in detachable belly packs.

American practice

In the USA there was an adherence to the machine-gun for the first-generation jets. With fighter speeds having increased only marginally over those of the reciprocating-engined types of the last war, the Lockheed F-80, Republic F-84 and North American F-86 used the M-3 machine-gun as fixed armament with few reported problems. Early USN jets were cannon-armed, the designation M-3 also being used for the 20mm weapons under the US system of that time. Both machine-guns and cannon were widely augmented by ground-attack weapons when the 'real war' of the 1950s broke out in Korea. The versatile Douglas AD Skyraider, with four 20mm cannon, showed that the way forward in the close-support role was not necessarily the sole prerogative of jets.

With United Nations' aircraft, including Seafires, Fireflies and Sea Furies of the RN, all armed with Hispano cannon, conducting multiple air strikes on ground targets, it was left to the Russians via their North Korean ally, to whom they supplied liberal quantities of MiG-15s, to up the stakes in air-to-air gun duels. Primarily in combat with F-86s, MiGs armed with two 23mm NR cannon on the lower port side of the nose and a single N37D 37mm weapon on the starboard side had the potential to cause fatal damage in dogfights. In the main, North Korean pilots generally proved to be too inexperienced to take full advantage of the MiG's performance, while Sabre pilots, even with their 'out-moded' guns, showed that superior training and tactics are often the key to success in combat.

While all the subsequent F-84 Thunderjet/Thunderstreak derivatives retained machine-guns, towards the end of the Korean conflict F-86 Sabres were fitted with four 20mm Oerlikon or American T-160 cannon in the 'Gun-val' operational testing programme. The success of this evaluation (six enemy aircraft were shot down) led to the installation of cannon in some succeeding Sabre variants, including the later F-86Hs and the F-86K. The F-86D differed in that it was given an all-rocket armament of twenty-four 2.75in (14.6cm) folding-fin aircraft rockets (FFARs) for the interceptor role, while the F-86Ls were updated D models.

Combat experience in Korea was instrumental in speeding up programmes designed to modernise the US air forces, although other nations saw the need to instigate similar updating. The USAF ordered an entirely new generation of jet types which explored a range of armament options. Some aircraft with innovative armament, such as the Northrop F-89 Scorpion, were already in service but had not been selected for combat in Korea.

The F-89 began its USAF service in July 1950 armed with six 20mm M-24 cannon in the nose, but the F-89D dropped the integral guns in favour of 2.75in (14.6cm) FFARs, nicknamed 'Mighty Mouse', housed in wingtip pods. A design begun in December 1945, the Scorpion was not given wing sweep and other advanced features, but it overcame some early technical problems to become one of the most reliable of the early jets. The Scorpion's revised armament appeared to point the way to the future for fighters, and rockets rather than guns were similarly adopted for the later versions of Lockheed's F-94 Starfire. Relinquishing the four 0.50in machine-guns of the F-94B, the C model of 1950 had forty-eight 2.75in (14.6cm) rockets set in a unique ring magazine around the nose. While the F-94A and B saw combat in Korea, the C model remained at home, seeing USAF and Air Guard service until 1959.

The USN continued to specify 20mm cannon for its fighters of the late 1950s/early 1960s, the Americans basing their M-39 gun on the German MG-213C. The Ford Motor Co and the Pontiac Division of General Motors produced the M-39E and subsequent models for installation in the Fury, Cutlass, Skyray, Tiger, Demon and Crusader, with AAMs and other ordnance being carried, depending on operational requirements.

The USAF followed a more diverse path in regard to aerial guns. There was a gradual reduction in the number of moveable guns carried by jet bombers, though 20mm weapons for tail defence were retained in the B-47 and B-66. Exceptions were the B-52, which originally had four 0.50in machine-guns in a remotely controlled tail 'stinger' (a single Minigun was later fitted in

An early production F-89 Scorpion salvoing its HVARs. The staple air-to-ground weapon of US jet fighters in the early post-war years, these missiles were drawn from old and new stock until they were all but exhausted during the Korean War to make way for the 2.75in FFAR based on the wartime German R4M.

some B-52Hs), and the B-57, armed with machine-guns and cannon in its early intruder variants.

In Russia, development of the 'baseline' MiG-15 led to the MiG-17 and MiG-19, and although there was a family resemblance, each design represented a significant increase in capability. The MiG-17P, armed with three NR 23 cannon, was the first radar-equipped jet interceptor to enter VVS service, and the MiG-17PFu became the first European fighter capable of firing AAMs. Making its service debut in mid-1955, the MiG-17 could carry four K-5 missiles on inboard wing pylons to augment its cannon.

Armament diversity was quite marked in the fighters of the 'Century Series' which represented a new generation of interceptors (those enemy bomber fleets were still probably coming). They were the F-100 Super Sabre, with four M-39E 20mm cannon; the McDonnell F-101 Voodoo, with four 20mm cannon; the F-104 Starfighter, with one 20mm General Electric M61A1 Vulcan gun; the Convair F-102 Delta Dagger and F-106 Delta Dart with no guns and the F-105 Thunderchief with one M61A1 Vulcan. The Super Sabre and Thunderchief were destined to excel more in the ground-attack role, although the 'Hun' equipped many interceptor squadrons as part of the US national

defence force for some years before the requirement for 'mud movers' in Vietnam. The F-105, disappointing at home owing to its variable reliability, became the mainstay of the USAF tactical bombing effort in Southeast Asia. The Starfighter's major deployment was in Europe in the hands of foreign air arms. As a fighter/interceptor the Voodoo's career spanned twenty-six years, a period that included highly successful war duty by the derivative RF-101 in Vietnam.

In armament terms the odd pair out were the Convair fighters. Both the F-102 and F-106 were missile carriers from the outset. The Delta Dagger entered service in mid-1956 armed with six Hughes AIM-4C/D missiles or two AIM-26B AAMs. In addition, it could carry twenty-four 2.75in (14.6cm) FFARs, a very widely deployed weapon of the period. In July 1959 Air Defense Command took delivery of the first F-106A, the two-seat F-106B making its first flight in April 1958. Both fighters saw service with the USAF at home and in Europe.

The single M61A1 Vulcan gun carried initially by the F-104 and F-105 represented a significant advance in aircraft cannon design. Consisting of six rotating barrels, the Vulcan was superior to a fixed battery of cannon in that installation and servicing were easier, cooling was more efficient and barrel wear evenly

The mighty M61 20mm cannon, operating on the Gatling principle of revolving multiple barrels, was one of the most significant aerial weapons of modern times. It enabled retention of a fixed gun as a backup to missiles on current US interceptors. With minor variations, mainly in the number of rounds of ammunition the drum held, the M61 has been fitted into aircraft of different configurations with little difficulty.

spread, even though firing rate was high. Tailored to fit aircraft of differing configurations, the gun had a total overall weight of 272lb (123.37kg), and its ammunition load and storage container usually varied only in terms of the number of rounds carried. All current USAF, Navy and Marine fighters which have guns are fitted with the M61A1.

European progress

In Europe there was less experimentation with all-missile armament for fighters. Tighter budgets saw the RAF interceptors of the 1950s and 1960s relying primarily on built-in cannon backed up by unguided rockets and the 'home-grown' infrared-seeking Firestreak (service debut August 1958) or Red Top (1964) AAMs. Protracted anti-terrorist operations over Malaya, which occupied the RAF until 1969, and the brief Suez operation in November 1956, required only conventional bombs and rockets.

Much the same 'no frills' policy on aircraft weaponry was followed by France, striving to build up a postwar manufacturing industry. From the 20mm DEFA cannon fitted to the straight-winged Dassault Ouragan of 1952, the Mystère and Mirage series switched to 30mm, a calibre which remains a clear French favourite today. Other nations followed suit. In Sweden the rotund Saab J 29 of 1948 was armed with 20mm Hispano cannon, as was the A model of the succeeding J 32 Lansen. In improved J 32B form this aircraft went over to Aden cannon of 30mm, as did the J 35 Draken.

A logical move

Extensive research and development programmes pointed to a significant increase in the potential lethality and increased range of the air-to-air missile over fixed armament. This caused McDonnell to opt entirely for missiles rather than a gun when it proposed the F4H Phantom II to the USN. In 1955 this aircraft promised

The de Havilland Firestreak was a substantial weapon carried by the first-line British fighters of the 1950s and 1960s. The Gloster Javelin could carry four of the 300lb (137kg) weapons.

Red Top was also a de Havilland-developed missile. Weighing 330lb (150kg), it was capable of a speed of Mach 3. Two were carried on forward-fuselage launching points on the Lightning fighter.

so significant a performance advantage over types then in service, including the then new Grumman F11F Tiger, that the idea of future fighters relying only on AAMs was accepted. Clearly guns would be even more old hat by the time the navy got the Phantom.

The USN had few problems with this radical change in fighter armament, even when it became embroiled in combat over Vietnam. Carrier crews flying F-4s shot down forty-one enemy aircraft (thirty-nine MiGs and two An-2s) using AIM-7 and AIM-9 missiles during the course of the war. Crusaders also claimed their share of kills, the F-8's acquired nickname 'Last of the Gunfighters' saying much about what had been on the cards for some time *vis-à-vis* the armament of USN aircraft.

It was only later, when the USAF purchased the Phantom, that the lack of a fixed gun was seriously criticised. Modified to take a centreline M61A1 cannon, the F-4E entered USAF squadron service in November 1968, in time to fly combat missions over Vietnam during the last stages of the US involvement. Of the total of 107 MiGs destroyed in Southeast Asia by all USAF Phantom models, five fell to F-4Es using the integral cannon. An additional MiG was shot down by a crew

using a combination of AIM-9 and gunfire. While this figure was small, the political situation in Vietnam and the short time the F-4E was in combat have to be taken into account – as well as the fact that, without a gun, the victories would probably not have happened at all.

Pod guns

One way the USAF resolved the fixed-gun shortfall on the Phantom, by far and away its most significant and important multirole aircraft, was to order guns that could be 'bolted on'. When F-4C deliveries began in 1963, wing and fuselage hardpoints were adapted to take guns in streamlined pods. Hughes and General Electric supplied the massive SUU-16 and SUU-23 to the USAF, both of which were used on the F-4C and D. The SUU-16 contained a 20mm M61 gun and was operated by a ram-air turbine, while the SUU-23 used gun gas as its actuating agent. Gun power was welcomed by aircrews, who began to bemoan the less-than-total ability of the mid-1960s models of the AIM-9 and AIM-7 to destroy their intended targets. Ten MiGs were downed by the crews of early-model Phantoms using only 20mm gunfire.

Powered by an external ram-air turbine, the SUU-16 pod containing an M61 20mm cannon was an early answer to the lack of fixed guns when the USAF ordered the F-4 Phantom. These guns were regularly used on combat missions in Vietnam, and the SUU-23 pod equipped British models of the aircraft.

The maximum configuration of three pods on wing and centreline stations was used in action by some F-4 pilots on strafing missions in Vietnam, although a single centreline pod was more common. Other aircraft, even those that did have fixed cannon such as the Douglas A-4 Skyhawk, occasionally used pod guns to increase the weight of fire they could lay down on tactical targets.

From these larger pods, smaller and lighter streamlined casings were developed. A range of one or more machine-guns or cannon, neatly enclosed in pods, emerged to uprate the firepower of lighter fixed-wing aircraft designed or adapted for battlefield support sorties.

In Britain, early postwar RAF and RN fighters of the 1950s and 1960s were almost universally armed with 20mm cannon. Four guns became the general standard, the exception being the F-86 Sabre, which the RAF used briefly during the early 1950s. Regarded only as stop-gap type – with the distinction of being the first swept-wing fighter operated by the RAF – the Sabre retained its six 0.50in machine-guns.

A major advance over the Second World War-vintage 20mm Hispano in that it could fire a heavier round, the Aden proved a reliable weapon in either fixed installations or pods. It equipped the Lightning, Jaguar, Harrier and Hawk, and the Phantom, which in RN and RAF service did not have fixed guns. Variants of guns in 30mm size were manufactured by DEFA and Oerlikon and saw widespread use in French and Swedish aircraft of the period.

In Germany, Mauser's heavier BK 27, an excellent gun offering a wide choice of ammunition, was selected for the Tornado, (including the RAF versions) the Alpha Jet and Sweden's JAS 39 Gripen fighter. Although it was good, its different calibre required separate stocks of ammunition and a further diversification from any NATO standard, which had become increasingly hard to achieve. This caused NATO-assigned units a considerable headache. On realistic 'war footing' exercises it was occasionally found that squadrons could not readily be rearmed during cross-base operations without pre-positioning of the right type of ammunition. Such a luxury could not realistically be counted upon in time of war.

With no perceptible international standardisation of weapons and equipment, world manufacturers (not necessarily those with a mainstream aerospace background) exploited lucrative, ready markets for aerial weapons. Conventional weaponry proliferated to fill all operational requirements and reflect the universal concentration on the tactical rather than strategic role.

Return of the gun fighter

In another category of aircraft developed in the 1960s, fixed guns were generally favoured. These were new designs put forward for the counterinsurgency (COIN) role and those based on existing variants used for training. The smaller European and Latin American air arms were particularly attracted by the economy and lower operating costs offered by such aircraft, which lacked fire-control radar and had 'limited' avionics but could carry an impressive amount of ordnance on wing and fuselage hardpoints. Exemplified by the Northrop F-5 Freedom Fighter (two 20mm cannon), the Folland Gnat (two 30mm) and the Fiat G 91 (four 0.5in machine-guns or two 20mm cannon depending on version), the small, economical strike aircraft found a niche in the world inventory of military aircraft.

Types such as the Cessna T-37 Dragonfly and North American T-28 Trojan helped bring about a widespread secondary role for those aircraft primarily ordered as crew trainers. That said, the T-37 was in a class of its own in terms of integral armament, for its single General Electric 7.62mm Minigun was one of the first adaptations for a fixed-wing aircraft of what was more widely regarded as a helicopter gun.

Gunships

A further application of the Minigun was in Douglas C-47 transports used in a nocturnal attack role. Over Vietnam the docile Skytrain became a tiger in the guise of a gunship which proved a devastating weapon against ground forces. Following early experiments with machine-guns to prove the concept, three Miniguns were adopted as standard, fired by the pilot using a gunsight. The Skytrain was held in a long, slow left bank for the duration of the firing run, but constant correction was necessary as the recoil action of the guns continually caused the aircraft to flatten out. A withering stream of shells could be aimed at the ground as long as the ammunition lasted; a typical four-second burst from one gun at a slant range of 4,500ft (1,371m) put 400 bullets into a circle 31.7ft (9.66m) in diameter. It was appropriate to give the armed transports an 'attack' designation and a nickname, and thus the AC-47 'Spooky' was born. It was a remarkable new role for an aircraft that was nearly thirty years old, and it proved that gunships had a place in a Vietnam-type war where highly sophisticated air power was continually frustrated by guerrilla tactics. However, when the enemy was able to retaliate with adequate firepower the AC-47 had little means of defending itself.

Adopting the generic word 'gunship', which had originated in the US Army's attack helicopter programme, such operations were extended to the Fairchild AC-119 Boxcar and Lockheed AC-130 Hercules, mainly as a result of the heavy losses sustained by the AC-47s and the proven need for larger, more modern aircraft to interdict enemy road transport. The AC-119 'Shadow' represented the USAF's Gunship 3 programme, the converted aircraft carrying Miniguns or 20mm Gatling weapons. The Hercules, the largest aircraft used in the gunship role, initially had Miniguns and later four

A war in which numerous new weapons and tactics were tested, Vietnam brought the fixed-wing gunship to prominence. Developed to increase the firepower that could be brought to bear by a single aircraft, the AC-130H carried 20mm M61 cannon, 7.62mm Miniguns and 40mm Bofors guns.

20mm cannon and 40mm Bofors guns in the cabin. But even this amazing firepower was topped when a single 105mm howitzer was fitted into the AC-130H in time to participate in blunting the 1972 Easter offensive by North Vietnamese forces.

Having proven the worth of fixed-wing gunships in specialised roles, the USAF scaled down the programme after Vietnam, although the Hercules operated as a gunship during the invasion of Grenada in October 1993. The 'toothed' version of the venerable Lockheed transport survives into the current inventory as the AC-130U, fitted with modern sensors and a GAU-12 125mm cannon replacing the M61s.

Backup fighters

Using guns fixed or in pods for pilot tuition in ground attack was but a short step from a 'dedicated' front-line backup role such as that currently adopted by some of the RAF's BAe Hawks. Lightweight gun packages can turn the humblest of trainers into combat aircraft, a trend which continues, making military pilot training much more economical than hitherto. Also, the availability of such weapons accessories can give smaller states or countries with limited military budgets a 'bargain basement air force'.

It was evident by the late 1960s that policies placing total reliance on missiles for military aircraft had not appreciated that air combat, taking place at relatively low altitudes and subsonic speeds, usually within visual range of the opposing pilots, was far from dead. In a realistic combat situation guns and missiles still tend to complement each other, but so much depends on the situation that develops, the skill of the opposing pilots, and the relative performance of their respective fighters. However, a certain transition from guns to missiles has occurred as the accuracy of AAMs has improved. This can be seen by examining the Israeli Air Force's (IAF) combat record. Having seen more action in its fifty-year history than most other air arms, the IAF progressed from being equipped entirely with French aircraft in the 1967 Six Day War to the current order of battle, which is composed of aircraft primarily of US origin. The Heyl ha'Avir also moved on from scoring all of its air-to-air victories with cannon fire in the 1967 war, to a ratio of 70 per cent:30 per cent in favour of missiles during the Yom Kippur War, and almost total missile kills (93 per cent) in operations over the Lebanon in 1982, even though its F-4s, F-15s and F-16s retained guns.

Moreover, numerous war sorties have proved that front-line tactical aircraft need, for the foreseeable future, to be able to accommodate numerous passive items as well as ordnance on fuselage and wing pylons. As electronics came to play an increasingly important role in war, carrying the necessary equipment became a simple matter of survival. Add cameras in external pods and the humble but vital fuel tank, and the underside of the average fighter can be pretty crowded before a single munition is attached. Multiple racks and conformal fuel tanks have made things easier, and gun pods can still be accommodated, but the need for them is clearly lessening. In recent years the trend once again has been to tuck the cannon inside the airframe. A gun remains the backup in close-in aerial combat, for a fighter which has expended all of its AAMs cannot be very useful, and today the world's front-line fighters and strike aircraft almost universally have fixed armament.

That said, the wheel appears to be coming full circle again with the fighter generation for the next century. Of these, the Lockheed F-117 Nighthawk has no fixed gun, the Dassault Rafale a single 30mm, the EF-2000 Eurofighter one 27mm and the Lockheed Martin/Boeing F-22 Raptor one M61A1.

Missiles

The first postwar guided-missile programmes, those that would ultimately result in weapons to meet most air, land and seaborne eventualities, were immeasurably helped by German developments under wartime conditions. By examining the history and operational record of the R4M, the world's first AAM, it was relatively easy for US industry to adapt this weapon into the 2.75in FFAR, variants of which saw service around the globe for many years. The Korean War saw widespread use of unguided ground-to-air rockets, the ubiquitous High-Velocity Aircraft Rockets (HVAR) in 3.5in (8.89cm) and 5in (12.70cm) sizes with 80lb (36kg) and 140lb (63kg) warheads respectively being expended liberally on ground targets. The USAF also used up stocks of the 11.75in (29.84cm) Tiny Tim, slinging a couple under the wings of F-51 Mustangs for a number of sorties, the results of which helped confirm that there was a place for air-to-ground missiles fitted with special warheads to deal with specific targets such as tanks and ships.

Sidewinder

Fitting infrared or heat-seeking warheads was found to be the most effective way of getting an AAM to bring down enemy aircraft. Lacking more-sophisticated guidance, such a missile was reliable enough provided the pilot could position his aircraft squarely behind the target, where the exhaust emission gave off its highest temperature. With a positive 'lock-on' the missile would invariably home on to the heat source. At the same time, AAMs needed ideally to be economical and simple enough to be carried by numerous aircraft types without substantial modification. An additional requirement was for mass production on a large scale, and this process really began with the Philco-Ford AIM-9 infrared (heat-seeking) missile of the mid-1950s. Said at the time to have fewer moving parts than the average radio set, the AIM-9 was successfully test-fired for the first time on 11 September 1953. Identified initially as the XAAM N-7, GAR-8 by the USAF, N-7 by the Navy and SW-1 by the development team, the early versions were made compatible with the F-86s sold to Nationalist China. It was this air force, battling its larger communist neighbour over Quemoy in October 1958, that recorded the first combat use of the Sidewinder when a number of MiG-17s were downed.

Vietnam also saw the AIM-9 Sidewinder heat-seeking AAM used extensively in combat for the first time. This is an AIM-9B on the port wingtip launcher of an F-104C Starfighter.

Missiles came under the force-wide US military air-craft redesignations of 1962, and the SW-1 became the AIM-9. Production had meanwhile geared up to supply the USAF and USN with the AIM-9B, which appeared on most US first-line aircraft of the period.

No combat action ever came the way of RN Super-marine Scimitar pilots, although this transonic fighter was the first British type to have Sidewinders. Initial live firings were made over Aberporth range on 21 October 1961, when a Meteor drone was destroyed. Service Scimitars flying combat air patrols were cleared to carry up to four AIM-9Bs on wing pylons. British association with the AIM-9 was limited, for it was not until the Phantom FG.1 entered service in April 1968 that the missile became part of the standard ordnance available to the FAA. After the Scimitar, the de Havilland Sea Vixen and Blackburn Buccaneer largely relied on the Red Top missile. In 1982, with the Phantom gone, the only Sidewinder-capable type was the BAe Sea Harrier, but its missiles then needed updating with the current AIM-9L when an urgent need arose to offer greater air combat capability over the disputed Falkland Islands. Stocks of the AIM-9L were consequently rushed to RN carriers in time for Harriers to give a good account of themselves in com-bat with Argentinian aircraft.

Improved models of the AIM-9 appeared regularly, the series having currently reached the AIM-9P, the ninth major production model. During its long service the Sidewinder has appeared under various guises and is licence-built in considerable volume outside the USA. The number of aircraft capable of launching

An important type in the Armée de l'Air inventory, the Mirage F 1 was a 'best-seller'. Although the internal cannon armament was retained, the aircraft's lethality increased substantially when armed with two R 550 Magic AAMs on the wingtips and four R 530 interception missiles. These were usually paired, one being a heat-seeker and the other radar guided.

Sidewinders expanded to include helicopters, and a larger Russian version was developed as the K-13A (Atoll) for front-line interceptors. Israel's development was the Shafir, also larger than the AIM-9 but having the same basic layout.

Radar guidance

Radar guidance appeared to offer a substantial advan-tage over infrared seekers for AAMs, and Hughes began development of the GAR-1, which became the AIM-4 Falcon series in 1962. The first radar-guided AAM in the world to see service, the Falcon reached initial oper-ating capability in 1956 as the intended armament of the F-89H Scorpion. Perfecting a triple-round retractable launcher for wingtip carriage on the F-89 proved chal-lenging to Hughes, but the system was made to work.

Success with the Scorpion system led to AIM-4s being adopted for the F-101, F-102 and F-106. All these aircraft carried missiles to destroy bombers, and it was not until 1963, when the AIM-4D appeared, that a version of the Falcon was intended for fighter combat. It was carried and used operationally by the F-4 in Viet-nam, where five aerial victories were scored with it despite the elderly Falcon not being considered the most important of the Phantom's weapons. The AIM-4D was the final production version.

Sparrow

The weapon that was most important to the Phantom and other front-line fighters and attack aircraft was the radar-guided Raytheon AIM-7 Sparrow. As the primary armament of the F-4, four AIM-7s were carried in semi-recessed bays in the fuselage undersides.

As widely known, but more expensive and second to the AIM-9 in terms of numbers built, the XAAM-N-2 Sparrow I appeared in 1961, the Sperry company being the main contractor. First tested in 1953, the beam-riding missile was fitted with dipole aerials which picked up sig-nals from the fighter's radar and powered cruciform delta wings to keep it aligned in the centre of the beam. A 52lb (23.4kg) blast/fragmentation warhead was activated by a proximity fuse. By late 1956 the Sparrow was in USN ser-vice, arming the Cutlass, Demon and Skyknight. The Sparrow and its derivatives have been the primary air-to-air weapons of many Western air arms for more than three decades. Sky Flash, the UK version, was built by British Aerospace Dynamics for delivery to the RAF from 1978.

By the early 1980s, research-and-development pro-grammes indicated that a far superior radar-guided mis-sile was possible using the latest computer technology. The result was the Hughes AIM-120A advanced medi-um-range AAM (AMRAAM). Designed to replace both the AIM-9 and AIM-7A by encompassing a very much more lethal warhead in a lighter and smaller body, AMRAAM had a full airborne interception suite built

After years of non-standardisation of weapons, NATO has in recent years improved this situation, one example being AIM-132 ASRAAM, a version of the US Hughes AIM-120, seen here on a Tornado F.3. Developed by British Aerospace in the UK and Bodenseewerk Geratetechnik in Germany, the missile has interoperability between a range of aircraft types within the alliance. Canada and other countries are also involved in the programme.

into it. This meant that, with the right basic co-ordinates fed in, the missile launched, switched on its own radar, used IFF to interrogate any friendly aircraft and went on to kill the intended target. Such a sophisticated system required a considerable investment of time and money, and the Hughes team faced daunting technical and budgetary problems, not to mention an embarrassing time delay. Surviving near-cancellation during the 1980s, AIM-120 emerged as a highly effective beyond-visual-range (BVR) weapon once its software programs had been debugged. By late 1988 the first USAF deliveries began, just in time for the AIM-120 to be carried into action during the Gulf War. It was not until the war ended that an F-16 pilot used one to shoot down an Iraqi MiG-25 with one shot. Two more single rounds, fired over the Gulf and Bosnia, made a total of three shots, three kills. This had never happened before with a new missile, and the fact that F-16 maintenance crews could tack on an AIM-120 in the space formerly occupied by an AIM-9 made it an instant favourite with pilots.

Deals were struck and the AMRAAM found customers in the UK, Norway, Sweden and Germany. A developed AIM-120C will arm the USAF's F-22A stealth fighter, and it will almost certainly remain in production until well into the twenty-first century.

Phoenix

Following the integrated weapons system philosophy to a logical culmination has led to programmes that remain more or less unique as a 'one-aircraft, one-missile' package. Such was the case with the intended primary armament of the General Dynamics F-111B fighter for the USN. When this aircraft, originated as

the TFX programme, ran into vast cost overruns, huge controversy and partial cancellation as the multirole, multi-service fighter it was intended to be, its weapons system, the AIM-54A Phoenix, was 'inherited' by the Grumman F-14 Tomcat. This at least kept it within Navy budgeting, as the F-14 was the Service's answer to the gap left by the stillborn F-111B. The F-111 also survived of course, to evolve as a successful USAF strike/ECM aircraft rather than a fighter, although the designation endured.

Meanwhile the Phoenix went to sea. Phenomenally expensive at around $1 million dollars a shot, the long-range, radar-guided AIM-54 is not a Tomcat pilot's first choice in 'limited' air engagements if a cheaper missile will do. An F-14 crew from VF-1 scored a single confirmed kill over an Mi-8 helicopter with an AIM-9 during the Gulf War. Phoenix remains an integral part of the Tomcat, up to six missiles being housed semi-recessed on the F-14A and B models, while two plus AIM-7s and AIM-9s are more typical on the F-14D. The missile itself has appeared in A, B and C versions, the last weighing 1,002lb (457.2kg). Outstandingly capable, with a speed of Mach 5 and a ceiling of 100,000ft (30,490m) plus, the Phoenix has a 132lb (59.9kg) warhead, making it one of the most powerful weapons in the world's arsenal.

Anti-radiation missiles

If the Second World War spurred weapons development far beyond the point reached at at the start of the conflict, the 'modern' wars in Korea, the Middle East and especially Vietnam spawned modernisation of systems in a considerably shorter timeframe. With the advantage of progressively miniaturised and versatile electronic components, missiles have greatly improved target-destruction ratios compared with those of the early 1960s.

Originally intended for the US Navy's General Dynamics F-111B, the costly AIM-54A Phoenix was inherited by the Grumman F-14 Tomcat. This F-14A of VF-32 is carrying its full complement of six AIM-54As on underwing and semi-recessed underfuselage mountings.

Missiles came increasingly into the expanding realm of countermeasures as Vietnam air operations developed. Aircraft losses to groundfire grew out of proportion to the perceived results achieved through bombing and interdiction, and the numbers attributable to Russian-built SAMs began to spiral. Missiles that could home on to SAM guidance radars were one sure counter, and by the end of the Vietnam War the anti-radiation missile had come into its own to represent what was, in most respects, a new class of weapon.

The first US tactical anti-radiation missile was the Texas Instruments AGM-45A Shrike. Ordered in 1963 as a relatively simple weapon that would destroy enemy land-based radars, the Shrike became synonymous with the USAF's Wild Weasel sorties over North Vietnam. When the NVPA used the SA-2 operationally for the first time on 24 July 1965 the war took on a new dimension. Fortunately for US strike forces, the enemy's profligate but not overly accurate expending of the Russian missiles gave plenty of opportunities for aircrews to work out evasive tactics, and only 2 per cent of those launched actually hit their targets. This did not mean that SAMs could be ignored; not when eight aircraft were downed in the space of the intervening months up to 27 November. That cost brought a trade-off of eight SAM sites destroyed – a not very acceptable ratio.

While the Shrike missile had its limitations, its use from May 1966 by F-100F Wild Weasel crews introduced a new mission that became an integral part of modern tactical air planning. Anti-radiation missiles were just one part of the complex 'search and destroy' operation that the Weasels represented. Expanded in scope, the programme acquired the F-105F Thunderchief as the main missile carrier, this duty eventually extending to the F-4 Phantom. By the end of the war USAF and USN strike aircraft were using improved Shrikes and the hefty General Dynamics AGM-78A Standard ARM.

Introduced in 1968 as a longer-ranging complement to the Shrike, Standard ARM had a range of 56 miles (90km) and a speed of Mach 2.5. The weight of the blast fragmentation warhead was 214.7lb (97.4kg), compared with the Shrike's 145lb (65.8kg). Much more important was the fact that the AGM-78B was given a memory. Data on enemy radars could be stored, thus eliminating the need to pre-tune the seeker before take-off, as was necessary with the older missiles. It meant that targets of opportunity could be attacked using the new version, an extremely important asset in a rapidly changing combat environment.

Although the Wild Weasel force was scaled down after Vietnam, the Texas Instruments AGM-88A HARM was introduced in 1983, reflecting the ongoing importance of the mission. Adopted for use with selected US first-line aircraft, AGM-88A refined the known parameters established with earlier ARMs. Its Mach 3-plus per-

Typically loaded, an F-4G Wild Weasel banks over a desert range on a tactical exercise. Tools of its trade include the massive Standard ARM and Shrike ARMs. After the F-100 and F-105, the F-4 took on the anti-radar role during the last stages of the Vietnam War.

formance allows enemy radar operators minimum shut-down time, and even if they have gone 'off the air' by the time HARM is in range they can still be detected and destroyed via a continual-homing capability.

Nonetheless, HARM remains a heavy missile, with a total weight including warhead of 791lb (362kg). To overcome this drawback, a BAe-Marconi collaboration in Britain resulted in ALARM, a Sky Flash-based anti-radiation missile that improved on AGM-88. As a 385lb (174,6kg) multimode weapon it has impressive fire-and-forget capability. After low-level release, ALARM can be programmed to zoom climb to 40,000ft (12,190m) before parachute retardation takes place. It then drifts downwards for several minutes while the seeker searches for hostile emissions. Once a radar has been selected, the drogue is released and ALARM dives on to the target.

Reliable television, infrared and radar guidance enabled air-to-ground missiles to expand substantially from the mid-1970s. Those produced in series with regular updates and guidance modifications resulted in a variety of weapons that were, theoretically at least, able to deal with any type of ground target. Included in this category are the Martin Marietta AGM-12C Bullpup, Hughes AGM-45 Maverick and BAe-Matra Martel, among many others. Some, such the Bullpup, were found wanting under combat conditions in Southeast Asia, while others served much of their production lifetimes in what can be termed a 'passive' security role, never being used in anger.

Closely associated with the Buccaneer, the main carrier aircraft in the UK, Martel is a versatile Mach 2 ASM which offers either TV or passive radiation seeking. An early result of British-French collaboration, the AS.37 anti-radar model has been widely used and developed in France.

The Second World War left a legacy of generally makeshift methods of destroying tanks from the air, so during the 1950s some thought was given to refining this gap in the world's aerial arsenal. It would take time for the best of these, the Hughes TOW and Rockwell Hellfire, to be perfected, and while these missiles have been applied more to helicopters than to fixed-wing aircraft, the AGM-65 Maverick is an important multirole ASM carried by USAF and USN aircraft. With TV guidance, the early Mavericks lacked the desired clear imaging latterly obtainable with infrared imaging using Rockwell laser homing. All modes are fire-and-forget, and Maverick's versatility has extended to a high night capability in conjunction with Low-Altitude Navigation and Targeting Infrared for Night (LANTIRN) and Forward-Looking Infrared (FLIR) systems. The AGM-65 is undoubtedly one of the foremost US air-to-surface missiles, but high cost is a factor in its operational deployment.

Historically, the destruction of tanks and other armoured fighting vehicles was often accomplished with

Part of the ongoing development programme for the later Harrier initiated by McDonnell Douglas was the night-attack version of the AV-8B for the US Marines. Equipped with Maverick missiles, Mk 82 500lb bombs and a 25mm cannon, the first example was test-flown at Twenty-Nine Palms Marine Base, California.

cannon firing armour-piercing (AP) ammunition designed to penetrate both protected and unprotected plated areas. Relatively few tanks have actually been destroyed by air attack since the last world war, and among the plethora of aircraft well able do so, only the Fairchild A-10 Thunderbolt II has had a major 'anti-armour' role. In this respect few weapons can rival the aircraft's 30mm General Electric GAU-8/A Avenger seven-barrel cannon. Huge at 9.5ft (2.896m) long and heavy (620lb (281.2kg)), it is the largest gun ever fitted to an aircraft. This gun proved more than a match for Iraqi armour during the Gulf War, as did the Maverick missiles carried by the A-10, some 230 of which remain in USAF inventory. Notwithstanding question marks over the type's survivability against more effective air opposition than was found in the Gulf, an additional role for the 'Warthog' is that of forward air control under the designation AO-10.

In a modern culmination of the Russian *shturmovik* philosophy of a heavily armoured ground-attack type with a high degree of airframe and aircrew protection in the face of liberal quantities of defensive fire, the Sukhoi Su-27 has also been tested in action. While the opposition fielded few tanks in Afghanistan, the Su-27 was heavily committed and flew numerous ground-attack sorties against guerrilla forces in difficult terrain. Lessons were learned by an operational test unit and modifications made, particularly to the engines, which are not as well protected as those on the A-10. In addition to a wide range of ordnance, the Su-27 has one fixed NNPU-8M 30mm cannon.

Sea targets proved particularly difficult for aircraft to destroy until dive and skip bombing with conventional bombs brought greater success than the torpedo,

Of great importance to the defence of Sweden in the 1970s and 1980s, the Saab J 37 Viggen was designed to carry a range of international weapons from the US Falcon and Sidewinder to Saab's RB 05A and RB 04 air-to-surface missiles. An example of the former weapon is seen in front of the aircraft in this view, with gun pods under both wings.

although the latter certainly had its day as an air-launched weapon. Giving the torpedo additional boost, better directional stability and more lethality seemed logical, although as regards air attack on surface vessels the modern war scenario would inevitably see very capable missiles such as the subsonic Aérospatiale AM.39 Exocet being deployed against ships. Proven in action in the Falklands by Super Étendard pilots of the Argentinian Navy, the Exocet has also figured in the Middle East conflict between Iran and Iraq.

Multi-purpose air-to-surface missiles now give attacking aircraft immense hitting power and stand-off protection against defensive fire. Kormoran and Penguin have joined the arsenals of those nations likely to have to deal with seaborne opposition, although such specialisation has been overtaken by the versatility of missiles such as the AGM-62 Walleye.

Conventional bombs

During the Second World War, Allied efforts in some military aviation fields, including weapons, seemed pedestrian in comparison with Germany's – apart from bombs. Britain developed a range of gravity bombs more destructive than anything produced elsewhere, dwarfing all such efforts by an otherwise innovative enemy. But what the Germans did achieve was much more significant, in that the first guided bombs, using

radio control, became a reality. The results of tests and operational use by the Luftwaffe were applied to some conventional Allied bombs, although most appeared too late to be used before the war's end.

The largest of the wartime British bombs developed for postwar use was the 12,000lb (6 ton/5443kg) Tallboy, which became the USAF's VB-13 Tarzon. With a streamlined casing to enhance flight characteristics and ground penetration, the Tarzon was fitted with annular tail fins containing a radio receiver. An operator in a B-29 Superfortress was thus able to steer the bomb visually in azimuth and range. Tarzon was the culmination of a series of American general-purpose (GP) bombs given radio guidance but no separate propulsion unit. Along with the VB-3 Razon, a 1,000lb (454kg) GP bomb also provided with tail guidance by radio signal, Tarzon was used operationally in Korea.

Boeing B-29s began using Razon bombs in 1950, mainly against Korean bridges. Some success was achieved, crews finding that it took an average of four bombs to demolish a bridge under good visual conditions. Later that year the Tarzon was tried for the first time, also against bridges, and although there was some success against these difficult targets the overall results – with an expensive weapon – were disappointing. Tarzons were withdrawn from use in the spring of 1951, by which time about thirty had been used.

While considerable effort went into miniaturising and streamlining nuclear bombs, it was soon apparent that 'limited wars' would see the continuing deployment of conventional high-explosive bombs. These had been relatively unchanged for years, standard 250lb (113kg), 500lb (226kg) and 1,000lb (454kg) bombs with unstreamlined casings having been used effectively by tactical fighter bombers, throughout the Korean War and beyond.

As tactical aircraft became larger and more operationally flexible by carrying mixed stores on multiple racks, increasing the weight of the 500lb bomb (226kg) by 25 per cent was a practical compromise. The 750lb (340kg) M-117 slotted between the older 500lb (226kg) and 1,000lb (454kg) bombs and enabled multiple rounds to be lifted by a wide range of aircraft without a prohibitive weight penalty. With an elongated 'slick' and more aerodynamically efficient casing, this bomb was very widely adapted for carriage on multiple-round racks from the 1960s onwards.

Most US GP bombs, particularly those in the '80s series' in weights ranging from the 250lb (113kg) Mk 81 and the 500lb (226kg) Mk 82 up to the 1,000lb (454kg) Mk 83 and 2,000lb (908kg) Mk 84, were given slick configuration, and vast numbers were delivered by the principal USAF, USN and Marine aircraft in Vietnam. The sheer weight of high explosive expended was bound to have some effect, but the accuracy of free-fall

bombs, even when delivered at ultra-low level by very capable fighter bomber pilots, has always left something to be desired. Rarely can the full load be relied upon to fall where it is aimed to break a 'hard' target. 'Short' or 'long' bombing has to be taken into account, particularly when the opposition is throwing up walls of AAA fire, not to mention SAMs. Dud rounds have always been a significant factor in bomb damage assessment.

It was therefore with some relief that air commanders in Vietnam were given Paveway, a new laser-guided device for directing standard bombs, in 1965. Laser technology had by that time advanced enough to enable combat aircraft to direct a narrow beam of energy towards a target. This laser 'basket' had to be maintained and, once again, clear conditions were important for success. The Paveway I seeker homed on to the laser basket and greatly improved the chances of target destruction, with the obvious bonuses of a very low number of rounds being needed compared with dozens of conventional bombs and far less exposure of crews and aircraft to the defences.

Paveway was a very apt name; Texas Instruments indeed pioneered a whole new family of sophisticated laser homing kits that could be fitted to standard low-drag 'dumb' bombs to turn them into 'smart' ones. The series expanded to bring in a different designation for the guidance element for bombs of various types and weights, with the prefix KMU.

China Lake is the USN's test range for ordnance of all kinds, and over the years numerous weapons systems have been tested for operational suitability. Not all of them made the grade, however, the ramjet-powered Supersonic Tactical Missile seen here under the wing of an A-7 Corsair II being one of the failures.

As soon as the laser guidance for Paveway bombs was perfected, air forces other than those of the USA adopted the system, which offered a manifold improvement in bombing accuracy, though at a substantial price. The RAF equipped most of its strike aircraft to use Paveway, a BAe Jaguar being seen here with two 1,000-pounders as well as the necessary laser-designator pods.

Paveway II (prefix BGU) was a simpler and cheaper system with a folding-wing aerofoil group added to the tail to improve manoeuvrability and lateral range. In 1987 Paveway III, the low-level laser-guided bomb (LGB), was introduced as a further improvement, with microprocessor controls and digital autopilot intended to cope with a European high-threat environment and reduced visibility.

The effectiveness of the Paveway series and other smart bombs grouped under the general heading of precision-guided munitions is hardly in doubt. On-board cameras record the increasing accuracy of laser guidance, though high cost tends to preclude their use against all but the most important targets. So, even though such sophisticated weapons systems are available to a number of air arms, the usefulness and economy of the 'dumb' or iron bomb has not passed.

The carpet bombing carried out by B-52s over Vietnam and, to a lesser extent, over Iraq reminded us that

strategic aircraft will probably continue to find roles that are predominantly tactical. Such air operations do not demand precision bombing or sophisticated weapons; and they have a significant psychological effect. In an age of the rapier, the bludgeon remains effective for some tasks. That much has hardly changed over the centuries.

Special bombs

Throughout the history of military aviation, bombs have been designed for use against specific targets which for one reason or another either could not be destroyed by conventional ordnance or had proved costly in terms of aircraft lost in repeat attacks. A number of these came to fruition and actual use in the Second World War, a conflict that saw even aircraft themselves being used as bombs. This idea was perpetuated in the use of F6F Hellcat fighters in Korea. On similar lines, the B-17s expended in early US missile-testing programmes pointed the way to airborne drones, either obsolete aircraft or custom-built remotely piloted vehicles (RPVs), and these are becoming increasingly important in proving new weapons, particularly missiles.

Numerous modern munitions can be grouped under the broad heading of anti-personnel or 'cluster bomb' weapons; a number of countries build and/or supply various combinations for carriage by military aircraft. These are invariably contained in a bomb casing with minimum streamlining to reduce drag and machined to split apart longitudinally to release showers of bomblets at a set altitude after release. These air-burst weapons spread grenades, darts, steel balls and the like across a considerable area to incapacitate hostile forces and disable soft-skinned vehicles. Runway denial munitions such as the Hunting Engineering BL755 work on much the same principle, and were used to good effect during the Gulf War by RAF Tornado units.

Napalm, despite creating spectacular explosions and a sea of fire, is limited. While it can be devastating to personnel and flimsy structures, it requires low-altitude delivery, preferably at modest speeds. Today's emphasis on stand-off precision delivery is tending to make napalm something of a secondary weapon in the arsenal of the large, modern air arm. Related 'fire bombs' are available in various configurations for numerous aircraft types. Large fuel-oil mix bombs create huge flat-trajectory explosions ideal for making 'instant landing areas' for helicopters. Size restricts their use to transport aircraft and helicopters.

Cruise

The cruise missile represents arguably the ultimate weapon in the bomber's armoury, as it can be delivered hundreds of miles out from a target without risk to crew or aircraft. The forerunners of these formidable munitions were large, air-to-surface missiles with air-breathing engines, the first of which entered service with the VVS in 1960. They were designed as anti-shipping weapons and had a relatively short range. These early missiles and a series of progressively improved ASMs were designed for the Tu-16, which was produced in many versions during its lengthy operational life. Although not cruise missiles in the modern accepted sense, the Russian ASMs were, like the US Hound Dog, Skybolt and SRAM, attempts to provide conventional bombers with reliable stand-off capability in a nuclear confrontation.

Boeing's AGM-86A actually made the world's first launch by an ALCM on 5 March 1976, a B-52 carrying it aloft. Designed as a strategic weapon with a nuclear warhead, this vehicle was joined by probably the best-known cruise missile, the General Dynamics AGM-109 Tomahawk. Developed in parallel with the AGM-86, the AGM-109H is designated as an airfield attack weapon and has a Teledyne Continental J402-CA-401 turbofan engine which provides 600lb (272kg) of thrust to propel the missile at 500mph (805km/h).

Cruise missiles aroused their share of controversy owing to their almost totally independent flight profile and an enormous range not far short of 2,000 miles (3,218km). Although ALCMs became a focal point of SALT agreements, they were retained to be deployed operationally in 1991, when the USA was able to add operational experience to the data accumulated in numerous test firings. The Gulf War saw B-52Gs from Barksdale Air Force Base, Louisiana, flying sorties of thirty-four-hours-plus duration to expend thirty-five

AGM-86C ALCMs with conventional warheads against Iraqi targets.

Stealth technology has been applied to weapons as well as aircraft, and extends to the current US cruise missile, the AGM-129A. Adaptable to conventional or nuclear warheads, this 2,750lb (1,248kg) weapon has a range of 2,070 miles (3,330km). Carried primarily by the B-52, it currently supplements the AGM-86C.

Obsolete though the B-52 may be, few can refute the psychological effect of the veritable rain of HE iron bombs it can deliver. 'Force projection' comes about as near to the ideal as possible with aircraft that fly so high that they are able to approach completely out of the sight and sound of those on the ground. Scores of sudden explosions 'marching' across the landscape offer the attacker an immense edge, the defenders knowing that this terrifying bombardment is usually only a prelude to the low-altitude delivery of munitions of all kinds by tactical aircraft. During the six-week Gulf conflict, cells of three B-52s flew most of their missions to neutralise Iraqi defences carrying 750lb HE bombs on standard fuselage and wing racks. About half the total 55,000 tons (55,880 tonnes) of bombs dropped by the Allied Coalition air forces during 'Desert Storm' are estimated to have been delivered to their targets by B-52s – not a bad record for an aircraft that first flew forty-six years ago.

Bibliography

Chant, C, *Modern Air Weapons* (Patrick Stephens, Cambridge, 1970). An excellent 'nuts and bolts' guide to weapons of the modern age, with historical notes on development.

Matra's Durandal was a rocket-powered area-denial weapon designed primarily to break up runways. Mirage F 1s were adapted to carry a total of eight under the wings and fuselage. The weapon was merely dropped, and was entirely independent of the carrier aircraft.

Clancy, T, *Fighter Wing: A Guided Tour of an Air Force Combat Wing* (HarperCollins, London, 1996). The author explains modern technology in simplified terms, and includes excellent notes on air weapons development and operation.

Frawley, G and Thorn, T, *The International Directory of Military Aircraft 1996/97* (Aerospace Publications, Canberra, Australia, 1996). A comprehensive and handy guide to the subject.

Gunston, B, *Rockets and Missiles* (Salamander Books, London, 1979). One of the few all-encompassing volumes on this important subject, giving comprehensive development from the earliest days up to 1978.

Fighters of the Fifties (Patrick Stephens, Cambridge, 1981). One of a number of books and articles by this prolific author covering the testing and service (in most cases) of the first jet types.

The Osprey Encyclopedia of Russian Aircraft 1875–1995 (Osprey, London, 1995). Recording virtually all Russian aircraft and armaments up to the historic post-*glasnost* period, this is one of the most important aviation books of recent years.

Wallace, G F, *Guns of the RAF* (William Kimber, London, 1972). Useful background on British aircraft armaments and the policy behind the weapons the RAF used, primarily in the Second World War, but with some modern equivalents.

Publications including data on weapons, particularly those of the early postwar period, are many and varied, but much is contained in such journals as *The Aeroplane*, *Air Pictorial*, *Aviation & Marine*, *World Airpower Journal*, *Air International* and *Detail in Scale*. The latter American publication was primarily a modelling journal that included very full articles on US ordnance from the Second World War to the present, including nuclear weapons.

3
The Jet Revolution
Jerry Scutts

Having begun the 'jet revolution' by being the first nation to bring turbojet and rocket-propelled combat aircraft into action during the Second World War, Germany had no choice after May 1945 but to leave further developments in this field to other countries. Industry-wide research and testing, culminating in a trio of aircraft that reached operational status – the Messerschmitt Me 262, Arado Ar 234 and Heinkel He 162 – had proved that jet propulsion had all but replaced the reciprocating engine as the power source for modern combat aircraft.

This fact had for some time been realised by groups of forward-thinking individuals in Britain and the USA. As the war ended the RAF had gained valuable experience by operating the Gloster Meteor under front-line conditions, although the only adversary pilots could note in their combat reports was the V1 flying bomb. A handful of USAAF pilots had flown sorties in P-80s over Italy, but the war had ended before Lockheed's jet fighter had any chance to prove itself.

With the coming of peace there was time for the war-winning Allied nations to evaluate the current 'state of the art' in respect of powerplants and airframes, to test-fly examples of former enemy aircraft and to examine research data and drawings of the many fascinating projects that German industry had worked up, some almost to the point of production, before hostilities ceased. Under the impetus of war, the Germans had explored virtually all possible means of powering military aircraft, the turbojet emerging as the most practical and economical.

In Britain, Frank Whittle's pioneering work on jet propulsion had led to his engine, the developed W.2B/23 Welland, being installed in production Meteor I fighters, which were first delivered to No 616 Squadron, RAF, in July 1944. The Welland powering the Meteor Mk I provided 1,700lb (770kg) of thrust, which was adequate but far from outstanding. Consequently the Meteor had, like the Me 262, the safety and 'insurance' of two engines. Rolls-Royce continued to develop the Meteor's powerplant, the 3,500lb (1,588kg) Derwent being installed in all but the first fifteen Mk IIIs.

The USA had also followed a similar 'safe' policy and installed two jet engines in the first non-propeller type to fly in that country, the Bell XP-59 Airacomet, powered by two General Electric Type I-A turbojets.

An example of the Whittle-designed turbojet with a centrifugal compressor was despatched to the USA and the I-A, based on this engine, was bench-tested for the first time on 18 March 1942. The XP-59A made its maiden flight, fitted with I-A engines, on 1 October. Thirteen YP-59s were built, these having the more powerful GE I-16 engine (which later became the J31) giving 1,600lb (725kg) of thrust.

Once they began to build in volume, engine manufacturers were quickly able to 'tweak' more power out of the early turbojets. This was demonstrated in November 1944, when a P-59A flew with two GE I-18s each rated at 1,800lb (816kg). While the P-59 significantly advanced knowledge of turbojet operation and endurance under numerous flight conditions, its performance was only slightly better than that of the fastest reciprocating-engined fighters of the day, and any plans to introduce it into combat were soon shelved.

That adequate performance to power a single-seat fighter could be derived from a single turbojet had been demonstrated by the He 162, the so-called 'People's Fighter', which was designed to be thrown into combat with barely trained pilots at the controls. Fitted with a 1,760lb (798kg)-thrust BMW 109-003E-1 or E-2, the He 162A-2 was capable of a maximum speed of 522mph (835km/h) and had an initial climb rate of 4,231ft/min (1,290m/min). Longevity and, indeed, long-term reliability were not prime considerations in this 'panic-measure' interceptor.

Much more of a future, albeit mainly a projected one, was envisaged for aircraft that would undertake bombing and reconnaissance sorties, the dual function of the twin-engined Arado Ar 234. With no counterpart elsewhere, the Arado bomber became operational with two 1,720lb (800kg) BMW 003A-1 turbojets.

As is well enough known, the Germans made more operational use of the Me 262 than all other innovative aircraft they built. Engine reliability problems, primarily as a result of substandard raw materials used for turbine blades, helped wreck any chance of the Luftwaffe gaining air superiority with Me 262s over Europe in the closing months of the war.

Budget restraints
Plans for Allied air force re-equipment after the war varied considerably. Military budgets came under close scrutiny, particularly in Europe, and in some countries precious little funding was allocated for research and new aircraft. For a time, new combat aircraft were low on the list of peacetime priorities.

In the USA there was a demonstrably great desire (and available funding, though drastically trimmed) to be at the cutting edge of technology. The Bell P-59 was not developed beyond a batch of twenty production models, as Lockheed had a highly promising programme in its single-engined XP-80. Further Airacomets were cancelled, and the remaining aircraft were used for evaluation and pilot training.

Lockheed produced the first XP-80 ahead of schedule and, in almost total secrecy, readied the prototype for its first flight. The engine intended to power it was virtually identical to the British Halford H-1 turbojet, built by Allis-Chalmers of Milwaukee. This engine was beset by numerous problems which soon proved to be insurmountable, and after the first flight, on 8 January 1944, the second XP-80 was re-engined with an I-40 (J33-11) developed by the Allison Division of General Electric, based in Indianapolis. Despite these minor setbacks, early flight tests indicated that, unlike the P-59, the XP-80 would be able to meet the USAAF's performance requirements for a jet fighter. The first acceptance took place, on time, during February 1945. Weathering a spate of crashes not attributable to engine trouble, Lockheed accelerated Shooting Star production, there being few problems in eventually extending the line to the T-33 trainer, the T2V-1 SeaStar and ultimately the F-94 Starfire. Engine power was gradually increased in Lockheed's 'Star' series to 6,350lb (2,880kg) thrust in the Pratt & Whitney J48 fitted in the F-94B night interceptor.

Four US companies, General Electric (which produced the J47), Pratt & Whitney (J48 and J57), Allison (J35) and Westinghouse (J30, J34 and J46) supplied turbojets for all the early postwar American fighters, fighter-bombers and trainers. The overall thrust level gradually increased to 7,800lb (3,538kg) in the RF-84F, which had a J65-W-7.

As the end of the war eased any pressure to get more Allied jet aircraft into combat in Europe, F-80 orders were cut back, although they remained large enough to meet immediate USAF requirements. With adequate numbers of P-47s and P-51s to maintain a substantial reserve force, jets equipped first-line fighter units as quickly as possible. As most people, including the budget holders on Capitol Hill, appreciated, the USA needed to be at the forefront of aeronautical technology.

On 28 February 1946 the third American jet fighter to be built, the Republic XP-84, made its maiden flight, powered by General Electric's 3,750lb (1,700kg) J36-GE-7. By starting out with a powerful turbojet for the XP-84, Republic was able to develop the original 'Thunderbolt replacement' into the RF-84F Thunderstreak and Thunderflash. The F-80 Shooting Star, F-84 Thunderjet and F-94 Starfire all received their baptism of fire over Korea, a war in which the turbojet proved its worth under less-than-ideal front-line conditions. There were some drawbacks, including lack of range and relatively modest firepower, but these early US jet fighter-bombers were only the first generation of a new class of combat aircraft.

The Soviet Union's windfall

In the Soviet Union there was also an urgency to bring turbojet fighters into VVS service. As a result the Yakovlev design bureau, notwithstanding valuable work by other concerns, achieved the distinction of completing the first Soviet jet fighter, the Yak-15, powered by a single RD-10 turbojet based on the German Jumo 004 and intended primarily for test and evaluation. The aircraft selected for production and VVS service was the Mikoyan and Gurevich MiG-9. Powered by a single RD-20 turbojet (a BMW 003 copy) this type did not have a great deal of development potential, but it was a start.

Allison was one of a small number of companies which made the 'first generation' of US turbojet engines a success and ensured that the country never lost the lead it had gained in the new powerplant technology. This is the J35, power source for a range of fighters, bombers and research aircraft.

The Soviets' early work in the turbojet field was aided by a thorough examination of German jet aircraft in advanced stages of construction in 1945 and the test-flying of those which had entered Luftwaffe service. Among the more exotic types was the two-seat rocket-powered Messerschmitt Me 163, plus standard Service examples of the Arado Ar 234B, Me 262A and He 162. Along with aircraft and hardware, large numbers of scientists and engineers, complete with their workshops and factories in some cases, were transported far to the East.

It was fortuitous for the Soviets that Britain, desirous of fostering better international relations, obtained permission to export the Rolls-Royce Nene. The Soviets could hardly believe their good fortune on taking delivery of the first ten engines in September 1946. Fifteen more followed in March 1947, and a total of fifty-five had been despatched by the end of that year. The Nene's arrival could not have been more timely, as it formed the basis for the entire Soviet powerplant manufacturing programme. What made it so important was the fact that it could be put into production, as the RD-45, without delay, the first units coming off the lines in August 1947. Built in enormous numbers and ultimately powering the MiG-15, Il-28 and Tu-14, the Nene/RD-45 was to become one of the world's most significant early turbojets. To the 39,000 engines originating from Soviet sources were added 8,500 from China under licence. Most of these were similar to the original RD-45, which, given the revised designation VK-1, was rated at 5,952lb (2,700kg). An afterburning model, the VK-1F, delivered 7,450lb (3,380kg).

With the Nene forming a firm basis for a modern aero-engine industry, the Soviets bought time to develop their own designs. Most of their earlier engines had been based on the Jumo 004 and BMW 003, German technology and scientists having been invaluable in establishing the basis for Soviet jet powerplants, but these early turbojets were rapidly surpassed in terms of reliability and rated power.

Britain marks time

In contrast to the forward thinking of the Americans and the Soviets, British rearmament policy *vis-à-vis* military aircraft powered by turbojets was muddled and beset by contradictory requirements in the immediate

Thanks to British government largesse, Rolls-Royce's Nene put the French and Soviet aero-engine industries on the map while the UK made little use of what was a very sound design. Most notoriously, the engine was given to the Soviet Union to power the MiG-15, which fought UN air power in Korea. After that the Soviets never looked back.

Activity at RAF Tangmere in August 1946 centres on the installation of the Rolls-Royce Derwent turbojets in a Gloster Meteor I before an attack on the world air speed record. The Meteor raised it to 616mph (991km/hr) in September 1946.

postwar period. There were many able designers and ideas were plentiful, but precious funds were spent by companies that had very small world (or home) markets with which to finance research.

Having produced the Nene, for a time the world's most powerful turbojet, Britain left it to other countries to exploit its full potential while little use was found for it at home. What was in effect a scaled-down version, the Derwent V, found application in the Meteor, though in early marks it gave a relatively low output. Capable of 3,500lb (1,588kg) thrust in standard form, the Derwent powered the record-breaking Meteors which achieved new absolute world air speed records of 606mph (975km/h) in November 1945 and 616mph (991km/h) in September 1946.

Governmental disinterest and lack of positive decision-making were instrumental in delaying the introduction of a swept-wing high-speed interceptor for the RAF by nearly a decade, although much valuable prototype testing was undertaken in the meantime. Much of this was ultimately wasted when promising projects were cancelled on the point of production after considerable sums of money had been spent. In lieu of anything better appearing, Meteor and Vampire production was stepped up, each type receiving progressively uprated engines. Extensive development programmes resulted in variants of these first-generation jet fighters becoming RAF mainstays by undertaking a wide variety

of important roles, including training, nightfighting and photo-reconnaissance. Britain also continued to establish jet records. On 4 November 1948 John Derry flew a Vampire from Hatfield, Hertfordshire, to Ciampino, Italy, at an average speed of 323mph (520km/h). Starting out (in February 1944) by designing engines for its own jet fighters, the de Havilland Engine Company concentrated on the 3,000lb (1,360kg) H.1 Goblin and 4,000lb (1,814kg) H.2 Ghost. Later came the H.4

Perhaps the best thing to do in the 1950s, when British government planning for future defence projects was uncertain at best, was to produce both the engine and the aircraft, as de Havilland did with the Goblin series powerplants for the Vampire and Venom interceptors and trainers. This is the Goblin I.

Any flight line of early de Havilland jet fighter bombers gave off characteristic plumes of smoke as the Goblin engine in each aircraft was started using a cartridge. These Venoms are based in the Middle East, familiar desert surroundings for RAF squadrons in the 1950s and 1960s.

Gyron. First run on 5 January 1953, this was abandoned after the government of the day decided that Britain would need no more manned jet fighters. When this ridiculous period passed, the Gyron Junior was built for the Blackburn NA.39, the Buccaneer. Rated at 7,100lb (3,220kg) for take-off, two Gyron Junior 101s gave the tough and capable Buccaneer a maximum speed of 720mph (1,158km/h) at sea level.

At Rolls-Royce much hope was pinned on the success of the Avon, envisaged as 'the Merlin of the jet age'. In RA.3 form the engine that powered the Hawker Hunter fighter developed 6,500lb (2,948kg). A cartridge start was almost always used, and direct pressure bleed was harnessed for cabin pressurisation. Continu-

ous Avon development pushed output to 11,250lb (5,103kg) in the RA.24 200 Series, which was type-tested in July 1956. This turbojet, at the same rating, was installed in the English Electric Lightning F.1 and 1A, twin engines enabling the aircraft, heralded as the RAF's 'last manned fighter', to reach Mach 2 with consummate ease and in F.1A form to achieve a maximum speed of 1,500mph (2,413km/h). More important for an interceptor was its initial climb rate of 50,000ft/min (15,240m/min), better than that of the later Phantom and early Tornadoes. Avon fighter engines culminated in the RB.146 300 Series for the Lightning (Avon 301 of 12,690lb (5,756kg) and the RM.6 for the Saab Draken.

On war service

In contrast to the misguided presentation to the Soviets of the engine that would enable UN aircraft to destroyed by the MiG-15 in combat over Korea, the bulk of the British air forces continued to fly piston-engined aircraft rather than jets. Consequently, when the FAA saw action in Korea it did so with reliable but outmoded types. No service jets had materialised to follow up the first carrier landing by a Vampire on 3 December 1945 and the first flights by the prototype Supermarine Attacker and Hawker Sea Hawk in July 1946 and September 1948 respectively. In the type of war that developed in Korea, where a great many ground-attack operations were necessary, jets were able to make faster target runs with a greater chance of evading ground fire. The pilots of piston-engined Fairey Fireflies and Hawker Sea Furies had their work cut out to modify tactics to compensate for any lack of performance over the front line.

Sweden took the bold step of establishing an independent aerospace industry to help guard her neutrality, with Saab as a cornerstone. The company was at the forefront of aircraft manufacture, with Volvo Flygmotor supplying engines such as the RM12 which powers the JAS 39 Gripen. A version of the General Electric F404 turbofan, the RM12 is seen here undergoing rig-testing.

When highly developed piston engines were being rapidly overtaken by turbojets, a number of aircraft were designed to incorporate both types of powerplant, with the aim of smoothing the transition training of pilots. Ryan's FR-1 Fireball was a relatively successful type in this category, though in the event few problems were encountered and mixed-powerplant aircraft were not really needed.

In stark contrast to the FAA, the American aircraft of Task Force 77 operating off Korea were clearly more modern. Like the USAF, the USN had also accepted the exciting challenge offered by jet power and by 1950 had flown the McDonnell XFD-1 Phantom I, North American FJ-1 Fury, North American XAJ-1 and Douglas F3D. In addition, the Vought F6U Pirate had been ordered for limited production. The interesting mixed-powerplant Ryan FR-1 Fireball fighter, with one 1,600lb (726kg) General Electric J31 turbojet and one 1,350hp (612kg) Wright R-1820-72W radial piston engine had all but completed its USN service. Most important of all, Grumman's F9F Panther and McDonnell's F2H Banshee were available to spearhead USN carrier strikes in Korea.

Continental progress

France, which had maintained a modestly sized aviation industry throughout the war (albeit run by the Germans), had also managed to design experimental jet engines in secret. Postwar, the industry gradually revived, and on 28 February 1949 the first Dassault Ouragan flew, powered by a licence-built Hispano-Suiza Rolls-Royce Nene 102 turbojet rated at 5,000lb (2,268kg). The company's Rolls-Royce licence for the Nene formed the basis for its own limited engine design, but the major work was with British engines. The third prototype Ouragan had a marginally uprated 5,057lb (2,294kg) Nene 104B, and this engine powered the 350 production aircraft, which were completed by 1954.

A final uprating of the Nene came in 1955, when India ordered the Ouragan as the Toofani. This version had a Nene 105A providing 5,180lb (2,350kg) of thrust, and although this output was by then being eclipsed by a considerable margin elsewhere, India, in

common with other nations, retained the first French jet fighter as a second-line type until the 1970s.

There was a concurrent desire on the part of the French government during these early revival years to be independent in all aspects of military aviation. After the war the catalyst was, in jet engine terms, ex-BMW designer Hermann Osetrich. His experience with the German concern ensured a firm foundation for the establishment of Atelier Technique Aéronautique Rickenbach (Atar) in Switzerland in 1945. The first Atar turbojet, rated at 3,307lb (1,500kg), was test-flown in a Martin B-26 Marauder during 1948. Subsequently run successfully at 3,750lb (1,700kg) mounted on a pylon above the fuselage of a Sud-Est Languedoc and at 5,181lb (2,350kg) as the Atar 101B2 in a Meteor, this engine was to form the basis for all French military powerplants for a decade. The nationalised group SNECMA, encompassing Gnome-Rhône, Renault, Regnier, SECM and GEHL, built the engine, and by early 1953 it was able to supply Dassault with the Atar 101C rated at 6,052lb (2,745kg) to power the Mystère IIC. The group also acquired Hispano-Suiza in December 1968, the company then having licence-built the Rolls-Royce Tay and produced the derivative 3,500kg (7,717lb) Verdon 350, which first flew in a Mystère in August 1953. It had also taken an active part in the Avon engine programme for both Dassault fighters and the Caravelle airliner.

Total concept

As Germany's wartime engineers had found, obtaining optimum performance from the simple early turbojets, which were of relatively low power, really demanded an entirely new approach to airframe design. The ideal jet aircraft needed a degree of wing sweep, a 'clean' fuselage with the minimum of drag-inducing protuber-ances, and a tricycle undercarriage to provide adequate ground clearance for the jet exhaust. These and other revolutionary but practical innovations were contained in the gauntlet thrown down by Germany. The effect of the jet revolution therefore extended far beyond engine power alone.

Consequently, North American Aviation regarded it as something of a gamble when it modified its XF-86 proposal for a USAF interceptor to incorporate 35° of wing sweep. The gamble was to pay off handsomely. Married to a General Electric J47 turbojet of 5,200lb (2,360kg) in the later A models, the F-86 achieved a top speed of 675mph (1,086km/h) and was transonic in a dive. The soundness of the F-86's design became appar-ent when USAF squadrons clashed with MiG-15s over Korea, as the Sabre was the only fighter able to take on the North Koreans on more-or-less equal terms. Pilots of No 77 Squadron Royal Australian Air Force, bemoaning the fact that they did not get Sabres but Meteor F.8s for combat in Korea, could only be grateful that their MiG encounters were mercifully rare.

Before it was obliged to fight, the F-86 established a new world air speed record of 670.981mph (1,078.03km/h) at Muroc on 15 September 1948. Fly-ing a standard F-86A with a full ammunition load, Major Richard L Johnson made four runs over a 4.82-mile (3km) course to set the new record, the first cap-tured by the USA after the war. In common with other early postwar jets, the F-86 was developed to keep pace with widening requirements, and by the time the F-86D appeared as a production model in March 1951, engine power, with the J47-GE-17, had been raised to 7,630lb (3,461kg) to boost top speed to 707mph (1,138km/h). Two more air speed records had also been captured by the F-86D, the second in July 1953 pushing the figure to 715.697mph (1,150.43km/h).

Two years or so after the end of the Korean War, American engines for USAF and USN combat aircraft performed well enough to sustain the high transonic speeds military aircraft were then routinely achieving. Despite the fact that the hypothetical strategic bombers these aircraft were largely designed to intercept never materialised, high performance had arrived. Nobody wished to turn the clock back. With the McDonnell Demon of 1955 turbojet power rating had almost reached the 10,000lb (4,536kg) mark as a routine out-put for Service aircraft, and the 9,700lb (4,400kg) Alli-son J71A-2 developed for the F3H-2 version showed that a single-engined fighter of the period could handle more thrust. The new engine transformed the Demon, which had always been considered underpowered, and the type served the USN for another ten years.

The 10,000lb-thrust mark was reached by the manu-facturers supplying powerplants for the USAF's 'Centu-ry Series' of interceptors, every one of which had a single

Once the practicality of turbojets was understood, little time was lost by countries with an established aerospace manufactur-ing industry. France was at the forefront of turbojet manufacture, the state-owned SNECMA building a wide range of engines, including the Larzac turbofan which powered the highly successful Alpha Jet.

A superb supersonic jet bomber and the epitome of USAF retaliatory power at the height of the Cold War, the Convair B-58 Hustler was powered by four General Electric J79 turbojets, one of which is seen on the servicing trailer on the right.

When the British government bought the McDonnell Douglas Phantom it contrived via Rolls-Royce to produce a J79 substitute which was disparagingly said to give the aircraft the slowest performance at the highest cost. The powerplant was the very sound Spey -25R turbofan, which unfortunately failed to deliver any great increase in performance over American models owing to the extensive engineering changes required to fit a larger engine into the Phantom airframe.

'Chuck' Yeager broke the sound barrier in the Bell X-1 on 14 October 1947. Pure research vehicles, the Bell record breakers were carried to altitude by B-29/B-50 mother ships to conserve rocket fuel, their endurance at full engine power being measured in minutes.

engine offering this power and, in most cases, considerably more. From the 10,000lb (4,536kg)-thrust General Electric J79 in the F-104, the Pratt & Whitney J75 P-17 leapt to 17,200lb (7,802kg) to make the Convair F-106, perhaps surprisingly, the most powerful of the series. The J75-P19W in the F-105D Thunderchief was rated at 16,100lb (7,303kg) in 'dry' condition and, illustrating how closely engine power and performance are related to airframe design and weight, the F-105D had a marginally better top speed than the F-106A although it was substantially heavier, tipping the scales at a gross weight of 52,550lb (23,836kg) compared with the Delta Dagger's maximum take-off weight of 39,195lb (17,778kg). With afterburner, the engines in both aircraft offered the same output of 24,500lb (1,113kg).

When the F-4 Phantom appeared, its General Electric J79 was rated at 11,870lb (5,384kg), and although this output was doubled by using two engines to give the Phantom an incredible performance for its time, there was a clear economic gain in increasing performance using one engine.

After Vietnam, the USAF particularly took note of the seemingly lost 'pull' exuded by the single-seat fighter, but the next-generation F-15 and F-16, plus the USN's F-18, would restore the 'one fighter, one man' philosophy. And while Pratt & Whitney was able subsequently to increase the thrust of the J75 to 17,000lb (7,711kg) in the Lockheed U-2 and to a massive 32,500lb (14,742kg) in the J58 fitted in the SR-71, these high-altitude reconnaissance aircraft were special cases. In order to double the power that was available to the fighter pilots of the standard dogfighters of the 1980s and 1990s a completely new engine was required.

Rockets for records

While the turbojet emerged as the most practical engine for front-line combat aircraft, rather than rockets, ramjets or mixed powerplants, all of the latter had some merit and practical application. Powerful rocket motors had a potential for very high speeds, albeit with a very much shorter endurance than was then possible with turbojets. Simpler and lighter airframes, without the need to incorporate external air intakes or internal trunking, could be produced for flight research. The Americans, particularly impressed by the speeds obtainable by German rocket-powered aircraft such as the Me 163, funded USAF and USN programmes using rocket aircraft to fly at and beyond Mach 1.

The USAF programme specifically aimed at reaching this milestone began on 27 July 1947. The vehicle was the Bell X-1, three of which were built. Gliding flights had already been made, and the first powered sortie took place on 11 April 1947. All of the X-1s had retractable undercarriages, but to conserve precious fuel they were carried to altitude under the belly of modified B-29s. This was a wise precaution, as at maximum thrust settings the X-1 carried sufficient fuel for only five minutes of flight. After carrying out the designated flight test, the pilot brought the X-1 down for a conventional landing. A speed of Mach 1 was officially reached by the Bell X-1 on 14 October 1947. Piloted by Charles 'Chuck' Yeager, the aircraft was powered by a single Reaction Motors bifuel XLR11-RM-3 engine with a maximum thrust rating of 6,000lb (2,722kg) at sea level. There was no throttle, but the pilot could fire each of four combustion chambers individually or in groups.

Three further Bell X-1s were completed, and the programme continued, the aim now being to determine the highest speed and altitude possible with the aircraft. Yeager attained Mach 2.44 (1,650mph; 2,655km/h) on 12 December 1953, and Major Arthur Murray reached an altitude of 90,440ft (27,566m) on 26 August the following year, this being an unofficial world altitude record.

Greater speeds and altitudes were achieved by the X-1E, a modified early model X-1, and the Bell X-2, which had a Curtiss-Wright XLR25-CW-3 two-chamber rocket engine. This engine did have throttle control, thrust rating being variable from 2,500lb (1,134kg) to 15,000lb (6,804kg). Again the boundaries were extended, the X-2 achieving a speed of Mach 2.8706 (1,900mph; 3,057km/h), another unofficial record, but the aircraft's main contribution to aeronautics was to provide data on the effects of heat on steel alloy skinning, and on pilot-ejection systems.

Supersonic

A steady increase in turbojet performance from the world's engine manufacturers pushed combat aircraft to ever-greater speeds. Better understanding of the aerodynamic parameters required for a fighter to achieve Mach 1-plus performance routinely in level flight, rather than in a dive, brought that goal closer. In the USA North American claimed this particular 'first' with the Super Sabre, which first flew on 25 May 1953 as the YF-100A. This pre-production aircraft set a new world speed record of 755.149mph (1,214km/h) on 29 October that year. Further records were established before the major production version, the F-100D, appeared in 1956. By then the powerplant was the 10,200lb (4,627kg) J57-P-21A, which bestowed a maximum speed of 892mph (1,435km/h) at 35,000ft (10,668m).

In England the English Electric P.1A/B pre-production prototypes had thoroughly proved the design's supersonic performance by the time the first production Lightning flew for the first time on 3 November 1959.

Mixing jets and props

Mention has already been made of the Ryan Fireball, an attempt to marry the traditional handling qualities of a piston engine and the new turbojets, primarily to ease pilot transition between aircraft with either powerplant. Other aircraft powered by a combination of turbojet and piston engines included the USN's Martin P4M Mercator and North American AJ Savage. Differing greatly in size, intended role and deployment, both were produced in only modest numbers. The Mercator had two Allison J33s mounted below its Pratt & Whitney R-4360 radials. The J33-A-23 in the P4M-1 gave 4,600lb (2,087kg) of thrust, enabling the aircraft to fly about 100mph (160km/h) faster than the rival P2V Neptune with its turbojets operating. But balancing the power of all four engines proved rather difficult, and the standard USN patrol mission became the task of the Lockheed design. The Mercator did, however, find a useful electronics countermeasure role as the P4M-1Q.

Designers with access to wartime German aeronautical research realised just what was possible, even without resort to exotic materials or rocket motors and special fuels. Some designs with backward- or forward-swept wings and variable-geometry or 'swing wings' which had developed beyond the project stage were studied with great interest, particularly the Messerschmitt P.1101, which had ground-adjustable wing sweep. This tadpole-fuselaged fighter design formed the basis for the Bell X-5, which flew with some American additions, including the engine. A 4,900lb (2,224kg) Allison J35 replaced the Jumo 109-004B specified for the German original, and the X-5 flew for the first time on 20 June 1951. Although it was not developed further owing to concerns over structural integrity (the second X-5 crashed in 1953), the aircraft provided the first practical variable-geometry data.

Wartime engine development had been a protracted business. For example, great effort was required to push

When Germany's aeronautical Aladdin's cave was opened in 1945, the Americans were quick to grasp the potential of variable-geometry wings. The Bell X-5 was one example of how Messerschmitt design philosophy was adapted, although creating a practical variable-geometry aircraft took much more investigation and time than the Germans might have realised. These June 1951 pictures show the X-5's ground-adjustable wing.

An aircraft with a variable-geometry wing enjoys a number of advantages over conventional swept-wing machines, and the USA, the Soviet Union, France and the UK all produced such aircraft. France was a leader with the stillborn Mirage G of 1967, the prototype of which is seen here with its wing in the fully forward position.

the reciprocating piston engine beyond the 2,000hp mark and to ensure its reliability under the demands of combat. Moreover, in the 1940s and early 1950s the option of redesigning new airframes and thereby unacceptably delaying entry to service was not universally adopted. Instead, two or four jet engines were installed in 'old' straight-wing aircraft to obtain the required performance.

The English Electric Canberra, the North American B-45 Tornado and the Ilyushin Il-28 are examples of jet-powered medium bombers that successfully used the basic configuration of an unswept wing and relatively low-powered turbojets. Not every warplane had to look as good as the F-86 Sabre or Hunter; 'traditional' designs were more than adequate in less-demanding roles.

Wringing the last ounce of thrust from turbojets without a substantial increase in overall dimensions and, inevitably, weight, was a continuing challenge, primarily to overcome the eternal conflict of thrust-to-weight ratio. More than one 1950s military aeroplane was handicapped by turbojet engines which prevented the full exploitation

of an otherwise sound design. Funding for upgrading was not always forthcoming, particularly in Britain, with the result that while it was perfectly possible to build a supersonic Hunter, for example, the potential was ignored.

Bombers

Impressive though SAC's Convair B-36 was, USAF chiefs soon began to voice doubts over its performance (not to mention the negative broadsides from USN admirals). Even with the addition of four J47s in underwing pods to boost the power of its six piston engines, the B-36J could only reach 411mph (357km/h) with all ten engines 'turning and burning'. An all-jet design was the way forward, and Boeing had the answer in the B-47, the world's first swept-wing jet bomber. Choosing the 6,000lb (2,722kg) J47-GE-25/25A engine and installing six on wing pylons, four in pairs and two outboard, the designers achieved a maximum speed of 606mph (975km/h) with an aircraft that had a gross weight of 206,700lb (93,759kg), compared with the B-36J's 410,000lb (185,976kg).

Following the B-47 came the mighty B-52, destined to become the USAF's standard strategic bomber. As it entered production in August 1954, Boeing engineers little realised that the Stratofortress would be around for the foreseeable future, and would still be flying missions in the twenty-first century. Boeing opted for four pairs of J47s, ultimately rated at 13,750lb (6,237kg) each in the B-52G to give a cruising speed of 510mph (820km/h) and a maximum speed of 600mph (956km/h), which enabled the aircraft to lift a gross weight of 488,000lb (221,515kg).

Soviet riposte

Nuclear weapons development sparked off an East–West arms race soon after the Second World War. The Soviet Union, perceiving as great a threat from the West as she herself posed to Washington and London, began building a defensive/offensive arsenal designed to equal anything her adversaries might deploy. In this the Soviet Union more than succeeded, but at huge, ultimately crippling cost.

War in Korea showed the expertise of Soviet designers Mikoyan and Gurevich in the fighter field, this bureau continuing the famous line to the present day. In sequence the MiG-17, -19 and -21 fighters were joined by a parallel family of strike and ground-attack aircraft, beginning with the MiG-23 of April 1967. Designed as a fighter, this machine had an excellent multi-role capability, its sparkling performance of Mach 2.35 being derived from a single 18,850lb (8,550kg) Tumansky (later Soyuz) turbojet which produced 28,660lb (13,000kg) with afterburner, an impressive figure. A similar output from a turbojet was achieved with the Soyuz R-29B-300 in the MiG-27 ground-attack aircraft, which although it did not require quite the power of the MiG-23, still had an impressive 17,637lb dry (8,000kg) and 25,353lb (11,500kg) with afterburner. The Soviets reached something of a peak of turbojet power in the MiG-25, which had two 24,690lb (11,199kg) R-15BD-300s. These gave the aircraft a maximum speed of Mach 2.8 and a service ceiling of 67,915ft (20,700m).

Not quite so prolific in terms of the different types entering service with the VVS, but no less capable, was the Sukhoi line of turbojet fighters and tactical strike aircraft. The Su-17, -20 and -22, which gave the Soviet Union, Warsaw Pact and selected Middle Eastern nations a potent ground-attack/strike fighter series, was powered either by Lyulka AL or Tumansky turbojets. The latter, for example, powered the Su-17M-2 and Su-22 export versions of their respective sub-types. Among the Sukhoi variants remaining in service is the Su-22M-4, which has a single AL-21F-3 rated at 17,200lb (7,802kg) dry and 24,800lb (11,249kg) with afterburner. Sukhoi's Su-24 variable-geometry long-range strike fighter of 1970 featured relatively unusual side-by-side seating for the pilot and weapons-systems operator. This feature alone placed it in the same class

as the General Dynamics F-111, which has a similar wing and cockpit layout. Designed to replace both the Il-28 and Yak-28 medium bombers, the Su-24 combines a substantial ordnance-delivery capability with good performance imparted by its two Saturn/Lyulka AL-21F-3A turbojets of 16,864lb (7,649kg) dry and 24,690lb (11,199kg) with afterburning.

However, it was with bombers that the Soviet Union achieved its greatest military fame – or notoriety, depending on your standpoint. A succession of long-range strategic types, from the Tu-16 to the mighty Tu-160, kept thousands of people in the West fully occupied on building interceptor fighters to counter each of them, not to mention bombers to strike back if the VVS hordes turned the Cold War hot. Regarding engines, the Soviets were unusual in relying to a significant extent on turboprop rather than turbojet power for one of the principal VVS bombers, the Tu-95. Beginning its long service life soon after the first flight of the prototype on 12 November 1952, the Tu-95 fulfilled a variety of roles. These including many associated with intelligence gathering and also the duties of cruise missile platform, aerial tanker and maritime reconnaissance aircraft. The powerplant of the still-current Tu-95MS comprises four 14,795ehp KKBM Kuznetsov NK-12MV turboprops driving eight-bladed contrarotating propellers.

Two turbojets provided the power for the Tu-22, namely Dobrynin RD-7M-2s producing 27,560lb (12,501kg) dry and 36,375lb (16,500kg) with afterburning. A supersonic bomber capable of a top speed of Mach 1.52 at 39,350ft (11,990m), the Tu-22 has its engines mounted at the base of the fin to allow undisturbed airflow and to free the fuselage of bulky and weighty intake ducting. Now largely performing an electronic-warfare jamming role, the Tu-22 remains in service with Iraq and Libya as well as with the Russian Federation.

Britain's main contribution to the Cold War as a nuclear power was the V force of bombers: the Valiant, Vulcan and Victor. The Rolls-Royce Avon-powered Valiant was the first in service, the four wing-root-mounted engines giving the aircraft a range of 4,500 miles (7,240km). In production B.1 form the Valiant had the Avon 204 rated at 10,050lb (4,560kg). The Avon engine had been progressively uprated since the initial flight of the second prototype, which had engines delivering only 6,500lb (2,948kg) of thrust. In comparison, the R.A.14 offered 9,500lb (4,309kg) in early production models. The Vulcan prototype was also powered by Avons, but production aircraft had four Bristol Olympus engines of 9,750lb (4,423kg) each. The Vulcan development programme, concurrent with increments in engine power, resulted in late-production B.2s having the 20,000lb (9,072kg) Olympus 301. With its role revised to that of lower-altitude stand-off bombing, the Vulcan had a maximum speed of 645mph (1,038km/h). The Victor B.1

used the power of four paired 11,500lb (5,216kg) Armstrong Siddeley Sapphire 202 or 207 turbojets in the wing roots, making it marginally faster than the Vulcan, although there was little to choose between the two bombers in this respect. The Victor B.2 was re-engined with the 19,750lb (8,960kg) Rolls-Royce Conway Mk 201 bypass turbofan, which only marginally increased maximum speed but resulted in an all-round increase in capability. However, the Victor began to show the strains of operating in the low-level role, and was destined to find its *métier* as a tanker, as older examples had already done.

Generally speaking, designers found that the low power delivered by the early turbojets necessitated the use of at least two engines to produce a worthwhile performance. A couple of decades on, smaller turbojets were a deliberate choice for a class of aircraft in which low operating costs were a prime factor. This was the so-called counterinsurgency fighter, designed around the smallest possible airframe and, in the case of the representative Northrop F-5, powered by engines originally developed for guided missiles. General Electric's J85, rated at 4,090lb (1,856kg), powered the YF-5A for its maiden flight on 31 July 1963. Thereafter the F-5 went from strength to strength, its engines being uprated to 5,000lb (2,270kg) with afterburning in the F-5E.

Turboshafts

The logical move of adapting the jet engine to the helicopter was pioneered by Bell. The traditional vertical mounting of piston engines in rotary-wing aircraft took up at least half the available fuselage space in the smaller machines, and freeing this by mounting the engines horizontally was only one of the huge advantages to be gained by persuading the turbojet to drive helicopter rotors. German expertise was again called into play when Dr Anslem Franz of Lycoming, who had worked on the Jumo 004, was able to adapt the gas turbine into a helicopter engine, the 600shp XT53. Bell's Model 204 (XH-40 under the USAF designation system), which became the UH-1, first flew on 22 October 1959, powered by a 700shp XT53-L-1 turboshaft.

The resulting increase in cabin space enabled the US Army to rewrite the book on battlefield tactics. Troop-carrying helicopters, exemplified by the UH-1D/H, replaced the truck, being fast and infinitely more versatile. In the armed UH-1B/C the Army also had the means to protect ground forces, dissuade the enemy from attacking landing zones and provide devastating fire support. Both models remain in service today, thousands of Hueys having in the meantime left the production lines. Although performance has to remain within the 100mph (160km/h) to 130mph (209km/h) mark, the Lycoming T53-L-9 or L-11 turboshaft now driving the familiar two-bladed main and tail rotors has been uprated to 1,100shp.

When UH-1B gunships were deployed in Vietnam, a dedicated helicopter attack role developed quickly. The armed transports were adequate, but something more suited to the role, which became increasingly demanding, was required by the US Army. Bell obliged with the AH-1G, the famed HueyCobra. A single-rotor attack helicopter, the Cobra had a 1,400shp Lycoming T53-L-13 turboshaft giving a maximum speed of 219mph

A casual glance at a turboshaft helicopter engine might belie its revolutionary concept. Imagine all the systems in view here tilted to the vertical, and the loss of fuselage/cabin space with a piston engine installation can be readily appreciated. In the Bell UH-1H the entire engine compartment is mounted above the cabin, which is thus available for carrying troops and freight.

(352km/h) in a dive and a cruising speed of 166mph (267km/h). War service in Vietnam led to an important engine modification, in that the exhaust had to be masked to prevent effective homing by SAMs. A shield that directed the hot gases upwards rather than aft, to be dispersed by the rotor wash, proved to be effective for the short time towards the end of the war when US Army AH-1Gs were exposed to sophisticated opposition.

Developed engines for the long Huey line included the Turbo Twin Pack, which provided the greater safety factor of twin engines and opened up a market for both military and civil orders. Canada was the launch customer for the Twin Huey, with a powerplant comprising two P7W PT6T-3 engines, similar to the first conversion, which used a Continental XT67-T-1 free turbine and two T72-T-2 model 217 turboshafts coupled to a common reduction gearbox and output shaft. This unit offered 1,200shp for take-off and 1,100shp in continuous flight. In the later Bell AB 412 Grifone and CH-146, which had four-blade main rotors, the power output was increased to 1,910shp. Two engines gave the CUH-1H (later CH-135) a cruising speed of 121mph (194km/h), compared with the UH-1H's maximum level speed of 127mph (204km/h).

Bell Helicopter's ability to diversify the basic AH-1 to suit numerous roles was hardly challenged for two decades, and today there is ample evidence around the world that the company's position remains strong. The biggest challenge in the attack role came from Hughes (later McDonnell Douglas) Helicopters, with its AH-64 Apache. Powered by two 1,695shp General Electric T1700-GE-710 or 1,890shp T700-GE-701C turboshafts driving four-bladed main and tail rotors, the AH-64 rep-

Sikorsky was among the first US manufacturers to offer turboshaft power for helicopters, there being few better examples than the long-lived H-3 series. Various European countries powered Sikorsky helicopters with 'local' powerplants, exemplified here by the Rolls-Royce H1400-1 Gnome installation in a Royal Norwegian Air Force SAR Westland Sea King.

resented a new generation of battlefield support helicopter when it first flew on 30 September 1975. With substantial US Army orders, the Apache is currently in service with five other countries and remains one of the most capable rotorcraft in its class anywhere in the world.

Turboshafts have since become the commonplace powerplant for military helicopters, with France very much at the forefront of development. The Alouette series was successfully converted to turboshaft power after the initial models operated on piston engines. Turboméca's Artouste turboshaft invariably drove a three-bladed rotor, while the Turmo in the SA 321 Super Frélon provided the power for a six-bladed main and five-bladed tail rotor.

Boeing Helicopters' CH-46 and CH-47 represent the largest helicopters developed in the West, but Russian rotorcraft manufacturers have long since dwarfed both, making them look tiny in comparison with such machines as the Mil Mi-22 and Mi-26. Both operate on twin-turboshaft power, the former using the 5,425shp Aviadvigatel (formerly Soloviev) D-25V, and the latter the 11,086shp ZKMB Progress (formerly Lotarev) D-136.

Kamov appears to keep the smaller end of the Russian helicopter industry going almost on its own, the specialised Ka-25, -27, -28 and -32 having been the mainstay types in the compact ASW helicopter class intended primarily for shipboard operation. Mil has of course entered the gunship field in a big way with the Mi-24, -25 and -26, a series that has combined the US concepts of the attack helicopter with troop-carrying. The Mil-28 dedicated attack helicopter uses a similar Klimov TV-3 turboshaft to its larger stablemate, its two 2,070shp engines giving it a formidable load-carrying capability. A top speed of 186mph (300km/h) makes it some 46mph (74km/h) faster than the Bell AH-1S.

While tactical and strategic aircraft monopolised the turbojet, other military roles such as antisubmarine patrol, invariably filled by turboprop aircraft, have seen some exceptions. The most notable is the BAe Nimrod, the 'born again' Comet airliner with uprated Rolls-Royce RB.168-20 Spey turbofans rather than Avon turbojets. The Nimrod's outstanding feature is its ability to loiter on ASW patrol for up to fifteen hours (unrefuelled), and to operate for substantial periods with two engines shut down. This not only conserves fuel but enables the crew to fly low and slow enough to spot small objects on the water.

Today's military jet transports, tankers, AEW aircraft and flying command posts such as the Boeing E-4 Sentry version of the 747 largely owe their origins to airliner development. These in turn have benefited from lucrative military contracts which ensured that future civil contracts could be fulfilled. Boeing, for example, hardly looked back after completing the first KC-135 for the USAF in 1957, the civil 707 programme thereby receiving the financial boost it needed. An upgrading from turbojet to turbofan power in line with front-line combat aircraft is evident in many of the transports and tankers currently operated by the world's leading air arms.

Jet flying boats

Jet flying boats were an interesting concept, but only the Soviet Union (notably the Beriev design bureau) took them beyond the prototype and pre-production stage. Britain explored the jet-flying-boat fighter with the single-seat Saunders-Roe SR-A/1, powered by two 3,300lb (1,497kg) (later 3,850lb (1,746kg)) Metropolitan-Vickers F2/4 Beryl turbojets, which first flew on 16 July 1947. Although the flying boat had proved successful in military service, its era had all but passed after the war, and nothing came of the Saro design, although it flew well enough.

America took jet-flying-boat design considerably further with the dramatic Martin XP6M-1 SeaMaster, which made its maiden flight on 14 July 1955. An ambitious attempt to provide the USN with a long-range, largely independent seaplane striking force capable of delivering nuclear weapons as well as conventional ordnance, the SeaMaster became a bit player in the USAF versus USN power game of the 1950s, which centred on the merits of carriers and strategic bombers, and the question of which Service could provide the best means to retaliate in the event of a nuclear attack on the West. Powered by four Allison J71s set into overwing nacelles to keep them clear of spray, the early SeaMasters had their share of problems, including rear-fuselage scorching as a result of exhaust emissions when the engines were in afterburner. Unfortunately, the remedying of this and other problems, which were not very critical, extended

the test programme another four years or so into 1959, the year that the first production SeaMaster, the P6M-2, was completed. This had four 15,800lb (7,167kg) Pratt & Whitney axial-flow J75s, giving a total thrust of 63,200lb (28,997kg) which enabled the aircraft to attain an unofficial top speed of Mach 1.02 on one test flight. Overtaken, like other promising aircraft, by time, newer technologies and in this case the nuclear attack submarine, the Sea-Master was cancelled in August 1959.

While the Western powers continued to use conventional flying boats in limited military roles well into the 1970s, as did the Japanese with the Shin-Meiwa PS-1, no operational types powered solely by turbojets emerged. Only the Soviet Union persevered with this considerable challenge, and in July 1956 the first flight took place of the Beriev Be-10, powered by two AL-7PB turbojets. Limited operational usefulness curtailed the Be-10's service, but it set four payload records in 1961. A replacement in the form of the Beriev Be-42 Albatross amphibian prototype first flew in December 1986. The world's largest amphibious aircraft, the Be-42 is powered by two 26,455lb (12,000kg) Aviadvigatel D-30KPV turbofans and two 5,510lb (2,500kg) RKBM RD-60K booster turbojets.

Vertical take-off

The often voiced but seldom addressed question of the vulnerability of conventional airfields, and the desired alternative of tactical aircraft having the ability to take off vertically from any convenient patch of ground, was finally answered by the advent of the Rolls-Royce Pegasus. This remarkable and for many years unique vectored-thrust turbofan with directional exhaust nozzles,

At one time the Martin SeaMaster was in line to form a US Navy flying-boat nuclear strike force. Desperate to offer a viable alternative to the USAF's Convair B-36, the Navy came up with the SeaMaster and, but for the ICBM-armed nuclear submarine, it might have fulfilled its potential as the core of a 'second force'.

first flown in the Hawker P.1127, enabled the later BAe Harrier to become the first Service aircraft in the world to take off and land vertically. Originally offering 9,000lb (4082kg) thrust as the BE.53 of 1953, it powered the first P.1127 into the air on 12 September 1961. Since then it has been improved and boosted from 19,200lb (8,709kg) in the Harrier GR.1 which entered RAF service in 1969 to 23,800lb (10,796kg) in its current F402-RR-408 form, and Pegasus derivative engines continue to power the Harrier GR.7 and Sea Harrier F/A2.

Following the Harrier's service in the US Marine Corps as the AV-8A from 1971, the USA provided substantial help in developing the aircraft beyond what appeared to be financially viable in the UK. Seeing the potential of a model capable of carrying a greater ordnance load, a limitation of the original 'small-wing' version, McDonnell Douglas, in collaboration with British Aerospace, designed the Harrier II for the USMC. A 21,450lb (9,737kg) F402 turbofan was fitted, and the wingspan was extended to 30ft 4in (9.25m). Deliveries of the AV-8B began in 1984, and the RAF's similar Harrier GR.5/7 flew for the first time later that year.

Today's Harrier development programme has, since the demise of the Soviet Union, re-established the aircraft as the world's most viable VTOL combat aircraft. Its challenger, the Yakovlev Yak-38 of 1971, was only the second Service aircraft to benefit from an operational lift engine, the 14,900lb (6,759kg) Tumansky R-27 turbojet, augmented by two RKMB RD-36-35FVR lift jets behind the cockpit. The Yak-38 was first deployed aboard the carrier *Kiev* in 1975, and as this vessel remains part of the Russian Navy at least some of them are understood to have been retained. A much-improved Yakovlev V/STOL fighter, the Yak-41, was cancelled in 1992, although design bureau research continues.

Turbofans

Compared with the turbojet, the turbofan offered a substantially higher performance and improved fuel burn for front-line combat aircraft, as was partly proven with the Pegasus. Emerging from years of political turmoil as the first aircraft to have afterburning turbofans and a variable-geometry wing, the General Dynamics F-111 was able to fulfil its undoubted potential. A current power output of 25,100lb (11,393kg) is obtainable from each Pratt & Whitney TF30 engine in the F-111F and G versions, the EF-111 Raven having two 18,500lb (8,398kg) TF30-P-3s. Fitting turbofans in the Boeing B-52H was a highly successful life-extension exercise for an aircraft more than forty years old. The output from eight 17,000lb (7,711kg) TF33-P-3s enabled range to be increased by about a third over that possible with turbojet propulsion.

Current first-line US fighters, including the F-14 Tomcat, F-15 Eagle, F-16 Falcon and F-18 Hornet, all derive an outstanding performance from afterburning turbofan

Quite distinctive owing to its four variable jet nozzles, the Rolls-Royce Pegasus has retained its place as the world's most practical V/STOL engine. Powering the highly versatile and successful British Harrier and American AV-8A/B, the basic Pegasus has also proved to be adaptable to considerable increases in thrust, in line with the larger and heavier but much more capable current Harrier series.

engines. In Europe the Panavia Tornado, the Dassault Mirage 2000 series and Rafale are similarly powered, all engines of European and US origin typically being in the 10,000lb (4,540kg) to 20,000lb (9,080kg) (dry) range.

Russia's turbofan-powered MiG-29/33 and MiG-31 are among the world's most potent fighters, the latter being the fastest with a maximum speed of Mach 2.83. Designed as an interceptor, not of mythical high-flying bombers but of infinitely more deadly cruise missiles and low-flying strike aircraft, the MiG-31 has two Aviadvigatel D-30F6 turbofans developing 34,170lb (15.499kg) with afterburning. The current parlous state of the Russian economy has meant that this potent aircraft has not been ordered for the VVS at the time of writing, and it remains to be seen if funding will become available. In the meantime, the VVS relies on the equally capable MiG-33, which is the redesignation applied to the updated MiG-29 following its initial production for the VVS in 1995. Two 19,355lb (8,779kg) Klimov/Sariskov RD-33K turbofans give this aircraft a top speed of Mach 2.35 and an initial climb rate of 64,960ft/min (19,800m/min).

Stealth challenge

One of the most difficult problems in designing effective stealth aircraft has been to suppress the heat exhaust from the engines. With the F-117 Night Hawk, Lockheed achieves this by mixing exhaust gases from each General Electric F404-GE-F1D2 non-afterburning turbofan with bypass air and dispersing it through 'platypus' exhaust gates. This effectively reduces the F-117's

Powered by twin TF30 turbofans, the General Dynamics F-111 weathered one of the most acrimonious political rows in history to emerge as a single- rather than tri-service attack and ECM aircraft. It was also the first successful US combat aircraft to employ variable geometry, as shown in this sectional drawing depicting the F-111 in fully swept, 'supersonic dash' form.

infrared signature and allows relatively low-powered engines of 10,800lb (4,900kg) to be used to give a normal maximum operating speed of Mach 0.9.

That the turbojet revolutionised air force equipment is undisputed; it led to today's highly efficient turboshafts and turbofans, yet maintained its place for certain applications. Like numerous advances in the scientific field it was not fully appreciated at the time of its conception, but what is commonplace today was too radical for some individuals to grasp in the 1940s. The engines currently powering military aircraft were matured through the dangerous years of the Cold War and enabled manufacturers to provide the world's air arms with highly capable aircraft. These have helped prevent the open international conflict that so many people feared and expected.

Engines are the heart of any combat aircraft, but the performance of the entire package – the airframe, avionics and weaponry – can only be fully tested under combat conditions. The Falklands conflict and the Gulf War offered important lessons in deployment of air power, particularly from the British point of view. The Harrier

Continuous running of a Pratt & Whitney F100-PW-220 turbofan on the manufacturer's test rig enables about nine years of operational service in F-15 and F-16 fighters to be simulated over a much smaller timescale.

Fans of the future. Two Turbo Union RB.199 Mk 104E engines were fitted in the Eurofighter 2000 prototype seen here, while the similar Eurojet EJ200 engine powered the third prototype and production aircraft. As of late 1998, Eurofighter remains a viable programme with an order book for 250 for the RAF, 130 for Germany, 130 for Italy and 87 for Spain.

made its combat debut over the South Atlantic, as did the Tornado, Jaguar and Buccaneer in the Gulf. Whatever problems these conflicts may have highlighted, there were few complaints about engine performance, a challenge that modern technology appears well able to meet for the foreseeable future.

Bibliography

Frawley, G and Thorn, J, *The International Directory of Military Aircraft 1996/97* (Airlife, Shrewsbury, 1996).

Guest, C-F, *Under the Red Star* (Airlife, Shrewsbury, 1993).

Gunston, B, *Russian Aircraft 1875–1995* (Osprey, London, 1996).

World Encyclopedia of Aero Engines (Patrick Stephens, Yeovil, 1995).

The Development of Jet and Turbine Aero Engines (Patrick Stephens, Yeovil, 1995).

Scutts, J, *UH-1 Iroquois/AH-1 HueyCobra: Modern Combat Aircraft No 19* (Ian Allan, Shepperton, 1984).

Swanborough, G and Bowers, P M, *United States Navy Aircraft since 1911* (Putnam, London, 1976).

Thetford, O, *British Naval Aircraft since 1912* (Putnam, London, 1982).

Aircraft of the Royal Air Force since 1918 (Putnam, London, 1995).

Wilkinson, P H, *Aircraft Engines of the World, 1946* (Pitman, London, 1946).

4
Aerodynamics and Structures
Dr David Baker

By the end of the Second World War the age of the modern combat aircraft had dawned. Piston-engined aircraft were reaching their limits, and a completely new range of performance was produced by aircraft designed to wholly new principles of aerodynamic design. Growth in performance and mission capability outpaced anything achieved before. During the 1940s, fighter performance went from a top speed of 350mph (563km/h) for the piston-engined Spitfire I to 675mph (1,086km/h) for the turbojet-powered F-86A Sabre. Maximum climb rate increased from 2,800ft/min (855m/min) to 8,000ft/min (2,440m/min).

In the 1950s and early 1960s the top speed of operational combat aircraft leapt to 1,500mph (2,414km/h). Some fighters, such as the English Electric Lightning, had an initial climb rate of more than 50,000ft/min (15,240m/min), and aircraft were under test that would exceed 2,000mph (3,220km/h) in level flight. A decade later a new generation of combat aircraft demonstrated climb rates in excess of 60,000ft/min (18,300m/min). In some areas manoeuvrability suffered from the uncompromising search for greater speed. Instantaneous turn rates actually went down, from 22°/sec for the F-86 to about 15°/sec for types such as the F-4 Phantom II. In the search for supersonic flight, wing loadings had increased, and that trend did not reverse until a new generation of technologies emerged in the 1970s, giving fighters like the F-14 snappy turn rates that pitch them against lightweights such as the Northrop F-5 in 'Top Gun' contests.

Much of the incredible increase in aircraft performance was achieved through progress in the development of the turbojet engine, which propelled airframes to hitherto unattainable speeds and altitudes. But not all the performance growth owed its origin to the engine. Greater understanding of the aerodynamic environment in which the supersonic combat aircraft operated added measurably to the efficiency of the design. The need to explore transonic and supersonic flight regimes through research in the air was emphatically brought home by a series of accidents in the last days of the piston-engined combat era. What pilots experienced as they rushed headlong to terminal velocity was unknown and unpredictable. In the Soviet Union, Britain, France and the USA companies and government research laboratories struggled to unravel the complexities of an entirely new age in aviation, one in which novel aerodynamic equations would open a fresh window on flight

and combine with the latest generation of materials to create the ultimate flying machine.

A harvest of research

The first decade of the Cold War brought quantum leaps in roles and requirements for all types of combat aircraft, built upon an extraordinary period in aeronautical development. Almost all of the new technologies that emerged during the Second World War were products of work begun and funded during the 1930s: pressurised cockpits, ejection seats, rocket and jet propulsion, etc. Later, Cold War developments diversified because governments balanced essential research and development against the introduction of new types with their associated production requirements. Those types that did progress from requirement to operational status during the duration of the conflict would play an important role in the new age of jet fighters and long-range (hemispheric) aircraft.

Central to postwar advancements was the jet engine, but the ability to step ahead of critical limits for propeller-driven aircraft opened a new era in aircraft design and combat capabilities. The enabling catalysts for high-speed aircraft were found in advanced aerodynamics, which up to then had been theoretical, and new and exotic structures. For the first three decades of powered flight aerodynamicists worked on the assumption that air, like water, was essentially incompressible. They were now to discover that this was not necessarily so. It was one of many lessons that would be learned in the decade following the Second World War and that would, by applying theoretical work to engineering applications, move aeronautics into the high-speed/high-performance arena which it occupies today. As design engineers were to learn, there is more to an efficient and effective combat aircraft than performance in a straight line.

Approaching the speed of sound

One phenomenon that came in for a lot of attention in the early 1940s, and would have important repercussions for postwar aviation, was compressibility. It first became apparent when fast piston-engined aircraft encountered stability and control problems at high speeds, and became a major challenge to aircraft design engineers in the late 1940s and early 1950s, as teams in Britain and the USA wrestled with seemingly insoluble problems to achieve transonic flight. At the core were the dramatic changes in the way air behaved around the lifting surfaces of fast-moving objects in the atmosphere. In high-speed test dives during 1941 aircraft experienced shaking and increased buffeting as they approached the point at which the air reached sonic velocity. Phenomena were encountered that seemingly defied explanation, and controls became ineffective. It was as though an impenetrable wall lay just ahead, coupled to the speed of sound. Thus was born the graphic but inaccurate journalistic phrase 'the sound barrier'.

The Austrian physicist Ernst Mach introduced a standard reference against which this 'sound barrier' could be measured. Called the Mach number, the ratio indicated how fast the aircraft was moving relative to the speed of sound, which changed with the temperature of the air. To the standard handbooks on aerodynamics were added the complexities of uncertainty. By the mid-1940s piston-engined aircraft had been pushed just about as far as they could go, and as the Second World War ended the new age of jet aircraft had dawned. Shaken from complacency by the work of Sir Frank Whittle, by 1943 US aircraft engineers realised the potential in turbojet propulsion, but knew that the problems encountered with compressibility would get worse as the speed of sound was approached.

Serious attention was paid to the problems of compressibility and sonic flight, which could be approached but not routinely experienced by piston-engined aircraft. The effects on a high-speed aircraft such as the P-51 or P-47 were considerable. Accelerating in a dive from Mach 0.75 to around Mach 0.86, the aircraft would achieve terminal velocity but in that relatively small margin of speed (a difference of Mach 0.11) drag would increase and lift would decrease massively. As the aircraft reached denser air the pressure of the atmosphere would increase and the temperature would rise. This had the effect of raising the speed of sound and reducing the Mach number of the aircraft, restoring it to the conventions of established aerodynamic principles.

Although reaction propulsion alone held the promise of sonic flight, the effects of compressibility appeared long before the first jet- or rocket-powered aeroplanes. Windtunnel research in the USA produced a laminar-flow wing which did not achieve the design objectives of laminar flow in flight, but served the unexpected and desirable function of delaying the critical Mach number. This number is defined as the aircraft flight Mach number where local flow over a reference surface, perhaps the upper wing, reaches unity. The higher the critical Mach number can be raised, the greater will be the aircraft's actual flight speed before it encounters compressibility. It was in an attempt to achieve this that the theoretical advantages of a laminar-flow wing were inadvertently found to achieve a design benefit.

The laminar-flow wing grew out of an attempt to minimise drag by smoothing turbulence in the bound-ary layer between the upper (lifting) surface of the wing and the air flowing across the aerofoil. A laminar-flow wing is one in which the line along which smooth flow of air gives way to turbulence is pushed back towards the trailing edge. In Germany in 1904 the Bavarian aerodynamicist Ludwig Prandtl had described the boundary layer and the concept of a smooth laminar flow to minimise skin friction and attendant drag. Between the world wars work in Britain showed that, to achieve this, maximum wing thickness should be around 40 per cent of the chord, and that, by reducing overall thickness, pressure drag caused by the air flowing round the wing would be reduced.

Work at the National Physical Laboratory in 1931 demonstrated the advantage of a carefully shaped laminar-flow wing by achieving a lower drag coefficient than a perfectly flat steel plate! In the USA an entire family of some 100 aerofoil designs were drawn up to provide low-drag sections designated by the National Advisory Committee for Aeronautics (NACA) and given NACA six-digit numbers, a menu from which airframe designers could select an optimised wing. It was entirely fortuitous that, in flight, the laminar wing helped delay the critical Mach number and, in a nice way, achieved what the protagonists desired, although in a different corner of the aircraft performance envelope. All this was vitally important, for it helped reveal to an industry struggling to ignore the onset of compressibility that it was an area of aerodynamic law that could be handled and understood. But they had been doing that for some time already without realising it.

Sonic shapes

The way air resistance increases with speed was known more than 300 years ago, when Isaac Newton asserted that resistance is proportional to the square of the diameter of a sphere and to the square of the velocity. It was Benjamin Robins, however, who predicted early in the eighteenth century that this neat linear theory was only roughly correct at relatively low velocities. His ballistics tests with objects propelled to a supersonic velocity of 1,200ft/sec (366m/sec) encountered compressibility. Robins recognised what was happening by determining that resistance close to sonic velocity jumps to very large values owing to elasticity of the air, but the implications were not appreciated. The next step to defining the transonic phenomenon was driven by the development of steam turbines, where the behaviour of fast-moving gases through nozzles was vital to defining the problem. The science of gas dynamics paved the way for theoretical studies of the properties of high-speed aerofoils.

In the 1930s efforts were made to improve the shape of propellers which, because their tips travel at a higher Mach fraction than the airframe, encounter problems with compressibility before the aircraft itself. Refinements were made to the aerofoil section, to twist distribution and to blade thickness/chord ratios. As a result the free-stream Mach number at which the propeller showed serious loss of performance increased. From this came the realisation that the propeller would itself be the limiting factor on aircraft performance. With the very real possibility of gas-turbine engines propelling an airframe to the transonic region, a definition of the speed of sound was vital. Newton had tried to calculate the speed of sound, but was low by about 15 per cent. It was left to the nineteenth-century French mathematician Pierre-Simon de Laplace to add the vital corrections to the formula. He concluded correctly that the speed of sound is determined entirely by temperature, and not by pressure. For aeronautical engineers this means that the speed of sound can vary at different points on a wing and at different geographic locations, heights and times of day and in different weather conditions.

In simplest terms, the drag coefficient begins to rise sharply as the speed of sound is approached and then gradually declines beyond the speed of sound, stabilising around Mach 1.5 at a value slightly higher than low subsonic velocities. The impact of compressibility and the effect of air upon an aircraft at sonic or supersonic speed would influence the design of jet aircraft more than any other factor, and it was important for engineers to understand what happened at transonic speed. As the aircraft approaches Mach 1 a pressure gradient builds up ahead of the wing until, at the speed of sound, it hits the relatively static air like an explosion, imparting rapid acceleration. Because the air is heated and expands, the pressure is reduced at the forward spanwise point, leaving a more normal pressure further back along the chord of the wing. This transition point from low pressure to normal pressure occurs violently and across a width measured in millimetres, creating a shock wave.

Over the entire aircraft the situation is complex because different rates of acceleration will push some air beyond supersonic speed when the airframe is still transonic. The exact position of the shock wave on the wing is determined by angle of attack, and as flow is disrupted it can break free, the loss of lift tending to cause a wing to drop, as several pilots found to their cost during high-speed dives. The build-up of pressure and turbulence can render control surfaces inoperable, and the effect on tail surfaces can be catastrophic. But the position of the shock wave along the top of the wing is also determined by the speed of the aircraft. As the aircraft accelerates beyond Mach 1 the shock wave moves slowly back toward the trailing edge. As the air accelerates over the forward upper portion of the wing and becomes more violent, an expansion wave forms at the leading edge, where the air suddenly speeds up, reducing the pressure.

These effects are normalised for a conventional wing shape such as that which would have been used on the earliest jet aircraft capable of transonic flight in a dive. Other wing sections will have different shock attachments. For instance, a symmetrical wing with mirrored upper and lower surfaces will have an expansion wave attached to the upper leading edge and a shock wave attached to the upper trailing edge, while the lower surface will have the shock wave at the front and the expansion wave at the rear. More complex sections such as double-wedge aerofoils will have expansion waves at the intermediate point of the wing where the two wedge profiles meet, and at the upper leading edge; shock waves will attach to the upper and lower trailing edge and lower leading edge. Much of this was known in theory, but design engineers who faced these complexities when producing a working aeroplane relied more on trial and error than on calculation.

For twenty years the shape of a wing had remained more or less unchanged. The theory of flight was simple and the solutions predictable – for relatively slow piston-engined aircraft. In the early 1940s engineers adopted a new set of wing-section designs in an attempt to achieve laminar flow, but ended up finding a way to delay the critical Mach number. High-speed aircraft of the period usually had wing thickness ratios of 14–18 per cent (that is, the thickness was 14–18 per cent of the chord), and the drag induced by wings, tail and fuselage could be calculated separately and added together with only minimal attention to the interference effects of the combined assemblies. That was to change as the traditional shape of the aircraft underwent a radical transformation. The greatest challenge lay not in cruising at speeds around the critical Mach value, but in achieving supersonic flight, where sufficient power is available to overcome drag in the transonic region.

Supersonic wings

In 1935 the German research scientist Professor Adolph Busemann presented a paper to the Fifth Volta Congress for High-Speed Flight in Rome in which he proposed a solution to compressibility, which was already becoming a detectable problem on some rounded parts of the airframe. He showed that by placing the leading edge of the wing at an oblique angle to the airflow, instead of at a right angle, the critical Mach number would be much reduced. By sweeping the wing back, the air flowing across its surface can be considered to have two components, one across the chord of the wing at the same angle as the sweep, and the other spanwise, which wastes itself along the swept leading edge to the tip. Because the sum of the two airflow streams can never be more than the total velocity of the airstream encountered, each component has a considerably lower velocity than the aircraft. Theoretically, if the aircraft is moving at Mach 1 the chordwise flow on a wing swept at 35° will be at Mach 0.82, while the spanwise bleed is at Mach 0.18. Chordwise flow for wings at 45° and 60° would be Mach 0.7 and Mach 0.5 respectively.

The theory works a little different in practice. The upward bending moment caused by lift on the wing varies across the span. The greatest effect is at the tip, which, being twisted downwards at the leading edge, lowers the angle of attack and decreases lift. In reality the exact place where the loads are applied, the torsional stiffness of the wing and the bending moment all dictate the degree of change to the incidence (twist) of the wing. Moreover, as the air speeds up across the upper surface the spanwise motion of the boundary layer moves it towards the tip, which further reduces lift and premature tip-stall. Because the wingtip loss will be behind the aircraft's c.g. it affects stability, causing the aircraft to wander in pitch. Loss of control in yaw can be induced when the aircraft is not directly aligned with the flow of air, because one wing will have less sweep than the other and will gain lift over the other wing, which will have much greater sweep. This can result in a rolling motion which, when coupled to loss of aileron stability owing to shockwave turbulence, threatens the safety of the aircraft.

In spite of all these potentially negative effects, the value of a swept wing for transonic flight was unquestionable. Later, when flight tests felt the atmosphere at multiple Mach numbers, it was seen that the advantages of a swept wing were less at supersonic speed and disappeared altogether at Mach 2, where the added stiffness of a straight wing was preferable.

The theoretical work of Adolph Busemann went unheeded everywhere except in Germany, where his work was immediately seized upon by the German Air Ministry and put under a security wrap. In 1931 another aerodynamicist, Albert Betz of Switzerland, showed that swept wings would delay the effects of compressibility, and several German aircraft with swept wings appeared before the end of the Second World War. Meanwhile, in the USA, Robert T Jones came to the same conclusion and prepared the way for the influx of German ideas at the end of 1945.

Jones was almost entirely self-taught, becoming an aerodynamicist at the NACA Langley Aeronautical Laboratory and head of its stability analysis section. Early in 1945 he extrapolated results obtained during airflow calculations for an experimental air-to-air missile to the compressibility problem of full-size aircraft. He noted that compressibility did not seem to influence slender, revolving objects. It became apparent that a swept-wing leading edge on a full-size aircraft would delay the effects of compressibility, an idea that would take root with force when a group of German scientists arrived in the USA during 1946. Among that group was Adolph

Early postwar evaluation of the swept-wing configuration was undertaken by the US Navy using this modified Bell P-63 King Cobra fighter, designated L-39-1, which had 35° of sweep. The extensive leading-edge slot is conspicuous.

Busemann, who came to work at the Langley Laboratory in May 1947. Senior engineers at Langley had been reluctant to publish Jones's work, but within a year the entire industry was alive with swept-wing designs.

There was, however, yet another form of wing design that offered considerable advantages and, in some respects, would prove superior to the swept wing. It, too, came from Germany. In the early 1930s Alexander Lippisch, a brilliant young design engineer, experimented with triangular wings and explored the aerodynamic qualities of tailless aeroplanes. During the war the prolific German aircraft research effort included studies of this planform, soon to become known as the 'delta', from the Greek letter expressed in the form of a triangle. The delta had advantages denied to the purely swept wing. It had the value of a swept leading edge, a thin section in relation to the chord (low thickness-to-chord ratio) and a low aspect ratio – factors that combined to delay the onset of compressibility. Some considered the delta preferable for transonic flight. Moreover, it had added advantages in structural rigidity and in the provision of space for engines, fuel and internal equipment.

Because of its extensive chord, the delta's wing root has considerable depth, affording a large increase in available space compared with conventional straight- or swept-wing aircraft. The highly swept leading edge offers minimum shock-wave drag and the advantages of a high critical Mach number. There is little or no probability of tip bending owing to spanwise loads, and the increased wing area gives better handling performance and manoeuvrability at transonic and supersonic speeds. Because the wing root chord provides enhanced stability there is less need for a tail, saving weight and reducing overall drag. Of course a balance has to be struck between the added structural weight of the larger wing and the weight saved by eliminating large rear-fuselage sections, integrating centre-fuselage structures in the wing and eliminating horizontal (and even vertical) tail surfaces.

One promising design developed by the Germans was the pure delta Lippisch LP-13a, which was to have been powered by a liquid-propellant boost rocket and a centrally mounted ramjet sustainer burning powdered coal. Never flown, it was calculated to be capable of 1,025mph (1,650km/h), and windtunnel tests indicated it would be aerodynamically stable to the limit of the tunnel, Mach 2.6. But not all German research focused on ultimate performance, and much effort was expended on potential improvements in handling and performance from refinements to the wing. This in turn had a significant effect on the structure of the aircraft. The all-metal stressed-skin monoplane that prevailed at the start of the war was outdated in the jet age. Conventional wisdom required fighters to have comparatively thick wings accommodating fuel, undercarriage and guns. The onset of compressibility argued for thin wings that

would have driven up landing speeds and restricted aircraft to concrete runways, whereas most aircraft of the period had to operate from grass strips.

High-speed aerodynamics

By the Second World War great advances had been made in the state of the art. Wing loadings were five times the value typical for a First World War fighter, combat aircraft were stressed to 12g and control effectiveness now gave aircraft a roll rate four times as great. In the postwar world of jet aircraft major changes were brought about by the way aircraft had to fly and fight. Wings could no longer grow thick, compensated by a larger chord to maintain an acceptable thickness ratio. Before the end of the war, airframes originally designed for much lower-speed regimes became highly evolved with more-powerful engines, and encountered conditions dangerously close to the limit. The Spitfire is a good example; engineers had to redesign its wing structure to accommodate its greatly enhanced performance with safety.

Rapid aileron deflection causes wing-twisting and decreases the amount of roll moment as a function of dynamic pressure, proportional to the square of the speed. Cantilever wings are usually stiff in bending but relaxed under torsional loads. This means they twist at the tip, causing aileron reversal. In such situations the control surface deflects the wing rather than the air, with potentially catastrophic effect where the rolling moment is inverted. In the design phase of any aeroplane it was essential to ensure that the speed at which aileron reversal would occur was well above the machine's maximum speed. The Spitfire's wing was highly advanced for its day and had great integral strength. With its low thickness-to-chord ratio, thin root and tip sections and washout to inhibit stall, its calculated aileron reversal speed of 578mph (930km/h) was more than adequate for an aircraft designed in the mid-1930s. However, with the advent of the Rolls-Royce Griffon engine, putting out 70–100 per cent more power than the original Merlin, later marks of Spitfire had clearly reached the design limit of the original wing. The only solution was to design a completely new wing with greatly increased torsional stiffness, which the designers did for the Mk 21.

In fact, if there was any aircraft that smoothly metamorphosed from the piston era to the jet age it was the line that began with the first Supermarine Spitfire and ended with the Vickers-Supermarine Swift, over a period spanning little more than twelve years. The key to that transition was the Spiteful, which had a new wing incorporating features resulting from NACA tests in the USA. The original Spitfire wing had a fairly conventional section, with the thickest part well forward of the centreline. Using laminar-flow design, the Spiteful's wing had the thickest part further aft, at 47 per cent of the chord. In 1942 a modified Spitfire with this wing achieved Mach

0.91 in a dive. The Spiteful had greatly increased vertical tail surface and the overall structure was stiffened considerably, but it was short-lived; even before it first took to the air work had begun on the jet-powered Attacker, incorporating a similar laminar-flow wing.

With wings developed from one of the last great piston-engined fighters, the Attacker was at best a stop-gap, and in 1946 the Air Ministry used German aerodynamic research to specify a replacement for the first RAF jet fighter, the Meteor, incorporating swept wings. Just as the Spitfire had been the monument to R J Mitchell in the mid-1930s, so would the new swept-wing jet be the legacy of his successor, Joe Smith, in the mid-1940s. When it appeared in 1948 the Type 510, precursor to the Swift, was the first British fighter to have sweep on the leading edges of wing and tail surfaces. But the revolution was universal. A year earlier in the USA North American had flown the all-swept F-86 Sabre, while in the Soviet Union, just a few months later, the all-swept MiG-15 took to the sky for the first time. Each displayed features pioneered by German aerodynamicists and engineers.

Although their swept wings enabled these aircraft to attain Mach 1 in a dive, aerodynamic design refinement was too immature and engine technology too basic to provide true supersonic capability. Brute force allowed the North American F-100 Super Sabre of 1953 to become the first aircraft capable of exceeding Mach 1 in level flight. With 45° leading-edge sweep, compared with 35° for the F-86, and an engine with almost three times the power, it conformed to basic principles. The marriage of new-age aerodynamics and aircraft design was still a legacy of the old way of doing business. There was simply too little data about sustained flight at transonic and supersonic speed to provide a basis for innovative design; there was still too much guessing in the dark.

Breaking the barriers

As a reference, the rocket-powered X-series research aircraft, beginning with the Bell X-1, had been the only means of obtaining information on the transonic and supersonic regime. Yet even these exotic 'hot-rods' were only marginally ahead of military combat aircraft already flying or on the drawing boards of aircraft companies across the USA keen to exploit the new technology and the fruits of victory over Nazi Germany. Moreover, they could fly at transonic or supersonic speed for a few minutes at most, and would not provide the systematic data essential to design of operational combat aircraft. Powered by a four-chamber rocket motor, the straight-winged Bell XS-1 (experimental sonic-1) was developed to collect transonic data. It officially exceeded the speed of sound during a brief flight on 14 October 1947, exactly two weeks after the first flight of the F-86.

When Mach 1.5 was exceeded for the first time, by the Douglas D-558-II rocket research aircraft in 1951, the Mach 1 F-100 was already well into the detail design phase, and when the same aircraft exceeded Mach 2 for the first time in November 1953 the precursor of the Mach 2 Convair F-106 for the USAF had already flown. The failure of that precursor, the F-102 Delta Dart, was to stimulate the first truly innovative step forwards in the development of high-speed combat aircraft since the Second World War and the introduction of the swept wing. For the first time new design laws would be applied to the fuselage rather than the all-important wing, clearing a path for modern combat aircraft design and engineering.

For the first five years of the jet age (1945–50), aircraft designers followed the received wisdom of Ernst Mach. Bullet-shaped devices would produce less drag than any other known shape. It was rule-of-thumb engineering, and it would put designers in trouble. Because the rocket propelled X-1 and its successors could not achieve sustained flight in the transonic or supersonic region, new windtunnels played an increasingly important part in defining optimum characteristics for fast jets. While working on optional shapes and wing-fuselage configurations in the 8ft Langley high-speed tunnel, Richard T Whitcomb tested ideas originating from 'schlieren' photographs that revealed unexpected shock-wave patterns. Apart from the anticipated shock where the air was pushed aside at the nose of the fuselage, there were two more: one where the wing and the fuselage combined to push more air out of the way, and a second coming off the fuselage close to the trailing edge of the wing. Whitcomb believed that the compressibility effect might be due in large part to these unseen 'aftershocks' emanating from the fuselage.

Conventional aerodynamics emphasised the importance of the wing. The fuselage had always been considered a structural necessity separating wing and tail, and the most logical place to put the pilot; it did not attract the attention that the wing did. Now, however, the fuselage was about to assume equal importance. Whitcomb believed that wing-fuselage interaction caused perturbations that integrated the separate equations for each, and he tested this idea on models in the windtunnel. But that was not where he fell upon an explanation. He made it a principle that some portion of each day would be taken up with creative thinking; doing nothing but thinking about problems. During one such session late in 1951 he literally 'saw' the solution. Air flowing around the fuselage was disturbed not only as a function of its diameter, but also by the total cross-section of fuselage, wings and tail.

What Whitcomb sought was a way to minimise the disturbance in the air as it flowed over and around the aircraft. He achieved that by reducing the diameter of the fuselage at the place where the wing added to the total area. His idea was to create a fuselage wasp-waisted in planform, literally pinched in where the wings were attached. The wasp-waisted fuselage, known to some as the 'Coke bottle' and to others as the 'Marilyn

Monroe' shape, was a way of adjusting the relationship between cross-sectional areas of the wing and body combination. Thenceforth the wing and the fuselage would be considered a blended whole, and the shaping would be known as 'area rule'. By April 1952 Langley's high-speed tunnel had provided sufficient data to give the idea credence, but it could still not be released as a proven fact. That would come with a vengeance when engineers from Convair visited Langley to evaluate problems with the F-102 in August 1952.

Powered by a powerful Pratt & Whitney J57, the F-102 had a knife-edge delta wing and should have slipped through Mach 1 with ease, but windtunnel models indicated that it would not, and Convair feared the USAF would cancel the project. Orders for the F-102, the most advanced air-defence fighter to date, had been placed as a result of the performance of a delta-wing precursor, the XF-92A, first flown in June 1948. Convair had chosen the tailless delta not only for the USAF air-defence requirement but also for a supersonic bomber that would emerge as the B-58 Hustler. Threatening to upset plans for two major development programmes, the fundamental problems with windtunnel models of the tailless delta sent shivers down the corporate spine. While Convair engineers sweated over the Langley results in mid-1952, the first YF-102 was coming together on the shop floor, and the company's supersonic tailless delta seaplane fighter, the XF2Y Sea Dart, was about to slip

First flown in July 1954, the CL-13C was a Canadair Sabre 5 with its fuselage modified by the addition of aluminium blisters to conform to Whitcomb's area rule. Built at the request of Canada's National Research Council, its performance proved to be the same as that of a standard Sabre 5, though its fuselage was of some 10 per cent greater volume.

into San Diego Bay. With so much invested in delta winged aircraft, the stakes were high.

During discussions at NACA Langley, Convair engineers heard of Whitcomb's area rule, and over the next several months worked with him to adapt the design of the YF-102 to the revolutionary new concept. Not wholly convinced that the idea would work, Convair completed the YF-102, put it to the air in October 1953 and flew tests which only served to prove that the pessimistic Langley windtunnel tests had been correct. While it could be forced to Mach 1.21 in a dive, it refused to

Exploiting area rule, a thin delta wing with four podded engines and widespread use of honeycomb sandwich panels, Convair's B-58 Hustler pushed design and manufacturing beyond the state of the art in the late 1950s.

cross the transonic region in level flight. By this time Whitcomb had been allowed to present his area-rule concept, and, while it remained classified, its principles were secretly described to appropriate engineers in relevant companies. What Convair did not know at the time was that Whitcomb had been to Grumman to see the design of their latest US Navy fighter, the F9F-1 (later F11F) Tiger, the world's first aircraft to incorporate area rule. On 16 August 1954 it became the first turbojet-powered aircraft to slip through Mach 1 without reheat.

Closely behind, Convair reworked the YF-102 into the F-102A by greatly increasing the length of the fuselage and improving the fineness ratio, incorporating a waisted, area-ruled midbody section and increasing the height of the fin. With other minor changes the redesigned aircraft took to the air in December 1954, achieving Mach 1.25 with ease on its second flight. While the area-ruled Tiger was the last of an unbroken line of feline Navy fighters from Grumman, the F-102A was the first of a successful line of tailless delta-winged

aircraft from Convair. The first fully refined area-ruled supersonic combat aircraft was the F-106, which had a delta wing relatively unchanged from that of the F-102A but a J75 turbojet 50 per cent more powerful than its predecessor. Changes to the location of air intakes and the cockpit, and to the shape and configuration of the fin, were applied from lessons on the F-102A. With these refinements the F-106 Delta Dart flew for the first time in December 1956 and in July 1959 the type began a career with the USAF that would last almost thirty years.

The F-102A/F-106 marked a watershed in modern combat aircraft design. Around the time that area-rule was transforming aero-engineering design, Lockheed pushed beyond the limits tested by X-series rocket research aircraft. Whereas the high-speed test programmes had touched Mach 2 for fleeting seconds, no aircraft had achieved sustained flight at twice the speed of sound. While the aerodynamic formula for wing-body interaction had driven the search for efficient and sustained flight beyond Mach 1, aerothermal equations and materials sci-

Adopting the area-rule principle pioneered by Richard Whitcomb, definitive versions of Convair's F-102 achieved predicted performance by means of the 'Coke-bottle' waisting of the fuselage, which delayed transonic drag.

ence would control flight to multi-Mach and hypersonic flight regimes. In a headlong rush for sheer speed Lockheed produced what many called the 'missile with a man in it', the F-104 Starfighter, which took to the skies for the first time in 1954. Radical in design, it consisted of a small, slender fuselage containing a single afterburning Wright J71 turbojet supporting tiny wings and a large vertical fin surmounted by a high-set tailplane. As the first combat aircraft capable of sustained flight at Mach 2 it was pushing ahead of the X-planes in a meaningful way.

Another design innovation from Richard Whitcomb was intended to raise the drag-divergence Mach number: the point at which shock waves appear. If it was achieved by reducing drag this would increase range for a given fuel load. Seeking an aerofoil shape that would produce a supercritical wing, known as such because it gives the wing a 'supercritical' Mach number, Whitcomb spent four years during the 1960s analysing various profiles. He settled on a wing with a flattened upper surface which reduced the tendency for shock waves to form. Lift lost through this feature was restored by adding a

downward curve at the trailing edge. An extensive test programme demonstrated the advantages of the supercritical wing, and many aircraft produced in the USA and elsewhere incorporated Whitcomb's wing. Its primary application, however, has been on transport aircraft.

Sustained supersonics

The way air moves around a supersonic object significantly affects not only the optimum wing shape, but also the design of the tail. In a subsonic aircraft the hinged elevator takes a meaningful bite at the air and achieves adequate pitch control. In supersonic flight the centre of lift moves rearward, calling for larger deflections of the tail surface. The effectiveness of the hinged elevator is reduced because it no longer influences the flow of air forward of the hinge line. When this problem was encountered on the F-86 it was solved by the adoption of an all-flying tail, in which the entire horizontal surface is pivoted, there being no fixed portion. This quickly became the standard solution, and was adopted for aircraft such as the F-104. Moreover, because the downwash effect of the wing can

With relatively low wing loading, this delta-winged Dassault Mirage 2000 displays the optimised shape for reduced transonic drag, and quarter-round inlets with boundary-bleed ducts.

seriously interfere with the effectiveness of the tailplane, this surface is best positioned high above the fuselage. As well as the F-104, the McDonnell F-101 Voodoo was given a high-tail configuration. Other designers chose different solutions. For instance, the F-100 Super Sabre had a horizontal tail set lower than the wing to avoid possible pitch control problems.

The first operational combat aircraft capable of Mach 1 in level flight, the F-100 was a development of the F-86. It was known at first as the Sabre 45, from its wing leading-edge sweep angle. The Sabre 45 was intended as an upgrade of the original Sabre, with greater speed and performance achieved by refining the design and installing an engine with almost twice the thrust. Devoid of area rule, it represented the end of the 'brute force' era but used creative ways to circumvent aerodynamic problems in the transonic region. For instance, the effect of aileron deflection on wing-twisting was reduced by putting the ailerons inboard of the tips on a stiffer part of the trailing edge, thus avoiding control reversal. With a longer nose than its predecessor, the aircraft was found to have a serious problem with yaw stability owing to the length-to-span mass ratio.

Compared with Second World War aircraft and first-generation jets, supersonic fighters had a more slender configuration with less mass distributed laterally. The comparatively low span-to-length ratio of the early production F-100A caused the loss of its distinguished pilot, George Welch, during a flight test in October 1954. Towards the end of a final series of performance-qualification flights Welch put the aircraft in a dive from 45,000ft (13,700m) to maximum dynamic pressure and pulled up at a planned 7.5g. This figure was only slightly exceeded when the nose of the F-100A yawed right 15°, and as it exceeded structural limits the aircraft broke up. All F-100As were immediately grounded while modifications were made to increase the wingspan by almost 2ft (0.6m) and the area of the vertical tail by 29 per cent. What the F-100 had experienced was inertial coupling, and in the F-100A incident the loads on the vertical tail exceeded its strength and it was torn from the airframe. The F-100A turned out to be a good aeroplane with great strength and adaptability, turning Mach 1.4 at altitude and only just below Mach 1 at low level. Another lesson had been learned, and the mechanics were applied to later types.

Although the F-100 is representative of the old approach to jet design – brute force, bigger engines, sheer speed – it pointed the way forward by incorporating about six times as much titanium alloy as the F-86. It was the first aircraft to make large-scale use of titanium, and this was a significant step, of which more later. It is true to say that, for all the extraordinary strides in engine power, efficiency and technology, and for all the advancements in high-speed aerodynamic theory, were it not for new and exotic materials none of this evolutionary develop-

ment could have taken place. Materials played a prime role in the enhanced performance capability of jets, and literally forged the modern combat aircraft of today. One classic example where their limitations were a serious concern in relation to the sheer performance of the aircraft concerned the last all-British fighter.

In a completely different approach to combat aircraft design, British manufacturer English Electric (already famous for its world-beating Canberra jet bomber) produced the RAF's first Mach 2 interceptor. Designated P.1, it too flew for the first time in 1954, but it was built to a very different design concept than the F-104, although in several respects they filled the same role and had similar shortcomings. The product of an Air Ministry desire to produce a truly supersonic fighter for the RAF, the P.1 had its design genesis as early as 1948, less than three years after the end of the war, but Ministry bureaucrats delayed development. It therefore represented the last product from an early postwar period when little innovation was seen other than the application of brute force over finesse. With a pair of 10,300lb (4,675kg)-thrust Sapphire turbojets the P-1 was capable of more than the Mach 1.2 for which it had been designed, and with two 16,300lb (7,400kg)-thrust Avons later marks of what was then the considerably redesigned Lightning were capable of Mach 2 – albeit for fleeting seconds.

Structurally, the P.1 was conventional yet clever in the way cross-sectional area was reduced and aerodynamic efficiency enhanced. The two turbojet engines were placed one above the other in staggered bays along the centre fuselage, feeding from a common snake inlet and exhausting through separate pipes. The upper engine was aft of the pilot's cockpit, some distance to the rear, and this innovation reduced the cross-sectional area of the huge slab-sided fuselage by 50 per cent. This had been deliberately sought as a means of reducing wave drag, an important prerequisite for supersonic flight without reheat (afterburning), which in the early 1950s was largely undeveloped. A considerable amount of drag was reduced by the single external compression intake, and further drag was reduced by the extreme, 60°, wing leading-edge sweep. The acute sweep did allow a thicker wing which held much-needed fuel for the powerful but thirsty engines. The tailplane had a similar 60° sweep. In early 'paper' designs the ailerons were placed on the wing at a streamwise angle, but to prevent flutter they constituted the wingtip, aligned at right-angles to the longitudinal axis and thereby lying on the torsional axis.

Led by W E W Petter, the P.1 design team evaluated several tailplane positions at a time when no one knew with certainty the optimum configuration for an aircraft intended to fly supersonic. In early designs the wing had anhedral angle of 5° and the tailplane was set about one-third up the fin, but one alternative design favoured a low tailplane and another had a T-tail. The Royal Aircraft

Establishment (RAE) backed the T-tail configuration, and flew a research aircraft, the Short S.B.5, to prove their point, but the results argued instead for the low tailplane. With a high tailplane the wing leading-edge vortices induced pitch-up, and to correct this the tail was set lower than the wing. In the early 1950s the majority contradicted many of the edicts from the young English Electric design team. They warned about the high tailplane selected for the Gloster Javelin, an appaling design seemingly plucked in desperation from the back of an envelope. Petter's people also warned about high-tail configurations, and predictions of dangerous deep-stall characteristics proved true over several succeeding decades on aircraft such as the BAC One-Eleven and Boeing 727 airliners.

The P.1 was a classic example of engineers' intuition. Technical experts argued at first that the wing sweep was too great and that the largely young design team were too radical in their approach. The S.B.5 again proved that the wing sweep was about right. However, there were to be several modifications to the operational version that transformed its appearance and adapted its aerodynamic qualities for speeds almost twice as great as the Mach 1.2 for which it had been designed. The pear-shaped inlet was changed to a circular inlet with a central cone housing the all-important target radar, and a supplementary ventral fuel tank with fins was added to the fuselage. A conspicuous increase in fin area improved stability at the top end of its performance range. However, as stated earlier, speeds were now pushing on the door of materials science, and the Lightning was among the first generation of operational aircraft to benefit.

New materials

What would soon be coupled as aerodynamic and thermal challenges had already begun to appear when design engineers began work on aircraft to probe flight at speeds beyond anything achieved up to then, aiming for flights in excess of Mach 3. The research aircraft which attained that performance was the Bell X-2, designed between 1945 and 1948, and the first of the X-series to incorporate swept-wing research from the blueprint stage. It was the first aircraft in the world to be fabricated from what were then considered to be sophisticated alloys. These were essential to ensure an aircraft's survival in the exotic flight regimes that combat aircraft were expected to reach in the decades following the powered flight tests which began in 1955. Fifty years on, modern combat aircraft design engineers have many different materials from which to manufacture aircraft parts – steel, aluminium alloy, aluminium-lithium, titanium alloys and composites – but these were not always available, and aircraft like the X-2, the F-100 and the Lightning pioneered the use of exotic materials.

The primary metal used in aircraft of the early 1950s was steel. Steel has high tensile strength, stiffness and density, and in the form of stainless steel has been used widely in landing-gear assemblies, wing-sweep mechanisms, engine supports, etc. Stainless steel has a high percentage of chromium (12–25 per cent) and good anti-corrosion properties. Wherever very high tensile strength or stiffness is required, steel has been retained but it has three times the density of aluminium alloys, and as such has a high weight-to-volume ratio. The X-2 introduced the use of stainless steel and a metal known as K-Monel, which contains 68 per cent nickel, 29 per cent copper and 3 per cent iron, manganese and carbon. Monel has high strength, good elongation, is resistant to corrosion and will withstand 400 °C, more than adequate for temperatures in excess of 300 °C expected at Mach 3. Almost the entire fuselage of the X-2 was fabricated from K-Monel, and the swept wing was covered with sheets of stainless steel. Only two X-2s were built, and only one was used for high-speed flight tests. It was lost on its twentieth flight, in September 1956, when inertia coupling caused it to crash after reaching Mach 3.2, killing its pilot.

By then, work was well advanced on the X-15, designed for Mach 7. The aircraft would experience external temperatures of 649 °C, generated through friction with the atmosphere, so a special alloy called Inconel-X was used for exterior skins. Like Monel, Inconels are a family of nickel-based steels with around 13 per cent chromium, 6 per cent iron and some manganese, silicon or copper. Although it proved highly successful, with a maximum recorded Mach number of 6.7, the X-15 operated in flight regimes no combat aircraft would attain. The materials used in its construction, however, were to feed across to the aircraft industry. Most combat aircraft use large quantities of aluminium alloys, but some have unique operating specifications and need

Managed by the USA's National Advisory Committee for Aeronautics and its successor, NASA, the North American X-15 (nearest) was the first aircraft to adopt incorporate exotic titanium alloys and Inconel-X in an airframe designed for Mach 6. The same company's Mach 3 XB-70 Valkyrie bomber (behind) pioneered the large-scale use of exotic materials.

special metals to protect them from heat or stress. An extreme example was the North American XB-70 Valkyrie of the early 1960s, which broke new ground in the large-scale use of exotic materials. Designed to cruise at Mach 3 on its own compression wave, the giant XB-70 had a dry weight of 150,000lb (68,088kg), of which 69 per cent was brazed stainless steel honeycomb sandwich and 8 per cent comprised three types of titanium alloy in addition to special materials such as Rene-41. Although the XB-70 did not go into service, it helped pave the way for widespread use of unusual materials.

As stated earlier, the F-100 was the first aircraft to use significant amounts of titanium. English Electric introduced titanium to the British aircraft industry through its application in the Lightning. Titanium was manufactured commercially for the first time in 1948, yet by the mid-1950s it was still very expensive and largely unexploited. Designed as the first truly supersonic aircraft for the RAF, the Lightning had a compact fuselage with systems equipment packed densely around the engines. This led to cooling problems, resolved in part by lagging and ventilation, but the heat generated by the engines and by friction with the atmosphere, which caused parts of the skin to reach up to 120 °C, threatened thermal fatigue. Titanium was the only solution for certain areas of the aircraft. Although it is 70 per cent heavier than aluminium, it has a much higher strength-to-weight ratio at high temperature and a much better fatigue life.

The balance between the aerothermal environment and materials science had a determining influence on the future of high-speed commercial aviation. To avoid excessive costs, Concorde used aluminium alloys, which retain their properties to a temperature of around 130°C. At altitude and a speed of just over Mach 2 Concorde would experience external skin temperatures of 120°C. To achieve higher cruising speed Concorde would have needed titanium, but even a modest increase in speed brings a high price in temperature. The Americans wanted to build a supersonic transport capable of Mach 2.7, but even that somewhat marginal commercial advantage over Mach 2.1 brought a temperature penalty 50 per cent greater than Concorde, making the use of titanium essential. With a price more than ten times that of aluminium, the extra cost of titanium was not considered worth the modest increase in speed made possible by this alloy, and the Anglo-French consortium decided to build Concorde to cruise at a more modest Mach 2.1.

Military aircraft rarely travel at such speeds for any length of time, although the unique Lockheed SR-71 is an exception. A product of the early 1960s, it was developed from the A-12, designed in 1958–9 to cruise at speeds in excess of Mach 3, making it one of the most advanced aircraft concepts of all time. Incorporating two J58 turbo-ramjets, the aircraft is still operational and unequalled today, and when it was designed it brought

special requirements from aerothermal engineering and materials technology. Almost 93 per cent of the aircraft's empty weight is a titanium alloy known as Beta B-120. At its cruising speed of Mach 3.2 external temperatures reach 350 °C, and the aircraft's survivability in this environment would have been impossible without lightweight titanium and a special paint incorporating microscopic metal balls which, among other things, dissipate more heat than they receive through friction with the air.

It was in an attempt to counter the anticipated threat of aircraft such as the XB-70 and the A-12 that the Soviet Union tackled similar problems of sustained high-speed cruise with the MiG-25. Its Mach 3-class airframe needed to survive heat soak temperatures of 300 °C. Designed in response to the new generation of US Mach 2-plus combat aircraft, which also included the B-58, it brought unique challenges. In 1961 the design team decided upon welded steel for most of the primary structure, with 11 per cent light heat-resistant alloy and 8 per cent titanium on the hottest parts. The aircraft was revealed publicly to Western eyes for the first time at a Moscow air show in 1967, and stimulated a quantum jump in combat aircraft design and engineering. This period, defined as the second phase of post-Second World War jet-combat-aircraft design, was drawing to a close, and the 'modern' era would begin by the start of the 1970s. Throughout the 1950s and 1960s, however, optional design preferences to solve common problems with supersonic and Mach 2 flight had almost become a matter of national identity. For the French it was the delta wing.

Segmented design

The French aircraft industry made a remarkable recovery after the Second World War, and a variety of experimental aircraft underwent trials in the 1940s and 1950s. In the mid-1950s Dassault received technical information from Fairey Aviation about its work on delta winged aircraft. The British manufacturer had built the supersonic F.D.2, an advanced delta aircraft which in 1956 achieved a world air speed record of Mach 1.7. Dassault wanted to exploit the full potential of delta wing shapes in high-speed combat aircraft, and gleaned much valuable data from Fairey. But France's own pool of expertise was already achieving outstanding results. Following the remarkable success of the delta-winged Nord Gerfaut I, which in August 1954 cruised through the transonic region without reheat, and the jet-and-rocket-powered straight-wing Sud-Ouest S.O.9000 Trident, Dassault took off with its Mirage family of delta-winged interceptors. They were destined to dominate French combat aircraft design for decades to come.

But it was the MiG-25 that led to a new era in combat aircraft design during the early 1970s. The experiences of fighter pilots flying Soviet-built aircraft in Korea inspired the MiG-21, the Soviet Union's most

Adopting several design innovations pioneered by German designers during the Second World War, Britain's Mach 1.7 Fairey Delta 2 of 1954 had a thin wing, a slender swept fin and rudder and blended intakes.

With thin wings of laminar-flow section and low aspect ratio, the French S.O.9000 Trident of 1954 incorporated an all-moving tail and hybrid propulsion comprising two wingtip-mounted turbojets and a single rocket motor in the rear fuselage.

83

successful post-Second World War fighter, and now fears of a Soviet leap in performance with the MiG-25 sparked innovative design trends. While public relations outlets for Western defence agencies continued to extol the virility of US and European designs, asserting the edge of quality over quantity, intelligence communities knew only too well that in an increasing number of instances Russian aircraft had a performance edge as well. Just as Korea revealed deficiencies in first-generation MiG-15s, so Vietnam revealed inadequacies in Western combat aircraft. It was sobering for F-4 Phantom II pilots to come under serious threat from MiG-21s flown by relatively inexperienced pilots from the communist bloc, and the solution brought the dawn of modern design trends.

In many respects the F-4 represented the final phase of the post-area-rule era, when aircraft were designed by slide-rule and computers had not been fully integrated into the design process. McDonnell made a good job of designing a twin-engine all-weather fighter for the USN, and the aircraft performed well in a very wide variety of roles for many air forces around the world, but it was a compromise from several separate design teams, and was adapted throughout its life for a broad range of missions. As such it was the last of its kind, designed not by a committee but by the next worst combination: individual engineering teams each determined to preserve their own elements of the configuration. While trying to create the world's first missile-carrying electronic interceptor, the size of the aircraft was determined by the need for a two-man crew (one to handle the electronics), and by the specified missile warload.

The F-4's fuselage design engineers continued the trend set by McDonnell with the single-engine F3H Demon, placing the tail over the exhaust outlet. Because the F4H had two powerful J79 engines the tailplane was positioned high on the fin to avoid efflux heat. Enlarged vertical tail surfaces were essential for longitudinal stability and good yaw control at supersonic speeds; the Demon was subsonic, whereas the Phantom II was good for Mach 2 at altitude. After the designers had opted for the preferred thin (6.4 per cent thickness-to-chord) wing like that of the Demon, and moved into detailed design, windtunnel studies showed undesirable non-linear pitch characteristics. These were corrected by giving 23° of anhedral to the horizontal tail. While this greatly improved pitch moment and longitudinal stability, the balance of the wing as an isolated surface was upset.

Already well along with their detail design, the wing team opted to retain the inboard structure and give the outer panels, designed to fold for carrier stowage, 12° dihedral in the downlock position to provide an 'average' 5° dihedral across the root-tip span. To correct poor lateral control at high angles of attack, caused by a lack of upper surface vortex, the leading edge was given neg-

ative camber. In addition, a dogtooth was placed at the outer panel anhedral line, and the wing chord was lengthened by 10 per cent. Thus the F-4 gained its unique 'tips up, tail down' appearance, a triumph, some said, of brute force over aerodynamics. That was not the end of the story. The prototype and early production aircraft were fitted with blown flaps, but later variants had seven different wing configurations, including leading-edge slats, leading-edge flaps, slats, trailing-edge flaps and spoilers. In this way engineers reconfigured the wing for different roles.

Mission-adaptive wings

In the 1970s a new and bolder initiative in aircraft structures and design exploited hitherto ignored corners of aircraft performance curves. If the F-4 could be said to have been a brute-force solution to the needs of the 1960s, the new designs were finessed and refined. The shortcomings of the variable-geometry F-111 led to one of the most influential designs of all time, the Grumman F-14 Tomcat. Variable geometry has been tried as a solution to problems with aircraft designed for a broad mission envelope. Small, thin, low-aspect-ratio wings were preferable for high supersonic speed, efficient high-speed flight at low altitude and good ride qualities close to the ground. Large, thicker, wings with reduced sweep and high-aspect ratio were best for sustained manoeuvrability, long-range cruise, long-duration loiter and short take-off and landing.

Both aspect ratio and thickness-to-chord ratio can be altered in flight by means of a variable-geometry (or swing) wing that can adapt its configuration to the optimum aerodynamic shape for different parts of the flight envelope. Since the Second World War a variety of engineering tests had been conducted on experimental aircraft with variable-geometry wings, but none had been a total success. During the 1970s and 1980s, however, an increasing number of aircraft with swing wings entered service in France, the USA, the Soviet Union, Britain, West Germany and Italy. The design of a successful combat aircraft incorporating variable geometry came at a time when flaps, spoilers and slats were being implemented for greater manoeuvrability, and not just for take-off and landing. When added to the swing wing, these aids could reconfigure an aircraft in flight, giving it a phenomenal performance range.

The maximum lift of the variable-geometry wing can be 60 per cent greater during take-off and landing, primarily as a result of the use of flaps and slats at minimum sweep angle. In combat at subsonic speeds it usually has 30 per cent greater lift owing to its high aspect ratio. Transonic speeds call for full sweep, the usual problems with thickness and area being taken care of by the reduced size of the wing. In combinations of sustained, high-thrust, manoeuvrability across a broad range of subsonic speeds the variable-geometry aeroplane can push further into the boundaries of the envelope, and the pilot has a greater range of options. Ride roughness at low altitude is considerably reduced owing to much-improved gust response, a variable-geometry aircraft at Mach 0.1 having about the same amplitude as a fixed-wing aircraft at Mach 0.5. Moreover, because drag is lower in all flight conditions, net fuel consumption is reduced, allowing increased mission radius or loiter time, or enhanced combat abilities.

However, there are disadvantages with a variable-geometry wing which bring unique problems for the overall design and performance of the aircraft. One is stability. At the fully swept position most of the lift (approximately 80 per cent) but only a small portion of the weight (about 15 per cent) moves rearwards. Because of this the centre of lift moves well aft of the c.g. For forward-swept flight regimes the centre of lift must still maintain a margin to the rear of the c.g., so by sweeping the wings aft the effect is magnified. This puts excessive downloads on the tail during manoeuvring

which, in addition to added weight brought on by larger tail surfaces, creates increased drag.

A big penalty is paid for variable-geometry wings in the extra structural weight incurred through single load paths at the wing pivot and additional fuselage stiffening needed to resist tail and rear-fuselage bending. Also, the volume taken up by the pivot mechanisms and the void for the inboard wing trailing edge in the swept position adds to wave drag, while additional structural stiffening to accommodate the cut-out adds weight. Finally, the sweep mechanism itself adds extra weight and, along with the void, reduces the internal space available for systems. Rearward shift in the centre of lift can be reduced by placing the pivot mechanism to the rear of the wing, so that as sweep angle is increased a larger section of wing rotates out of the forward slot. It can also be reduced by increased taper (wing root-to-wingtip chord ratio), or by the use of forward lifting surfaces. A compromise solution is to place the pivot point well outboard of the fuselage, leaving a large portion of the wing centre section fixed.

Serious problems with engine performance were made worse in the General Dynamics F-111 by poor inlet geometry. The design, which featured a moveable cone and ejector plate outboard of the pronounced boundary layer bleed plate, was compromised by conflicting design options.

The F-111's designers sought to reconcile very different specifications from the USAF and the USN by means of 'brute force' solutions typical of the 1960s. It was the first US combat aircraft with variable geometry, and it had serious design flaws. The wing pivots were placed close to the leading edge, the wing inboard sections accommodating quarter-round engine inlets. This forced external stores positions out to the swing wings, adding to the rearward shift in mass and requiring complex stores pivot mechanisms at the three pick-up points on each wing. Glove vanes at the leading-edge wing root were used to improve longitudinal stability and pitch trim.

Like most aircraft with variable-geometry wings, the F-111 (and the Mirage G and the MiG-23) maintained roll control in full sweep via differential use of the flying horizontal tail surfaces, which operated as tailerons. In a remarkable flowering of swing-wing combat aircraft, the F-111, the Mirage G two-seat fighter and the Soviet Union's Tupolev Tu-22 *Backfire* bomber appeared simultaneously in the late 1960s. Hard on their heels came the revolutionary Grumman F-14 Tomcat, which opened the decade of the 1970s and a new generation of truly modern combat aircraft. Developed to a new and expanded specification left vacant when the F-111 failed to satisfy USN requirements, the F-14 was designed and developed as an entire weapons system. Engineers put the shape together from a synthesis of separate, fused design considerations. Whereas the F-111 had been compromised by poor engine inlet/fuselage geometry, the F-14 incorporated clean inlet boxes with a direct flow path to the podded engines located either side of a flat underbody optimised for carrying weapons, fuel tanks, reconnaissance pod or other stores. The wing pivot points were placed outboard of the fuselage on a broad, reflexed, section known as the 'pancake', to which

'Elephant-ear' intakes ingest clear air ahead of the McDonnell Douglas AV-8B's supercritical wing. Note the tufts attached beneath the wings to reveal localised vortex patterns during test flights.

the forward nacelle carrying the crew and radar, the tail, and the undercarriage would be attached.

To confirm the integrity of its design, Grumman studied alternatives and found that to get anywhere near the payload/mission capability an aircraft with a conventional wing would need an area of 745ft^2 (68.41m^2), compared with the F-14's 565ft^2 (52.49m^2) and would weigh 4,920lb (2,236kg) more. Moreover, because the engines would have been buried, it would have inlet/boundary-layer bleed problems similar to those that plagued the F-111. Early in the design's evolution, extendable glove vanes were proposed to improve longitudinal stability, but Grumman had other ideas about performance aids for the wing which obviated the need for such a system. The aircraft was designed with high-lift devices including leading-edge slats and trailing-edge flaps with spoilers, but had no ailerons. The tailplane surfaces double as tailerons. The two outer flaps are supplemented at the 20°, fully forward sweep position by two inner flaps, while the four-section spoilers on each wing supplement the tailerons to a pitch angle of 5°, beyond which differential elevator rates are sufficient for roll control.

New inlets for old

In addition to the relative geometry of wings, engines and stores positions, a design aspect of vital concern was the geometry of the engine inlets and exhaust nozzles. Integrated blending of aerodynamic and propulsion requirements into a common design was a unique feature of the F-14, ending decades of evolving technologies in structures and materials. In the 1940s jet aircraft made do with fixed inlet geometry, perhaps supplemented by auxiliary inlet doors to increase the air ingested at slow speeds. Transonic requirements of the 1950s were accommodated by similar inlet designs incorporating bypass systems to match ingested air to engine needs. In the 1960s designers went for straight-line speed in the belief that aircraft were evolving into missile platforms, and this requirement was met by straight inlets clear of boundary air and wing/fuselage turbulence. By the end of that decade a new requirement forced radical changes in design. Aircraft were now required to fly and fight at maximum performance levels right across the flight envelope, and lessons from Vietnam killed the myth that dogfighting combat aircraft were redundant in modern air warfare.

Weighing 33 tonnes fully loaded, the F-14 was required to perform high-g manoeuvres in close-in dogfights that would tax a lightweight fighter. The F-14's two-dimensional wedge-shaped inlet provided external compression, facilitated via three horizontal variable-geometry ramp doors along the flat upper surface of the forward inlet box. These provided high-pressure recovery, low distortion in the airflow rates and density levels and, consequently, minimal turbulence. The wide spac-

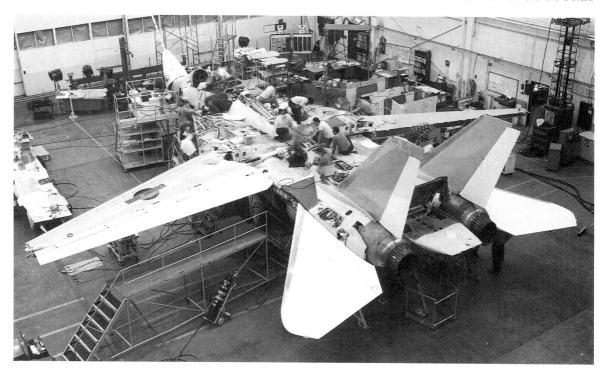

Grumman's F-14 Tomcat introduced new composite materials and advanced production methods to herald a revolution in air-craft manufacturing, with design evolution uniting all the elements of airframe and powerplant. Note the widely spaced engines, all-flying tailplane and outboard wing pivots facilitating generous weapons carriage on the fuselage and inner wing sections.

ing and ample boundary bleed region between the rec-tangular box section and the oval-shaped forward fuse-lage nacelle keeps clean air and engine compressors accessible to controlled airflow at all times. The advan-tage and superiority of the design lies in its simplicity. Gone are the spikes, cowls, suck-in doors and the variety of circular, half-round and quarter-round inlets of the fighters of the 1950s and 1960s. The rectangular box inlet revolutionised high-performance aircraft, opening the performance band right across the flight spectrum.

Combat aircraft with this engine inlet configuration quickly appeared in several countries. The American F-15 in 1972, the Panavia Tornado in 1974 and the Soviet MiG-29 and Sukhoi Su-27 in 1977. The need for large fin area has been stated earlier, and it grew with the highly manoeuvrable, high-alpha (angle-of-attack) flight profile that the F-14 and others of its type pos-sessed. The deterioration in longitudinal stability with higher Mach number was covered by lessons learned on the F-100 and the P.1/Lightning. However, large fins lose their effectiveness through tip twist from high aero-dynamic loads causing rudder deflection and spanwise twist. Two fins can be an asset, biting air otherwise masked by a wing during high-alpha banking, etc. Increasingly, ventral strakes were seen as an added advantage, minimising upper fin height and providing a

stiffer structure engaging a better aerodynamic flow with the underbody.

Finally, trends set by the F-14 included equal consid-eration of engine exhaust outlets. Much time and effort was spent selecting an optimum exhaust configuration to take advantage of the widely spaced engines. After-body effects are dynamic and never passive, up to 35 per cent of total drag being incurred in this region in poor designs (such as the F-111). Afterbody effects are significant in single-engine jets, and the power of mod-ern propulsion systems renders them worse for twin-engine layouts where cross-flow and plume interference is a major obstacle to good interaction between the efflux and the airflow. In the F-14 Grumman opted for a convergent/divergent iris system, opening up for high power levels and closing up like the iris of an eye at low thrust. The wide range of exhaust outlet configurations allowed engineers to select optimum shapes for specific aircraft performance requirements. In designing the exhaust outlets for the F-15, McDonnell Douglas chose the same basic design but had different aerodynamic problems owing to the close spacing between the engines.

Not only was the F-14 typical of the new engineering approach. By integrating every element as part of a total system it also provided a new level of automation and avionics support for pilot activity in the cockpit. Operation

Another product of the 1970s revolution in combat aircraft design, the Rockwell B-1 incorporates features pioneered by high-performance fighters, including a blended wing-body shape and boxed inlets in undisturbed air.

of the variable-geometry wing is a typical example. Although manual mode is provided, allowing the pilot to control the degree of sweep physically, a Mach sweep programmer (MSP) is available for fully automated control of sweep angles. A separate air-data computer automatically controls the position of the engine inlet compression ramps, which optimise the flow of air according to speed and angle of attack. Combined, these two systems allow the pilot to keep his attention out of the cockpit and on the air battle. In the next twenty years this trend would grow to dominate combat aircraft design, but some manufacturers chose a different route. When General Dynamics designed the F-16 for the USAF lightweight, low-cost, fighter competition it shunned the use of expensive titanium structures and resorted to stainless steel.

Super-structures

The design of aircraft structures was transformed by the use of titanium alloys and exotic, expensive materials such as aluminium/lithium. A naturally occurring element, lithium is the least dense solid, and has traditionally been used in alloys, in the preparation of tritium and as a lubricant with high moisture resistance and temperature tolerance. In production since the 1920s, aluminium/lithium has been difficult to produce and was not well defined for aerospace applications. Manufacture and quantity production were difficult, but its advantages were well known. It has 10 per cent less density and 10 per cent greater stiffness than most ordinary alloys. It has been selected for some forgings on the Eurofighter 2000, though optimism about its extensive use was ill-founded and only about 5 per cent of the aircraft is fabricated from this material, mostly thick plate and wing frames. The most ambitious use of alumini-

um/lithium was in the manufacture of ultra-lightweight external propellant tanks for NASA's Space Shuttle, the first example of which was launched in June 1998.

Nevertheless, the materials revolution persisted through the use of carbonfibre composites (CFCs). As strong as aluminium alloy but 20 per cent lighter, they can make an enormous difference to aircraft structures and overall performance. Developed in the mid-1960s at RAE Farnborough, CFCs were at first introduced gradually into aircraft structures, but use of composites has accelerated greatly in the 1990s. Again it was the new generation of fighters at the end of the 1960s and in the early 1970s that made the quantum leap into exotic materials. The first of its kind to incorporate significant quantities of these (then) new materials, by weight the F-14 had 36 per cent aluminium alloy, 24.4 per cent titanium, 18 per cent steel and 1 per cent boron. Applying new manufacturing and joining technology, the industry acquired new skills and built new machines to fabricate aircraft parts using alloys and CFCs.

This first generation (F-14, F-15 and F-16) had 1–3 per cent composites by weight, but by the end of the 1970s this had risen to around 10 per cent, as in the Mirage 2000, for example. In 1980 26 per cent of the structural weight of the McDonnell Douglas AV-8B was composite material, and by the early 1990s the Lockheed Martin YF-22 had 35 per cent composites and the Eurofighter 2000 had 40 per cent. Yet there are penalties. Lockheed uses conventional alloys in alternate wing ribs on the F-22 owing to the poor damage propagation characteristics of composite materials. Survivability was enhanced when alloys replaced carbon-based composites in primary structure.

In twenty years the application of CFCs had outstripped all projections, and the transformation in the avionics industry was similar. At the end of the Second World War electrical elements in a typical fighter were less than 5 per cent of the flyaway cost. By the 1950s that figure had increased to about 12 per cent for aircraft like the Hunter. A major leap forward occurred in

Following in the style of the F-14, the fixed-wing McDonnell Douglas F-15 had rectangular boxed inlets and an integrated design affording clean airflow across its wing and tail surfaces.

Whether their structures are of metal or carbonfibre, combat aircraft must be able to withstand the stress of high-g combat manoeuvres. This McDonnell Douglas AV-8B Harrier II airframe withstood forces equal to ten times its own weight without deformation or failure when sixty tons of force was distributed through it by tension pads and straps which applied loads from computer-controlled hydraulic systems.

the F-14, which had 27 per cent of its cost in avionics. By the mid-1970s that value had risen to more than 35 per cent, as in the Panavia Tornado. In the mid-1990s 55 per cent of the cost of the F-22, arguably the most advanced combat aircraft of the twentieth century, is in its avionics equipment, and this trend will grow into retrofits of most combat aircraft.

There has been a price to pay for increasingly capable combat aircraft, in the form of increased demand on ground servicing and maintenance. At the war's end a typical fighter absorbed fifteen man-hours of maintenance for every flight hour. In the 1950s aircraft like the Hunter, F-86, F-100 and F-104 required twenty to thirty maintenance man-hours per flight hour, and just a few years later types such as the F-105, F-101 and F-106 required thirty-five to forty-five maintenance hours. By the late 1960s the trend already in reverse. The figure was down to between twenty-two and thirty-two hours for the F-4, while the F-15 needed just under twenty hours. Incredibly complex for its day, the F-14 shot through the roof to fifty hours. Today's fighters, such

Typifying the ultimate combat aircraft of the twentieth century, Lockheed Martin/Boeing's F-22 epitomises fifty years of modern jet fighter evolution. With its unprecedented quantity of composite materials, stealthy aerodynamic design and supersonic cruise capability in military power, the F-22 embodies all of the major developments in aeronautical science.

New manufacturing methods and composite materials were evaluated in radical designs for test projects. Here, engineers prepare a windtunnel model of the forward-swept-wing Grumman X-29 for test, displaying its close-coupled canard configuration and proud engine inlets.

as the F-22 and Eurofighter 2000, use enhanced avionics, electronics and self-diagnostic systems to reduce the commitment to between ten and fifteen hours.

Super manoeuvres

The prolific Second World War German research effort that resulted in work on swept wings for delayed compressibility effects correctly identified tip stall and loss of aileron control as a serious problem for transonic aircraft. When Junkers produced its Ju 287 jet bomber it was given forward- rather than aft-swept wings in an effort to eliminate this problem. Boundary air flowing across an aft-swept wing migrates spanwise towards the tip, producing unsatisfactory stalling conditions. With a forward-swept wing (FSW) the boundary layer flows inboard, leaving the outboard control surfaces unaffected. However, aeroelastic effects (the interaction of aerodynamic forces with the elastic properties of an airframe) require additional stiffness and extra weight in the wing structure. Nonetheless, Junkers felt that the cost in added structural weight was worthwhile. Flight trials revealed some problems, largely due to the wing flexing during turns or in gusts, but generally the Ju 287 flew well.

After the war Ju 287 designer Hans Wocke persuaded the Hamburger Flugzeugbau to build a business jet with

forward-swept wings. The HFB-320 flew in 1964, and fifty were built, including sixteen for the German Air Force, but the concept was swamped by design data on conventional swept wings and failed to catch on. In the 1970s it was revived as a means of achieving sustained high-g turns and good high-angle-of-attack performance, and in 1982 Grumman built a small-scale FSW prototype, the X-29. It had a thin supercritical wing and was inherently unstable. An all-flying canard surface mounted forward of the wing provided longitudinal control, and strakes extending aft of the trailing edge assisted pitch control. The X-29 had an aluminium and titanium primary structure and a carbon epoxy skin. In 450 flights between 1984 and 1992 it demonstrated a 15 per cent better transonic lift-to-drag ratio than expected and good roll control at high angles of attack, but its overall drag was greater than expected. So far, the only FSW combat aircraft is the Sukhoi Su-37, a prototype of which first flew in September 1997.

In the 1990s combat aircraft are required to be manoeuvrable at all levels of the performance envelope. Gone are the mythologies about missiles replacing the manned aircraft, although studies increasingly point to pilotless combat vehicles by 2025. As early as the 1960s electronic control-of-flight surfaces promised benefits over mechanical linkages. Through a system of active

Engineers prepare a main wing box, fabricated from composites, for the X-29. Such projects led to a wider use of materials for new generations of combat aircraft.

sensors that detect small and unwanted motion in air-craft attitude, an active electronic-hydraulic command system (fly-by-wire, or FBW) delivered corrective signals to the aerodynamic control surfaces. This brought advantages not only in performance, manoeuvrability and agility, but in the very nature of the aircraft's design. By flouting convention and designing a combat aircraft to be inherently unstable, great improvements in aerodynamic performance could accrue. By using active control systems to keep the aircraft stable in the air, aerodynamicists and design engineers exploited a wider range of theoretical possibilities to give combat aircraft unprecedented agility.

Known as relaxed static stability (RSS), this was a product of advances in electronics, avionics and fighter design. The first aircraft to exploit it was the General Dynamics (now Lockheed Martin) F-16, and it represented a complete departure from accepted practice. With authority for control and stability deferred to black boxes and carbonfibre wire, the pilot was more of a mission manager than a driver. Relegation of basic control tasks to automated systems gave the pilot greater freedom to 'fly' the aeroplane vigorously in combat, knowing that the prohibited corners of the envelope were electronically protected. The introduction of the F-16 into service in 1979 was the last major change of the decade, bringing combat aircraft out of the 'brute force' era and into an age of sophisticated design and technology trends driven largely by electronics and avionics. Today, all modern fighter aircraft are designed with RSS and FBW.

High transonic turn rates, high angles of attack and rapid pitch movement are prerequisites for gaining the advantage in the modern air-combat arena. Over several decades attempts have been made to improve these factors dramatically. In the 1950s highly swept or slender-delta wing planforms were sought to counteract the effects of compressibility at high speed, but they induced flow-separation across the wing. It was discovered that a sharp leading edge would counteract this, producing stable overwing vortices and increasing low-speed lift. The straight-wing Lockheed F-104 with a sharp wing leading edge was designed to exploit that effect. A decade later Northrop developed its highly successful T-38 trainer into the F-5 fighter and adopted a small leading-edge extension, or LEX, which increased lift 10 per cent at high angles of attack and greatly improved turn performance.

In a further development of the F-5, Northrop adopted a much larger LEX on a moderately swept wing for its YF-17, designed for the USAF lightweight fighter competition of the early 1970s. Later in the decade McDonnell Douglas used the concept in its highly successful F-18, in which a strong vortex field was induced on the LEX itself as well as on the wing. The advantage of 'preparing' the airflow for the wing

Changing economic priorities mean that combat aircraft are now required to perform several different roles. Added life for the McDonnell Douglas F/A-18 Hornet is provided by a new supercritical wing and leading-edge extensions which greatly improve aerodynamic performance and weight-carrying capability.

surface by preconditioning the flow field is the main reason why foreplanes have become such a common sight on modern combat aircraft. Although the 'canard' might be expected to cause instability, changes to the aircraft's c.g. eliminate that problem. A strong but stable vortex field can improve lift by up to 30 per cent, and by eliminating the tailplane on delta-wing types the aircraft can be set up for better manoeuvrability.

In addition to having active control systems, aircraft such as the Dassault Rafale are built around a high-performance wing/foreplane design, while Sweden's Saab Gripen has a similar, close-coupled all-moving canard which doubles as an airbrake on landing rollout. In the USA, research into design innovation for high-performance combat aircraft centres on existing types adapted with new technology, or experimental aircraft such as HiMAT (Highly Manoeuvrable Aircraft Technology), a research project of the mid-1970s. Unlike European aircraft manufacturers, the US industry has been reluctant to pick up foreplane design concepts and employ them in operational aircraft. Russian design bureaux have been quick to adapt existing types to new roles, or to develop variants with enhanced performance, using foreplanes to improve airflow over the wing and as supplementary control surfaces. Several high-performance aircraft from Sukhoi now feature canards along with a greater emphasis on coupled controls.

A new development focuses on pushing manoeuvrability to the limit of human endurance by the use of

Research into highly manoeuvrable combat aircraft designs accelerated during the late 1970s. Here, the Rockwell HiMAT pilotless research vehicle is prepared for air-drop flight tests. (See page 229.)

Robert Jones of NASA attempted to rewrite conventional aerodynamics with his low-drag oblique wing concept, tested on NASA Dryden's purpose-built AD-1 research aircraft in the early 1980s. In fact the idea dates back at least to the Second World War, when Blohm und Voss designed the P.202 single-seat jet fighter with a wing that could be slewed to an angle of 35°.

thrust-vectoring engine nozzles. Several experimental projects involving a specially adapted F-16 and the X-31 have demonstrated the effectiveness of this technology. In flight trials during 1993 the thrust-vectoring F-16 demonstrated new ways of gaining the advantage over a fixed-nozzle adversary. Emulating a high angle-of-attack manoeuvre known as the 'cobra', demonstrated by the Sukhoi Su-27, in which the aircraft briefly seems to perform a back-flip, the F-16 was able to show a transient angle of attack of 110° and a sustained angle of attack of 80°. Conducted as part of a USAF evaluation of multi-axis thrust vectoring, these tests demonstrated the advantage in briefly pitching the aircraft beyond the vertical to 'paint' a target across the other side of a turn loop. In another, evasive, manoeuvre made possible by thrust vectoring, a sudden 360° rotation virtually along the flight path forces a pursuing fighter to overshoot and come within lock-on range ahead. To date, the only operational aircraft with this capability is the Lockheed Martin F-22. Powered by two Pratt & Whitney F119 engines vectored in pitch, it is scheduled to enter service in 2005.

A stealthy approach

Perhaps the ultimate challenge in matching aerodynamics and structure came with the first demonstration of a low-observables, or 'stealth' combat aircraft. Following several early efforts at reducing the cross-section of an aircraft's radar image, major research conducted by several US aircraft manufacturers resulted in a 1970s development project shrouded in secrecy. It began when engineers at Lockheed designed an aircraft with faceted surfaces to reflect and disperse radio waves away from the signal source, thus making it difficult to detect. For the first time, aerodynamics did not set the primary guideline which determined the shape of the aeroplane. It would have been impossible to design, and impossible to fly, without computers, and as such represented a departure from traditional methods. The operational successor to test aircraft was the Lockheed F-117A stealth fighter-bomber which, although not completely invisible to radar, causes sufficient uncertainty to enable it to get in to the target and out again with the highest probability of escaping unscathed achieved by any combat aircraft.

The basic construction of the F-117A is simple, using conventional aluminium alloys with radar-absorbent-materials attached with epoxy resin to form the outer surface. In studies conducted in the 1960s Lockheed discovered that rounded, blended surfaces reflect less radar energy back to the antenna than flat ones. Paradoxically, the company designed the F-117A with flat surfaces, but the facets were angled to divert energy away from the source of the beam. Blended contours were, however, selected for Northrop's low-observable bomber, the B-2.

None of these stealthy projects would have been possible without computer-aided design (CAD) and the

Design innovations aimed at eliminating unwanted radar reflections control aerodynamic and engineering considerations for stealth aircraft. This intake grill shrouds bright radar features inside Lockheed's F-117A.

use of computational fluid dynamics (CFD). The former came of age during the second half of the 1980s, and from this came a computer-integrating-manufacturing (CIM) programme from which assembly of the B-2 was to benefit. The B-2 is essentially a flying wing, and there have been several attempts in the past to produce what amounts to an almost perfect, aerodynamically clean, heavier-than-air flying machine.

In the 1940s and 1950s Northrop built two bombers, the propeller-driven XB-35 and the jet-propelled YB-49, embodying the flying-wing concept, but for several reasons they failed. The secret behind the B-2's success is CAD and a sophisticated fly-by-wire system to keep the aircraft in the air. Just as the F-117A relies on sensors to 'fly' the control surfaces and keep it from falling out the sky, so the B-2 uses a complex flight-control system to sort out its quirky way of reacting to the air. Aerodynamically, a flying wing behaves in a very different way to an aeroplane with a slender fuselage and a tail unit. In theory a flying wing could have a payload range 25 per cent greater than a conventional aircraft. Span loading is more uniform and has better distribution, bringing a consequent reduction in stress fatigue.

To help keep it stealthy the B-2 has a sawtooth trailing edge carrying nine flight-control surfaces along its entire length. The centrebody flap, also known as the beavertail, is used for gust alleviation. Two pairs of inboard elevons control roll and pitch, and an outer elevon panel on each side doubles as an aileron. Finally, horizontal split drag rudders near the wingtips are used to control yaw, much as a split rudder in the vertical plane of a conventional aircraft can be employed as a drag brake. On the B-2 these work by one or the other opening and closing to slew the aircraft to port or starboard, but they are not stealthy. In a full combat mode, in which the aircraft operates at the lowest state of visibility, yaw control is effected by differential

Aerodynamics and airframe structures were adapted to specific needs in the stealthy B-2 programme, producing an aircraft impossible to control without fly-by-wire. Note the suppressed frontal profile, upper-surface inlets and shrouded exhausts for air-cooled exhaust gases to reduce the infrared signature.

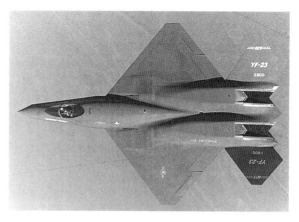

Several design features of the Northrop-McDonnell Douglas YF-23, such as its large-area trapezoidal wing, canted fins and low-infrared exhaust channels, are likely to appear in unmanned, high-g combat aircraft of the future.

engine thrust settings. The thick centre section is close to the maximum possible before flow-separation, giving the aircraft deep weapons bays, and the upper and lower surfaces comprise continuous, unbroken blends of complex curves. The wing has a modified laminar-flow section, combining the necessary camber for optimised aerodynamics with a sharp leading edge.

The materials used in the construction of the B-2 are employed in other aircraft, but none of them rely on composites to the same extent. The B-2's centre section and intermediate wing sections are built around large carry-through structures fabricated from titanium, but elsewhere the primary structure is formed from composites. Much of the outer skin is bonded to secondary structure before assembly, ensuring continuity of surface finish. The fractional misalignment of panels and skins found in conventional aircraft was totally unacceptable on the B-2; it had to be made to levels of tolerance and accuracy never before achieved in a production aircraft. Even modest distortion in surface panels would play havoc with the the bomber's stealth characteristics, and small changes to its exterior shape caused by buffet and turbulence could ruin its mission. Working to a precise database, its builders align each part of the aircraft with a basic co-ordinate system and a reference grid. Carbonfibre-epoxy panels are bonded together for a seamless finish without external fasteners, giving a blemish-free surface.

After almost a century of powered flight, aviation has penetrated barriers once thought impregnable. Compressibility experienced at sonic and transonic velocities has been overcome, the thermal barrier has been tackled with new and exotic materials, and the use of computers for design and manufacture has made possible shapes and configurations few dreamed of just twenty years ago. Since 1945 aviation has progressed far beyond the expectations of those who produced the great combat aircraft of the most destructive war ever waged. Yet, despite all the genius and ingenuity of design teams around the world, none of this would have been possible without the test pilots, many of whom have lost their lives demonstrating the ideas of others and proving the combat aircraft of the last fifty years.

Bibliography

Baker, D, *Grumman F-14 Tomcat* (Crowood, Marlborough, England, 1998). Contains a detailed semi-technical description of the evolving trends in fighter design throughout the period 1950–70.

Burns, B, 'Fundamentals of Design', *Air International*, 1979–80. Various articles describing the basic aspects of aerodynamics and aircraft design.

Huenecke, K, *Modern Combat Aircraft Design* (Airlife, Shrewsbury, England, 1987). A technical treatise on the subject with some good mathematics and formulae; useful as a background reference for design engineers.

Loftin, K, *Quest for Performance* (NASA, Washington DC, 1985). A good reference on the development of military aviation and the search for ever greater speed and performance.

Stinton, D, *The Anatomy of the Aeroplane* (Granada, St Albans, England, 1966). The basic principles of aerodynamics, with comprehensive coverage of many aspects of aircraft design pertinent to combat aircraft.

5
Military Avionics since the Second World War
Norman Friedman

Most of the currently familiar types of airborne radar can be traced back to the Second World War: the airborne interception sets which fighters use to find bombers, the ground-mapping and sea-search sets which bombers use to find their targets, and even airborne early warning. The great difference between then and now is that the wartime radars stood virtually alone, being integrated into the functioning of the aeroplane by the crew. For example, a nightfighter's radar could detect a target but could not control the fighter to track the target; nor could it aim guns without human intervention.

The great postwar development was integration, combining sensors with other elements of the aircraft as a combat entity. This was driven by a series of urgent needs. First came the need to improve interceptors (and associated systems) to the point where they could deal with jet bombers carrying nuclear weapons. Second was the need to keep tactical bombers useful and survivable despite their increased speed and the presence of enemy anti-aircraft missiles. Third was the need, within NATO, to deal with the sheer mass of Soviet forces, both on land and at sea, which made for dramatic changes in command and control systems. Finally, there was the need to maintain air superiority on an aeroplane-to-aeroplane basis.

Integration was possible because electronic technology itself underwent a revolutionary change. In 1945 it was all analogue. The face of a radar display, for example, showed blips whose brightness was roughly proportional to the strength of the radar return from a given direction at a given range. The display, then, was analogous to what the radar antenna received. It did nothing to analyse that signal. Similarly, the dials on the aeroplane's instrument panel indicated in analogue fashion: as the aeroplane climbed, for example, the hand on the altimeter moved. Moreover, the information presented on an analogue screen or dial generally could not be used directly by some other device. To feed it into that device, someone had to produce a new analogue signal, perhaps by placing a cursor on the radar blip, or by following the marker on the dial. A target-tracking radar typically produced error signals, which an operator had to follow to keep the radar pointed at its target. There was no automatic way of reading target speed into an associated fire-control system.

Where computation was required (as in fire-control devices such as bombsights), it was carried out by circuits or by mechanical devices which formed analogues to the mathematical steps involved. Computation could

Gloster G.41C Meteor Mk 3 EE348 had the proven Second World War American AN/APS-4 radar housed in its transparent acrylic nose radome for 'assisted target-ranging'. The intention was to provide the pilot with quick reference of a target ahead in marginal weather, and supply range information for weapon-firing, thereby eliminating the need to set the sight's graticle selector switch manually. In Britain this radar was designated Airborne Interception (AI) Mk 15. Claimed to be the first turbine-powered fighter to be fitted with AI radar, EE348 was tested at the Central Radar Establishment from late 1945.

Apart from the changes brought about by the new form of powerplant, the cockpits of the early jets differed little from those of their piston-engined forebears. Prominently displayed on either side of the reflector gunsight in this Meteor 3 are the revolution counters for the two Rolls-Royce Derwent I engines.

be quick, but no analogue computer was very flexible. To adapt it to a different problem, it had to be rewired or rebuilt.

Autopilots were the most highly advanced analogue avionic devices. They sensed aircraft motion, and automatically moved control surfaces to maintain an ordered course. However, an autopilot flew a straight path at a constant speed, rather than performing any sort of desired manoeuvre. Alternatively, it could be used to sense aircraft motion, as part of a bombsight – for a specific weapon, with specific characteristics.

Digital systems are very different. Because they handle only numbers (i.e., quantities represented in common form, whatever their significance), the same computer can be programmed to do many sorts of calculation. Moreover, the numbers coming out of any one calculation can be fed into another (or into a numerically driven control mechanism). Thus the computer can easily integrate sensors with, for example, fire control; or it can feed data from an aeroplane's instruments into a flight-control program, which in turn can control the aeroplane itself. In some sense digital systems are self-conscious, in that they can examine the data flowing through them. A radar is a case in point.

In the simplest radar the display is an A-scope. It measures signal strength against time (which equates to range). With an analogue radar the operator decides that particular peaks in the display correspond to real targets; this process is called detection. In a digital radar the same input is converted into a series of numbers, giving the signal strength at short intervals in range. The radar detects by associating any peak above a set value (set to avoid false alarms due to noise) with a real target, more or less as the human operator does, but in this case detection is automatic. It reports the range corresponding to what it decides is a real target. That number can feed into some other process, such as that used in fire control. If the radar scans, then the read-out is a range and a bearing, and the system can compare read-outs scan by scan to measure the movement of the detected target. In an analogue system the human operator would do the scan-to-scan comparison, often using a grease (or chinagraph) pencil. He could use the vector (target course and speed) he had deduced to plot an intercepting path. Similarly, the computer can use its deduced target path to determine how the fighter should manoeuvre to intercept. In the end, the difference is that the analogue fighter needs considerable crew effort to intercept, whereas the computer can simply instruct the pilot via, say, a head-up display. The faster the aircraft, the greater the difference the digital computer makes.

Another important difference is that the digital computer need not treat all the data it obtains identically. In the radar example it might be that, at some ranges, reflections from the ground would swamp echoes from aircraft, whereas at others aircraft would probably stand out. The range in question would depend on the angle at which the aeroplane's radar was pointing. The digital system can adjust the detection threshold (the signal strength demanded of a real target) to match. The human operator would have to guess where the boundary lay. The computer could automatically take into account the aeroplane's altitude (fed in digitally by the aeroplane's altimeter), disregarding strong echoes probably coming from the ground.

The postwar fighter problem was complicated because interceptors were losing their speed edge over the bombers. By 1945 some bombers were flying at fighter speeds, making them almost impossible to intercept. Some early jet bombers were actually faster than the fighters assigned to destroy them. Many later fighters were credited with supersonic speed, but they could not maintain that speed for very long. Non-afterburning speed, particularly for a fighter burdened with long-range fuel tanks, was often less than typical bomber speed. The problem became much more urgent with the advent of nuclear weapons.

Tactics therefore had to change radically. The fighter had to be steered into a collision course, approaching from ahead of the bomber. That required not merely that the fighter detect the bomber, but that it be coached on to the required path. Even then it would have only a very short time to attack, so its weapon had to be much more lethal.

Postwar experiments, both on land and at sea, showed that manual plotting techniques limited the number of separate targets (raids) a system could handle each hour. The faster the targets, the lower the number. The limitations had not been too serious in wartime, because bombers had to attack in large numbers to damage big targets. With the appearance of atomic weapons, however, bombers would probably attack in ones and twos, widely separated.

The first response to this problem was to simplify it. Vectoring might well be impossible, but a fighter could surely calculate the path to a single target. The fighter controller would broadcast the plotted positions of incoming bombers, assigning the closest fighter to each target. If the fighter knew just where it was, a simple onboard computer

might suffice. Air navigation thus became crucial, leading to the development of automatic aids such as the tactical air navigation system (Tacan), in which an aeroplane finds its position from a beacon's reply to its interrogation. Tacan became standard in the late 1950s. The need for onboard computation helps explain why most of the all-weather jet interceptors of the 1950s had two seats.

Even with self-vectoring fighters, a manual air-defence system could not handle large numbers of fast-moving targets. In the early 1950s, then, both in Britain and in the USA (and probably in the Soviet Union), interest turned to computers. The British developed an analogue comprehensive display system (CDS). It raised US hopes, and the USAF began work on a fully digital system, semi-automatic ground environment (SAGE). SAGE and its many offshoots automatically compiled a picture of the ongoing air battle, on the basis of which fighters could be assigned to their targets. However, the computer had to be able to command the interceptor into position to attack.

Thus SAGE went hand in hand with the creation of a datalink, by means of which it could guide a fighter. The Convair F-106 was built specifically to work with SAGE.

The 200 black boxes that comprised the Convair F-106 Delta Dart's Hughes MA-1 navigation-and-control system earned the aircraft the nickname 'plane with a brain'. The system flew the all-weather interceptor to its target, directed it on its attack course and then, at a precisely computed moment, fired its air-to-air missiles.

The ground system would bring the aeroplane into position to attack a bomber, and command it to fire its missiles. The first SAGE operations centre became operational in 1958, the system having been ordered in 1954.

Because SAGE required large numbers of computers, the programme forced US manufacturers, particularly IBM, into mass production. The growing military and civilian demand for computers led in turn to the development of smaller and less-expensive types, which became crucial to airborne use. When SAGE was conceived, computers used vacuum tubes to store data for computation. During the programme the first solid-state (transistorised) devices appeared. At this stage all the parts of a computer were mounted separately on circuit boards. The next step was integrated circuits, in which several devices were manufactured together and mounted together. As integration increased, these circuits became the now-familiar chips.

In the US case, SAGE was soon followed by SAC's big command system. SAC needed a computer merely to monitor and display the status of its widely dispersed force. Not all of its bombers could possibly be ready to go on any given day. The computer could keep track of their condition, and it could continuously change attack orders so that all the important targets were covered.

However, SAC soon discovered that automation was a slippery slope. The computer had to digest information from the many bomber bases. Computers were expensive, so the only one in the Command was that at headquarters. Information therefore came in by teletype and telephone; operators at SAC headquarters had to translate it to enter it into the one big computer. This took so long that, in an early exercise, the computer fell 1½ hours behind reality. Sometimes it was 6 hours behind. SAC found that it needed a networked system, with secondary computers (at the headquarters of the three numbered air forces comprising SAC's force), feeding the main one. They in turn had to be fed by the bomber airfields. Again, telephone data laboriously punched into a computer was too slow. The controlling computer literally had to know which bombers were ready to go at any moment, since some had to be assigned to any crucial targets left uncovered. For example, it would hardly do to leave key Soviet air-defence sites unattacked. In February 1958 the USAF approved development of a 'real time' command and control system, 465L.

The aeroplane's weaponry was the other end of the air-defence system. Fighters could now be vectored into position to shoot, but, given high bomber speeds, they would have very little time in which to do so. By about 1950 the USAF was arming its new F-86D, F-89, and F-94 interceptors exclusively with unguided rockets which could be fired in large salvoes to ensure hits. Fire-control systems proved difficult to develop, probably because of the complexity of integrating analogue computers with analogue radars.

Moreover, the rockets were inaccurate; in flight they soon spread out. The first really successful Western guided missile, Sidewinder, was conceived as a way of making a standard 5in rocket accurate enough to hit an aeroplane. Missiles were complex and, in an age of tube electronics, unreliable. In the early 1950s the US government considered the threat of Soviet nuclear bombers so urgent that it approved an interim solution, Genie, a nuclear-armed unguided rocket. Inaccurate it might be, but its explosion would bring down any nearby bomber.

The problems of jet-versus-jet combat created the first major new avionic systems, radar-oriented fire controls. To hit a target in a deflection shot, a pilot needs to know the course, speed and range of the target. He can then point his aeroplane so that the stream of bullets will arrive at the same point as the target. With a wartime lead-computing sight a pilot placed 'pippers' around the image of the target. The sight contained a gyro (a reference point and direction in space), so when the pilot kept the pippers on the target, the gyro could measure relative target motion. That was only in angular terms. However, the pilot also adjusted the size of the ring formed by the pippers to surround the target. In effect he was estimating target range. Given both angular speed and target range, the sight's analogue computer could calculate the appropriate firing (deflection) angle.

Lockheed's F-94C Starfire was armed exclusively with Mighty Mouse 2.75in unguided folding-fin rockets; twelve in each of the two wing pods and twenty-four arranged in a ring round the nose radome, covered by retractable fairings which have been opened in this photograph. Entering service in March 1953, the F-94C had a Hughes E-5 fire-control system.

The main drawback of the system was that the pilot rarely accurately measured target range, because the target was generally at an angle to him. The solution was to add a range-only radar to the gunsight. In a typical system of the early 1960s (in the USN's Crusader fighter), the pilot selected an interception course towards the target. The computer decided when he should open fire, and emitted an appropriate tone in his headphones (it also ordered cease fire).

The Sidewinder missile used much the same solution. When its seeker picket up a target's infrared (IR) signature, the pilot heard a tone. Unfortunately the fact that the missile was pointing at a target did not necessarily mean that it could manoeuvre effectively to hit it; the missile could only pull so many gs, for example.

Because it homed on the target's hot tailpipe, Sidewinder was ineffective in the most likely case of a bomber interception, a collision-course attack from ahead (eventually Sidewinder received a seeker sensitive enough to hit from ahead). The solution was a radar-guided missile. Ideally it would be entirely self-contained, using its own radar to lock on to a target designated by the attacking pilot. Until the 1980s, however, it was very difficult to accommodate the appropriate radar within missile dimensions.

The two alternatives placed in service both traded complexity in the fighter for complexity in the missile, and both demanded large fighter radars. The simplest was beam-riding. The fighter radar locked on to the target and generated a separate guidance beam, which usually rotated. A missile flying down the beam could sense how far from the beam centerline it was. Unfortunately it was difficult to keep the narrow beam locked on to a manoeuvring aeroplane, and the beam broadened with range, rendering the system effective only at relatively short distances, perhaps up to 5 miles (8km). Because it was simple both the USA and Soviet Union adopted it, in Sparrow I and in the Soviet R-5 series (NATO AA-1 'Alkali'). In the Soviet case, beam-riding made it easy to adapt the missile to ground attack, and the R-5 formed the basis for the first Soviet tactical air-to-surface missile, the Kh-66/Kh-23 (NATO AS-7). When the Soviets learned of Sidewinder they adopted infrared guidance, modifying the R-5 so that it beam-rode to an acquisition basket near the target, then switched to IR. In 1958 the Soviets gained access to early Sidewinders and copied the US missile outright.

The RAF did not adopt radar guidance. Instead, it opted for the IR-guided Firestreak and Red Top. These offered a fire-and-forget capability (one fighter could attack several bombers in quick succession), but they also required the fighter to get into an attacking position on the bomber's tail (Red Top reportedly offered head-on capability).

The next step, still in widespread use, was semi-active homing. The missile homes on radiation from the

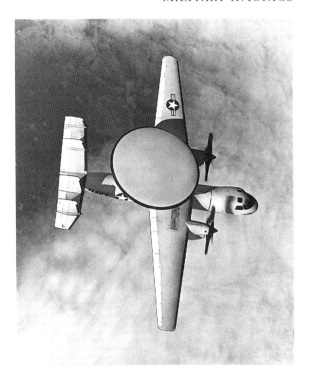

From September 1974 the Grumman E-2C Hawkeye, with its 24ft-diameter Rotodome, comprised the US Navy's primary airborne warning-and-control system. Its advanced radar could automatically detect hundreds of aerial and surface targets simultaneously within a 3-million-cubic-mile surveillance envelope, and a total tactical picture could be transmitted via datalink to the area commander for real-time assessment while the aircraft controlled multiple strike and interceptor forces.

fighter radar, which is reflected from the target. The rub is that it generally cannot use the intermittent pulses of a conventional radar, because there is too much time between pulses. Typically, then, an aircraft radar designed to support a semi-active missile produces an additional steady illumination (continuous-wave (CW) radiation). Modern semi-active missiles detect both the reflected radiation and the radiation coming directly from the radar. Comparing frequencies, they measure the Doppler shift due to target motion. Given that information, the missile can estimate the target's course and speed and thus can fly towards an interception point, rather than simply following the target. This makes the missile's flight path far more energy-efficient, increasing the weapon's range.

By about 1960 it was clear that computers would soon be compact enough to fit on board large aircraft. SAGE functions shrank sufficiently to fit on board the carrier-borne Grumman E-2 Hawkeye, which was conceived to handle 400 targets simultaneously.

SAGE roughly coincided with the rise of anti-aircraft missiles such as the US Nike and the Soviet S-75 (SA-2 in Western parlance). The death of the large bomber seemed to be at hand. However, those who operated bombers disagreed, pointing out that both SAGE and the missiles depended heavily on radars, which were ineffective against low-flying aircraft. The lower the bomber flew, the shorter the radar's horizon and, therefore, the less the warning time it offered. Moreover, radar beams tended to distort at very low angles. Airborne radars could, in theory, see low-fliers at greater distances, but any radar looking down tended to see the Earth.

The main solution was pulse-Doppler radar. Signals reflecting from a moving target are shifted in frequency, a phenomenon exploited in the modern semi-active missiles described above. The train of echoes received by a radar can be analysed in frequency to extract that shift. The problem is that the train of signals already has a frequency given by the rate at which the radar puts out pulses, its pulse-repetition frequency (PRF). The radar suffers from two types of ambiguity. The first is in range. It cannot automatically distinguish a nearby echo from a much more distant one which is received after the next pulse is sent out. In effect, its PRF determines the greatest range it can measure unambiguously: the range to which a pulse can go out and return before the next goes out. This phenomenon encourages radar designers to choose long PRFs for long-range radars, typically about a hundred pulses a second. Unfortunately the frequency set by the PRF is the lowest for which the radar can measure Doppler shift (due to speed) unambiguously. Aircraft speeds generally equate to thousands of pulses per second. The pulse-Doppler radars on modern fighters therefore operate at thousands or even hundreds of thousands of pulses per second. They typically estimate target range by shifting among several PRFs and comparing the apparent target range in each. One important advantage of such radars is that they can distinguish aircraft against the ground.

Probably the first important military pulse-Doppler radar was the APG-59 (AWG-10 system) in the F-4J version of the Phantom; the British F-4K and -4M had the AWG-11 and -12 versions of the same system. The F-14 combat system, AWG-9, was built around another pulse-Doppler radar at about the same time. Such radars are now quite standard.

Another major change in radar technology roughly coincided with pulse-Doppler: tracking techniques. During the Second World War, radar designers learned to track targets by having a slightly off-centre radar beam spin around the axis of the radar. If the radar were pointed directly at the target, the target's echo would be slightly less than if the beam had been on the axis, but it would not vary much as the beam spun. If the target were off-axis, target strength would vary radically, and this variation itself could be used to correct direction. Called conical scanning (conscan), this technique was applied to many kinds of radars.

There were two drawbacks. First, conscan was very vulnerable to jamming, since it associated a direction in space with a time in its cycle. A strong jammer, varying over time, could confuse the scanner, convincing it that it was pointed in the wrong direction. As it happened, Sidewinder and many other IR missiles used an IR analogue of conscan, so they were vulnerable to flashing countermeasures using fixed IR sources. For a conscan radar the second drawback was that a manoeuvring aeroplane might not have a constant radar return even if a radar were kept pointing at it. A conscan tracker would find any fluctuation very confusing, particularly in the case of a radar looking down on an aeroplane.

The solution, which first appeared in the 1960s, was monopulse. The radar now put out four beams, each a little off-centre, and the returns from all four were continuously compared. If they balanced, all four were seeing the same target; it they differed, an error signal was generated. More than twenty-five years later, monopulse devices are still very difficult to counter.

For semi-active missiles, monopulse tracking made it possible to use the reflections of pulse-Doppler radars rather than the CW illumination of the past. A monopulse seeker could find the direction of each pulse; a conscan seeker needed a lengthy illumination to find direction. Given a sufficiently smart processor, a missile can average out the reflections of the intermittent pulses to find the way to its target. Moreover, like the radar, the missile can now distinguish radar echoes from a target from those from the ground, so it can be fired effectively in a snap-down engagement.

The other major radar innovation of the 1960s was the synthetic aperture, for ground observation. The larger a radar, the narrower its beam, and the better its ability to distinguish objects close together. To produce an image of the ground far from the aeroplane, a radar would need a really large antenna, generally larger than a usable aeroplane. However, if the radar could send and receive signals while going in a straight path, it might be made mathematically equivalent to a radar with an antenna the length of the path during which it continued to receive the signals sent out earlier. That would not work if the radar were observing a rapidly moving object, such as another aeroplane; but it was perfectly adapted to observing the ground or, for that matter, slowly moving craft on the sea. Synthetic-aperture radar (SAR) superseded an earlier side-looking airborne radar (SLAR) technique in which the antenna was made as long as possible but used conventionally. Perhaps the most noteworthy recent use of SAR techniques is in the US JSTARS, in which SAR is married to a moving target indicator (MTI) to detect moving vehicles.

A Royal Navy Sea Harrier escorts a prying Soviet Ilyushin Il-20DSR multi-sensor reconnaissance aircraft. The large housing beneath the forward fuselage for its sideways-looking aircraft radar is conspicuous, as are a variety of antenna for other Elint and Sigint equipment, operated by the aircraft's twenty mission specialists.

Most SAR radars use long antennas, but in SAR techniques can be – and are – used by a small antenna pointed sideways. For example, reconnaissance Hornets (F/A-18s) used by the US Marine Corps have software which provides their APG-65 radars with a SAR mode. Some maritime patrol aircraft have inverse SAR radars (ISARs), in which the Doppler shift due to the rolling of a ship provides a measure of the ship's profile (higher or lower parts of the ship have different Doppler shifts, since they are further from or closer to the axis around which the ship rolls). Such radars are called synthetic apertures because the motion of the ship in effect narrows the radar beam in the vertical direction, improving its resolution.

Radar emissions reveal the presence of an aeroplane. That is true even of a radar altimeter. To supplement or even to supplant radar, two kinds of IR sensor have appeared, the forward-looking (FLIR) and the search/track (IRST). A FLIR is in effect an IR television, a night-vision device capable of seeing objects on the ground in considerable detail. FLIRs first became important during the Vietnam War, when US pilots were assigned to attack supply trucks running down the Ho Chih Minh Trail at night. In some cases pilots now use night-vision goggles (NVGs), which provide night vision using a very different technology, amplifying the very faint light provided by the Moon and even the

stars. That light falls on a photo-sensitive material which emits an electron when it is hit by even one photon. The electron then enters a multiplier tube, in which it is accelerated and in which it knocks more electrons out of the material. The stream of electrons generated by the single one then hits another surface, in which electrons produce the photons which appear on the device's eyepiece. Such devices can be recognised by their accelerator tubes; NVGs look like pairs of binoculars. A full night-vision cockpit combines night lighting with a FLIR display and NVGs for the pilot and crew. In some cases there is also a laser radar to detect obstructions such as power lines.

The IRSTs had a very different origin. They were a way of detecting air targets, usually against the cold background of the sky, without using radar, and hence without alerting the targets. The concept dates back to the late 1950s, and it has been tried many times. IRSTs can currently be seen on board a variety of Western and Russian fighters, sometimes in combination with a laser rangefinder. In contrast to a FLIR, no image is formed; instead, the IRST shows the positions of the targets it detects. In the Russian Su-27 and MiG-29 the IRST is considered part of an electro-optical radar, the other element being a laser rangefinder. The Russian view is that it is vital to avoid emissions in intercepting a target.

Typically the radar operates in dormant mode. A clear-air target is acquired and tracked by IRST (which incorporates a laser ranger); the radar is used only when it disappears into cloud.

There are also stabilised optical cameras. In Vietnam, US fighters equipped with long-range (beyond visual range) Sparrow missiles could not use them effectively for fear of hitting friendly aircraft. They were forced to adopt a tactic of coming alongside the potential target to identify it visually before falling back to fire (the missile had a finite minimum range). Postwar, the USN introduced a stabilised telescope feeding a television camera, specifically to allow pilots to identify their targets before firing.

While missiles of various sorts were being developed, the nature of defensive avionics was drastically changed by the advent of nuclear weapons. The bombers of SAC were expected to penetrate Soviet airspace singly or in small formations, so each aeroplane would have to deal with defences on its own. To do that it could jam or deceive long-range surveillance radars; but every pound of electronic warfare equipment carried reduced fuel or weaponry. Hence the importance, in the 1960s, of the switch to low-altitude tactics and to the advent of stand-off missiles. At the least, the missiles could be expected to destroy missile bases standing between bomber and target.

As defensive missiles improved, aircraft had to fly lower and lower at high speed. They therefore needed some assistance in avoiding terrain. The first approach to this problem was the terrain radar in the Grumman A-6 Intruder. A video screen in the cockpit showed the terrain ahead, and the pilot steered accordingly. In later aircraft, such as the General Dynamics F-111 and the Panavia Tornado, terrain avoidance (ground-following) was automated, a specialised radar connecting directly with the flight controls.

For their part, the Soviets adopted stand-off weapons to counter Western air defences. Khrushchev in particular considered classical bombers obsolete; no aeroplane, he thought, could fly above or very near its target unscathed in the face of the new anti-aircraft missiles. In 1954 the Soviets formally ordered development of stand-off weapons, to be carried on board modified versions of bombers (which they called missile carriers). By 1957 Khrushchev had gone further, cancelling production of the bombers altogether, but allowing continued work on missile carriers.

The Soviets' view was that a bomber was reasonably safe until it came within a few hundred miles of its target. That was the effective range of interceptors based near the target, and missiles would not be used until the bomber came even closer. Missile support avionics could be limited to a big long-range surface search radar, which the bomber would use to detect its target. The missile itself would be guided by autopilot, the sheer power of its thermonuclear warhead making up for any drift. Protective jamming was not particularly necessary.

The opened nose of a General Dynamics F-111A reveals the main scanner for the APQ-113 search radar, the smaller scanners for the TI APQ-110 terrain-following radars behind and below it, and the main avionics bay immediately behind that, with all modules in standard racking to allow easy replacement.

A prominent feature of the Grumman EA-6B Prowler was the large fin-top housing for a passive receiver antennae for hostile signals. The large underwing pods, which had Garrett windmill turbogenerators in their noses, emitted high-power jamming transmissions, and chaff dispensers were located in the underside of the rear fuselage.

There was an important exception: an attack against a naval force. In that case the Soviets planned to deploy regiments of bombers, flying in formation. Ships might well be spaced widely enough that even nuclear warheads would destroy only one or two of them. Thus it would take several bombers to deal with any naval force. Moreover, the main targets, the carriers, might well not be in the centre of the formation. In addition, the ships would use their jammers to conceal the targets, so the bombers would have to press on to try to identify the targets.

The concentrated bomber force would need electronic protection, which the Soviets planned to provide in three forms. First, specialised aircraft could lay chaff corridors down which the bombers would fly. Second, escort jammers would fly with the bombers, jamming specific air search radars within the naval force. Finally, aircraft would have their own self-protection jammers, presumably to deal with individual attackers. Special chaff-laying and escort-jammer versions of the standard naval bomber, the Tu-16, were developed. Escort jamming was so important that when a new high-speed bomber, the Tu-22M, replaced the Tu-16, it could not be used as planned because the escort-jammer version proved unsuccessful (presumably jamming interfered with vital avionics). Thus through the 1980s Tu-22M formations, which might have profited enormously from their speed, had to fly instead at Tu-16 (subsonic) speeds all the way to their targets. Only just as the Soviet Union collapsed did the escort jammer Tu-22M prototype appear.

Much of the jamming effort went into negating anti-aircraft missiles. At first the missiles were scarce and expensive, but soon after the outbreak of the Vietnam War Soviet missiles began to appear in North Vietnam. It became clear that the tactical aircraft the USA was using to bomb North Vietnam would need some means of protecting themselves. The initial US response was escort jamming, using such aircraft as the Douglas EB-66, the Douglas EF-10 Skyknight and the EA-3. For individual strike aircraft, the best countermeasure to missiles was violent manoeuvring. They needed some means of warning, and they were fitted with simple radar warning receivers (RWRs). The Soviet missiles were command-guided, receiving their commands on rear-facing antennas, so it was difficult for a target aeroplane to jam them. However, it was worthwhile to jam many of the directing radars. While the USAF developed a series of jamming pods which its strike aircraft could carry, the USN preferred internal jammers.

Both Services also developed hard-kill countermeasures in the form of anti-radar missiles (ARMs), beginning with Shrike. The USAF developed a force of radar-hunting aircraft, Wild Weasels, armed with Shrikes and cluster bombs and equipped with special sensors to locate offending radars. They were intended to precede a strike, neutralising enemy missile sites by hitting their radars. The USN, which had many fewer aircraft, preferred to carry its ARMs on board standard strike aircraft. It reserved its smaller number of specialist aircraft, eventually EA-6B Prowlers, for escort jamming. Only well after Vietnam were the Prowlers equipped with ARMs, and even then most such missiles went aboard strike aircraft.

One other offensive avionics development of this period deserves mention. By about 1960 US strategists were becoming concerned that nuclear weapons might be used without authorisation. The fear was that a commander faced with destruction might fire to save his command, thus touching off uncontrollable escalation. This view was particularly strong in the Kennedy administration, and it coloured the government's entire strategy. At the time, the USAF in Europe had nuclear weapons loaded on board quick-reaction (QR) fighter-bombers sitting on runways. The solution adopted at the time was a permissive action link (PAL), essentially a coded lock which precluded weapon operation unless the proper code was supplied. The particular aeroplanes assigned to QR duty had special wiring, generally connected to a series of keys in the cockpit. Unless the wiring was activated, the bomb under the aeroplane could not be armed. Often the bomb had its own PAL. Until the advent of digital systems, then, only some US and NATO aircraft could carry nuclear weapons, because only some were wired for that purpose. Thus of two apparently identical F-100s, for example, only one might be nuclear-wired.

Nuclear-wiring had real consequences for NATO. In theory, the alliance expected to fight a non-nuclear battle before considering any resort to nuclear weapons. However, a NATO commander knew that if he lost his nuclear-wired aircraft during the non-nuclear phase of the war he would be losing his ability to mount a nuclear attack if he had to. He would therefore hold back those aircraft during the initial non-nuclear phase. Since nuclear-wired aircraft might form a large part of the NATO air force, that threatened to cripple the alliance's non-nuclear capability.

There was another problem, too. SAC was designed to retaliate in the event of the USA being attacked. The Kennedy administration badly wanted to install PALs on its aircraft, but SAC argued that in that case it would pay the Soviets to obliterate Washington and thus prevent the arming codes from being sent. Similar arguments applied to strategic submarines.

The Soviets had fears of their own. Given their politics, clearly they also feared that a malcontent might choose to use the bomb against their own government. Until the mid-1960s their strategic forces, including their bombers, could not go on alert because all bombs were stored separately, under control of the KGB, the Communist Party secret service. After the Cuban missile crisis, however, the Kennedy administration was much concerned that the Soviets might deploy nuclear-armed forces and give them the freedom to fire (we now know that was not the case in Cuba). It therefore revealed PAL technology to the Soviets, the ironic result being that for the first time Soviet strategic forces could go on alert and thus could not be destroyed by a US

first strike. In the case of bombers, the Soviets went a step further from the Americans. At least ultimately, they linked their arming circuits to the aeroplane's autopilot, so that their bombs could not be delivered except against preselected targets.

Another important computer application of the mid-1960s was to large antisubmarine aircraft (the Lockheed P-3C Orion and the British Nimrod). The computer could maintain the tactical picture formerly plotted by hand, assembling the mass of information provided, for example, by sonobuoy-analysis operators. It could also do much more. It could guide the pilot to lay a planned sonobuoy field much more accurately, and could assemble the aeroplane's tactical picture into a form which could be sent to another aeroplane via a datalink. Thus a P-3C relieving another on station could exploit the first aeroplane's tactical information.

By the end of the 1960s a powerful computer could fit aboard a single-seat tactical aircraft. The A-7D/E Corsair II was an important early example. Its fire-control computer was fed by the aeroplane's flight instruments, so that at any instant it knew airspeed and aircraft attitude. When bombing a target, a pilot in effect aimed the aeroplane at it. However, dive bombing was quite dangerous, not least because the aeroplane came too close to the target. In theory, an aeroplane could toss a bomb on to a target, but no pilot could aim properly. Toss-bombing was therefore seen, until the end of the 1960s, as a nuclear bombing tactic, in which a little imprecision made no great difference.

Enter the computer. A pilot approaching the target could input target position by placing a cursor on the target as seen through the windscreen. The aeroplane's radar measured target range and depression angle, locating the target precisely. The aeroplane's fire-control computer already contained ballistic data on the bomb to be dropped. It could compute a toss-bombing path which would place the bomb on target. In the A-7E the computer ordered the pilot to follow the computed path, and released the bomb at the optimum point. The pilot might find himself manoeuvring to evade enemy anti-aircraft fire. As he did so, the computer could recalculate optimum path and release point.

In this case the virtues of the digital computer were important in several distinct ways. First, only a digital system could automatically take data from the radar and the flight sensors. Second, only a digital system could be programmed to handle a variety of different bombs. Finally, only a digital system could smoothly adjust as the pilot changed flight path.

The computerised fire-control system in the A-7E appeared just after the advent of 'smart' bombs, which a pilot flying at high altitude could lock on to a target. The most common, which are laser-guided, require the pilot (or some other operator, e.g. on the ground) to hold a laser on the target as the bomb drops. In effect an onboard fire-control system is a different way of distributing intelligence between munition and aircraft. It makes possible reasonably accurate delivery of inexpensive 'dumb' bombs. In the 1980s the USAF much preferred laser designation; the USN preferred to rely on aircraft fire-control systems, although its A-6E Intruders had laser designators. One reason was that aircraft often had to discard their weapons before returning to carriers; the USN was loath to lose expensive laser-guided bombs. Experience during the Gulf War suggested that the USAF was right. Even though unguided bombs could be delivered fairly accurately, they could not hit critical pinpoint targets such as bridge girders.

Ground attack raised another question. Targets such as tanks and trucks do not have very distinctive signatures. A pilot can certainly distinguish them by eye, but then he has to command weapons against them. Beginning in Vietnam, there were attempts to devise a sensor which could do better. Some were extremely ingenious. For Vietnam, for example, US scientists realised that the ignition system in a truck tends to create radio noise, which can be detected and exploited. In the 1980s the USAF ran an unsuccessful programme using a Doppler radar to detect the motion of tank tracks, as part of its overall LANTIRN programme.

Given the failure of tank-detecting sensors, most ground-attack weapons are now laser-guided. The aeroplane carries a laser designator, which the pilot or bombardier locks on to a target on the ground. Typically it can swivel and depress, so that the aeroplane has some freedom of manoeuvre. The problem is that the lock-on depends on an electro-optical tracker. Typically it fastens on the centroid of an area of contrast in the target,

Ferranti's laser ranger and marked target-seeker, destined for the Sepecat Jaguar and British Aerospace Harrier, is seen here in prototype form in the nose of English Electric Canberra B.2/8 hybrid WJ643 during trials at RAE Farnborough in the early 1970s.

or on an edge (which it may follow off the target). On the other hand, designating a target from a distance gives the pilot a much better chance of survival.

As it happens, that also gives him a much better chance of seeing the target in the first place. That is, the farther away the object, the more slowly it seems to move. Hence, the longer the pilot has to realise it is there. The pilot of a jet flashing past at low level may not realise that a target is present until after he has passed it. Yet, given modern anti-aircraft weapons, a second pass is usually fatal. That is why air forces lost interest in ground attack as they adopted jets. The attempt to retain ground-attack capability demanded weapons which could be fired from a distance, i.e., which corresponded to the new conditions under which targets could be seen. Hence the importance of forward-firing rockets and then of simple guided missiles such as Bullpup and the Soviet AS-7 (Kh-23) – and then of the designator/computer combination in the A-7E.

The A-7E computer provided data to the pilot in a new way. He could hardly afford to look down into the cockpit to see a computer screen; he was flying far too close to the ground. The computer therefore projected data (in symbolic form) on to a glass in front of the windscreen. This was the first important example of what is now quite common, a head-up display (HUD). It is the means by which the aeroplane's central computer displays to the pilot the integrated picture it has produced of what he faces, and what he can do about it.

The A-7E pilot generally navigated to the target area, and once there relied mainly on his eyes to acquire the target. However, the potential existed for a much greater degree of integration. By the early 1970s inertial-navigation packages had progressed to the point where they could fit aboard tactical aircraft. They could be programmed to guide the pilot through a series of way points en route to his target, using his central computer to present headings on the HUD.

This possibility had already been realised in the USN's last carrier-based strategic bomber, the A-5 Vigilante. Central to its design was the use of a non-radiating (i.e., inertial) navigation system. In the 1960s the Vigilante had the first HUD, by means of which its navigational computer instructed its pilot, who could hardly afford to look down while flying at high speed at very low altitude.

Virtually all modern aircraft have HUDs. They display not only the data generated by the aeroplane's mission (combat control) computer, but also some essential instrument read-outs. The amount of data a pilot can process is inherently limited, and the computer can help by filtering (integrating) some of the relevant data, and also by combining them in more usable form.

An aeroplane carries numerous air and tactical data sensors, and to display all of them would be to cover the

This BAe Harrier cockpit has a Smiths Industries Specto Avionics head-up display system. Above the crash protection pad is the combining glass, on which electronically generated symbols and alphanumerics are presented in the pilot's line of vision.

HUD in symbols. Therefore HUDs are designed to show only a fraction of the available data, the pilot selecting alternative programmes (e.g., for cruise, for air-to-air combat, for particular bombing tactics). The pilot must still look almost directly ahead to see the HUD superimposed on the sky. That must be distracting during violent manoeuvres, as in close air-to-air combat. The ultimate HUD displays its data not on a fixed screen in the cockpit, but on the visor of the pilot's helmet.

Until the late 1980s missions were generally planned by hand, using maps of the terrain and the best intelligence of items such as enemy radar and anti-aircraft coverage. Computers, however, can generate three-dimensional views of terrain as it should appear to the pilot. Moreover, they can be used to generate the best possible path to the target, taking all factors into account. The avionics side of this development is that the planned path can be fed into an aeroplane before it takes off, to be entered into its central mission computer, so that the necessary instructions can show up on the HUD, or even in the aeroplane's autopilot. Moreover, individual mission plans can be integrated together for a mass strike, the aeroplanes arriving simultaneously over a target from different directions (to make defence difficult). Perhaps the greatest significance of computer planning and cockpit automation is that strikes can be

When this photograph of a production McDonnell Douglas/BAe AV-8B Harrier cockpit is compared with the earlier cockpit in the illustration above, the great changes wrought by the advent of digital avionics become evident.

mounted very much more quickly than in the past, at least in theory.

Experience in the Gulf War showed that critical targets might pop up very rapidly, perhaps even after an aeroplane is in flight. There is therefore considerable current interest in retargeting. Clearly the aeroplane's mission computer can receive data from a special link. It may also be possible to display target images in the cockpit, so that the pilot can recognise what he has to hit.

The A-7E fire-control device roughly coincided with a drastic change in missile fire control. Missiles, like aeroplanes, have manoeuvring limits. A pilot watching a target is unlikely to be able to check his (and the target's) altitude, airspeed, and turning rate and range against the envelope in which the missile is designed to manoeuvre. Analysis of the failure of US missiles in Vietnam, particularly Sidewinder, revealed that out-of-envelope shots were probably largely to blame. The solution was to insert a computer which could keep track of the variables, and which had in it details of the envelope involved. This was clearly a step towards a modern computerised fighter fire-control system.

Feeding a fighter's radar signals into a computer had profound implications. The computer could decide that a target had been detected, and could log that detection in a track file. As the radar scanned it could update that track file, and it could form others. Because each file was updated only when the radar scanned back in that target's direction, the track was based only on intermittent observation of the target. Even so the radar could, in theory, maintain several target tracks simultaneously. The slower the target, the more accurate the track. Moreover, because the track files were digital, the computer could send target data (including speed and heading) to an aeroplane's fire-control computer. The computer tracking technique is called track while scan (TWS). It was the key to providing a single aeroplane with the ability to deal with multiple attackers.

There had always been a real fear that an enemy could swamp an air-defence system by presenting it with far more targets than it could engage in the short time available. That had engendered modern computer-based ground systems like SAGE. In the air, the problem was much the same. A fighter could shoot down a bomber with a semi-active missile, but it would have to focus its radar on that target throughout the flight of the missile. Meanwhile, other bombers could slip past. The problem was most acute for naval forces, since they could support only a very limited number of fighters. About 1959 the US Navy conceived a solution, Eagle-Missileer.

The Missileer fighter would carry a very-long-range air-to-air pulse-Doppler radar, to find bombers as early as possible. The fighter would sacrifice performance, since it had to carry the big, high-drag radar and as many long-range Eagle missiles as possible, for as long as possible. Clearly the radar would see many of the bombers in a raid, and Eagle would have to deal with them more or less simultaneously. To this end its radar had to operate in TWS fashion. Moreover, it had to be able to guide several missiles at the same time. No single missile could expect to rely entirely on radar reflections from its target. Instead it would have an autopilot to keep it on course between illuminations. The Eagle radar would illuminate each target in turn. As the missile neared the target it could no longer expect illumination just as needed. It would rely instead on its own active radar. Because the active seeker would be needed only for the last part of the missile's flight, it did not have to be very powerful.

Missileer was cancelled in favour of a more fighter-like aeroplane, initially the F-111B and then the Grumman F-14 Tomcat. Eagle became the Phoenix missile. The combination, which became operational in 1975, offered the greatest range of any air-to-air system, largely thanks to its intermittent-guidance technique and the autopilot incorporated in the missile (it also helped that, using the autopilot, the missile could be commanded into an energy-efficient up-and-over trajectory). Thanks to its track-while-scan radar/computer system, an F-14 could track up to twenty-four targets and engage six simultaneously. Because its tactical data were all digital,

Grumman's potent F-14 Tomcat carrier-borne air-superiority fighter combined the AWG-9 pulse-Doppler radar weapons-control system with the Phoenix missile, which incorporated its own autopilot.

it could send its data to an accompanying radar aeroplane (an E-2) or to the carrier controlling it, and digitised instructions could be sent up to the F-14 in return.

On a less rarified level, the standard Sparrow missile was modified so that it could deal with multiple attackers. It was provided with an autopilot set at launch time, which allowed it to fly a considerable distance before it needed to see any illumination (or, for that matter, to accept intermittent illumination). The step beyond is AMRAAM, an active-radar missile with an autopilot – and with a link back to the firing aeroplane. Using that link, the aeroplane can update the missile to fire at a manoeuvring target, all the while guiding the missile into position where its seeker should be effective.

These ideas are not unique to US aircraft. For example, the current long-range Russian air-to-air missile, R-27 (AA-10 Alamo), has an updatable autopilot linked to a TWS radar on the launching aeroplane.

Applying a computer to a radar can have other implications. The computer can generate the waveform the radar emits, making it easy to change the radar's function. Initially radars were designed for very limited roles, such as air-to-air or air-to-ground. A pulse-Doppler radar, for example, is hardly likely to be effective for mapping the ground or for ranging against targets on it. The APG-65 in the F/A-18 Hornet was the first computer-controlled radar. The F/A designation reflects a conscious belief that the same radar could be switched between air-to-air and air-to-surface applications, and

that it could be equally effective in either (indeed, it made it possible to merge two separate aircraft projects).

Computer treatment of a radar's output has its own consequences. In the past it was generally accepted that radars designed for different roles were easy to distinguish. For example, an airliner's weather radar was very different from a sea-search radar used to set up attacks against ships. However, US experiments with a standard airliner weather radar showed that, with computer filtering and an improved display, the radar could quite adequately locate naval targets. The improvement was not externally detectable because nothing was done to change the radar's emissions.

Quite aside from such trickery, multi-mode radars can be very difficult to identify. For example, in 1987 an Iraqi Mirage fighter fired two Exocet missiles at the US frigate *Stark* in the Persian Gulf. The fighter had a multi-mode Agave radar, which was being used in a ship-attack role. The ship's countermeasures operator thought the radar he was detecting was a US-built AWG-9 (which also has an anti-ship mode) on board an Iranian F-14. The two radars naturally use similar waveforms to accomplish similar ends, and the operator was much influenced by the expectation that the Iranians were hostile, whereas the Iraqis were relatively friendly. The lesson is that attempts to identify radars by their emissions, which are the basis for countermeasures (including airborne types), are less and less effective. Once radar waveforms are software-controlled, identification may become almost impossible.

The Hughes APG-65 watercooled pulse-Doppler multi-mode radar in the McDonnell Douglas F/A-18 Hornet can track ten targets and display eight of them. It has raid-assessment mode, and Doppler beam-sharpening gives good air/ground clarity.

A US Navy pilot sights 'hostiles' in a Hughes Weapons Tactical Trainer designed to teach experienced pilots the combat use of the F/A-18 Hornet strike fighter. A 360° computer-generated image of the sky, targets and the ground provides a realistic training environment. The almost complete absence of instruments in the cockpit is noteworthy.

Clearly visible in this study of a General Dynamics F-16A cockpit is the sidestick control on the right and the throttle on the left; the embodiment of the hands-on-throttle-and-stick (HOTAS) system, in which every commonly used control is at the pilot's fingertips on one or other of these grips, enabling the aircraft to be operated instinctively.

The caveat, which may become increasingly important, is that it is possible that each radar set imposes 'fingerprints' on the signal it emits. To the extent that military aircraft of the future are likely to use radar receivers to sense the environment around them, they may have to rely on some form of fingerprinting, with all that entails in computer processing power – and in intelligence-gathering to obtain fingerprints of an opposition's radars.

The big radar-guided missiles are generally effective at long range. For shorter ranges, the weapon of choice is still the self-guided IR missile, the descendant of Sidewinder. The missiles themselves are violently manoeuvrable, but the most important change has been in the supporting element on board the aeroplane. In the past the seeker head in the missile was either caged to look straight ahead or slaved to the aeroplane's radar. In a dogfight, however, the pilot tends to move his head to see a target. In the 1970s the idea arose of slaving the missile seeker to the pilot's head – specifically, to his helmet. The helmet visor could be given an aiming reticle, and the pilot could activate the missile seeker when the target occupied it. A missile with sufficient manoeuvring power could exploit this kind of aiming. Generally the aircraft combat system connects with the helmet via cockpit sensors which track it. In the early Russian systems, for example, a television tracked lines painted on the back of the helmet.

The USN seems to have been the first to try a helmet sight, but it proved unsuccessful. Helmet sights were developed by the Israelis (for the Python missile), by the South Africans (for the Darter missile), and by the Soviets. The latter used theirs (introduced in 1985) on Su-27 and MiG-29 fighters to control the extremely manoeuvrable R-73 (NATO AA-11) short-range missile. The system's advantages became obvious when US pilots began flying ex-East German MiG-29s in 1991. Using US tactics they could acquire targets in thirty times the volume of air available to an F-15, and estimated exchange rates greatly favoured the Russian fighter. German pilots flying MiG-29s against F-16s (which are more manoeuvrable) got the first shot most of the time, even though the F-16s were clean and the MiGs were carrying belly tanks, six missile pylons, and two training rounds. Western tactics did work in many-on-many fights, in which the MiG's limited target-tracking was a major disadvantage. As it happened, rigid Soviet tactics hardly exploited the combination.

Hitherto, dogfighting capability had generally been equated to the aeroplane's ability to manoeuvre violently. Given that ability, a pilot could get on a target's tail. If, however, the missile could be fired far off-boresight (i.e., when the aeroplane was not yet pointing towards the target), then perhaps the missile could do more of the work. That might be particularly important for a

The Westinghouse APG-66 I/J-band pulse-Doppler radar in the nose of the General Dynamics F-16.

stealthy fighter, which would have a much smaller radar cross-section in some directions than in others. Manoeuvring violently to deal with a close-in target, such an aeroplane might well expose itself to a long-range shot by a fast radar-guided missile. For that matter, the advent of extremely manoeuvrable helmet-cued dogfight missiles might drastically reduce the value of fighter manoeuvrability in general. That raises questions about the design sacrifices the new Eurofighter makes to achieve its manoeuvring power. Helmet sights have also been adopted for other purposes. The AH-64 Apache ground-attack helicopter uses a simple helmet sight to control its turret-mounted cannon.

Meanwhile, aeroplanes themselves were changing. By the mid-1950s it was clear that supersonic aircraft generally would not be inherently stable, at least not in all flight regimes. The solution was to provide a limited form of controlled change to the movement of the aeroplane's controls. This was the beginning of fly-by-wire. Ultimately, the pilot's controls would feed the pilot's intentions into a flight-control computer, which would decide which control-surface movements should be made (based on such factors as speed and aircraft attitude). The computer could also move control surfaces without being commanded to do so, to keep the aeroplane on course at altitude.

Using a computer, then, an inherently unstable aeroplane could be flown safely. Aerodynamic design could be subordinated to other considerations. In the 1970s, for example, the US government became very interested in aircraft designs which might minimise radar reflectivity. The hope was that a properly-shaped aeroplane could reflect radar signals away from the transmitter, so that they would not be picked up. Very large computers could be programmed to predict the radar cross-section associated with any particular detailed aeroplane shape. The result was the 'faceted' F-117, which could not be flown without computer control. Have Blue, a radar-carrying aircraft which looked like a slightly streamlined winged brick, was a more extreme version of the same concept.

For computer control to work, the aircraft's instruments have to feed into its control computer. Ideally their outputs should be digitised. There is no longer much reason for outputs to be presented to the pilot on analogue dials, since the dials would require separate means of translating back from digital data into analogue form. It is much simpler to send the digital data to a display computer which can construct synthetic dials on display screens. A pilot does not need most of his instruments most of the time, and the ones he does need vary according to what the aeroplane is doing. The screens can, therefore, display only a selection of the instruments, perhaps in expanded form (hence easier to scan). The same screens can display the aeroplane's radar or FLIR pictures, or other tactical data. This computer-controlled 'glass cockpit' is now common on airliners as well as combat aircraft. It has some important drawbacks. It is becoming clear that pilots familiar with the old standard dials do not automatically realise what the display computer is not showing, and do not always associate the synthetic dials they see (often showing only part of the dial face) with the old analogue ones. The problem is bound up with the decisions inherent in the software of the fly-by-wire computer.

As in most computer applications, errors can occur, and they can be quite subtle and difficult to detect. An example is the B-1 bomber, which uses fly-by-wire control. Unfortunately, when it was redesigned B-1B the flight-control software was not rewritten. The new aeroplane was quite different from its predecessor, and a prototype crashed on a low-level test flight. Fly-by-wire computer problems were also blamed for an early Swedish Gripen crash and for an Airbus crash during a demonstration (reportedly the system refused a pilot's attempt to climb it out of a stall). A Russian pilot reportedly pointed out that fly-by-wire will force a pilot into a stereotyped reaction to an extreme manoeuvre (e.g., near a stall), and that an opponent familiar with that reaction may be able to exploit it to shoot him down. On the other hand, the C-17 transport was required to be able to land in a very short distance, and only fly-by-wire could provide the exquisite level of control required. Unfortunately the program could not easily be tested, since failure would have destroyed a valuable prototype. The solution was to carry out a series of dummy landings at 10,000ft (3,000m). Ultimately the high cost of the C-17 programme itself was ascribed mainly to the cost of writing software and, worse, testing it.

Computer aerodynamic control (fly-by-wire or, using fibre optics, fly-by-light) has many other aspects. Wires can be duplicated for better survivability and, in theory, the software in the flight computer can be designed to take account of the way the airframe changes owing to battle damage. Thus in theory a fly-by-wire aircraft should be far more survivable than a conventionally controlled one. That is quite apart from the fact that reduced stability ought to permit much greater manoeuvrability. The flight computer can also protect a pilot from undertaking dangerous or fatal manoeuvres.

Moreover, the pilot himself has physical limitations. Motions become more and more difficult as the aeroplane manoeuvres more and more violently. The new Eurofighter, which is designed specifically for dogfighting, has a voice-recognition feature in its cockpit; it can (at least in theory) respond to a pilot's voiced commands. Presumably, then, he will be able to order some manoeuvres even though he is unable to move his controls. Moreover, he may be able to voice commands before executing them with his hands or feet. In a somewhat similar vein, the US Defense Advanced Research

Agency has worked on a program called Pilot's Associate, which would allow a pilot to put his aeroplane into a tight manoeuvre even though it might cause him to black out. The Pilot's Associate would have sufficient artificial intelligence to follow through. Such action might be particularly valuable in evading missile fire.

The advent of computers has changed aircraft design in a subtle but very important way. In the past, each instrument or device in an aeroplane was wired directly to some other element. For example, a radar would feed directly into a radar scope, or an altimeter would be wired to the dial on the aeroplane's instrument panel. A sophisticated aeroplane such as an F-4 might have several miles of wire, adding considerable weight. Moreover, changing any one element of the aeroplane required rewiring.

The more modern alternative is a databus. Each device or readout is connected to the bus. Data move as addressed messages. For example, when a radar detects a target it sends out a message, which the radar scope reads and translates into part of a display. The same message may be picked up by the aeroplane's central mission computer. It may, for example, be translated into a datalink message, to be sent down to a control centre or out to an accompanying aeroplane. It may also register with the computer controlling the projector on to the pilot's HUD.

From a constructional point of view there are no longer massive numbers of point-to-point connections. Instead, there are buses (which may be duplicated, for survivability) to which each device is connected. Much obviously depends on bus capacity, since an overloaded bus can lose messages by allowing them to interfere. However, given an appropriately designed bus, it is relatively easy to modify an aeroplane by plugging in new elements, or by removing existing ones. The current world standard is the US-developed 1553B bus.

The bus concept also has important consequences for the aeroplane's ability to deliver weapons. In the past, aircraft were specifically wired to carry particular weapons. A pylon might be stressed for, say, 1,000lb (450kg), but its wiring, and the wiring of the aircraft's fire-control system, determined just which 1,000lb stores it might accommodate. Specific wiring also carried specific arming and release messages (which might not be any more complicated than the release of a magnet) to the pylons. A bus, connected to a stores-control computer, can theoretically accommodate a very wide variety of different weapons, perhaps the entire variety that an air arm uses. The behaviour of a particular shape, once it has separated, depends in part on the aerodynamics of the dropping aeroplane. A ballistics (weapons-aiming) program will, therefore, have to be arranged for each combination of aeroplane and weapon. Hence the continuing need for integration testing.

Overall, it seems inevitable that the extent of integration, i.e., the extent to which the central tactical system combines different sensor outputs, will expand. The new Joint Strike Fighter (JSF) is a case in point. Current aircraft treat radar and electronic countermeasures data quite separately. In the JSF a single set of broadband receivers is used for all electromagnetic signals, whether they are echoes of the aircraft's radar or messages sent by datalink – or enemy radar signals. All are placed (in digital form) on the same bus, to be picked off by the relevant processors. The processors' data in turn is sent to the aeroplane's central tactical computer, also by bus (in this case, a different bus). The computer uses all this data to form the tactical picture it presents to the pilot. In this case the data previously used only for warning (in an RWR) becomes part of the pilot's overall situational awareness. One consequence of using a single set of antennae for all signals is that enemy sources of radar signals will be located far more precisely than has been usual for tactical aircraft. In that case the standard JSF may have unusually good capability to locate and destroy enemy radars.

By the late 1970s Western military avionics was facing yet another challenge. It was fairly clear that, should Europe explode into war, neither side would cheerfully resort to nuclear weapons. The Soviets and their allies had built up massive tank forces. Western anti-tank missiles wielded by troops (and carried on board helicopters) might well blunt an initial assault, but the Soviets banked on exhausting the initial defence and then smashing through with forces which had assembled well behind the front lines. The challenge was to locate and destroy these forces without resorting to tactical nuclear weapons.

The solution was SAR radar, which could be used to direct either ground-based rockets or anti-tank aircraft. Any radar facing ground targets encounters a potentially fatal problem, that the ground is covered in objects which are not too distinctive. In the 1970s the answer was to concentrate on moving vehicles. At first it seemed that radar range would be relatively short, so the radar aeroplane might have to fly well beyond the front line. The USA developed an odd-looking stealthy aeroplane, Have Blue, for just this purpose, with flat sides housing big SAR radars. It transpired, however, that radar range was so great that the radar aeroplane did not need to go anywhere near the front line. It could be the quite conventional Boeing 707 which was converted into the E-8 JSTARS platform. In this case the aeroplane had to be large not because of the size of its radar, but because it had to accommodate a mass of computers and operators. It turned out that a quite effective radar could be carried on board a fighter, in a pod, with a digital link down to the users.

An early graphic depiction of an E-8 JSTARS aircraft equipped with a multi-mode moving-target indicator and synthetic-aperture radar for ground surveillance, and an extensive command, control and communication system to conduct attacks against ground targets.

The military applications drove the avionics, but by the 1970s it was beginning to appear in commercial aircraft. Probably the first major development was inertial navigation. Large airliners, probably beginning with the Boeing 747, have inertial devices which register the point of take-off and a series of waypoints. Typically the pilot is alerted as he approaches a waypoint, after which he makes the turn on to the new heading. This procedure was highlighted when an apparent failure to set an inertial system correctly brought Korean Air Lines Flight 007 into collision with Soviet air-defence forces over Sakhalin in 1983. Now another military-inspired system, the network of Global Positioning Satellites

(GPS), provides even the smallest aircraft with accurate positional information and may make the complex inertial systems redundant.

A second important transfer from the military world was the combination of glass cockpit and fly-by-wire. The current versions of most airliners use glass cockpits instead of the earlier collections of analogue dials. There has been some question as to whether the change has been for the best, as pilots sometimes find the computer outputs confusing or illogical; reportedly they have often not been designed properly from the pilot's point of view. Full fly-by-wire has appeared in such aircraft as the later Airbuses and the Boeing 767 and 777.

6
Offensive Aircraft in a New Age
Robert Jackson

The strategic bomber

In broad terms, the function of a strategic-bombing force is to bring about the progressive destruction of an enemy's military, industrial and economic systems, and to undermine the morale of its people by attacks on population centres to the point where their capacity for armed resistance is fatally weakened. That doctrine, first formulated by the Allied leadership in January 1943 at Casablanca, and specifically aimed at Nazi Germany, remains unchanged today. What has changed is the awesome nature of the aircraft and weaponry available to implement it. This is epitomised by one aircraft type alone, the Boeing B-52 Stratofortress, which has remained at the heart of the West's airborne strategic nuclear deterrent forces ever since it entered service with the USAF Strategic Air Command in 1955. Its operational career is worth examining in detail, for it spanned almost all of the Cold War era. In addition, the B-52 has experienced the full range of technical and operational changes that have proven necessary to enable the strategic bomber to survive in an intensely hostile environment, particularly one dominated by sophisticated surface-to-air missiles (SAMs).

The B-52 was the first aircraft to be armed with a long-range, stand-off, air-to-surface missile, the North American GAM-77 Hound Dog, a system designed to enhance the bomber's chances of survival. The 43ft (13m) missile had small canard foreplanes, a rear-mounted delta wing fitted with ailerons, a small fin and rudder, a very slim fuselage and a Pratt & Whitney J52-6 turbojet in an underslung rear pod. It was designed to carry a 1-megaton warhead over a range of between 500 and 700nm (926 and 1,297km), depending on the mission profile, and it could operate between tree-top level and 55,000ft (16,775m) at speeds of up to Mach 2.1. The weapon was fitted with a North American Autonetics Division inertial system, which was linked to the aircraft's navigation systems and continually updated by a Kollsman astro-tracker in the launch pylon.

All B-52Gs and, later, B-52Hs armed with the Hound Dog carried one pylon-mounted round under each wing. The Hound Dogs's turbojets were lit up during take-off, effectively making the B-52 a ten-engined aircraft, and were subsequently shut down, the missile's tanks being topped up from the parent aircraft. After launch the missile could follow a high- or low-flight

A Boeing B-52G Stratofortress armed with two GAM-77 Hound Dog air-to-surface missiles.

A B-52H armed with short-range attack missiles.

profile, with dog-legs and diversions as necessary. Later, anti-radar and terrain-contour-matching (TER-COM) modifications were introduced. At the missile's peak in 1962 there were 592 Hound Dogs on SAC's inventory, and it is a measure of the system's effectiveness that it remained in operational service until 1976.

Meanwhile, considerable strides had been made in the development of other airborne offensive weaponry. In the 1960s the miniaturisation of nuclear warheads had led to studies of an air-launched weapon which was small enough to be carried by a fighter-bomber and launched against a target from a range of about 100 miles. Boeing, the eventual prime contractor, began detailed studies of this short-range attack missile (SRAM) in December 1963, and in the following year the USAF drafted an operational requirement, SOR-212, which led to the development of the weapon system under the designation WS-140A. A dummy SRAM was dropped from a B-52 in December 1967, followed by two test launches in 1969, and later that year the first drop was made from a General Dynamics FB-111.

The first SRAM assigned to SAC was delivered to the 42nd Bomb Wing (BW) at Loring AFB, Maine, on 4 March 1972, the missile subsequently equipping all B-52H and B-52G units and SAC's two FB-111 wings. The B-52 was capable of carrying twenty SRAMs, twelve in three-round underwing clusters and eight in the aft bomb bay, together with up to four Mk 28

thermonuclear weapons, while the FB-111 could carry up to six SRAMS, four on pivoting underwing pylons and two internally.

The SRAM's primary function was to neutralise enemy defences such as radar sites, SAMs and other AA systems, greatly enhancing the bomber force's penetration capability. Powered by a solid-fuel Lockheed SR-75-LP-1 rocket motor, the missile was only 14ft (4.27m) long and 18in (0.45m) in diameter. Including its 200kt W-69 thermonuclear warhead, it weighed only 2,230lb (1,012kg). Designated AGM-69A in USAF service, it carried a Singer-Kearfott KT-70 inertial guidance system, with a Declo Magic computer and terrain-avoidance altimeter. Four flight programmes could be loaded into it: terrain-following, pull-up from under the radar followed by inertial dive, semi-ballistic, and combined inertial and terrain-following. Its speed was in excess of Mach 3.0, and its range was between 35 and 105nm (65–195km), depending on the selected flight profile. The first launch of an operational SRAM was made over the White Sands Missile Range, New Mexico, by a B-52 crew of the 42nd BW on 15 June 1972. Between that date and March 1977, seventy-two missiles were test-fired with only two malfunctions, an impressive record by any standard.

Weapons such as these gave SAC crews flying B-52s and FB-111s at least a fighting chance of breaking through a screen of Soviet air defences which were growing increasingly more effective, and in the latter stages of the Vietnam War the B-52s had a taste of how effective Soviet air-defence weaponry could be. This happened during Operation 'Linebacker II', which was authorised by President Richard M Nixon in May 1972 in the context of a major North Vietnamese Army offensive against the South and a stalemate at the Paris peace talks. The operation is worth examining in some detail, because in support of an intensive strategic bombing campaign it brought together all the photographic intelligence and electronic intelligence resources, as well as all the ECM facilities, employed so far in Vietnam. As part of the renewed offensive, B-52s ventured into heavily defended North Vietnamese airspace for the first time in May and June to make limited night attacks on airfields and oil-storage facilities, and also to lay mines in the waters of Haiphong and other strategic ports. These minelaying operations, carried out by modified B-52Ds, were also flown under cover of darkness, and no losses were sustained.

On 20 October 1972, when it seemed as though the Paris talks were at last leading to an agreement that would end the war, air operations over North Vietnam were once more halted. They were resumed when the peace talks again broke down amid indications that the

North Vietnamese were preparing to renew their offensive in the South. There followed an eleven-day bombing campaign against the North which developed into the heaviest bombing offensive of the war, with round-the-clock attacks on targets which had mostly been on the restricted list until then. They included railway yards, power plants, communications facilities and petrol, oil and lubrication (POL) stores and ammunition supply dumps, as well as the principal North Vietnamese Air Force (NVAF) fighter bases and SAM sites. The target list numbered thirty-four strategic objectives, over 60 per cent of which were situated within a 25-mile (40km) radius of Hanoi.

The original plan called for the B-52s to attack at night, in three waves, with F-111s and A-6s continuing the offensive in daylight. The B-52 bomber streams were to be preceded by F-111 interdictors, attacking fighter bases at low level, and F-4 Phantoms dropping *Window* (metallic strips designed to confuse enemy radar). The B-52s were to approach their target areas from the northwest, using strong high-altitude winds to give them a much-increased ground speed, and after bomb release they were to swing away from the target in tight turns in order to clear SAM defences as quickly as possible. Attacks were to be made by cells of three

A close-up of the B-52E's tail armament of four radar-directed 0.5in guns with 600 rounds apiece. The tail gunner in the pressurised turret could escape in an emergency by jettisoning the entire turret.

aircraft, generally bombing from 33,000ft (10,065m). The three aircraft were to fly in close formation to pool their ECM resources, which included the GE ALQ-87 and ITT ALQ-117 jammers and the Lundy ALE-24 chaff-dispensing system. In fact, the B-52D was better equipped with ECM than SAC's main-force B-52Gs, some of which were brought in to augment the bombing force during 'Linebacker II'.

The operation began on the night of 18/19 December 1972, when 129 B-52s took off from their respective bases in Thailand and on Guam. Thirty minutes before the first cells arrived over their targets, F-111s carried out strikes on enemy airfields and F-4s sowed two chaff corridors to screen the attacks on the target areas of Kinh No and Yen Vien, north of Hanoi. Unfortunately, the strong northwest wind had dispersed the chaff before the B-52s arrived.

The first B-52 wave to attack the Yen Vien railway yards flew over a cluster of SAM sites as it began its final run-in to the target, and 'Charcoal 1', the leading aircraft in the 'Charcoal' cell, sustained a near miss from an SA-2 just as its bomb doors were opening. Crippled and out of control, with its pilot, copilot and gunner either dead or incapacitated, the bomber began its long plunge to the earth. The navigator, radar navigator and electronic warfare officer ejected and were taken prisoner. A second B-52, attacking with the 'Peach' cell in the second wave four hours later, was luckier. It was also crippled by an SA-2, this time just after completing its bombing run, but managed to reach friendly territory with wing and engine fires before its crew were forced to abandon it.

The third wave of eighteen B-52s, attacking five hours later, encountered fierce opposition over the target (the Hanoi railway repair shops). More than sixty SAM launches were observed, but the bombers' ECM worked well and there were no losses, although one aircraft was damaged by a near miss. Another wave of twenty-one aircraft, attacking from the west, also encountered heavy opposition from eleven SAM sites in the Hanoi area and lost the leading aircraft in the last cell to bomb, 'Rose 1'. On this first night of 'Linebacker II', therefore, in which the enemy had launched more than 200 SAMs and expended massive quantities of AAA ammunition, the SA-2s had destroyed three B-52s and damaged three more. The B-52s suffered no casualties on the night of 19/20 December, when 120 bombers attacked several targets in the Hanoi area. However, the North Vietnamese had by now realised that the bombers were approaching their target areas along the same tracks each night, and they evolved new tactics that included sending up MiG fighters to shadow the incoming bomber stream and verify its altitude, so that the defences could fuze their missile warheads and AAA shells accordingly.

During the third night of operations, on 20/21 December, SA-2s knocked down two B-52s as they completed their bombing runs, and both of them crashed in Hanoi. A third B-52, badly damaged, struggled back to Thailand, only to crash on landing, killing four of its crew. Two more B-52s in the last wave that night were destroyed by SAMs; a third was crippled and crashed in Laos. In the nine-hour operation the enemy had fired 220 SAMs and claimed six B-52s, four of which were B-52Gs.

On the fourth night, 21/22 December, the tactics employed by the bomber stream were modified somewhat. The time between attacking waves was greatly reduced, attacking altitudes were varied, and the cells were randomly spaced. In addition, individual crews were given freedom of action in evasive manoeuvring; most favoured a shallow post-attack turn followed by a dive to low altitude and a high-speed run clear of the Vietnamese defences over the Gulf of Tonkin. All sorties on this night were flown from U-Tapao, the Guam-based B-52s being released for Arc Light missions (carpet-bombing attacks on suspected NVA troop movements in the South), and there were no losses.

The B-52 force was stood down for thirty-six hours over the Christmas period, but on the night of 26/27 December 120 B-52s, flying in tightly compressed waves and accompanied by 113 defence-suppression and ECM aircraft, attacked ten targets in Hanoi, Haiphong and Thai Nguyen, the more vulnerable B-52Gs being assigned to the last two objectives. Two streams attacked Hanoi from the northwest, flying in from Laos and out over the Gulf of Tonkin, while two more attacked on a reciprocal track. All the bombers passed through the target areas within fifteen minutes, and only one B-52 fell to the SAM defences, although a second, severely damaged, crashed short of the runway while attempting to land at U-Tapao in Thailand.

The last three nights of Operation 'Linebacker II', in which sixty B-52s were committed on each night, cost SAC five more bombers, all victims of SAMs. By this time the North Vietnamese defences had been virtually neutralised, and the enemy had expended most of their stock of around 1,000 SA-2s. On 30 December North Vietnam announced that it was ready to resume peace negotiations. In all, 729 B-52 sorties had been flown during the operation, and more than 15,000 tons of bombs dropped out of a total of 20,370 tons. Fifteen B-52s had been lost to the SAM defences, and nine damaged, while thirty-four targets had been hit and some 1,500 civilians killed. Of the ninety-two crew members aboard the shot-down US bombers, twenty-six were recovered by rescue teams, twenty-nine were listed as missing presumed dead, and thirty-three baled out over North Vietnam to be taken prisoner and eventually repatriated.

Many lessons were learned in Vietnam that would be applied to future airborne intelligence-gathering and offensive systems. Foremost among them was that, for a manned reconnaissance or strike aircraft to be relatively certain of survival in a hostile high-technology air-defence environment, it had to be virtually invisible to radar and other electronic sensors as it carried out its mission. Research that would lead to the production of an operational 'stealth' aircraft was already more than a decade old when the Vietnam War ended, but it was that unhappy conflict that accelerated the programme and made the Lockheed F-117A strike/reconnaissance aircraft and the Northrop B-2 bomber realities.

Operation 'Linebacker II' underlined the already-known fact that strategic bombers such as the B-52, lacking the evasive manoeuvrability of smaller strike aircraft, could not operate at high altitude over the territory of a nation armed with long-range SAMs without suffering heavy casualties. However, a planned reduction in the size of SAC's B-52 fleet was anticipated, for SAC was now expecting the early introduction of the Rockwell B-1 variable-geometry supersonic bomber, designed to replace the B-52 and FB-111 in the low-level-penetration role.

The B-1 prototype first flew on 23 December 1974, and subsequent flight trials and evaluation progressed rapidly. On 21 April 1975 a SAC KC-135 tanker crew of the 22nd Air Refueling Squadron conducted the first flight-refuelling trials with the new bomber, and on 19 September it was flown for the first time by a SAC pilot, Major George W Larson of the 4200th Test and Evaluation Squadron at Edwards AFB. Major Larson handled the controls for about one-third of the 6½hr flight.

Trials continued throughout the following year, and on 2 December 1976 the US Secretary of Defense, Donald H Rumsfeld, after consultations with President

The Rockwell B-1B, the operational version of the supersonic bomber which incorporates a good deal of 'stealth' technology in its design.

Gerald Ford, authorised the USAF to proceed with production of the B-1. In September, however, Congress had restricted funding of the B-1 programme to $87 million per month, slowing down the programme and effectively leaving the decision on the B-1's future to President Jimmy Carter, who would take office on 20 January 1977.

The decision hung in the balance until 30 June 1977, when Carter delivered his bombshell and stated in a nationwide television address that the B-1 would not be produced. He said:

This has been one of the most difficult decisions that I have made since I've been in office. Within the last few months I've done my best to assess all the factors involved in production of the B-1 bomber. My decision is that we should not continue with deployment of the B-1 and I am directing that we discontinue plans for production of this weapons system. The Secretary of Defense agrees that this is a preferable decision.... The existing testing and development now under way on the B-1 should continue to provide us with the needed technical base in the unlikely event that more-cost-effective alternative systems should run into difficulty.... In the meantime, we should begin development of cruise missiles using air-launched platforms such as our B-52s, modified as necessary.

At a Pentagon Press Conference on 1 July, Secretary of Defense Harold Brown sought to elaborate on the decision, stating:

My recommendation to the President, and his decision not to proceed with the production of the B-1, were based on the conclusion that aircraft carrying modern cruise missiles will better assure the effectiveness of the bomber component of US strategic power in the 1980s. Both the B-1 and the cruise missile offer high assurance of survivability and penetration. But the President and I are convinced that the cruise missile will provide more certainty for our defense.

The cruise missile to which Carter and Brown were referring was the Boeing AGM-86A air-launched cruise missile (ALCM), which originated in a design study of 1963–6. This originally led to the AGM-68 subsonic cruise armed decoy (SCAD), a miniature aircraft powered by a Williams WR19 turbofan and designed to replace the Quail, an earlier decoy missile, in SAC service. SCAD went into full-scale development in July 1970, but in June 1973 it was cancelled in favour of a long-range ALCM based on SCAD technology. Unlike SCAD, which had only a secondary attack capability after fulfilling its primary decoy role, ALCM was designed as a nuclear delivery vehicle from the outset.

The AGM-86A first flew, at the White Sands Missile Range, on 5 March 1976, and the missile was achieving most of its flight-test objectives by the following year, when it was subjected to a fly-off against the General Dynamics AGM-109 cruise missile then under development for the US Navy. The AGM-86A was designed to be compatible with the B-1's weapons bay, but when the B-1 was cancelled Boeing went ahead with the full-scale development of an improved version, the AGM-86B ALCM-B, which would have been too big for the B-1. The AGM-86B was finally selected to be SAC's air-launched cruise missile in March 1981; the plan was that it should be carried by all SAC B-52G bombers, the first squadron becoming operational in December 1982. Mating the ALCM with the B-52G would extend that aircraft's operational life by at least ten years, and the early introduction of the missile would enable the bomber force to shoulder a greater proportion of the Triad responsibility (the nuclear triad being the airborne force, the land-based ICBM force and the submarine-launched deterrent) until the advent of the M-X ICBM. In practice, marrying the ALCM with the B-52 was to be neither as simple nor as cheap as President Carter had earlier implied.

With some modifications, ALCM could be carried on the launcher developed for SRAM, so that the two missiles could be operated side by side. The last of 1,500 SRAMs was delivered to the 320th BW at Mather AFB, California, on 20 August 1975.

The requirement to extend the B-52's useful life as a cruise-missile carrier generated a major modification programme designed to sustain the aircraft as a viable weapons system into the 1990s. Modification programmes were by no means unusual for the B-52, but this latest one, the offensive-avionics-system (OAS) retrofit programme, which got under way with a $129 million contract to Boeing Wichita in August 1978, was to be the most expensive to date.

Major structural modifications to the B-52 were begun in 1964, when the type was first adapted for low-level operations, and continued at intervals thereafter. In 1975–7, under a programme called Pacer Plank, eighty B-52Ds each had 30,000lb of original structure removed and replaced, including new upper and lower wing skins, rebuilt wing leading- and trailing-edge structures, reinforced cockpit windows, modified engine nacelle fairings and large areas of fuselage skinning. Pacer Plank cost $208 million and added about 3,400lb (1,542kg) to the all-up weight of each aircraft, mainly through the specification of thicker skins and the substitution of aluminium for many magnesium components. At the same time, all B-52Gs and Hs were fitted with cartridge starters which could be fired to start all engines simultaneously, reducing the start-up time by two minutes.

The aircraft also underwent numerous systems modifications, including one called Rivet Ace. This began in 1974 and added new ECM sets, designated as Phase IV equipment. The most notable external feature which appeared on the B-52 in the 1970s was the electro-optical viewing system (EVS), which was fitted to all B-52Gs and Hs between June 1973 and early 1976. This featured steerable Westinghouse AVQ-22 low-light TV sensors and Hughes forward-looking infrared sensors, housed in nose blisters and designed to give the degree of visibility needed to maintain an accurate flight path and to designate waypoints and targets during low-level attack. The data from either sensor was shown on a multi-function cathode-ray-tube (CRT) display mounted to the right of the pilot's main instruments.

A B-52H ejects an air-launched cruise missile from its weapons bay during trials over the White Sands Missile Range, New Mexico, in 1976.

The OAS was intended to be fitted to all 96 B-52Hs and 173 B-52Gs in SAC service in 1979, under an ongoing programme that was to cover the best part of a decade. The overall aim was to improve navigation and weapon-aiming accuracy by at least 30–40 per cent. All OAS-modified B-52s were to receive new sensors, excluding the main radar. The programme included modifications to the Raytheon ASQ-38 forward-looking radar, the addition of a new Teledyn Ryan Doppler downward-looking radar and a Honeywell radar altimeter, the latter being linked to a TERCOM unit, and a Honeywell AN/ASN-131 gimballed electrostatic aircraft-navigation system. Other equipment included an IBM central avionics computer and new Sperry navigational-control and display equipment. Three systems operators would be retained, giving a six-man crew of pilot, copilot, navigator, radar navigator, ECM operator and gunner. All of the OAS-modified B-52s were also to be fitted with new ECM equipment, including the Westinghouse AN/ALQ-153 tail warning radar and the Northrop AN/ALQ-155 ECM suite.

In conjunction with the OAS programme, SAC's B-52G force was to be modified to carry the ALCM, the first sixteen-aircraft squadron to be operational by December 1982. The first OAS-modified, ALCM-capable B-52G flew in September 1980 and embarked on a year-long test programme entailing some fifty-eight flights. While this was in progress, the first two AGM-68B ALCMs were delivered to the 416th BW at Griffiss AFB on 11 January 1981, to be used initially for environmental testing and maintenance training. The first OAS-modified B-52G was delivered to the 416th BW on 15 August 1981, and a month later a crew of

this unit conducted the first ALCM training flight, a 9hr mission designed to gather data on the aircraft and missile systems. The B-52 was armed with twelve ALCMs carried externally and eight SRAMs in the bomb bay. Operationally, the B-52G would launch its ALCMs from launch points well clear of the enemy coast. The missiles would fly over the sea under their inertial guidance system, sustained at Mach 0.7 by their Williams Research F107-WR-100 turbofan engine and updating their navigation system by means of a TERCOM fix taken soon after crossing the coastline. With a range of 1,400nm (2,594km), the AGM-86B was capable of delivering its 200-megaton W-80 warhead on targets within 85 per cent of Soviet territory.

On 2 October 1981 President Ronald Reagan's new US administration took the decision to resurrect the Rockwell B-1 programme. Between 1977 and 1981 the USAF had used the B-1 prototype in a bomber-penetration evaluation, and this had resulted in a unique opportunity to rate the combat effectiveness of an advanced bomber already cancelled as a production programme, with no pressure to prove the case one way or the other. The conclusion reached was that, with skilled crews and flexible tactics, the bombers were getting through to their targets more often than the computers had predicted, a fact that was firmly presented in a report submitted to Congress early in 1981.

The operational designation of the supersonic bomber, 100 of which were to be built for SAC, was to be B-1B, the prototypes already built now being known as B-1As. The primary mission of the B-1B would be penetration with free-fall weapons, using SRAMs for defence suppression. The aircraft would also be modified

A Rockwell B-1B climbs away from a practice low-level penetration attack run through mountainous terrain.

to carry the ALCM, being fitted with a movable bulkhead between the two forward bomb bays to make room for an eight-round ALCM launcher.

The first B-1B flew in October 1984 and was well ahead of schedule, despite the crash several weeks earlier of one of the two B-1A prototypes taking part in the test programme. The first operational B-1B (83-0065) was delivered to the 96th Bomb Wing at Dyess AFB on 7 July 1985, although it was the fleet prototype, 82-0001, which underwent the SAC acceptance ceremony, the other aircraft having suffered engine damage from ingesting nuts and bolts from a faulty air-conditioner.

Despite a series of problems with avionics and systems, B-1B deliveries to SAC reached a tempo of four per month in 1986. In January 1987 the trials aircraft successfully launched a SRAM for the first time, and in April an aircraft from the 96th BW completed a 21hr 40min mission that involved five in-flight refuellings to maintain a high all-up weight, the aircraft flying at approximately 400kt (741km/h) and covering 8,175nm (15,148km). This operation was in connection with the development of operational techniques involving the carriage of very heavy loads over long distances. Most B-1B missions are flown at high subsonic speeds; the aircraft is fitted with fixed-geometry engine inlets which feed the engines through curved ducts incorporating streamwise baffles, blocking radar reflections from the fan. These reduce the maximum speed to Mach 1.2; the earlier B-1A had external compression inlets and could reach Mach 2.2, but its radar signature was about ten times that of the B-1B.

A good deal of so-called 'stealth' technology has been built into the B-1B, greatly enhancing its prospects of penetrating the most advanced enemy defences. The aircraft carries a phenomenal weapons load, including 84,500lb (38,320kg) of Mk 82 or 24,200lb (10,974kg) of Mk 84 iron bombs in the conventional role, twenty-four SRAMs, twelve B-28 and B-43 or twenty-four B-61 and B-83 free-fall nuclear bombs, eight ALCMs on internal rotary launchers and fourteen more on underwing launchers, and various combinations of other underwing stores. Low-level operations are flown with internal stores.

Formidable though the B-1B undoubtedly is as a weapons system, it was the venerable B-52 that went into action during the Gulf War of 1991, carrying out saturation attacks from high levels against Iraqi forces in Kuwait (which it was able to do with impunity once the threat of Iraqi SAMs and fighters had been eliminated). At the time of writing, the operational career of Boeing's strategic jet bomber seems set fair to span half a century, a tribute to what can be achieved by the constant upgrading of airframe, engines and systems.

The development of strategic bombers in the former Soviet Union had followed roughly the same lines as that in the USA, although on a smaller scale. At the annual air display held at Tushino, on the outskirts of Moscow, on 9 July 1961, Western observers were startled to see what appeared to be the prototype of a Soviet four-engined supersonic bomber, which flew overhead flanked by MiG-21 fighters. The aircraft was in fact the Myasishchyev M-52. Western intelligence had known about it for some time (the NATO code name *Bounder* had already been allocated to it), but it was an experimental one-off, and it never went into production. On the other hand, an operational supersonic jet bomber did make its debut at Tushino in 1961. This was the Tupolev Tu-22 *Blinder*, designed as a supersonic successor to the *Badger*. The Tu-22s seen at Tushino were pre-series trials aircraft, and first deliveries of the type to the *Dalnaya Aviatsiya* (Soviet Strategic Air Force) would not be made until the following year. The first operational version, codenamed *Blinder*-A, was pro-

The Myasishchyev M-52 Bounder *experimental high-speed bomber at Tushino on 9 July 1961, escorted by a MiG-21.*

122

Tupolev's Tu-22 Blinder *was the Soviet Union's first operational supersonic jet bomber.*

duced in limited numbers only, its range of about 1,400nm (1,853km) falling short of planned strategic requirements. The second variant, *Blinder*-B, was equipped with a flight-refuelling probe.

The original Russian bomber trio of the 1950s, the Myasishchyev M-4 *Bison*, Tupolev Tu-16 *Badger* and Tupolev Tu-95 *Bear*, continued to form the backbone of the Soviet strategic bomber fleet, and in the early 1960s their operational capability was greatly enhanced by the deployment of the first Soviet air-to-surface missiles (ASMs). The earliest such missile, the KS-1 *Komet* – a

large, unwieldy weapon resembling a pilotless, scaled-down MiG-15 – had in fact been deployed since 1957 with the Naval Air Force, where it equipped anti-shipping *Badgers*. The second Soviet ASM, the K-10 *Kipper*, first seen at Tushino in 1961, was larger still and also resembled a scaled-down aircraft. Like its predecessor it was powered by a single turbojet and had a relatively short range of about 100nm (185km). It had a very large conventional warhead and was also primarily an anti-shipping weapon, cruising at about Mach 1.2 and then entering a Mach 2 dive on to its target.

The Myasishchev M-4 Bison *was not a success as a strategic bomber, and was later converted to undertake the electronic intelligence role. This is a 3M* Bison *on a surveillance mission over the North Atlantic.*

The Soviet Union's first really viable strategic jet bomber was the Tupolev Tu-16 Badger.

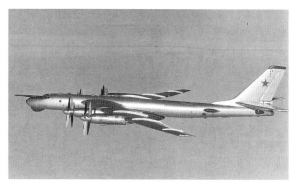

A Tupolev Tu-95 Bear *on an intelligence-gathering mission over the North Atlantic.* Bears *regularly deployed from their Murmansk bases to Cuba.*

If the AS-2 was large, the Kh-20 *Kangaroo* was massive. It, too, made its appearance at Tushino in 1961, slung under a *Bear*, and its large size indicated that it had a nuclear warhead. Its range was estimated at about 400nm (740km). *Kangaroo*'s swept-wing configuration appeared to owe a great deal to an experimental lightweight fighter design of 1956, the MiG Ye-2A. Yet another disclosure at the 1961 Soviet Aviation Day was the AS-4 *Kitchen*, a supersonic delta-wing ASM that appeared recessed beneath the fuselage of one of the ten *Blinders* that took part. This, too, appeared to be an anti-ship weapon.

In 1969 US intelligence estimated that the Soviet air and naval forces still had 150 strategic bombers deployed,

with about 230 warheads at their disposal. Most of these were free-falling weapons, the *Bison* and *Bear* reportedly being able to carry four 8-megaton weapons each, but their vulnerability was such that they would be unlikely to survive a nuclear mission in a hostile environment.

However, the day of the manned strategic bomber in the USSR was not over. In 1969 American satellite reconnaissance identified the prototype of a new variable-geometry bomber at Tupolev's manufacturing plant at Kazan in central Asia. Designated the Tu-26 (also known as the Tu-22M) *Backfire*, the bomber reached initial operational capability (IOC) in 1973 and, during the years that followed, replaced the Tu-16 *Badger* in Soviet service. *Back-*

A Tu-16 in service with the Indonesian Air Force, armed with two AS-1 Kennel *air-to-surface missiles.*

A Tu-95 Bear *carrying a Kh-20* Kangaroo, *the largest-ever production air-to-surface missile.*

fire is supersonic and, with afterburning, can reach a ceiling of 62,000ft (18,910m). It can be armed with either conventional or nuclear weapons, and although according to the Russians its primary mission is 'to perform peripheral (non-strategic) attack and naval missions', with in-flight refuelling it undoubtedly has a strategic capability.

Russia's supersonic four-engined strategic bomber, the Tupolev Tu-160 *Blackjack*, began flight-testing in 1982, and was deployed operationally from 1989.

Somewhat larger than the American B-1, *Blackjack* carries four AS-15 *Kent* (Russian designation RK-55) subsonic, 1,000nm (1,850km)-range cruise missiles, which also arm the Tu-142 *Bear* H. The Tu-142 carries six RK-55s on an internal rotary launcher, but it can be configured to carry an additional two under each wing root and a cluster of three between each pair of engines, making a total of sixteen.

In modern air warfare the dividing line between strategic and tactical air power has become somewhat blurred, with strategic aircraft sometimes being used in

The Tu-22M Backfire *strategic bomber gave the Soviet Navy the capability to attack NATO shipping at long range.*

Russia's answer to the USA's B-1 was the Tupolev Tu-160 Blackjack *variable-geometry supersonic bomber.*

a tactical role. The saturation bombing of Iraqi troops by B-52s in the Gulf War is just one example. But one aircraft type in particular will have a clearly defined strategic role in the twenty-first century. This is the Northrop B-2 Spirit strategic penetration bomber, the embodiment of 'stealth' technology pioneered operationally by the Lockheed F-117A fighter-bomber.

Development of the B-2 was begun in 1978 and the USAF originally wanted 133, but by 1991 successive budget cuts had reduced the requirement to just twenty-one aircraft. The first B-2 (880329) was delivered to the 393rd Bomb Squadron of the 509th Bomb Wing at Whiteman AFB, Missouri, on 17 December 1993, with a second squadron, the 715th BS, also scheduled to be equipped with bomber, bringing the 509th BW's establishment up to sixteen aircraft.

The B-2, which is powered by four 17,300lb st General Electric F118-GE-100 non-afterburning turbofans, has two weapons bays mounted side by side in the lower centrebody, each fitted with a Boeing rotary launcher assembly. The bomb cells can accommodate sixteen AGM-129 Advanced Cruise Missiles, or alternatively sixteen B-61 or B-83 free-fall nuclear bombs, eighty Mk 82 500lb bombs, sixteen Joint Direct Attack Munitions, sixteen Mk 84 2,000lb (906kg) bombs, thirty-six M117 750lb (340kg) fire bombs, thirty-six CBU-87/89/97/98 cluster bombs, and eighty Mk 36 560lb (304kg) or Mk

62 sea mines. With a typical weapons load the B-2 has a range of 6,500nm (12,045km) at high level and 4,400nm (8,153km) at low level.

In designing the Advanced Technology Bomber (ATB), as the B-2 project was originally known, Northrop decided on an all-wing configuration from the outset. Although the company had built and flown the B-49 experimental flying-wing bomber in 1947, this had little influence on the decision to pursue an all-wing solution for the B-2; the all-wing approach was selected because it promised to produce an exceptionally clean configuration for minimising radar cross-section, including the elimination of vertical tail surfaces, with added benefits such as span-loading structural efficiency and a high lift-to-drag ratio for efficient cruise. Outboard wing panels were added for longitudinal balance, to increase lift-to-drag ratio and to provide sufficient span for pitch, roll and yaw control. Leading-edge sweep was selected for balance and transonic aerodynamics, while the overall planform was designed to have neutral longitudinal (pitch) static stability. Because of its short length, the aircraft had to produce stabilising pitch-down moments beyond the stall for positive recovery.

The original ATB design had elevons on the outboard wing panels only, but as the design progressed additional elevons were added inboard, giving the B-2 its distinctive

The Northrop YB-49, designed as a strategic jet bomber in the late 1940s, was a failure, but gave Northrop invaluable experience with flying wings.

Forty years later, Northrop's flying-wing experience was embodied in the B-2 Spirit 'stealth' bomber.

'double-W' trailing edge. The wing leading edge is designed so that air is channelled into the engine intakes from all directions, allowing the engines to operate at high power and zero airspeed. In transonic cruise, air is slowed from supersonic speed before it enters the hidden compressor faces of the General Electric F118 engines.

A stores management processor handles the B-2's 50,120lb (22,730kg) weapons load, and a separate processor controls the Hughes APQ-181 synthetic-aperture radar and its input to the display processor. The Ku-band radar has twenty-one operational modes, including high-resolution ground-mapping. The B-2 lifts off at 140kt (260km/h), the speed being independent of take-off weight. Normal operating speed is in the high subsonic range, and maximum altitude around 50,000ft (15,000m). The aircraft is highly manoeuvrable, with fighter-like handling characteristics.

With the deployment of the B-2, the emphasis has shifted somewhat from deterrence (a concept that might mean little to a hostile government driven, say, by fanaticism of one kind or another) to the ability to carry out quick and effective pre-emptive surgical strikes on targets such as factories producing weapons of mass destruction. The deterrent forces of the Cold War were a guarantee that the world would not be turned into a radioactive wasteland, but now the old controls have gone, and the world is a dangerous place, made more so by perverted religious and scientific dogma. The danger of a nuclear holocaust may have receded with the reduction of the superpowers' arsenals, but its spectre is still there, lurking in a different guise just beyond the horizon.

Interdiction

While the strategic bomber's mission is to strike at the heart of an enemy's industrial and economic infrastructure, the task of the interdictor, striking hard and fast and using precision weapons, is to neutralise command, control and communications. In practice this means military headquarters, radar sites, airfields, supply and ammunition dumps, convoys, and road and rail links, the whole mission being designed to prevent the reinforcement of the battle area.

The basic concept of interdiction is not new. It was used on a large scale for the first time in the spring of 1918, when the Royal Flying Corps (which became the RAF on 1 April that year) launched a massive day-and-night effort to slow down the German offensives on the Somme and Lys by attacking roads, railways and marshalling yards, bridges and other communications bottlenecks. Specialised night interdiction was developed by

One the most successful offensive aircraft of all time was the English Electric Canberra. The American licence-built version, the Martin B-57, is seen here over Vietnam.

the RAF in 1943, using the de Havilland Mosquito, and in the weeks preceding the Allied invasion of Normandy in 1944 the role was assumed by virtually the whole of the Allied strategic air forces, which mounted a massive and successful campaign against the enemy's transportation system. During the Korean War the principal interdictor aircraft was the Douglas B-26C, which afterwards was replaced in this role by the Martin B-57, a licence-built version of Britain's English Electric Canberra. The RAF also used two Canberra variants as interdictors and intruders, the B(I).6 and B(I).8; both carried underwing bomb armament and a ventral gun pack.

The USAF's Martin B-57Bs saw widespread service in Vietnam, beginning interdiction sorties against enemy supplies on the Ho Chi Minh Trail in April 1965. These missions were carried out in conjunction with Lockheed C-130 or Fairchild C-123 flare ships and the Douglas EF-10B Skyknight electronic warfare aircraft. The highly specialised B-57G evolved from these operations. This aircraft, barely recognisable as a Canberra variant, carried a low-light-level TV system, forward-looking infrared (FLIR) equipment and a laser guidance system, all of which were operated by a systems specialist in the aircraft's rear seat. The relevant information was fed by the systems operator into a computer and was displayed in the pilot's cockpit so that he could select the appropriate weapons combination. The modified aircraft could carry the same ordnance as the B-57B, except that the

laser guidance system now made it possible to fit four 500lb 'smart' bombs on its underwing pylons.

The Vietnam War saw the combat debut of an aircraft that has become synonymous with interdiction; the General Dynamics F-111. The development history of the F-111, which is still one of the world's most potent combat aircraft, and was years ahead of its time in terms of technology, goes back to 1962, when the General Dynamics Corporation, in association with Grumman Aircraft, was selected to develop a variable-geometry tactical fighter to meet the requirements of the USAF's TFX programme. An initial contract was placed for twenty-three development aircraft, including eighteen F-111As for the USAF and five F-111Bs for the US Navy (in the event, the Navy cancelled its order). Powered by two Pratt & Whitney TF30-P-1 turbofans, the prototype F-111A flew for the first time on 21 December 1964, and during the second flight on 6 January 1965 the aircraft's wings were swept through the full range from 16° to 72.5°.

In total, 160 production F-111As were built, the first examples entering service with the 480th Tactical Fighter Wing (TFW) at Nellis AFB, Nevada, in October 1967. On 17 March the following year six aircraft from this unit flew to Takhli AFB in Thailand for operational evaluation in Vietnam (Operation 'Combat Lancer'), making their first sorties on 25 March. The operation ended unhappily when three of the aircraft were lost as a result of metal fatigue in a control rod, but the prob-

The General Dynamics F-111A, shown here in typical Tactical Air Command camouflage and with wings fully swept, first saw action over Vietnam.

lem was rectified and in September 1972 the F-111As of the 429th and 430th Tactical Fighter Squadrons were deployed to Takhli and performed very effective service in the closing air offensive of the war ('Linebacker II'), attacking targets in the Hanoi area at night and in all weathers through the heaviest anti-aircraft concentrations in the history of air warfare.

The F-111E variant, which superseded the F-111A in service, featured modified air intakes to improve performance above Mach 2.2. Re-equipment of the 20th TFW at Upper Heyford in the UK was completed in the summer of 1971, and the unit was assigned the war role of interdicting targets deep inside hostile territory as part of NATO's 2nd Allied Tactical Air Force (ATAF). The other UK-based F-111 TFW was the 48th; based at Lakenheath in Suffolk, it was assigned to 4th ATAF in its war role and had the ability to interdict targets as far away as the Adriatic. The 48th TFW was armed with the F-111F, a fighter-bomber variant combining the best features of the F-111E and the FB-111A (the strategic bomber version) and fitted with the more powerful TF30-F-100 engines. The 48th TFW's aircraft were equipped to carry two B43 nuclear stores internally, as well as a variety of ordnance on six wing hardpoints, and formed the core of NATO's theatre nuclear strike force.

In the conventional role the F-111F's primary precision-attack weapon system was the Pave Tack self-contained pod containing a laser designator, rangefinder and FLIR equipment for use with laser-guided bombs such as the 2,000lb (906kg) Mk 82 Snakeye, the GBU-15 TV-guided bomb or the Maverick TV-guided missile. The Pave Tack pod was stowed inside the

An FB-111A armed with the short-range attack missile.

F-111's weapons bay in a special cradle which rotated through 180° to expose the sensor head when the system was activated. The sensor head provided the platform for the FLIR seeker, the laser designator and rangefinder, so that the weapons system operator (WSO) was presented with a stabilised infrared image, together with range information, on his display.

As the F-111 ran in at low level towards its target the WSO's primary display showed a radar ground map which enabled major course corrections to be made. All the information from the aircraft's systems was processed by a CP-2A digital computer, which presented it to the crew in intelligible form. The aircraft's General Electric APQ-113 multi-mode radar operated in the J-band; as well as providing accurate air-to-ground navigation, it also supplied ranging and weapon-delivery facilities, and in the air-to-air role it could track and scan hostile targets and control the aiming and launch of defensive Sidewinder AAMs.

The WSO activated Pave Tack at a range of about four miles from the target. This provided more accurate steering information, and at the same time the infrared image appeared on the display. After selecting the correct infrared field of view the WSO centred a reticule on the target and fired the laser, which was kept in target by the F-111's inertial navigation system even when the aircraft was taking violent evasive action to avoid enemy defences. The WSO used a hand controller to fine-tune the laser's line of sight. With the laser illuminating the target, the F-111's CP-2A computer initiated a pull-up and automatically released the weapons at the optimum height for an accurate toss-delivery attack. As the aircraft turned away from the target, Pave Tack's sensor head rotated so that it continued to illuminate the target until bomb impact. The pod was then retracted and the 'cleaned-up' F-111, having pulled round hard and dived back to low level, accelerated to supersonic speed for its escape from the target area.

The use of Pave Tack and the F-111's associated weaponry was dramatically demonstrated under operational conditions when, in the early hours of 15 April 1986, F-111Fs of the 48th TFW struck at targets in Libya in a calculated response against a growing tide of international terrorism allegedly being supported by that nation. Fifteen F-111Fs took off from Lakenheath in the UK at 2130hrs on 14 April and were joined by three EF-111 Raven electronic-warfare aircraft. The total length of the outward flight, which was planned to avoid French and Spanish airspace, was 2,800nm (5,188km), and as the F-111F's combat radius with a 6,000lb (2,718kg) bomb load was about 1,000nm (1,583km), three refuelling contacts were required. The first two contacts were made at high level, the F-111s descending to medium level for the third, over the Mediterranean off the Algerian coast.

With this final contact completed, the F-111s descended to low level, turning south at a point to the west of Sicily and bypassing the island of Lampedusa as they headed towards their assigned Libyan targets. There were three of these: the Libyan Air Force side of Tripoli Airport, the Sidi Bilal port facility ten miles west of Tripoli, and the Al Azziziyah barracks in Tripoli itself.

The aircraft tasked with the strike on the airfield and port were armed with Mk 20 Rockeye 500lb (226kg) laser-homing cluster bombs, while those assigned to the attack on the Tripoli barracks area and its associated command centre carried Mk 82 2,000lb (906kg) laser-guided bombs for greater effect against hardened targets. At the same time, fifteen Grumman A-6 Intruders and Vought A-7 Corsairs from two US carriers, also armed with laser-guided weapons, headed in across the Gulf of Sirte to hit two targets near Benghazi: the Al Jumahiriya Barracks, which according to US Intelligence was a backup command centre to the one at Tripoli, and the military airfield at Benina.

Throughout the operation, which was carried out in the face of moderate and disorganised AAA and SAM fire, top cover was provided by US Sixth Fleet F-14 Tomcats and F-18 Hornets, directed by Grumman E-2C Hawkeye command and early warning aircraft. Effective countermeasures were provided by the EF-111 Ravens, and also by US Navy Grumman EA-6 Prowlers. The F-111s flight-refuelled on the way back to the UK; one aircraft failed to return as a result of the operation. Post-strike reconnaissance showed that all the assigned targets had been hit, albeit with a certain amount of collateral damage to civilian property in Tripoli. The UK-based F-111s were also deployed to Turkey during the 1991 Gulf War, using their weaponry to destroy bridge targets in Iraq.

The F-111's successor in the interdiction role is the McDonnell Douglas F-15E Strike Eagle, the attack version of the air superiority fighter, which played a major role in the Gulf War and proved what the F-111 had already demonstrated six years earlier: that modern combat aircraft can deliver precision-guided weapons on to heavily defended point targets. One of the F-15E's primary tasks in Operation 'Desert Storm' was to seek out and destroy Iraqi *Scud* missiles at night, working in conjunction with the Boeing E-8 joint surveillance target-attack radar system (J-Stars). Developed from the Boeing 707 airliner, the E-8 carries very advanced surveillance systems to detect second-echelon ground concentrations deep behind enemy lines. The aircraft's computers then broadcast target information to both ground and air forces, directing tactical and strike aircraft, missile strikes or artillery fire as required. Once the E-8 had located an objective, the F-15E's WSO would use the aircraft's low-altitude navigation-and-targeting-infrared-for-night (LANTIRN) sensor to pin-

An F-15E with prototype LANTIRN pods and conformal fuel tanks under test by McDonnell Douglas in 1987.

point the missile and its launcher and destroy them.

Developed by Martin Marietta, LANTIRN comprises two pods, one for navigation and one for targeting. The AAQ-13 navigation pod contains a FLIR sensor and a terrain-following radar, while the AAQ-14 targeting pod houses a steerable FLIR, laser designator and missile boresight correlator. The navigation FLIR enables the crew to maintain high speeds at night and at low altitude, beneath bad weather. Infrared images of the terrain ahead of the aircraft are projected on to the pilot's Kaiser wide-angle HUD; compared with the F-15C's HUD, the F-15E display has a wider field of view – 20° in elevation by 30° in azimuth – made possible by holographic optics.

The navigation pod's Ku-band terrain-following radar enables the crew to avoid obstacles while flying at high speeds and low altitudes. The pilot can manually follow commands displayed on the HUD, or alternatively couple LANTIRN to the digital automatic flight-control system for 'hands-off' terrain-following at altitudes down to 200ft (60m) at speeds up to 520kt (960km/h). The companion targeting pod contains a high-resolution stabilised, steerable FLIR for target-acquisition and tracking at ranges greater than 8nm (18km). A laser boresighted to the FLIR designates targets for precision-guided weapons. Alternatively, a missile boresight correlator can hand off targets to imaging infrared Maverick missiles. The F-15E/LANTIRN system was tested and evaluated during Operation 'Desert Storm' and produced some spectacular results. Although the primary targets were *Scuds*, command and control links, armour, airfields, roads and chemical, biological and nuclear weapons storage areas were also attacked in the course of more than 2,200 sorties, and only two of the forty-eight F-15Es deployed were lost. While flying night-time anti-*Scud* patrols, the aircraft usually flew in two- or four-ship elements, covering a large patrol area.

The F-15E concept arose out of a USAF requirement, identified in 1982, for a new long-range interdiction aircraft, and the first of 200 production examples flew for the first time in December 1986. The F-15E is powered by two Pratt & Whitney F100-229 engines producing 29,000lb (130kN) of thrust, enough power to enable it to dogfight with types such as the MiG-29 and Su-27. The aircraft is stressed to withstand 9g at combat gross weight, and its weapon system can be reconfigured from air-to-ground to air-to-air mode at the flick of a switch. For air combat the F-15E can carry four AIM-7F/M Sparrow radar-guided AAMs and four AIM-9L/M Sidewinders, or up to eight AIM-20 AMRAAMs; a 20mm M61A1 six-barrel Gatling gun with a 512-round magazine is mounted in the starboard wing root. The F-15E can also carry a wide variety of 'smart' weapons, including GBU-10, -12 and -24 laser-guided bombs, BBU-15 glide bombs, GBU-28 laser-guided penetration bombs (developed in only seventeen days during the Gulf War to destroy Iraqi bunkers) and AGM-65 Maverick missiles.

The F-15E's radar is the Hughes APG-70, a development of the APG-63 installed in earlier-model F-15s. While retaining the APG-63's air-to-air capability, the APG-70 has a synthetic-aperture, high-resolution mapping mode. Terrain maps of near-photographic resolution are 'drawn' during rapid radar sweeps up to 45° either side of the flight path, and these can be 'frozen' on the cockpit displays for navigation and targeting purposes, minimising the risk of radar emissions being detected. The aircraft can lift a maximum warload of 24,500lb (11,113kg) and has a maximum range of 2,400nm (4,450km); maximum combat radius is 685nm (1,270km).

NATO's other principal interdiction aircraft since the early 1980s has been the IDS (Interdictor/Strike) version of the variable-geometry Panavia Tornado, which resulted from a 1960s requirement for a strike-and-reconnaissance aircraft capable of carrying a heavy weapons load and of penetrating all foreseeable defensive systems by day and night and in all weathers. It needed to be endowed with an excellent low-level performance and to be capable of hitting a pinpoint target, such as a bridge, in a single pass, for which it would need to be equipped with the most advanced avionics.

Three European nations – Britain, West Germany and Italy – participated in the Multi-Role Combat Air-

craft (MRCA) programme, as it was originally known, and a consortium of companies was formed under the name of Panavia. In November 1969 the MRCA was adopted as a NATO programme, and in July 1970 Britain and West Germany signed a Memorandum of Understanding to launch development, Italy joining the programme officially in October.

The first of nine Tornado IDS prototypes flew on 14 August 1974, by which time the aircraft's roles had been clearly defined as nuclear strike, counter-air (airfield attack), interdiction, close air support, tactical reconnaissance and maritime strike. The aircraft itself would remain constant for these varying missions; only the weapons fit would change.

Aside from tactical nuclear weapons – the British WE177 tactical nuclear bomb – the Tornado IDS carries a wide range of conventional armaments up to a total weapons load of 16,000lb (7,248kg). One of its principal systems is the Hunting Engineering JP233 airfield-attack-weapon system, comprising two disposable airborne dispensers, the first housing thirty cratering submunitions and the second area-denial mines, the idea being to produce a line of craters overlaid by a minefield, thereby destroying runways and taxiways and denying repair personnel access to the runway. The system was used during the Gulf War to neutralise several key Iraqi airfields, but the RAF Tornado crews using it suffered heavy losses in percentage terms compared with the other Allied strike forces. The Tornado/JP233 combination had been developed for operations in

A Tornado IDS discharges runway-cratering and area-denial submunitions from its JP233 dispensers.

A chaff and flare dispenser on the outboard underwing pylon of a No 617 Squadron Tornado GR.1 at RAF Marham, Norfolk.

Europe, where factors such as variable weather (which for much of the time would preclude accurate bombing from medium altitude) and the need to minimise exposure to Warsaw Pact air-defence radars and fighters had led to the RAF and most other NATO air forces adopting techniques of low-level penetration and attack. In Iraq it was the Tornados that consequently came under the most intense AAA and short-range SAM fire. With longer-range SAMs and enemy fighters neutralised in the first days of the war, other strike aircraft, bombing from medium level, were far less vulnerable.

Medium-level attacks by Tornados carrying laser-guided bombs had to be carried out in conjunction with Buccaneer aircraft fitted with the Pave Spike laser designator pod, a twenty-year-old system that had no thermal imaging and could therefore only be used by day. At a later date Tornado was equipped with a system called thermal-imaging airborne laser designator (TIALD), manufactured by GEC Marconi Avionics. The first two TIALD pods (known affectionately to their RAF operators as 'Sandra' and 'Tracey') were used operationally in the latter stages of the Gulf War. In the course of 91 sorties against hardened aircraft shelters, 229 direct hits were obtained.

That record was bettered by only one other interdictor used in the Gulf War; the Lockheed F-117A 'stealth' aircraft. The F-117A is a single-seat, subsonic strike, defence-suppression and tactical-reconnaissance aircraft, powered by two General Electric F404 turbofans with shielded exhausts designed to dissipate heat emissions and so minimise the aircraft's infrared signature. The use of faceting (angled flat surfaces) in its construction scatters incoming radar energy, while radar-absorbent materials and transparencies treated with conductive coating further reduce the F-117A's radar profile.

The Gulf War vindicated the USAF's enormous expenditure in stealth technology. The twenty or so F-117As deployed to Saudi Arabia during the crisis bombed all their assigned targets on the first night of offensive operations. These were mostly command, control and communications centres in built-up areas,

The Lockheed F-117A Nighthawk 'stealth' fighter-bomber in flight.

which had to be bombed accurately and with minimum collateral damage. Pilots made good use of their aircraft's ability to remain undetected in the target area for lengthy periods while targets were verified. As the air campaign progressed, the F-117As crippled Iraq's nuclear and biological weapons production facilities.

Defence suppression: the 'Wild Weasels'

Interdictor aircraft have to contend with an enormous variety of defensive systems arrayed against them before they reach their target areas. In breaking through this barrier they are assisted by a concept which, like so many others, was born in the Vietnam War: the anti-radar 'Wild Weasel' aircraft.

From mid-1965 onwards, USAF and USN strike aircraft operating over North Vietnam faced one of the most formidable air-defence systems ever devised: a massive array of AAA guns, automatic weapons, SAMs and a modern interceptor force. As a result, an electronic war developed between US tactical aircraft and the enemy's electronic defence layers, with Douglas EB-66 and EF-10 electronic warfare aircraft combining with F-100s or F-105s to detect emissions from an enemy *Fan Song* radar, indicating that the launch of an SA-2 *Guideline* SAM was imminent, and then destroying the installation with bombs or missiles. Aircraft tasked with these operations were given the codename 'Wild Weasels'.

The lessons of Vietnam led to the provision of airborne equipment to fulfil the defence-suppression role, and the modification of aircraft to carry it. The requirement was for an aircraft that was in effect a self-contained weapons system, capable of carrying both the necessary electronics and the weaponry to hit enemy radars effectively. The McDonnell F-4 Phantom was the best choice available; 'Wild Weasel' trials were carried out with two F-4Ds in 1968, but later studies showed that the F-4E variant was easier to modify. Consequently, USAF funding was obtained to convert 116 F-4Es to F-4G standard under the Advanced 'Wild Weasel' programme. Modifications included a torpedo-shaped fairing on top of the fin to house an APR-47 radar antenna, which was also carried on the side of the fin and along the upper surface of the fuselage. The F-4E's M61A1 cannon was removed to make space for the installation of the computer systems associated with the F-4G's sensory radar. With this equipment the F-4G crew could detect, identify and locate hostile radar emissions and select the appropriate weapons system for use against them.

'Wild Weasel' aircraft can operate independently, but more usually they operate as an integral component of a strike force. F-4Gs of the 35th Tactical Fighter Wing, normally based at George AFB in California, operated in support of Allied strike aircraft during Operation 'Desert Storm', using Texas Instruments AGM-88

HARM high-speed anti-radiation missiles. HARM operates in three modes: target of opportunity (TOP), pre-briefed (PB) and self-protect (SP). In the TOP mode its guidance system detects, locates and classifies radar systems and the information is displayed in the cockpit, enabling the crew to launch HARM towards the highest-priority target. In the PB mode, threat radar locations are loaded into the weapon's computer before the mission. After a predetermined stand-off launch position has been reached, possibly in the target's blind zones, the missile can be launched in the general direction of the objective. On attaining a pre-set altitude it scans ahead, identifies radar emissions corresponding to those stored in the computer, and attacks, homing directly on to its objective at Mach 2 plus.

Other anti-radar missiles, such as the British Aerospace air-launched anti-radar missile (ALARM), have different attack profiles. ALARM is intended for use in conjunction with attacks on targets whose radar defences are well documented. Before a planned attack the weapon would be programmed on the ground with a library of radar signatures, enabling its seeker to compare and identify the signals it receives, and a list of target radars arranged in order of priority according to the threats most likely to be encountered on a particular mission. Armed with these two sets of data, ALARM can be launched without lock-on and without being tuned to a particular threat by the carrier aircraft's radar warning receiver. During development, a digital databus was incorporated into the missile itself, enabling the crew to reprogramme the weapon in flight, an obvious advantage in the event of a change in mission priority.

ALARM's primary mode of operation is indirect attack, which would be used against a heavily defended target. In this, the missile is launched at low level, climbs to around 40,000ft (12,200m) and deploys a parachute,

A Tornado GR.1 carrying British Aerospace ALARM anti-radar missiles.

Fairchild A-10 Thunderbolt IIs display their unusual configuration.

loitering while it searches for radar emissions. It then selects its target, according to threat priority, and dives on it unpowered at high speed. If the radar ceases to transmit, an on-board inertial navigation (INS) guidance system keeps the missile on course. The secondary mode is direct attack, in which the missile is fired towards the target with or without lock-on. If it fails to acquire a target within a predetermined distance it climbs to altitude, deploys its parachute and searches for another.

Offensive battlefield air support
The US Army's Air Land Battle Doctrine puts the battlefield air support case quite simply:

> The best results are obtained when powerful blows are struck against critical units or areas whose loss will degrade the coherence of enemy operations in depth, and thus most rapidly accomplish the mission. From the enemy's point of view, these operations must be rapid, unpredictable, violent and disorientating. The pace must be fast enough to prevent him from taking effective actions.

During the Vietnam War it became apparent to the Americans that they had a serious lack of an aircraft designed specifically for ground attack and close support. The immediate result was a series of stopgap measures (which in practice worked quite well), involving the use of aircraft such as the North American T-28 trainer and the Douglas A-1 Skyraider. What NATO urgently needed, however, was a modern ground-attack aircraft for use in the European environment against a massive assault by Warsaw Pact armour; an aircraft that could destroy enemy tanks in all weathers and survive in an environment dominated by SAMs, fighters and the deadly ZSU 23/4 *Shilka* anti-aircraft artillery. Very heavy armour and high manoeuvrability were the essentials of the requirement.

In December 1970 Fairchild Republic and Northrop were each selected to build a prototype of a new close-support aircraft for evaluation under the USAF's A-X programme, and in January 1973 it was announced that Fairchild Republic's contender, the A-10, had been selected. It was to prove one of the most remarkable (and one of the ugliest) combat aircraft ever developed.

Fairchild met the armour requirement by seating the pilot in what was virtually a titanium 'bathtub', resistant to most firepower except a direct hit from a heavy-calibre shell, and added to this a so-called 'redundant structure policy' whereby the pilot could retain control even if the aircraft lost large portions of its airframe, including one of its two rear-mounted engines. The core of the A-10's built-in firepower was its massive GAU-8/A seven-barrel 30mm rotary cannon, which was mounted on the centreline under the forward fuselage. The gun fired up to 4,200 rounds per minute of armour-piercing

A close-up of the A-10, showing the seven-barrel General Electric GAU-8/A 30mm high-velocity, high-energy rotary cannon.

ammunition with a non-radioactive uranium core for greater impact, and was quite capable of destroying a light tank or armoured personnel carrier. The aircraft also had eight underwing and three underfuselage attachments for up to 16,000lb (7,248kg) of bombs, missiles, gun pods and jammer pods, and carried the Pave Penny laser system pod for target designation. It was fitted with very advanced avionics including a central air-data computer, an inertial navigation system and a HUD.

The A-10 was designed to operate from short, unprepared strips less than 1,500ft (457m) long. The operational tactics developed for the aircraft entailed two A-10s giving one another mutual support, covering a swathe of ground two or three miles wide, so that an attack could be quickly mounted by the second aircraft once the first pilot had made his firing pass on the target. The optimum range for engaging a target was 4,000ft (1,220m), the A-10's gunsight being calibrated for this distance. As the highly manoeuvrable A-10's turning circle was 4,000ft (1,220m), this meant that the pilot could engage the target without having to pass over it. A one-second burst of fire would place seventy rounds of 30mm shells on the target, and as a complete 360° turn took no more than sixteen seconds, a pair of

A-10s could bring almost continuous fire to bear. The 30mm ammunition drum carried enough rounds to make ten to fifteen firing passes.

In order to survive in a hostile environment dominated by radar-controlled AAA, A-10 pilots trained to fly at 100ft (30m) or lower, never remaining straight and level for more than four seconds. One of the aircraft's big advantages in approaching the combat zone was that its twin General Electric TF34-GE-100 turbofan engines were very quiet, enabling it to achieve total surprise as it popped up over a contour of the land for weapons release. Attacks on targets covered by AAA involved close co-operation between the two A-10s. While one engaged the target, the other stood off and engaged anti-aircraft installations with its TV-guided Maverick missiles, six of which were normally carried. The A-10 also had a considerable air-to-air capability, the tactic being for the pilot to turn towards an attacking fighter and use coarse rudder to spray it with 30mm shells.

A Russian requirement for an attack aircraft in the A-10 class materialised as the Sukhoi Su-25 *Frogfoot*, which was selected in preference to a rival design, the Ilyushin Il-102. The Su-25 saw considerable operational service during the former Soviet Union's involvement in Afghanistan, and as a result of lessons learned during

The Sukhoi Su-25 Frogfoot, *the Soviet equivalent of the A-10, first saw action in Afghanistan.*

that conflict an upgraded version, the Su-25T, was produced, with improved defensive systems to counter weapons like the shoulder-launched Stinger and Redeye surface-to-air missiles. An infrared jammer was installed in the aircraft's tail, optimised against the Stinger and Redeye frequencies, and measures were taken to reduce the engines' infrared signatures.

Optimised for attacks on armour, the Su-25 is fitted with an electro-optical target-acquisition system. This has a 1° field of view and provides 23× magnification on a cockpit CRT, enabling the pilot to identify and designate the target. The Su-25 carries sixteen anti-armour missiles in two packs of eight launch tubes; the missile's maximum range is 4.3nm (8km). The aircraft is also equipped with a radar-warning receiver capable of carrying out threat evaluation, and can carry two X-58 (AS-11 *Kilter*) anti-radar missiles, one on each inboard wing pylon.

A key element in modern offensive battlefield support is the short take-off, vertical landing (STOVL) aircraft, epitomised by the British Aerospace/McDonnell Douglas Harrier. Although the British were responsible for the early development of this remarkable aircraft, it was the US Marine Corps who identified the need to upgrade their original version, the AV-8A. The Harrier's airframe design and construction, and its systems, used 1950s technology, and by the 1970s, despite systems

updates, this was restricting further development of the aircraft's potential. In developing the USMC's new Harrier variant the basic design concept was retained but new technologies and avionics were fully exploited.

One of the major improvements was a new wing, with a carbonfibre composite structure, a supercritical aerofoil and greater area and span. The wing has large slotted flaps linked with nozzle deflection at short take-off unstick to improve control precision and increase lift. Leading-edge root extensions (LERX) are fitted to enhance the aircraft's air-combat agility by improving the turn rate, while longitudinal fences (LIDS, or lift improvement devices) are incorporated beneath the fuselage and on the gun pods to capture ground-reflected jets in vertical take-off and landing, giving a much bigger ground cushion and reducing hot-gas recirculation.

A prototype AV-8B Harrier II first flew in November 1978, and production deliveries to the USMC began in 1983. Delivery of the RAF's equivalent, the Harrier GR.5, began in 1987, and production GR.5s were later converted to GR.7 standard. This version, generally similar to the USMC's night-attack AV-8B, has FLIR, a digital moving-map display, night-vision goggles for the pilot and a modified HUD.

Although aircraft such as the A-10 and Harrier have provided a vital component of NATO's battlefield support armoury, the search for the optimum ground-attack

A US Marine Corps AV-8B Harrier II releases a pair of Mk 82 retarded bombs.

aircraft is ongoing. Such an aircraft would be capable not only of destroying all types of enemy armour (although that would be its main role), but also of engaging enemy aircraft, battlefield helicopters and remotely piloted vehicles (RPVs). It would have to possess very high agility, which studies made so far have defined as the ability to turn through 180° in five seconds at Mach 0.4. This would enable the small agile battlefield aircraft (SABA) to meet a fighter in the F-16/MiG-29 class head-on and engage it with infrared missiles before the enemy could get out of range. At the same time, SABA would have to transit the battle area at 400–450kt (741–833km/h) to increase its own chances of survival. Other requirements include the ability to operate from an 820ft (250m) rough dirt strip, and an endurance of more than four hours with a full warload.

One of the leading SABA studies was carried out in the late 1980s by British Aerospace, whose designers considered several airframe configurations. These included the P.1238, a pod-and-twin-boom layout powered by a single-disc unducted fan. Its metal airframe was inherently stable, and it would have needed a fly-by-wire system to produce the necessary high agility with carefree handling. Armament was envisaged as six short-range attack missiles, two under each wing and one on each wingtip.

Another was the P.1234-1, designed to be powered by a Rolls-Royce Adour turbofan. Helicopter suppres-

sion was seen as the main role when this design was being studied, and armament comprised two air-to-air missiles and a 25mm cannon in a belly-mounted cupola that could be trained through 360°, the idea being that the aircraft could engage targets throughout a spherical envelope by combining the cannon's 360° traverse and the aircraft's 360° of roll.

A modified design, the P.1234-3, took this concept a stage further. The instantaneous turn rate was calculated to be 40° per second. Instead of a cannon, the turret would fire hypervelocity missiles from two tubes, with about twelve missiles carried internally. These would be aimed by inputs from three sensor turrets, one in the nose and two mounted dorsally on either side of the fuselage waist. The weapon envelope was +/–20° in pitch in the 360° azimuth plane of the aircraft, and a spherical engagement envelope was possible by rolling the aircraft.

The idea was too complex, and the BAe team reverted to a more conventional weapon-launch concept, combining the extremely agile P.1233-1 design with a highly agile dogfight missile. An unducted fan was chosen as the powerplant because of its economical high power, and BAe based performance figures on the Avco-Lycoming T55 engine. A canard layout was chosen for the design because the inflow to the disc would dominate a conventional tailplane. Pitch control was by means of the canards, and yaw control by a forward-mounted ventral rudder. A dorsal air intake was incorporated to reduce the risk of foreign-object damage, while the foreplane and wing vortices would ensure a clean flow to the intake at high angles of attack.

The P.1233 was designed to give a very low radar signature; it would also have been very quiet and hard to detect visually. In addition, it would have had a low infrared signature, reduced still further by the application of anti-IR camouflage paint. The engine exhaust, the primary source of IR detection, was cooled by the airflow and then cooled and dispersed further by passing through the fan.

Fascinating and plausible though SABA and similar projects appeared, they were negated almost overnight by the experience of the Gulf War, when the lion's share of the damage to enemy armour was inflicted by fast jets – Jaguars, Mirage 2000s, F/A-18s and F-16s – carrying out blistering attacks with huge loads of conventional ordnance, rather than smart weapons, from medium altitude after defence-suppression aircraft had dealt with the SAM threat. Furthermore, had the enemy's most modern agile jet fighters appeared to challenge the attacks, most of the attackers were themselves equally as agile, if not more so, and could have fought as air-superiority fighters once their air-to-ground weaponry had been released.

The first priority in achieving successful battlefield support, therefore, is to neutralise the enemy's SAM and radar-controlled AAA systems, leaving the way clear for medium-level attacks – beyond the envelope of small arms and shoulder-launched missiles – by large numbers of fast, agile aircraft armed with substantial warloads and equipped with the necessary targeting systems to deliver those loads with great accuracy in all weathers and at night. In these circumstances they need not be new, costly or even stealthy aircraft, but they must be aircraft whose basic, inherent design is capable of ongoing development to accommodate new equipment and of meeting the evolving demands of air warfare, one of the fundamental tests of a truly successful weapons system.

One such aircraft is the Lockheed Martin F-16 Fighting Falcon. Designed and built by General Dynamics, the F-16 had its origin in a 1972 USAF requirement for a lightweight fighter, and first flew in February 1974. In service with many air arms other than the USAF, it carries an advanced GEC-Marconi HUD-and-weapon-aiming computer system (HUDWACS), in which target designation cues are shown on the HUD as well as flight symbols. The HUDWACS computer is used to direct the weapons to the target, as designated on the HUD. The F-16 HUDWACS shows horizontal and vertical speed, altitude, heading, climb and roll bars, and range-to-go information for flight reference. There are five ground-attack modes and four air-combat modes. In air combat, the 'snapshoot' mode lets the pilot aim at cross-

ing targets by drawing a continuously computed impact line (CCIL) on the HUD. The lead-computing off-sight (LCOS) mode follows a designated target; the dogfight mode combines snapshoot and LCOS; and there is also an air-to-air missile mode.

The F-16's built-in armament is a General Electric M61A1 multi-barrel cannon mounted in the port side wing and fuselage fairing, with provision for 515 rounds of ammunition. The aircraft has a combat radius of up to 866nm (1,604km), depending on the mission profile. There is a mounting for an AIM-9L Sidewinder at each wingtip, an underfuselage centreline hardpoint, and six underwing hardpoints for various stores. All of the hardpoints are stressed for manoeuvres up to 9g, enabling the F-16 to dogfight while still carrying weaponry.

The Fighting Falcon is powered by either a 131.6kN (29,588lb st) General Electric F-110-GE-129 or a 129.4kN (29,100lb st) Pratt & Whitney afterburning turbofan, and can lift many combinations of air-to-surface weapons. A typical stores load might typically include the two wingtip-mounted Sidewinders, four more on the outer underwing stations, a podded GPU-5/A 30mm cannon on the centreline, drop tanks on the inboard underwing and fuselage stations, a Pave Penny laser spot tracker pod along the starboard side of the nacelle and bombs, ASMs and flare pods on the four inner underwing stations. The aircraft can carry advanced beyond-visual-range missiles such as Sparrow and Sky Flash, Maverick ASMs, HARM and Shrike anti-radar missiles, and a weapons dispenser carrying various types of submunition including runway-denial bombs, shaped-charge bomblets, and anti-tank and area-denial mines.

Firmly proven in battle with the US and Israeli air forces, the F-16 has been the subject of almost continual development since it first flew, and this pattern is likely to continue well into the twenty-first century. One of the most exciting proposals entails adapting the aircraft for the uninhabited combat aerial vehicle (UCAV) role; this envisages modifying some of the large number of redundant F-16As held in storage to serve as pilotless long-endurance stand-off weapons carriers. The cockpit and its associated life-support systems would be deleted and a new, almost straight wing would be fitted. This would have a span of 60ft (18.3m), almost double that of the manned F-16, and an area of 533ft² (49.5m²). Internal fuel capacity would be increased to 22,000lb (9,979kg), giving an endurance of eight hours.

The UCAV could be used for battlefield support and strategic interdiction, defence suppression and reconnaissance missions in high-threat areas, remotely controlled by sensory equipment in other aircraft. An additional role might be the interception of ballistic and cruise missiles during their critical launch phase, the aircraft using hypersonic interception weapons.

The French ALAT, using the Sud Alouette fitted with pylon-mounted Nord SS-10 anti-tank missiles, was the first air arm to recognise the value of the helicopter as an attack aircraft.

The Soviets tested the Mil Mi-1 with Falanga anti-tank missiles as early as 1961.

7
The Attack Helicopter
Elfan ap Rees

By the year 2000 the attack helicopter will finally be achieving dominance on the battlefield, making the tank obsolete and replacing the fixed-wing, ground-attack aircraft in terms of close support for the ground forces. It has been a long time coming.

Early production helicopters in the 1940s and at the start of the 1950s were of questionable value as war machines despite their unique capabilities. Performance was so poor that there was a constant wavering between payload and fuel; even the crew was marginal in some missions. Thus the prolonged French war in its colony of Indo-China, the British anti-communist campaign in Malaya and the early days of the Korean conflict saw the helicopter being used primarily for casualty evacuation and transportation, but rarely in an offensive role.

The need to arm helicopters was of course recognised, especially by those in the field, but initially it was more to defend than to attack. Hand-held Bren guns and door-mounted, general-purpose machine-guns were thus introduced, and the US Marine Corps (USMC) even carried out limited trials with strap-on rocket launchers, but it was not until the mid-1950s that formal efforts began to arm the helicopter for the attack role.

By this time French colonial problems were centred in Algeria, where the rugged terrain much favoured the rebel freedom fighters. The French soon realised that helicopters bringing in troops were especially vulnerable during the landing approach or when hovering. After losing three Sikorsky H-19s in as many days, they first attempted to use fixed-wing aircraft to strafe rebel positions in advance of a helicopter assault and then, when that failed, they armed several helicopters as escort ships.

The very first trial in 1955 positioned an armed soldier in a casevac litter on the skids of a Bell 47, but an inevitable shortage of volunteers led, in 1956, to the French Air Force fitting an H-19 with a forward-firing 20mm cannon and two rocket launchers, plus a second 20mm cannon and three machine-guns installed in the cabin. Unfortunately once the ammunition, fuel and essential crew were added, the helicopter could not get airborne. After removing some weapons and experimenting with others, such as an eight-tube rocket launcher, the final choice was one 20mm cannon and two 12.7mm machine-guns on flexible mounts, installed in the cabin doorway. Although this installation was awkward and relatively inaccurate, it served to keep rebel heads down while the accompanying unarmed assault helicopters delivered their loads.

The arrival of the larger and more powerful Sikorsky H-34 in 1957 gave the French Air Force a new opportunity, and a prototype attack version was secretly converted in Algeria for combat trials. Progressive weaponry improvements soon reached the maximum payload. Known as the 'Pirate', this single armed H-34 carried one 20mm cannon, four 73mm three-tube rocket launchers, one 68mm rocket launcher and four reloadable 73mm bazookas, all firing forward, plus one 20mm cannon, two 12.7mm machine-guns and one 75mm machine-gun firing through the cabin door and window openings. Although this was impressive, the field trials soon showed that the helicopter was slow and unwieldy, and eventually the armament of the H-34 'Pirate' conversions standardised on a pintle-mounted 20mm cannon in the doorway and three 12.7mm machine-guns at window openings. All French Air Force H-34s were fitted with the fixed fittings necessary to mount these weapons, allowing a rapid role change in the field from transport to fire-support when required. The Army also tested heliborne weapons on their Piasecki H-21 tandem-rotor helicopter, including eighteen-tube 68mm rocket pods on each side of the fuselage and two machine-guns attached to the forward undercarriage.

The Algerian campaign was especially notable for the introduction of the first helicopter-launched air-to-ground guided missile, of particular value in winkling out rebels positioned in caves and similarly inaccessible mountain locations where shorter-range guns and unguided rockets were less effective. This type of missile had been under development as a ground-based anti-tank weapon since the Second World War, and in France Nord Aviation successfully developed the SS-10 and subsequently the SS-11 for Army use. The SS-10 had a maximum range of a mile (1.6km), travelled at about 186mph (300km/h), and was guided by the operator sending signals down wires to actuate control surfaces inset in the cruciform wing-root trailing edges. Its launch weight was 33lb (15kg). Although relatively basic, the SS-10 was the only anti-tank missile available for helicopter use at the time of its development in the mid-1950s, and could be extremely effective in skilled hands. Not surprisingly, the Aviation Légère de l'Armée de Terre (ALAT) experimented with mounting the SS-10 on the Bell 47G and Sud SO.1221 Djinn, an unusual two-seat helicopter designed primarily for observation and training roles, and using a turbine engine to pressurise air which was then directed via the rotor system to cold-jet effluxes at the blade tips. This system gave the Djinn a rapid rate of climb and excellent performance, but over a limited range and with a limited payload.

In 1956 the arrival of the larger Sud Aviation SE.3130 Alouette II allowed ALAT to begin the deployment of armed attack helicopters on a more permanent basis. The first turboshaft-engined helicopter to enter production, the Alouette II marked a major step in helicopter development. Its light 320lb (145kg) Turboméca Artouste turbine provided some 400shp, compared with 200hp from the Franklin piston engine powering the contemporary and similar-sized Bell OH-13, or 600hp from the Pratt & Whitney radial piston engine in the larger H-19. Much of the weight saved translated straight into more payload and better performance.

The choice of armament for the Alouette II soon settled down to either seventy-two 37mm rockets or four SS-10 missiles, later superseded by the SS-11 variant. The SS-11 had a range of up to 9,840ft (3,000m), at which distance it was still capable of penetrating 0.4in (1cm)-thick armour plate; at closer range it could penetrate 24in (60cm). In action, the operator first acquired the target via a stabilised magnifying optical sight, and then guided the missile on to the target by using a joystick to transmit signals down control wires to the missile. The powerplant was a two-stage, solid-propellant rocket, and directional control was achieved by varying the thrust of the two rocket effluxes. The SS-11 weighed 66lb (29.9kg) at launch and travelled at about 360mph (580km/h), taking about twenty seconds to reach a target at maximum range. By the end of the 1950s the French commanders in Algeria were regularly using the H-34 and Alouette II in an attack role, supporting surprise assaults on rebel camps and attacking positions that fixed-wing aircraft could not reach.

Elsewhere, use of the helicopter in attack operations was proceeding more slowly. In Southeast Asia the Indo-Chinese and Korean conflicts were in a state of uneasy truce, the British campaign in Malaya was virtually over, and there was generally no incentive to accelerate such development. In addition, army field commanders had yet to recognise the helicopter's potential, and the air forces continued to guard their own fixed-wing ground-attack role jealously.

There was some development, however. In the UK, firing trials of the SS-11 missile were carried out using the turbine-engined Westland Whirlwind 10, and in the Soviet Union early efforts to arm the Mil Mi-1 were followed by trials with the Mil Mi-4, fitted with weapons pylons for ground attack, and using rockets and podded machine-guns and a single machine-gun position in a ventral bath tub. In the USA both the Army and the Marine Corps were experimenting with various weapons combinations, including test-firings of SS-11 missiles. By 1963 things were beginning to change rapidly.

The Vietnam War

The catalyst was the involvement of the USA in the second Indo-Chinese conflict, better known as the Vietnam War. United States helicopter forces first arrived in South Vietnam at the end of 1961, and by mid-1962 it had been realised that a dedicated ground-attack helicopter was needed, capable of destroying armour and fortifications as well as soft targets. A US Army study group recommended the development of Air Cavalry combat brigades and the design of a dedicated helicopter to equip them. As an interim step fifteen Bell UH-1A Hueys were modified with 70mm rocket pods and a machine-gun, and issued to a new unit, the Utility Tactical Transport Helicopter Company (UTTCO), established initially at Okinawa in Japan and then deployed in October 1962 to Vietnam, where eleven UH-1Bs were added. The latter aircraft had a more powerful engine, allowing the weapons load to include two 7.62mm M-60C machine-guns in a hydraulically operated turret, installed on an outrigger on each side of the fuselage. The two turrets, aimed by the copilot using a roof-mounted sight, could traverse and elevate together and provided much more firepower than the fixed gun installation in the UH-1A. The rocket pods were retained, the complete armament system being designated M-6C3.

In May 1963 a new weapon system, the XM-3, was introduced on the UH-1B. Replacing both the turrets and rocket tubes of the earlier system, the XM-3 introduced two pods of twenty-four rockets each, which could be fired singly, in ripple, or all at once. The following year saw another alternative available, the XM-16, which retained the M-6E3 subsystem but added two XM-158 seven-tube 70mm rocket pods. Also introduced was the M-5 subsystem, which comprised a traversing nose turret containing an M-75 grenade launcher which could fire 40mm rounds at a rate of 220 per minute out to a range of some 4,920ft (1,500m).

While the armed Huey could be very effective, the problem that now began to emerge was one of speed; the heavier gunships were slower than the transport helicopters they were intended to protect. This meant that assault formations had to slow down to match the speed of the gunships and, even worse, had to wait for them to catch up in the event of an en-route attack. The stage was set for another sea change. Following the decision in August 1962 to initiate development of a dedicated attack helicopter to replace the armed Huey, in 1964 the US Army launched its Advanced Aerial Fire Support System (AAFSS) competition, calling for an ambitiously fast, armoured and heavily armed tandem-

The need for ground-attack capability in Vietnam led to early Bell UH-1 Hueys being fitted with rocket pods and fixed forward-firing machine-guns, often supplemented, as seen here, by hand-held firearms.

seat helicopter. Bell, Lockheed and Sikorsky each entered individual designs, based on preliminary studies and research that had been under way for some time.

In Bell's case this dated back to 1958, when the company had first begun to look at ways in which the bulky silhouette and profile of the UH-1 might be reduced and armed to produce a fighter helicopter. The resulting Model D-245 was further developed over the next four years into the D-255 Iroquois Warrior, which retained the dynamic system of the UH-1C Iroquois variant, as well as the basic tailboom and powerplant bay, but introduced a new forward-fuselage section with a stepped tandem cockpit housing the gunner in front of and below the pilot, a ventral ammunition bay and weapons compartment, a nose-mounted gun turret and stub wings able to carry various external loads, including SS-11 missiles and 2.75in rocket pods. Its skid undercarriage was fully retractable. A full-scale mockup of the new helicopter was shown to US Army officials in June 1962, and undoubtedly spurred the AAFSS decision two months later.

In the meantime, Bell test-flew the tandem-seat concept with the Bell 47 Sioux Scout and invested further company funding in its AAFSS entry, the D-262. This incorporated many of the features introduced in the Iroquois Warrior, but to no avail. Bell and Sikorsky, whose S-66 utilised H-3 Sea King dynamics married to a similar low-profile, tandem-seat fuselage, were to lose the AAFSS competition to the more innovative Lockheed AH-56 Cheyenne.

Despite this setback, the engineers at Bell remained convinced that the Iroquois Warrior concept was right, and that there was a need for a less-sophisticated attack helicopter that could be brought into service in a short timescale. Work therefore continued at the company's Fort Worth factory, and in early March 1965 the senior management gave the go-ahead for construction of a single company-funded prototype, the Model 209.

The new design was powered by a single 1,100shp Lycoming T-53L-11 turboshaft engine with a UH-1C main gearbox and tail-rotor-drive system. Its main rotor was the two-blade Model 540 door-hinge design with

The precursor of the dedicated attack helicopter was the very inoffensive and experimental Sioux Scout, developed by Bell from the Model 47G to demonstrate the principle of tandem cockpits, chin turret and stub-wing weapon mounts.

The Sikorsky S-66 was one of several competing designs that failed to get beyond the drawing board in the US Army AAFS competition. A variant retaining the conventional tail rotor was built as the S-67 Black Hawk, but was written off in a crash at the 1974 Farnborough Air Show.

increased chord to improve performance and manoeuvrability, but with the rotor stabiliser bar replaced by a stability-control augmentation system (SCAS). Compared with the UH-1, the fuselage width was slimmed down by 5ft (1.5m). The proposed armament included a 7.62mm Minigun, housed in an Emerson electric nose turret, with 4,000 rounds of ammunition. Each stub wing had a single pylon for the carriage of additional weaponry.

Although Bell had foreseen an Army change of mind and had accelerated construction of the Model 209, the helicopter's first flight, on 7 September 1965, had already been overshadowed by events. A month earlier the US Army had realised the urgency and announced a requirement for an interim gunship helicopter to meet immediate combat needs in Vietnam, with first deliveries by mid-1967. Bell was quick to respond, and proposals were also submitted by Boeing-Vertol, Kaman, Piasecki and Sikorsky. With one exception, however, the competing designs were all armed variants of existing conventional helicopters. By April 1966 the Model 209, already unofficially named the Cobra, had been declared the clear winner and a production order for 110 aircraft plus spares was in the bag.

Designated the AH-1G (in the H-1 Huey series), the first pre-production Cobra differed from the prototype in having a fixed skid undercarriage, larger and strengthened stub wings and a new chin turret. First flown on 15 October 1966, it was followed by a second example five months later. Full production deliveries to the US Army began in June 1967, standardising on the uprated 1,400shp Lycoming T53-L-13 powerplant.

The AH-1G's initial armament included the TAT-102A tactical armament turret, developed by Emerson Electric and housing a GAU-2B/A Minigun six-barrel 7.62mm machine-gun, with 8,000 rounds. This turret was later superseded by the XM-28 sub-system in a TAT-141 turret mounting two Miniguns with 4,000 rounds each, or two XM-129 40mm grenade launchers, each with 300 rounds, or one Minigun and one XM-129. Structural provision was made to enable the airframe to accept a turret subsystem capable of firing the M-61A1 20mm Vulcan gun, the XM-197 three-barrel 20mm gun, or a three-barrel 30mm gun. Four external store attachments under the stub wings could accommodate various loads, including a total of seventy-six 2.75in rockets in four SM-159 packs, and two SM-18 or XM-18E1 Minigun pods. In normal operation the copilot/gunner controlled and fired the turret armament, using a hand-held pantograph-mounted sight to which the turret was slaved. The TAT-102 turret could be fired throughout a field of 230°, 50° down and 21° up, and the TAT-141

The arrival of the AH-1 in Vietnam saw the first operational use of a dedicated attack helicopter on the battlefield.

could be fired throughout 115°, 60° and 25° respectively. The crew was protected by armoured seats, side panels and a windscreen, and other panels protected vital areas such as the engine compressor.

Operational deployment of the Cobra in Vietnam began in September 1967, when the 1st Platoon 334th Armed Helicopter Company re-equipped, replacing the armed UH-1s which had served since the unit's origin as UTTCO in July 1962. Although it took a while for the crews to adjust to the performance and other advantages of the AH-1G, the firepower it was able to bring to bear gave the US Army a distinct aerial advantage for the remaining years of the Vietnam War. Total orders for this variant were to reach 1,126 by 1971, and new tactics were developed to maximise effectiveness and minimise the risk to the helicopter. Steep dives from a relatively high altitude were the favoured method, attacking at right angles to friendly ground forces whenever possible, to avoid fratricide. In this way a crew could accurately place machine-gun fire and rockets within 164–229ft (50–70m) of their own troops, even down to 33ft (10m) when necessary.

Despite the Cobra's success in Vietnam, it remained deficient in two respects. The first was the lack of all-weather and night-vision aids. The US Army did experiment with the latter, developing the Nighthawk system in 1965, which comprised a Xenon searchlight, with both infrared or white light, mounted in the cabin of a UH-1 and accompanied by a starlight telescope as a night-observation device. Escorting gunships attacked any target illuminated by the searchlight or detected by the telescope. Later, in November 1969, three Iroquois Night Fighter and Night Tracker (INFANT) systems were tested by the 1st Cavalry Division. Installed in a UH-1H, INFANT comprised a low-light television with an infrared searchlight, inte-

grated with the M-21 armament subsystem. The trials were successful enough to warrant the formation of four INFANT platoons, equipped with the UH-1M, but development did not go further.

The second deficiency was the lack of anti-tank armament. Again trials had been under way, initially evaluating the UH-1 with the French SS-11 missile and then developing and testing a new tube-launched, optically tracked, wire-guided (TOW) missile. Originally designated XMGM-7A and initially developed by Hughes Aircraft for ground forces, the TOW system consisted of a lightweight missile powered by a two-stage, solid-propellant motor, housed in a tubular glass-fibre launcher and guided via electronic signals down two wires connected to the missile's control surface actuators. With a range of 4,100yds (3,750m), TOW was successfully ground-fired against tank-size targets in September 1965 and was ordered into production at the end of 1968. Airborne firing trials were carried out concurrently, and during the late 1960s Hughes developed a three-missile TOW pack as the XM-26 missile-launcher-sight subsystem intended for the Cheyenne, with a gyro-stabilised tracking sight to eliminate the effects of aircraft vibration and manoeuvring.

In Vietnam the TOW missile made its first appearance in 1971, when two UH-1B trials aircraft were hurriedly airlifted to the war zone in April 1972 to help counter the surprise introduction of Soviet tanks by the North Vietnamese during a push southwards through the Vietnamese highlands. The first missile was launched in anger on 2 May against a captured American M-41 tank during a battle at Kontum. Over the next five weeks eighty-one TOW missiles were fired and fifty-seven targets destroyed, including twenty-four tanks. During the same period six UH-1Ms armed with the SS-11 fired twenty missiles against just three tanks,

The M-22 anti-tank missile system, introduced on a limited number of Hueys, featured Nord SS-11 missiles mounted on stub pylons on either side of the rear fuselage.

destroying two and damaging one. The success with TOW was to encourage the US Army to arm the Cobra with this system after Vietnam.

The Vietnam experience put the attack helicopter firmly on the tactical map. It spawned a new family of weaponry, and formed the basis for the USA's development of next-generation helicopters during the 1970s.

Enter the *Hind*

In the Soviet Union the early trials with the Mi-1 and Mi-4, armed with guns, rockets and Falanga anti-tank missiles, gave way in the late 1960s to a definitive variant of the Mi-4, armed with the K4V helicopter weapons system. This included a 12.7mm machine-gun in the ventral pod, and outriggers carrying four Falanga M missiles plus ninety-six C-5 rockets in six pods. Some 130 Mi-4s were rebuilt to this configuration, pending the introduction of the new Mil Mi-8TB variant in 1975, which mounted the same system.

Meanwhile, Mil was also developing a more dedicated attack version of the Mi-8 under the 'air infantry combat vehicle' concept. This envisaged an armoured troop carrier also capable of carrying heavy weapons, including guns and anti-tank missiles. The concept therefore differed considerably from the emerging American attack-helicopter doctrine, pointing instead towards a fast and powerful armoured helicopter, capable of inserting combat troops into a defended area and of using its own weapons to suppress enemy fire. By 1969 this project had progressed to the manufacture of the first prototype Mi-24, which used the dynamic components of the Mi-8, including two 1,700shp Isotov TV12-117 engines, married to a revised fuselage incorporating an eight-seat cabin, a side-by-side 'glasshouse' cockpit and a straight stub wing with four pylons able to carry rocket pods or 500kg bombs. Launchers for four Falanga missiles were attached under the fuselage, and a 12.7mm machine-gun was mounted in the nose.

First flown on 19 September 1969, this first Mi-24 was followed by an initial evaluation batch which revealed the need for several modifications. These included the adoption of a 16°-anhedral stub wing to overcome dutch roll, a longer nose section and relocation of the Falanga missile mountings to the wingtips, where the missiles were less likely to foul the underwing pylons on launch. The next batch of aircraft, designated Mi-24A *Hind*, incorporated these changes, and some 250 were built for use by the Soviet Air Force, to develop new tactics and to gain experience of attack-helicopter operations.

Meanwhile, the Mil Design Bureau was continuing to test the next Mi-24 variant with new weapons, including Falanga-P missiles and the semi-automatic Raduga-F guidance system, the Yakushev-Borsov four-barrel

YakB-12.7mm machine-gun and the KPS-53A stabilising sight mechanism. Two prototypes, designated Mi-24B, were used for these trials during 1971–2, but development was then interrupted when pilots complained of the bad view from the second pilot position and the poor field of view for the Raduga-F. At the beginning of 1971, therefore, the Mil designers began a redesign of the nose section, with new separated pilot cockpits, over-pressurised for operation in a nuclear/biological/chemical (NBC) environment. The second problem was solved by relocating the Raduga-F under the nose.

The bureau planned to install the new *Shturm* anti-tank-missile system on this variant, initially designated Mi-24V, but tests of the new system were still delayed, and instead the new version was tested with the Mi-24B weapons system. This half-Mi-24B/half-Mi-24V modification was designated Mi-24D. To overcome a yaw-control deficiency under certain flight conditions – for example when hovering and moving laterally close to the ground in side-winds – the tail rotor was relocated from the starboard to the port side, changing its direction of rotation and resulting in an increase in its power. At the same time the uprated 1,900shp TV3-117 engine was adopted. By late 1974 the Mi-24's outward appearance was finally frozen, even though the problems with its weapons system persisted. Between 1973 and 1977 the Arsenyev and Rostov plants produced some 350 Mi-24Ds.

Meanwhile, in 1972, tests of the *Shturm*-V semi-automatic anti-tank missile for carriage aboard the Mi-24V finally began. This variant could carry up to eight *Shturm* missiles, and also introduced a new ASP-17V automatic sight. Mi-24V trials were finished only a year after the completion of Mi-24D development, and both variants were officially delivered to the Soviet Air Force on 29 March 1976. At this date the Service had some 400 Mi-24As and Mi-24Ds. Between 1976 and 1986 some 1,000 Mi-24Vs were built, and the aircraft remains

The early Mil Mi-24A Hind *variant featured a 'glasshouse' cockpit layout that was unpopular with crews.*

The Mi-24D was the first Hind *version to see action, being used during the Russian invasion of Afghanistan.*

the basic attack helicopter in the modern Russian army. The export Mi-24V has the designation Mi-35.

From the beginning, Mil's designers wanted to equip the Mi-24 with an anti-tank cannon, but concerns over the recoil of such a gun meant that it was not included on the early Mi-24 variants. A go-ahead to develop a cannon-armed variant came in 1974, and the bureau selected the twin-barrel 30mm Griazer-Shipunov GSh-30, already used in fixed-wing fighter-bombers, and installed it in a fixed position on the starboard side of the Mi-24V. The YakB-12.7mm machine-gun was removed. This variant was designated Mi-24P (*Pushka*, cannon). Proving the installation took several years, and there were a number of development difficulties, particularly during firing trials, the gun designers eventually having to increase the cannon's barrel length. The end result gave the Mi-24P a powerful weapon, although its use severely limited airframe fatigue life.

Between 1981 and 1990 the production plants built some 620 Mi-24Ps, and this variant also served with distinction in the Afghanistan War. However, the cannon in the Mi-24P was a fixed installation. The next development, therefore, was to move the weapon to the nose, where it replaced the YakB-12.7mm machine-gun on a moveable mounting. This resulted in yet another Mi-24 variant, the Mi-24VP. In 1989 the Rostov plant built a

number of Mi-24VPs before the changing political and world scene overtook events.

A wide range of weaponry has been carried by the Mi-24, including weapon pods under the wings with four-barrel YakB-12.7mm and two TKB-621 (7.62mm) machine-guns, the AGS-17 Plamia 30mm grenade launcher, GSh-23 cannon, C-5 (57mm), C-8 (80mm), C-13 (130mm) and C-24 (1,250mm) rockets, night flares, various bombs, minelayer pods etc. The R-60, R-73 and Igla air-to-air missiles were also tested, and during the Afghanistan War some Mi-24s had additional defensive 12.7mm and 7.62mm infantry machine-guns installed in the main cabin. By 1995 proposals had been made to upgrade the Mi-24 further, in particular by installing Western avionics and mission systems to provide an all-weather/night-attack capability, and the dynamics system from the Mi-28. Funding problems in Russia have frustrated the development, but a prototype, designated Mi-35M, was displayed at the 1995 Paris air show.

The European theatre

While the Russians were gaining attack-helicopter experience in Afghanistan, the USA and her NATO allies had been benefiting from lessons learned in the European theatre. Here, the Warsaw Pact forces had long held a significant numerical advantage when it came to

148

Later Hinds *were fitted with an offset 30mm cannon on the starboard side of the fuselage.*

tanks and other armoured ground forces. At the beginning of the 1970s NATO could put up only a few anti-tank helicopters against the threat, most armed with the now ageing Nord AS-11 missile and none developed specifically for the attack-helicopter role. Although the UK and France dallied briefly with the idea, proposing a tandem-seat variant of the new Westland Lynx, the European armies moved instead to arm a new generation of utility helicopters with either the TOW or the competitive high-subsonic, optically guided, tube-launched (HOT) anti-tank missile developed jointly by Aérospatiale and Messerschmitt-Bolkow-Blohm.

Thus it was left to the USA to develop the dedicated attack helicopter to meet the Warsaw Pact threat, and by 1969 it had become evident that the original AAFSS programme aircraft, and in particular the Lockheed Cheyenne, were fatally flawed. The Cheyenne was an advanced concept. It was a compound helicopter with a four-bladed, gyro-stabilised rigid main rotor with a forged titanium hub, a four-bladed tail rotor mounted at the tip of the port horizontal tail surface and a pusher propeller in the extreme tail. Its powerplant was a single 3,435shp General Electric T74-GE-16 turboshaft. For high-speed cruising almost the entire engine output was directed through the propeller, only some 300shp being diverted to the feathered main rotor to minimise wind-

milling drag. Stub wings helped to offload the main rotor as well as providing attachment points for up to four TOW missiles, rocket pods etc. A nose turret carried an Aeronutronic XM129 40mm grenade launcher or a General Electric 7.62mm Minigun, and a ventral turret with a 360° traverse housed an Aeronutronic XM140 30mm cannon. The weapons operator was positioned in the front cockpit, in a seat on a stabilised platform which could swivel through 360°, while the pilot sat in the raised rear cockpit.

Comprehensive equipment for all-weather operations was provided, including automatic terrain-following radar, an automatic flight-control system, Doppler radar and an inertial navigation system. The helicopter also had to be able to self-ferry 21,000 miles (38,892km) so that it could leapfrog from the USA to Southeast Asia via Hawaii. Its gross overload VTOL take-off weight was 22,000lb (9,980kg), rising to 30,000lb (13,608kg) for a rolling STOL take-off in the self-ferry role. Maximum level speed was intended to be 253mph (408km/h).

The prototype AH-56A first flew in May 1967. It was followed by nine similar aircraft over the next twelve months, for test and evaluation by the US Army. In January 1968, 375 production aircraft were ordered, only to be cancelled a year later as various teething problems emerged. The project was too ambitious and too costly,

149

In Europe, conventional helicopters were modified for the anti-tank attack role in the 1970s. West Germany, for example, mounted the HOT missile system, with a roof sight, on the MBB Bo105P, and put more than 200 in service on the Warsaw Pact frontier.

and had in any case been overtaken by events. In August 1972 the US Army finally decided to start again, this time placing greater emphasis on the anti-armour capability and less on the high-speed escort role, and the whole Cheyenne programme was ended.

Both Bell Helicopter and Sikorsky reacted immediately, the latter offering its S-67 Black Hawk using the S-61 dynamic system, and Bell proposing its Model 309 King Cobra. This was offered in both single- and twin-engined configuration, the company funding construc-

Lockheed's AH-56A Cheyenne was the result of an over-ambitious US Army specification for a high-speed, low-level attack helicopter. It had a rigid main rotor, a four-bladed tail rotor and a three-bladed pusher propeller.

tion of two prototypes in 1971. The King Cobra was based on the AH-1G, scaled-up and strengthened to operate at a gross weight of 14,000lb (6350kg), and using the dynamic system of the experimental heavy-lift Model 211 Huey Tug with its wide-chord main rotor. In addition to new all-weather avionics and navigation systems, the aircraft could carry up to sixteen TOW missiles under extended stub wings. Evaluation of the Black Hawk and King Cobra took place during 1972 but, by the year's end, the US Army had rejected both proposals and created an Advanced Attack Helicopter (AAH) task force to develop a new set of specifications.

At the same time plans advanced for upgrading the 'interim' Cobra for the European theatre, developing its anti-tank capability and introducing new survivability features. Under a contract signed in March 1972, Bell launched an Improved Cobra Armament Programme (ICAP), modifying eight AH-1Gs with the TOW missile system and a helmet-directed fire-control sighting subsystem. Following flight trials in 1973, an initial contract to convert 101 AH-1Gs to the new configuration as AH-1Qs was awarded in January 1974. The AH-1Q was equipped to carry eight TOW missiles, but the increase in gross weight caused a deterioration in performance. To counter this, Bell upgraded the dynamic system, introducing the 1,800shp Lycoming T53-L-703 and a new transmission, plus the Model 212 tail rotor and, eventually, new composite main blades. Cobras completed to the new standard were designated AH-1S

Following the Vietnam War, the Cobra was transformed into the AH-1S dedicated anti-tank helicopter with the TOW missile system.

(Mod), followed by the AH-1S (Prod), with newer survivability modifications such as a flat-plate canopy in 1977, the AH-1E (enhanced armament including a new 20mm turreted gun system), AH-1F (enhanced armament plus a new Kaiser fire-control system), and AH-1P (formerly AH-1S (Prod)).

In parallel with development of the single-engined Cobra, Bell also pursued development of a twin-engined variant. Initially this was for the USMC, which preferred the option of a second engine for its overwater

The Bell King Cobra was offered to plug the gap following the cancellation of the AH-56A Cheyenne programme. Instead, the US Army decided to start afresh.

The AH-1J was the first twin-engined variant of the Cobra to enter service, being developed especially for the overwater operations conducted by the US Marine Corps.

missions. In 1969 Bell therefore introduced the navalised AH-1J, with an 1,800shp Pratt & Whitney (Canada) T400-CP-400 coupled TwinPac. Sixty-nine were ordered by the Marines, followed by 202 for the Imperial Iranian Army Aviation. The latter funded a powerplant and transmission upgrade, introducing the 1,970shp T400-WV-402 TwinPac, and also the adoption of TOW missile armament. Both changes were subsequently adopted by the USMC, leading to the AH-1T variant from 1976.

While Bell developed the Cobra family the AAH competition had been launched, calling for a helicopter with day/night and adverse-weather capability, able to survive battle damage from 12.7mm and 23mm rounds, capable of cruising at 167mph (268km/hr) and climbing vertically at 449ft (137m)/min with a load of eight missiles and thirty drums of 30mm ammunition, and having almost two hours' endurance. Five companies responded to the request for proposals, including Boeing-Vertol, Lockheed, and Sikorsky, but the winning designs came from Bell and Hughes. In June 1973 the US Army selected both for competitive evaluation before making a final decision. Bell's design, the Model 409 (YAH-63), retained the traditional two-bladed rotor system, with 42.6in (13m) wide-chord main blades and a semi-rigid hub. Power was provided by two well-separated 1,500shp General Electric T700 turboshaft engines. The proposed armament included up to sixteen anti-tank missiles or seventy-six 2.75in rockets under

the stub wings. A chin turret mounted a triple-barrel 30mm General Electric XM-188 rotary cannon.

Surprisingly, perhaps, bearing in mind the company's unique experience with the Cobra, the YAH-63 neither 'looked right' nor performed well. The first flight was delayed until 10 October 1975, and one of the two prototypes was damaged in a heavy landing at the beginning of June 1976, on the eve of the four-month competitive evaluation process. In December 1976 the US Army ruled out the YAH-63 and Bell returned to concentrating on further developing the Cobra.

The Hughes AAH entry, the Model 77 (YAH-64), was also powered by T700 engines in separated nacelles, but otherwise differed greatly from the YAH-63. The main rotor was four-bladed and of conventional design, while the tail rotor used a novel scissors layout, with unequal spacing between the four blades. This layout reduced noise levels considerably compared with the Bell design. In the nose, the targeting-and-night-vision system was mounted right at the front, the 30mm cannon being moved to a swivel position below the front cockpit and the weapons operator. Hughes selected its own XM230 Chain Gun for the YAH-64 rather than the competing General Electric XM188, and the TADS/PNVS (target-acquisition-and-designation system/pilot night-vision system) was to be competed for by Martin Marietta and Northrop. Avionics was mostly placed in side blisters on each side of an otherwise narrow fuselage, for ease of access during field maintenance.

Although Hughes Helicopter lacked the attack helicopter experience of its main competitor, its YAH-64 won the US Army 1976 Advanced Attack Helicopter competition.

While the two helicopter designs were fighting it out, competitions were also under way to select the major subsystems, not least the anti-tank missile to be carried. In this competition the wire-guided Hughes TOW was competing with the new Rockwell AGM-111 Hellfire (helicopter-launched fire-and-forget) laser-guided missile. In addition to its superior guidance system, the Hellfire offered a 9.6-mile (6km) range and a high subsonic speed, plus better development potential. In February 1976 the US Army chose the Hellfire. Subsequently Hughes learned that its single-barrel Chain Gun had been selected in preference to the General Electric XM188.

The first of five YAH-64A prototypes made its maiden flight on 30 September 1975, and, following selection of the Hughes AAH at the end of 1976, some five years were devoted to trials and testing before a first production order was authorised in March 1982. A month later the US Army announced that it had chosen the Martin Marietta TADS/PNVS for the new helicopter, now designated AH-64A Apache, and the way was clear for full production.

The first production Apache was flown in January 1984, coinciding with the take-over of Hughes Helicopters by McDonnell Douglas. Service entry began a year later, when AH-64As were delivered to Fort Rucker and Fort Eustis for crew and maintenance training. The first combat unit, 3/6th Cavalry Division at Fort Hood, Texas, was cleared for active operation eighteen months later.

The AH-64A Apache earned itself an awesome reputation during the Gulf War, when film of its night-attack capability and weapons system accuracy and firepower was televised worldwide.

153

To meet the Italian Army requirement for a dedicated attack helicopter, Agusta developed the TOW-equipped A.129 during the 1980s.

In Europe it was gradually realised that the adaptation of utility helicopters such as the Gazelle, Bo 105 and Lynx for the anti-tank and attack/escort role was less than ideal. Consequently, several countries, including Germany, France, Italy and the UK, began to reconsider the development of dedicated attack designs. However, the sheer cost of such ventures led to prolonged discussions between governments and various joint projects. Eventually two distinct designs emerged, the Italian Agusta A.129 Mangusta and the Franco-German Eurocopter Tiger. Both were smaller than the Apache, but took advantage of new composites technology to save weight without sacrificing structural strength.

The Mangusta was developed to meet an urgent need for the Italian Army, which in the 1970s still lacked an anti-tank helicopter other than a few modified Agusta A.109s used for TOW missile familiarisation and training. The new A.129 followed the now established tandem-seat, narrow-fuselage, stub-wing formula but laid heavy emphasis on survivability and advanced avionics.

The construction of five prototypes, including a ground-test vehicle, was 70 per cent funded by the Italian government, and the first aircraft made its maiden flight in early September 1983. The initial aircraft were primarily airframe and dynamics test machines, but the fourth prototype, first flown in mid-1985, introduced the Harris digital integrated multiplex system, controlling the communication, navigation, armament, engine, power-distribution and utility subsystems. The fifth prototype was representative of the production A.129, with the full TOW armament and sighting systems.

The A.129 has a fully articulated four-blade main rotor and a two-blade, semi-rigid tail rotor. The glass-fibre blades are designed to have a ballistic tolerance against hits from 12.7mm ammunition and considerable tolerance against 23mm hits. The 70 per cent composite airframe is also resistant to 12.7mm ammunition, including the transmission, which has a thirty-minute run-dry capability. Power is provided by two 952shp Rolls-Royce Gem 2 engines. The pilot's night-vision FLIR, sensor and sighting systems are mounted in the extreme nose. Armament is carried on four weapons pylons below the stub wings, and typically comprises eight TOW missiles in the outboard positions and podded rockets, guns, bombs or other stores inboard. Both passive and active protection systems are included, with radar- and laser-warning receivers, jammers and a chaff/flare dispenser.

Sixty A.129 Mk 1s were ordered for the Italian Army, deliveries starting in October 1990. However, the

Re-engined with LHTEC T800 engines and fitted with a new five-bladed main rotor, Agusta's A.129 International has been developed to offer an upgraded attack capability.

changing military and technological scenario led to a slow-down in production, only thirty being delivered by early 1995. Since then an upgrade programme has been initiated on fifteen aircraft to install a 20mm multi-barrel cannon in a chin turret, plus Stinger air-to-air missiles, for the scout/escort role.

In contrast, the Franco-German Tiger project had the benefit of a later development timescale and, arguably, a less urgent need, since the two prime customers had relatively large numbers of anti-tank helicopters in service. This was probably just as well, as each government had subtly different requirements, which inevitably led to prolonged discussions and specification changes. Eventually three distinct variants were finalised. The first of these was the French Army HAP (*hélicoptère d'appui et de protection*), armed with a 30mm cannon in a chin turret and 450 rounds of ammunition, four Mistral air-to-air missiles, plus up to forty-four 68mm rockets. Its role was to offer day/night escort protection to the anti-armour variant against enemy aircraft and light armoured vehicles, as well as providing ground-attack support for ground forces.

Complementing the HAP was the HAC (*hélicoptère anti-char*), designed to carry eight of the new Euromissile Trigat fire-and-forget anti-armour missiles, plus four

Mistrals for self-defence. The specification called for the ability to carry out an attack by day or night and in adverse weather over a firing distance of not less than three miles (5km). To reduce detectability, the roof-mounted optronics of the HAP were relocated to a mast-mounted position, allowing the crew to scout and identify targets while remaining hull-down behind cover.

The German requirement was specifically for the anti-armour role, designated the PAH-2 and with a similar basic layout to the HAC but introducing some equipment variations. Originally 212 PAH-2s were required, but the collapse of the Warsaw Pact, and the consequent reduction in the tank threat during the 1990s, caused a rethink. Eventually, in 1996, Germany opted for a multi-role combination of the HAC and HAP, designated the UHU. A year later a launch contract was signed, marking the go-ahead for the manufacture of 312 HAC and UHU variants at the German Donauworth factory, and a further 115 HAPs at the French Marignane plant. Deliveries are due to begin in 2001.

The basic Tiger airframe employs 80 per cent carbon- and Kevlar-based composites, including frames and beams, and features a high standard of crew crash protection as well as claimed radar 'stealth' advantages over its contemporaries. The main rotor is a rigid, four-bladed,

Due to enter French and German service early in the new millennium is the Eurocopter Tiger, being developed as a multirole combat Unterstützungshubschrauber (UHU) version with mast-mounted sight for the German Army and the HAP variant with roof-mounted sight for the French ALAT.

hingeless fail-safe system, with ballistic tolerance and a thirty-minute run-dry main gearbox. Power is provided by two 1,170shp MTR-390 turboshafts, developed jointly by MTU, Rolls-Royce and Turboméca. An undernose turret houses a 30mm cannon, with ±90° azimuth and ±30° elevation, slaved into the fire-control system. Helmet-mounted displays and sighting are available, along with cockpit multifunction colour displays, dual redundant mission computers, and other advanced avionics and navigation aids.

Replacing the *Hind*

In the former Soviet Union, the emergence of the new-generation Western attack helicopters prompted the development of potential *Hind* replacements in the late 1970s. The specification called for a rugged attack helicopter that could be deployed on to the battlefield, and be self-supporting for up to two weeks in terms of maintenance and day-to-day operations. It also had to have high survivability. Armament was to include both anti-tank missiles and anti-tank cannon.

From the outset, such a design concept meant mechanical simplicity and reliable engineering, with protective armour and similar defensive technology

being used to maximise aircraft and crew survivability. Mil's bid in the competition was the Mil Mi-28, first flown in November 1982 and incorporating a dynamics system developed from the Mi-24 but with a new slimmer fuselage, an elongated nose with radar, chin sensors, and a fixed crashworthy landing gear. Power was provided by two Klimov TV3-117 turboshaft engines, as used in the *Hind*, but mounted further apart, on either side of the main transmission and above the stub wing for added protection.

A well-proven powerplant, if less efficient than Western engines of comparable power, the TV3-117 in the Mi-28 is flat-rated at 2,200shp, but to an altitude of at least 6,550ft (2,000m), and with a single-engine fly-away capability. The main gearbox on the Mi-28 is a typically solid and heavyweight piece of Soviet hardware, much bulkier than that of the Apache, and with conventional reduction gears rather than the planetary type used in the US helicopter. The main rotor mast is relatively short, but has a 5° forward tilt to give a 13.5° rotor disc clearance over the tailboom. This combination permits the Mi-28 to be air-transported in the Ilyushin Il-76 with only the main rotor blades removed. Immediately behind the main gearbox is an auxiliary power unit to provide

The Mi-28 Havoc has been developed as a successor to the Mi-24, but has been delayed by a lack of funding. Aircraft 014 was modified in 1997 as the first Mi-28N, with mast-mounted radome and night-vision capability.

full autonomy in the field. Large access panels open up to expose all the engine and transmission areas, simplifying in-field maintenance.

The five-bladed articulated main rotor head, which appears relatively conventional, bears more than a passing resemblance to the French Spheriflex design. De-icing heaters are built into the leading edges of the composite main blades, which have a 4 per cent offset. This gives the helicopter a high degree of agility, including a +3g to −5g capability. Roll rate is said to be plus 50° per second, and Mil test pilots have looped the aircraft.

All of the early Mi-28 prototypes flew with a conventional three-blade tail rotor, similar to that used on the Mi-24, but in 1989 a new scissors 'quiet' unit was introduced, with the blades intersecting at a 35° angle rather than the 55° of the Apache unit. The tail rotor driveshaft runs along the top of the tail boom, and is protected by armoured fairings.

The fuselage is built largely of aluminium, but with composite materials used locally as armour protection and in some non-critical areas. The two crew are seated in armoured tandem cockpits able to withstand direct hits from 7.62mm and 12.7mm machine-gun bullets or fragments from 20mm cannon shells. Also included is a small cabin/cargo bay, capable of carrying spares,

ammunition, missiles and rockets or two/three passengers. This gives the helicopter the ability to deploy into the field with ground support, or to rescue downed crews from front-line battle areas, the result of Russian experience in the Afghanistan conflict.

The Achilles' heel of the new Russian attack helicopter was its lack of sophisticated avionics and sensors. With Russian avionics development still lagging behind that of the West, the basic cockpit instrumentation in the Mi-28 is largely mechanical, except for a single centrally placed CRT, with all the instruments needed for take-off clustered on the right and those for flying grouped on the left. At the present time the CRT provides only a basic TV function, but FLIR and LLTV are available as options. Above the CRT is the HUD, while on either side of the seat are the various electrical switches and radios, etc. To reduce pilot workload an autopilot is installed to allow auto-hovering and heading hold for fire control. In addition, pulling on the collective automatically increases the angle of attack, keeping the helicopter very stable and further reducing the workload.

Although its electronic aids are limited, the Mi-28 does have a basic system able to remember and recall targets, linked to the sighting system. The latter includes a laser rangefinder integrated with Doppler INS and

Despite the introduction of the Mi-28, efforts have been made to upgrade the Hind, *the Mi-35M variant offering Mi-28 dynamics, night-vision equipment and shortened stub wings able to carry a range of offensive weaponry.*

daylight-only optics in the nose turret. This turret is removable in its entirety simply by unclipping fasteners around its periphery.

The standard anti-tank armament comprises sixteen 9M114 Kokon guided missiles or the improved laser-guided 9M120. Other weapons include 80mm and 122mm rocket pods, bombs up to 500kg or other assorted munitions on the stub-wing pylons. In flight the stub wings contribute up to 15 per cent of the total lift, depending on speed. An important armament decision was the mounting of the specified 30mm cannon, the well proven 2A42, which has a selective feed for two types of ammunition and is the standard Russian army weapon on the BMP infantry fighting vehicle. Used in Afghanistan under combat and field-tested in all climates and conditions, the 2A42 is known to have excellent armour-piercing qualities and to operate trouble-free in dusty and sandy conditions. These qualities were seen as being compatible with the need for reliability in the field, where maintenance, spares and special ammunition might not be available. Although the 2A42 weighs three times as much as a comparable aircraft gun (551lb/250kg overall installation weight), its use was considered feasible provided the aircraft's structure was built to take the weight and recoil. Despite the difficulties Mil chose to mount the cannon in a ventral turret, able to traverse through 220° horizontally and through +13/−45° vertically, synchronised with the elec-

tro-optical sighting system. The ammunition (250–300 rounds) is contained in boxes mounted on each side of the cannon, eliminating the need for flexible feed chutes. The total weight of the turret installation, with ammunition, is 1,366lb (620kg).

Later development of the Mi-28 has concentrated on the Mi-28N. This variant introduces a millimetre-wave radar and avionics/sensor system upgrades to provide a day/night adverse-weather capability. However, it is likely to depend on foreign systems rather than domestic alternatives until Russian technology catches up. The first Mi-28N, which also incorporated an uprated transmission to improve performance and maximum gross weight, made its first flight in late 1996.

Competition for the Mi-28 came from Kamov, with a very different design which drew on the bureau's long experience of the coaxial, contrarotating-rotor configuration. Traditionally, of course, Kamov had been responsible for naval helicopter development in the former Soviet Union, while Mil had supplied the battlefield support helicopters. This gave Mil an immediate psychological advantage in the ensuing competition, enhanced by its success with the *Hind*, which had itself beaten an earlier Kamov design, the Ka-25F, in the 1960s armed assault helicopter competition.

After careful study of the new attack-helicopter specification the Kamov bureau recognised that hot-and-high performance, manoeuvrability, survivability and in-field reliability were going to be crucial in the final evaluation and selection process. Consequently the team spent time researching the success record of the *Hind* in Afghanistan and other war theatres. The first important design decision was to choose a rotor system. Kamov evaluated various options, but eventually decided to retain its 'trademark' coaxial rotor. Although seen as controversial, this decision was based on sound reasoning, especially when matched against the Army specification. This configuration offered several apparent advantages over the more conventional approach adopted by the Mil Bureau. First, the absence of a tail rotor, together with its associated gearboxes and driveshafts, reduced vulnerability to tail strikes. Indeed, even with the entire tail shot away, the Ka-50 can be recovered and flown to a safe landing. A secondary advantage was the considerable saving in weight, not only due to the absence of the dynamic components, but because there was no need for the rear fuselage to be a load-bearing structure.

Another major benefit of a coaxial system is the amount of power available. With no bleed to a tail rotor, the contrarotating main rotors receive 100 per cent of the power from the TV3-117 engines, giving 12 per cent more lift than an equivalent conventional main-and-tail-rotor design. For the Ka-50, which may need to hover at low level in hot-and-high conditions with a full load of anti-tank missiles, every ounce of power is advantageous. The same benefits apply to nap-of-the-Earth (NOE) manoeuvrability, for the coaxial system is virtually unaffected by crosswind conditions, rotor diameter and overall dimensions can be smaller than those of equivalent conventional designs, and rapid climbs, descents and turns are possible. Kamov believed that these advantages far outweighed the drag factor of the tall rotor mast with its double swash plates and contrarotating control linkages.

Yet another virtue of the coaxial rotor, which Kamov decided to exploit in the Ka-50, is its inherent stability, especially when matched to a four-channel digital automatic flight-control system. Kamov recognised that this would help reduce pilot workload to a point where it might be possible get away with the biggest competitive gamble of all: a single-seat cockpit. Such a decision was bold, and the company also had to convince the customer that one man could handle both the helicopter and its fighting systems. It also meant rewriting some of the chapters on attack-helicopter operations, and rethinking weapons and sighting methods to comply with the single-crew doctrine.

The attack role of the Ka-50 naturally dictated that the armament would include a mix of guided anti-tank missiles, unguided rockets and at least one heavy-calibre gun, all of which would need to be aimed and fired by the pilot. Once again Kamov looked for unconventional solutions to the problem. To begin with, new laser-guided missiles, such as the supersonic AT-9 Vikhr, could be employed against targets with the aid of a ground observer or a second aircraft able to provide VHF radio datalink information and to illuminate targets for the attacking helicopter, thereby relieving the pilot of this particular responsibility. Indeed, the Kamov team argued that two pilots in two Ka-50s would be more valuable than two crew in one, with the second helicopter able to laser-designate targets from a

The developed Ka-50 Hokum, *represented here by a pre-production prototype, is an extremely powerful and manoeuvrable helicopter. Its coaxial rotor system enables the single pilot to fly in a tight turning circle to concentrate fire on a pinpointed target.*

safe distance. The use of a secondary source to provide the laser guidance also considerably reduces the threat to attacking aircraft from return fire, as well as providing scouting and defensive support.

The Vikhr has a range of 8–10km and is capable of penetrating 900mm of reactive armour. By selecting a different fuze (proximity or contact) the pilot can also use the AT-9 against other aircraft. The Ka-50 can carry up to sixteen AT-9s on the two outer stub-wing pylons, together with the tube-launched unguided rockets on the inboard pylons. Other underwing weapon options include twin 23mm cannon pods, AA-8 Aphid and AA-11 Archer air-to-air missiles, AS-12 Kegler missiles, FAB500 bombs and up to eighty S-8 80mm air-to-ground rockets. The pylons themselves are in two parts, with the bottom portion articulated to allow a 10° downward elevation. For long-range ferry operations each of the four pylons can carry an external fuel tank, or alternatively a field pod containing selected spares and maintenance tools for off-base operations.

The Mil decision to sling the cannon below the nose in a free-mounted turret was not seen as a good idea. Instead, Kamov mounted the cannon in a semi-fixed position alongside the load-bearing centre fuselage. Hydraulics provide a limited elevating movement (12° up/30° down) to help the gun remain on target, but the helicopter itself provides most of the traversing element, although the hydraulics system does provide a 15° traverse movement to the right. Nevertheless, the aiming of the weapon is primarily achieved by the pilot pointing the whole helicopter at the target. This simplistic approach is made easier because the position of the gun, together with up to 500 rounds in two ammunition boxes in the centre fuselage, gives no stability, handling or c.g. problems for the pilot.

As with the Mi-28, domestic avionics and sensor equipment in the Ka-50 suffer from a lack of technology. However, a HUD adapted from that used in the MiG-29, helmet-mounted sights, on-board target-marking lasers and other sensor equipment are available for the Ka-50 pilot acting entirely alone against ground targets, to reduce cockpit workload. Flight information is shown on the HUD, while other essential data, including weapons and health monitoring, can be overlaid. For Russian army operation the Ka-50 has a mechanical moving-map display, and a stabilised day targeting

The need to develop a full night and all-weather attack-and-training capability in the Hokum *has led to the two-seat Ka-52 variant, with an unusual side-by-side crew arrangement.*

160

The new AH-64D Apache variant is said to multiply the attack and survival capabilities of the original AH-64A many times over. Deliveries of the upgraded version to the US Army began in 1998.

sight/laser rangefinder and designator, with low-light TV as the main optical means of target-identification and tracking. For night operations a nose-mounted forward-looking infrared (FLIR) sight is proposed.

Apart from the benefit of eliminating the tail rotor (30 per cent of helicopter combat losses in Afghanistan were due to tail related damage), the Ka-50 includes a number of survivability features now found in most attack-helicopter designs, including composite rotor blades and built-in crash shock protection. However, the Kamov team concentrated especially on the personal protection of the pilot. Cockpit armour plating was one obvious solution, using a 772lb (350kg) two-wall steel plate. This armour, which protects against radar-guided guns and is capable of withstanding 23mm cannon rounds from 328ft (100m), is backed up by 12.7mm-proof armour-plated glass in the cockpit canopy.

The most revolutionary survivability feature incorporated in the Ka-50, however, is the pilot-ejection system, a world first in an operational combat helicopter. Developed by Zveda, the zero-zero system is centred on the rocket-assisted K-37 seat. To provide a safe ejection trajectory, the six main rotor blades are automatically blown off by explosive bolts when the pilot pulls two handles at the base of the seat. Next, in close sequence, the canopy is blown off, the seatback is positioned parallel to the rotor mast, and a rocket pack (mounted above the head-rest) is launched vertically into the air, pulling the seat out of the cockpit by cable. Once seat and pilot are clear of the aircraft, seat separation and parachute deployment follow in the conventional manner. The complete sequence takes about two and a half seconds.

Initial flight tests in 1982 of the new helicopter, designated Ka-50, were shrouded in secrecy, with the

161

prototype carrying civil Aeroflot colours and having extra cockpit glazing and cabin doors painted on the fuselage to confuse Western observers. Consequently it was not until the late 1980s and the collapse of the Soviet Union that details of the design emerged. Since then, about a dozen prototype and pre-production aircraft have been built, along with a two-seat side-by-side Ka-52 prototype intended for pilot training and the airborne command role.

In the meantime, US intelligence experts became convinced that the new helicopter was not in competition with the Mi-28, but was an entirely new air-to-air combat helicopter. This conclusion ignored established Soviet design competition doctrine and helped foster, especially in the USA, a call for new-generation fighter helicopters to counter the assumed threat. This eventually led to the Boeing-Sikorsky RAH-66 Comanche programme, currently under development as an all-weather armed reconnaissance helicopter with secondary air-combat and light-attack roles. Still in the early stages of development, the Comanche is unlikely to enter US Army service before 2007, when it will begin replacing the Bell OH-58D scout and the remaining AH-1 Cobras, and will operate alongside an upgraded version of the Apache.

The latter is the AH-64D Longbow Apache, an extensively reworked variant with new systems and sensors designed to increase its capability and survivability on the battlefield in day/night adverse visibility conditions. One major improvement is the introduction of a new mast-mounted millimetre-wave fire-control radar, able to penetrate fog and smoke on the battlefield and provide comprehensive target information. Demonstrations with prototype AH-64Ds have shown that, in less than thirty seconds, the crew can unmask and remask behind cover, the radar having scanned through 360° and recorded all activity within range in the meantime. On-board processors then locate the precise position, speed and direction of up to 265 targets, classify each one and prioritise it in terms of threat. The information can then be passed to the helicopter's own weapons system, or transmitted instantly by datalink to accompanying AH-64Ds or to a ground commander for battlefield planning. By 1997 the AH-64D had become the preferred attack helicopter for several nations, including the UK and the Netherlands.

Two other dedicated attack helicopters are also under development for service entry early in the twenty-first century. The first of these is the Denel Rooivalk, conceived during the final days of apartheid in South Africa

The South African Rooivalk, developed by Denel Aviation, incorporates a dynamic system based on French Super Puma technology but married to a dedicated attack helicopter airframe. Limited production for the SAAF was launched in 1997.

By the late 1980s Bell had developed the Cobra into the twin-T700-powered AH-1W for the US Marine Corps, carrying up to eight new-generation Hellfire anti-tank missiles. Further development under way in 1998 will lead to a four-bladed rotor, an upgraded cockpit and additional weapon pylons.

and necessarily making use of domestic technology, gained through development of the licence-built Aérospatiale SA.330 Puma. This led to the Oryx, which introduced the upgraded dynamics and Turboméca Makila engines of the Super Puma.

Development of the Rooivalk began concurrently in the mid-1980s, with two Pumas being used as testbeds for weapons systems and other components. The project was delayed in 1988 when the government withdrew funding following the scaling down of the war in Namibia, but Denel decided to continue work and rolled out the first prototype in January 1990. In general the design follows the now classic attack-helicopter layout, with a slim fuselage, two crew in tandem cockpits, separated engines each offering around 1,800shp, and stub wings able to carry eight anti-tank missiles, two rocket pods and four air-to-air missiles in total. A 20mm cannon is mounted under the nose below the ball-mounted IR/PNVS sighting system. Described as a medium-weight attack helicopter (maximum take-off weight is 19,290lb/ 8,750kg), the Rooivalk is designed to be air-transportable in a Lockheed C-130 Hercules. As a result of South African experience in the Angolan

and Namibian conflicts, ease of maintenance in the field was seen as a priority, and access hatches and work platforms were incorporated along the length of the fuselage.

By mid-1998 three flight-test prototypes were involved in the development programme and the first production aircraft was close to completion for the South African Air Force. Twelve aircraft are currently on order, with service entry due in 1999. Denel is also offering the Rooivalk overseas.

The other twenty-first-century entrant is the Bell AH-1Z Super Cobra, an upgrade of the re-engined AH-1W variant. The AH-1W, which introduced twin 1,626shp General Electric T700-GC-401 powerplants to the US Marine Corps AH-1T airframe, had already shown a substantial improvement in hot-and-high performance. This was exemplified in the Gulf War, where AH-1Ws destroyed more than 200 armoured vehicles and tanks and achieved a 92 per cent mission readiness rate in temperatures of 60 °C.

The new AH-1Z introduces a four-bladed bearingless main rotor system to improve performance payload and agility and reduce maintenance and vulnerability.

The new dynamics allows the maximum take-off weight to increase to 16,800lb (7,720kg), including 3,914lb (1,775kg) of stores on new stub wings fitted with three weapons pylons instead of two. Also included in the upgrade is a 'glass cockpit' with an integrated weapons-management system, an advanced mission computer and other improvements designed to bring the ubiquitous Cobra into the twenty-first century.

The attack helicopter of 2001 is far removed from the limited day-only, soft-target Cobra of the mid-1960s, and a totally different animal from the concept originated a decade earlier in the Algerian War. The new-generation attack helicopter is arguably the most sophisticated weapons system available on the battlefield, able to carry out surgical strikes against almost any target, under almost any weather conditions, at any time of day or night. Furthermore, such attacks can be carried out from a cloaked position, without warning, and with full target and designating co-ordination between ground units, accompanying attack helicopters and other forces available to the digital battlefield commander. Meanwhile, helmet-mounted displays, automated flight-control systems, digital moving maps, GPS, terrain-avoidance, threat warning and other devices are all helping to reduce the cockpit workload and make life easier and more survivable for the attack-helicopter crew.

In the foreseeable future it is computers and avionics that will drive further advances in attack helicopter design, rather than revolutionary airframe and dynamic system changes. Development of the latter is likely to be geared more towards weight reduction and enhanced survivability to improve the mission profile. In just over forty years the attack helicopter has certainly come a long way.

Bibliography

ap Rees, E, *World Military Helicopters* (Jane's Information Group, London, 1986).

'Mi-28 Havoc', *Helicopter International* (Avia Press Associates), Vol 13 No 2, September 1989.

'Kamov Ka-50', *Helicopter International*, Vol 16 No 4, January 1993.

'Bell AH-1W', *Helicopter International*, Vol 17 No 4, January 1994.

'AH-64 and Longbow Apache', *Helicopter International*, Vol 17 No 5, March 1994.

'Euro Tiger', *Helicopter International*, Vol 17 No 6, May 1994.

Everett Heath, J, *Helicopters in Combat* (Arms & Armour Press, London, 1992).

Mikheyev, V, 'Mil Mi-24 Development', *Helicopter International*, Vol 18 No 4, January 1995.

Pelletier, A J, *Bell Aircraft since 1935* (Putnam, London, 1992).

Taylor, M (ed), *Brassey's World Aircraft & Systems Directory 1996/1997* (Brassey's (UK), London, 1996).

8
The Modern Defensive Fighter
Robert Jackson

The air-superiority aircraft

Ever since the aircraft became a viable fighting weapon, the outcome of land battles has been decided by the control of the air above them; in other words, by the ability of one side to deny the attacking aircraft of the other access to the airspace over the battlefield. The ongoing quest for air superiority is a state of affairs rather than a role or a mission, and it has led to the evolution of a succession of specialist fighter aircraft.

In the USA the lessons of the Korean War, in which Sabres and MiG-15s battled for supremacy in the stratosphere close to the Yalu River, resulted in the new 'Century' series of fighters, including the North American F-100 Super Sabre, the first combat aircraft in the world capable of sustained supersonic level flight, and the Mach 2 Lockheed F-104 Starfighter, armed with air-to-air missiles and increasingly sophisticated weapon systems for high-speed interception at great altitudes. The Soviet counterpart of the F-100 was the MiG-19, given the NATO codename *Farmer*; the first Soviet fighter with supersonic capability in level flight, it had a maximum speed of Mach 1.4 and entered series production in 1955. It was followed, in 1959, by the MiG-21 *Fishbed*, a lightweight delta-wing fighter with a Mach 2 capability. This aircraft, more than any other, enabled the Soviet Air Force to challenge NATO's battlefield fighter supremacy in the 1960s.

The development of fighter technology in France followed a similar pattern, the subsonic Dassault Mystère IVA fighter giving way to the supersonic Super Mystère,

equivalent to the F-100 and the MiG-19, which was a stepping-stone to the highly successful Mach 2 Mirage series. Only Britain made the jump from subsonic to supersonic fighter with no transonic intermediary, replacing the Hawker Hunter day fighter and the Gloster Javelin all-weather fighter with the Mach 2 English Electric (later BAC) Lightning. Like the F-104 Starfighter, the Lightning was developed as a supersonic missile-armed interceptor, but it had none of the Starfighter's limitations. In fact the Lightning was the world's only supersonic pure *fighter* aircraft until the advent of the McDonnell Douglas F-15, and by the time the latter flew in prototype form the Lightning had already been in RAF service for twelve years. The Lightning certainly had its fair share of problems, including an inadequate weapons system, but its ability to get off the ground very quickly and climb to 30,000ft (9,000m) in a little under two minutes was an important asset in an era when it was assumed that an East–West war would begin with a nuclear attack on airfields, with minimum warning time.

In the late 1960s the air war over Vietnam showed that the latest aircraft designs had deviated from the practical lessons; speed and sophistication were no substitutes for manoeuvrability, and an all-missile armament was no substitute for guns. Aircraft such as the McDonnell F-4 Phantom, designed for combat at supersonic speeds and for multiple roles, found themselves fighting nimble MiG-17s and MiG-21s in turning combats at 500kt (926km/h) or less, and they had to be retrofitted with 20mm cannon for this close-in work.

North American's F-100 Super Sabre was the first fighter capable of sustained supersonic speed in level flight.

Lockheed's F-104A Starfighter was designed for high-speed interception at great altitudes.

The MiG-19, the first Soviet fighter with supersonic capability in level flight, entered service in 1955.

In the 1960s the MiG-21 lightweight Mach interceptor enabled the Soviets to challenge NATO's battlefield air superiority.

France's equivalent of the F-100 and MiG-19 was the Dassault Super Mystère B.2, the stepping-stone to the successful Mach-capable Mirage series.

An English Electric (BAC) Lightning F.6 armed with two Firestreak air-to-air missiles. The original Lightning was, in effect, an experimental aircraft with a weapons system built into it.

The modern air-superiority fighter is a highly manoeuvrable aircraft that is capable not only of engaging an opponent in close combat and winning, but also of engaging him with missiles at beyond visual range. It must excel in three main areas: detection of targets, agility and weaponry. Its radar must have sufficient range to match the enemy threat, and be resistant to hostile jamming. The radar must also have look-up and look-down capabilities and incorporate an illuminator if semi-active radar-guided missiles are to be carried.

In 1965 the USAF and various aircraft companies in the USA began discussions on the feasibility of just such an aircraft and its associated systems to replace the F-4 Phantom, and four years later it was announced that McDonnell Douglas had been selected as prime airframe contractor for the new aircraft, then designated FX. As the F-15A Eagle, it flew for the first time on 27 July 1972, and first deliveries of operational aircraft were made to the USAF in 1975. Urgent impetus was

given to the programme following the appearance of the Soviet Union's MiG-25 *Foxbat* interceptor, an aircraft that was itself developed to meet a potential threat from a new generation of US strategic bombers including the North American XB-70 Valkyrie, a project that was subsequently cancelled.

Simply stated, the F-15 Eagle was designed to outperform, outfly and outfight any opponent it might encounter in the foreseeable future, in engagements extending from beyond visual range (BVR) right down to close-in turning combat. Irrespective of starting conditions, most air combats come down to speeds around or below Mach 1.2, often falling to subsonic speeds, so manoeuvrability must be optimised for these conditions. The pilot who enters combat with most aircraft energy, either in the form of height or speed, will have the advantage in manoeuvrability, but if the combat continues this advantage is soon lost, superiority passing to the aircraft with most latent energy. In simple terms this means the aircraft with the most excess thrust, a measure of the aircraft's ability to accelerate and climb. This potential is described as specific excess power (SEP), and its highest value occurs at high subsonic speeds, at the foot of the drag curve. As the airspeed increases, supersonic drag begins to appear and intake pressure recovery falls as a result of shock waves (wave drag), reducing the thrust available.

In a sustained turn, when a pilot is endeavouring to get into the best position for a gun attack, the maximum rate of turn and the minimum turn radius are achieved when the drag generated in the turn is equalised by the available thrust. The maximum rate of turn depends either on the available lift or on the maximum g forces the airframe can stand. However, it is difficult to sustain a maximum-rate turn without losing height. Everything depends on the thrust-to-drag and lift-to-weight ratios, key factors which must be taken into account in the design of an agile air-superiority fighter's wing.

The F-15's wing, for example, is a very neat piece of aerodynamic design, with a conical camber and an aerofoil section optimised to reduce wave drag at high speed. The last 20 per cent of the chord is thickened to delay boundary layer separation and so reduce drag. Manoeuvre performance is also enhanced by the slab

tailplanes, which operate differentially, in concert with the ailerons, in the rolling plane and together for pitch control. They compensate to a great extent for loss of aileron effectiveness at extreme angles of attack, a vital factor in tight air combat. The aircraft's twin fins are also positioned to receive vortex flow off the wing in order to maintain directional stability at high angles of attack. The F-15C, the main interceptor version, has a wing loading of only 54lb/ft^2 (25kg/0.9m^2) and this, together with two 23,450lb st (104.3kN) Pratt & Whitney F-100 advanced-technology turbofans, gives it an extraordinary turning ability and the combat thrust-to-weight ratio (1.3:1) necessary to retain the initiative in a fight. The high thrust-to-weight ratio permits a scramble time of only six seconds, using 600ft (180m) of runway, and a maximum speed of more than Mach 2.5 gives the pilot the margin he needs if he has to break off an engagement.

To increase the F-15 Eagle's survivability, redundancy is incorporated in its structure. For example, one vertical fin, or one of three wing spars, can be severed without causing the loss of the aircraft. Redundancy is also inherent in the F-15's twin engines, and its fuel system incorporates self-sealing features and foam to inhibit fires and explosions.

A Tupolev Tu-95 Bear *electronic-intelligence aircraft under surveillance by two McDonnell Douglas F-15 Eagles from Keflavik, Iceland, in 1986.*

An F-15 Eagle launches an AIM-7 Sparrow air-to-air missile, 1984.

A pair of MiG-25 Foxbat *strategic interceptors armed with semi-active radar-homing AA-6 Acrid missiles.*

The F-15's primary armament is the AIM-7F Sparrow radar-guided AAM, with a range of up to 35 miles (56km). The Eagle carries four of these, backed up by four AIM-9L Sidewinders for shorter-range interceptions and a General Electric 20mm M61 rotating-barrel cannon for close-in combat. The gun is mounted in the starboard wing root and is fed by a fuselage-mounted drum containing 940 rounds. The aircraft's Hughes AN/APG-70 pulse-Doppler air-to-air radar provides a good look-down capability and can be used in a variety of modes. It can pick up targets at around 100nm (180km) range and, in the raid-assessment mode, can resolve close formations into individual targets, giving the F-15 pilot an important tactical advantage.

When the radar detects a target in the basic search mode the pilot directs the AN/APG-70 to lock on and track by putting a bracket over the radar return, using a selector mounted on the control column. The locked-on radar will then show attack information such as the target's closing speed, range, bearing and altitude separation, and the parameters governing the F-15's weapons release. When the target enters the kill envelope of the weapon selected, the pilot decides whether to attack using his head-down, virtual situation display, which gives a synthetic picture of the tactical situation, or to go for a visual attack using his HUD.

Another useful AN/APG-70 mode is the velocity search. When this is selected the radar shows only target velocities at long range, so if the pilot sees a return that is bowling along at Mach 3 and 70,000ft (20,000m) with no identification friend or foe (IFF), he can be fairly certain that he is dealing with a MiG-25R reconnaissance *Foxbat*. The radar can also be used to scan the field of view displayed in the HUD for up to 10 miles (16km) ahead of the F-15; in this mode it automatically locks on to the nearest target, which is then interrogated. If an IFF response shows it to be friendly, radar lock is broken and the radar continues to search for the next priority target.

The concept of the F-15 as an air-superiority fighter was first proven in the summer of 1982, when the Israeli Air Force, which was then rearming with the American aircraft, embarked on a period of intensive action in support of the invasion of southern Lebanon. Israeli and Syrian combat aircraft had been involved in a series of skirmishes over Lebanese territory since 1979, and in the course of these F-15s encountered MiG-25s for the first time. Since the F-15 had been brought into service to counter the MiG-25 in the first place, the results of these actions, which were firmly in the F-15's favour, attracted a lot of attention. The Israelis reported that the *Foxbat* was fast at high altitude but that its manoeuvrability was poor, as was the visibility from the cockpit. At medium and low altitudes the heavy MiG-25's speed fell away markedly and its handling qualities were sluggish.

An F-15C Eagle refuels from a McDonnell Douglas KC-10A tanker. Flight refuelling greatly extends the time an air-superiority fighter can remain on patrol.

The MiG-23 *Flogger*, according to the Israelis, was a much better proposition, but the Syrian tactics left much to be desired. A senior Israeli Air Force officer, speaking in an interview about the air battles that took place over the Beka'a Valley in the summer of 1982, said:

Their pilots behaved as if they knew they were going to be shot down and waited to see when it was going to happen and not how to prevent it, or how to shoot us down. Which was strange, because in the 1973 [Yom Kippur] war the Syrians fought aggressively. This time it was different, so it was difficult to compare the aircraft. They could have flown the best fighter in the world, but if they flew it in the way they were flying, we would have shot them down in exactly the same way. It wasn't the equipment at fault, but their tactics. Look at the area of operations and the restrictions we had. We couldn't enter Syria. They were only two minutes from their bases, while we were between ten and forty minutes from base; some of our aircraft had to come from Ouvda, down in the Negev.

Most of the kills, 85 to 90 per cent, were in the Beka'a Valley, less than a minute from the Syrian border. It meant we only had two minutes from them crossing to crossing back if they only wanted to sweep the Beka'a area. If we didn't succeed in two minutes then we couldn't follow them across the border. That was a difficult situation for us. They fired missiles, they fought, but in a peculiar way. I don't mean they were sitting ducks, but in our view they acted without tactical sense. Maybe in their view the best tactic was to get away from ... I don't know what. But the results show it was very strange.

History was to repeat itself. During the Gulf War, F-15s claimed no fewer than thirty of the thirty-nine Iraqi aircraft destroyed in air combat. In every case the Iraqi pilots failed completely to get the best out of their aircraft, even though some were MiG-29s, which in theory were a match for the F-15.

The MiG-23 Flogger *multirole combat aircraft, featuring variable geometry, was one the Soviet Union's success stories and was widely exported.*

The MiG-29 Fulcrum *was the first of the Soviet Union's high-technology air-superiority fighters. From the outset, design emphasis was placed on high agility.*

Just as the F-15 was developed to counter the MiG-25 *Foxbat* and the MiG-23 *Flogger*, both of which were unveiled in the late 1960s, the MiG-29 *Fulcrum* and another Soviet fighter, the Sukhoi Su-27 *Flanker*, were designed in response to the F-15 and its naval counterpart, the Grumman F-14 Tomcat. The two Soviet aircraft share a similar configuration, combining a wing swept at 40° with highly swept wing-root extensions, underslung engines with wedge intakes, and twin fins. The combination of modest wing sweep with highly swept root extensions, designed to enhance manoeuvrability, is also used on the Lockheed Martin (formerly General Dynamics) F-16 Fighting Falcon and the McDonnell Douglas F-18 Hornet.

The MiG-29, the first of the new Russian air-superiority fighters to enter service, is powered by two Klimov RD-33 two-spool, low-bypass turbofan engines which, at the aircraft's normal take-off weight of 15 tonnes, give a thrust-to-weight ratio of 1.1. Design emphasis from the start was on very high manoeuvrability and the ability to destroy targets at distances of between 660ft (200m) and 32nm (60km). Forty per cent of the MiG-29's lift is provided by its lift-generating centre fuselage, and the aircraft is able to achieve angles of attack at least 70 per cent higher than earlier fighters.

The aircraft has an RP-29 pulse-Doppler radar capable of detecting targets at around 62 miles (100km) against a background of ground clutter. Fire-control and mission computers link the radar with a laser rangefinder and infrared search/track sensor, in conjunction with a helmet-mounted target designator. The radar can track ten targets simultaneously, and the system allows the MiG-29 to approach and engage targets without emitting detectable radar or radio signals. The *Fulcrum*'s primary armament is the AA-10A *Alamo*, the equivalent of the F-15's AIM-7 Sparrow, with the AA-8 *Aphid* infrared AAM as the close-range weapon. A 30mm gun, with 150 rounds, is fitted in the port wing-root leading-edge extension.

Like the F-15, the larger, longer-range Sukhoi Su-27 is a dual-role aircraft. In addition to its primary air-superiority task it was designed to escort Su-24 *Fencer* strike aircraft on deep-penetration missions. (During the Gulf War USAF F-15s escorted strike aircraft as well as fulfilling their primary counter-air task.) The Su-27 also has a lift-generating fuselage and is capable of quite extraordinary angles of attack. It can carry up to ten AAMs.

The primary missions of the dual-role Sukhoi Su-27 Flanker, *above, are air superiority and long-range escort for types such as the Su-24* Fencer *deep-penetration strike aircraft, below.*

171

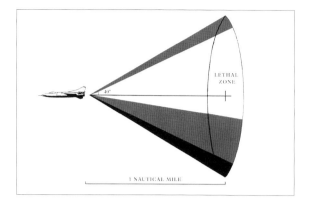

Lethal cone.

The advent of modern, purpose-built air-superiority fighters like the F-15 and Su-27 has brought about a revolution in air-fighting tactics. Previously, a fighter pilot's success and survival depended on his ability to keep the area behind his aircraft, the 'six o'clock' position, clear while manoeuvring into his opponent's six o'clock position in order to discharge his weapons into the so-called lethal cone, radiating at an angle of about 40° from the tail of the target aircraft and extending rearwards for a mile or so. If a pilot could keep his adversary out of this cone, the chances of the enemy aircraft getting off an effective shot with guns or heat-seeking missiles were slim.

The 40° lethal cone theory led to the development of several classic air-combat manoeuvres in both defence and offence. The simplest defensive manoeuvre, unchanged since the First World War, is the break, in which the defending pilot uses maximum g and performance to turn the aircraft towards his attacker and, hopefully, cause the latter to overshoot if his closing speed is high.

Another defensive manoeuvre is the high-g barrel roll, which depends on the opponent having excessive closing speed and also on very accurate timing. The defending pilot watches the attacker coming in and then, at the critical moment, throttles back, extends his airbrakes and pulls his aircraft up into a barrel roll, losing speed all the time and pulling as much g as possible. The theory is that the attacker's high speed will take him through the centre of the roll, whereupon the defender completes the manoeuvre, 'cleans up' his aircraft and increases speed to dive after his opponent, having turned the tables on him. The problem with this manoeuvre is that it has to be started at exactly the right moment; too soon, and the attacker will pull up and then dive down to attack the defending aircraft while the latter is halfway round the roll, its energy dissipated.

One of the more classic offensive combat manoeuvres is the yo-yo, which was devised by Russian MiG-15 pilots in the later stages of the Korean War and subsequently adopted by the Americans. There are two kinds: high speed and low speed. In the high-speed yo-yo, which is used to prevent overshooting a hard-turning target, the attacker rotates the nose of his aircraft high, aileron-turning to keep the target in sight. As his speed falls away, reducing the radius of turn at the top of the manoeuvre, he pulls hard over the top and drops down into a firing position inside his opponent's turn. The low-speed yo-yo, on the other hand, is designed to gain the advantage over an opponent who is turning at an equal or faster rate than the attacking aircraft. The attacker enters a diving turn, gaining speed, and then rolls across his opponent's turning circle, achieving a firing position on the latter's tail; although by the time the manoeuvre is completed the target aircraft will have increased the distance considerably.

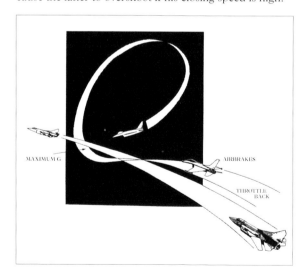

High-g barrel roll.

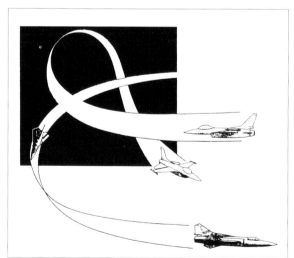

High-speed yo-yo.

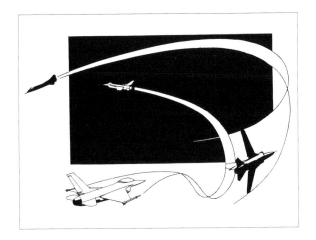

Low-speed yo-yo.

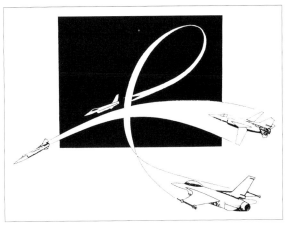

Lag pursuit roll.

During the Vietnam War American pilots flying heavy aircraft such as the Phantom, which do not turn well at lower speeds, found that they had a problem when fighting lighter and nimbler aircraft like the MiG-17 and MiG-21. In some cases their higher speed brought them so close to the target that it reduced their weapons envelope considerably. To remedy this they developed a manoeuvre called the lag pursuit roll, in which the attacking aircraft pulls up across the target's turning circle and then rolls, dropping down into a position outside the opponent's radius of turn and about a mile astern. If the opponent keeps on turning, the attacker will be in his blind spot; if the target breaks in the opposite direction he will fly across the attacker's cone of fire.

One combat manoeuvre which was developed during the Second World War and is still used by today's generation of fighter pilots is the scissors, in which each aircraft flies as slowly as it can, continually reversing its turn in an attempt to make the opponent overshoot. It is not recommended for fighters with dissimilar manoeuvrability, because the more manoeuvrable aircraft should always win. A variation is the rolling scissors, in which the two opposing aircraft roll round and round one another, descending all the time. It is the ultimate game of 'chicken', because the pilot who pulls out first is dead, and if both pilots leave it too late they are both dead.

The basic fighting element of two aircraft, the pair, has remained much the same ever since the Germans devised it during the Spanish Civil War. Today's pairs of fast jets fly in line abreast, with between one and three miles between the two aircraft, and all air-combat tactics are built around this basic element. On combat air patrol, the task of a pair of fighters is to locate a suspect aircraft, turn towards it, identify it by making a close pass, force the enemy pilot into a situation where his actions are predictable, and shoot him down.

Scissors

Rolling scissors.

173

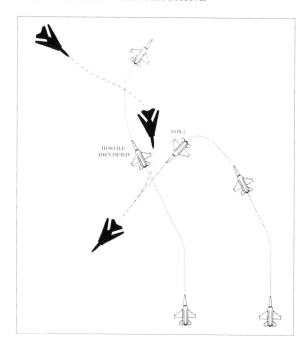

Wing drop.

The usual technique in a two-against-one situation is for the lead aircraft of the combat air patrol (CAP) pair to make a fast head-on run towards the enemy aircraft with his wingman some distance out to the right. As the lead pilot flashes past the opponent at close range he makes a positive identification and pulls hard right astern of the enemy aircraft, whose pilot will almost certainly have dropped a wing to make his own identification. As the enemy pilot turns in pursuit of the aircraft that has

Bracket avoider.

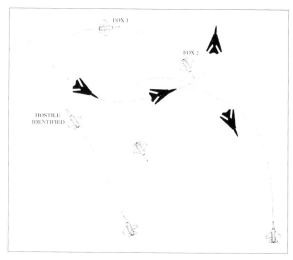

Sandwich.

just gone past him, the wingman will have an opportunity to get on his tail for a shot with a heat-seeking missile. Although the latest generation of heat-seeking AAMs are extremely agile weapons that can be fired head-on, a tail shot still brings the best chance of success.

If the enemy pilot has detected both fighters he will probably ignore the lead aircraft as it makes its fast head-on pass and instead turn towards the number two, in which case the CAP pair will have him effectively boxed in. If the enemy pilot realises his mistake and reverses his turn it will put the lead CAP aircraft, which is also turning hard, in a position for a shot with a radar-guided AAM from the beam, and if he continues his turn towards the wingman the lead aircraft will pull round on his tail for a heat-seeking AAM shot. If the enemy pilot evades this he will still have to contend with the wingman, who will pass him head-on at high speed and then turn hard to make his own attack from astern or from the beam.

Another option, known as the eyeball/shooter, aims to destroy the enemy aircraft in the shortest possible time without becoming committed to a turning fight. The lead CAP fighter makes his fast head-on pass to identify the enemy aircraft, but his wingman, who is some distance astern of the leader, fires a radar-guided or heat-seeking AAM from a direct head-on position. Combat agility may be greatly enhanced by fitting moveable exhaust nozzles that angle the thrust up, down or sideways. Known as multi-axis thrust vectoring (MATV), this is a more flexible version of the vectoring in forward flight (VIFFing) technique used by pilots of the British Aerospace Harrier. The aerodynamics of a modern fighter aircraft are so finely balanced that it needs a computer to co-ordinate everything. Signals from the principal flight controls – the control column, rudder pedals and throttle – are fed to the computer, which flies the aircraft by mak-

vertical the aircraft picks up speed and the pilot returns to level flight, heading back the way he came. Pilots of the V/STOL Harrier use a somewhat similar technique in combat manoeuvre called a 'flop'; the pilot selects 30° of nozzle and augments it with full back stick, which gives a pitching movement of about 40° per second – in effect, a very tight loop in which the Harrier seems to revolve round its own axis. In combat, the 'flop' is used to change quickly from nose-up to nose-down. Using VIFF, the Harrier can pull up to 122° angle of attack.

Whether all this extra manoeuvrability will enhance an air-superiority fighter pilot's prospects of success, though, is arguable. Some designers believe that future combats will be fought with short-range fire-and-forget missiles like ASRAAM. With such weapons, and a helmet-mounted sight, all a pilot needs to do is look at the opposing aircraft, fire, and let the missile complete its work of destruction.

The strategic interceptor

While the task of the air-superiority fighter is to achieve control of the air over the battlefield and the approaches to it, the role of the strategic interceptor is to destroy enemy bombers and cruise missiles before they come close enough to friendly territory to present a threat. To this end, the strategic interceptor must be able to remain on CAP for lengthy periods, must be able to accelerate to supersonic speed to investigate a threat, and must be armed with long-range air-to-air missiles.

The advent of bomber aircraft armed with stand-off weapons (the Boeing B-52 Stratofortress and the North American Hound Dog ASM, for example) gave urgent impetus to the development of Soviet strategic fighters in the early 1960s, and resulted in the appearance, at the 1961 Tushino air display, of the Tupolev Tu-128, a long-range, missile-armed, all-weather interceptor. With a length of 85ft (25.9m) and a wingspan of 65ft (19.8m), the Tu-128, given the NATO codename *Fiddler*, was the largest interceptor to see service anywhere, and Western experts noted with interest, after they had gathered

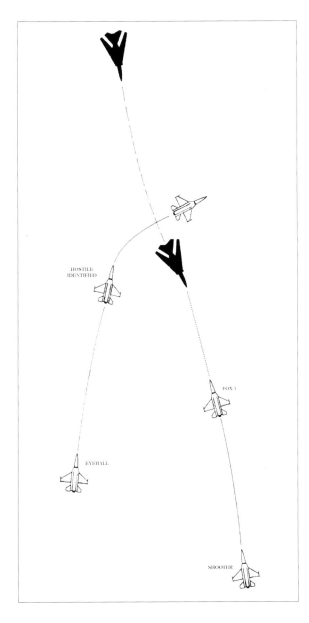

Eyeball/shooter.

ing the necessary inputs to the flight-control surfaces. If an aircraft has MATV (as does the Sukhoi Su-37, another highly agile Russian counter-air fighter, which made its first flight in this configuration in April 1996), the system is computer-controlled, the pilot having no direct control over the angle of thrust during a combat.

Multi-axis thrust vectoring can produce manoeuvres such as the one known as the J-turn, in which the nose of the aircraft rises quickly until it is pointing vertically upwards. The aircraft continues to travel horizontally, but loses speed. The pilot then flicks the aircraft to left or right through 180°, and as the nose comes down towards the

Tupolev's Tu-128 Fiddler *long-range, missile-armed interceptor was designed to counter Boeing B-52s armed with the* Hound Dog *stand-off weapon.*

A Sukhoi Su-15 Flagon *strategic interceptor of the type that shot down a Korean Air Lines Boeing 747 over the Sea of Japan in 1983.*

more intelligence on the aircraft, that its designation carried the suffix 'P' for *Perekhvachnik* (interceptor). The interesting point was that this suffix was applied only to the designations of Soviet aircraft which had been adapted to the fighter role, indicating that the Tu-28 had originally been designed as a low-level strike aircraft, possibly in the anti-shipping role, and that its adaptation as a fighter was the the result of an urgent Soviet Air Defence Forces requirement for an aircraft capable of intercepting SAC B-52s while the latter were still outside missile launch range. The Tu-28 was estimated to have a combat radius of about 1,500nm (2,780km) with maximum fuel, and it was armed with four *Ash* AAMs on underwing pylons.

The MiG-25 *Foxbat*, powered by a pair of Tumansky engines giving it a high-altitude speed of Mach 3.0, was rushed into service to counter the potential threat of the North American B-70 supersonic bomber, and the cancellation of the B-70 left the MiG-25 in search of a role.

It eventually re-emerged as a reconnaissance, precision-strike and defence-suppression aircraft, the strategic interceptor role having been assumed in the meantime by the Sukhoi Su-15 *Flagon*. It was an aircraft of this type that achieved brief notoriety in September 1983, when it shot down a Korean Air Lines Boeing 747 over the Sea of Japan with the loss of 269 lives.

The Su-15 was in turn progressively replaced by the MiG-31, a greatly developed version of the MiG-25 that received the NATO reporting name *Foxhound*. Initiated to counter the threat to the Soviet Union from B-52s and B-1s carrying air-launched cruise missiles, the MiG-31 is a two-seat, all-weather, all-altitude interceptor designed to be be guided automatically to its targets and to engage them under ground control. It is equipped with an electronically scanned phased-array fire-control radar (known as *Flash Dance* to NATO) which has a search range of 110nm (200km) and can track ten targets, engaging four simultaneously. In a typical mission profile an interception

Design of the MiG-31 Foxhound, *which replaced the Su-15 as Russia's main strategic interceptor, was initiated to counter the threat from cruise missiles.*

would be made by a flight of four aircraft, the leader being linked to the AK-RLDN ground radar-guidance network and the other three linked to the leader by APD-518 digital datalink. This arrangement permits a line-abreast radar sweep covering a zone some 485nm (900km) wide. The MiG-31 carries four AA-9 *Amos* semi-active radar-homing long-range AAMs on ejector pylons under the fuselage, plus two AA-6 *Acrid* medium-range infrared AAMs and four AA-8 *Aphid* short-range infrared AAMs on underwing pylons. One variant of the MiG-31, the MiG-31D, is a dedicated anti-satellite aircraft.

For the former Soviet Air Defence Forces, which had to cope with the threat of air attack from virtually any direction, the deployment of strategic interceptors in considerable numbers around the country's vast periphery was of paramount importance during the years of the Cold War. The USAF, on the other hand, faced a threat of attack by manned bombers flying over the Arctic, and was consequently able to place its strategic fighter defences well forward, in Alaska, Greenland and Iceland. For many years the front line was held by the Convair F-102A Delta Dagger and its development, the F-106 Delta Dart, armed with the Douglas AIR-2 Genie or Super Genie nuclear-tipped AAM. These older aircraft were later replaced by the F-4 Phantom and, ultimately, the F-15 Eagle.

Although the threat from Soviet manned strategic bombers was never particularly great at the height of the Cold War, the Soviet leadership having opted instead for the development of advanced strategic missiles, it was revived in the latter years with the deployment of a version of the Tu-95 *Bear* armed with cruise missiles and of the Tu-160 *Blackjack* supersonic variable-geometry bomber, the broad equivalent of America's B-1.

The USA's principal NATO partner, Britain, also faced an air threat from one main axis, but the British air defences had to expect a much shorter warning time. It was therefore imperative to deploy an aircraft with a rapid reaction time, and in this respect the BAC Lightning was excellent. With the aircraft off the ground interception was a fairly straightforward matter, even though the main medium between pilot and controller was voice communication. (It had always been intended to equip the Lightning with a datalink for the passage of data from a ground-based computer to the aircraft's auto-attack system, but this was never fitted.) In a rear-sector attack using the Lightning's Firestreak AAM missiles the target would have been well within visual range during the final stage, provided it was daytime, so there was little danger of engaging a friendly aircraft.

The replacement of the Lightning by the McDonnell Douglas Phantom FG.1/FGR.2 brought some dramatic

A McDonnell Douglas Phantom FGR.2 of No 41 Squadron, RAF Coningsby, armed with seven BL755 cluster bombs, four Sparrow and four Sidewinder air-to-air missiles.

changes in the RAF's Rules of Engagement, because the Phantom carried an impressive array of weapons, including some with a genuine BVR capability, and this raised many issues of identification, classification and tactics which had to be solved by tighter controls and realistic training if the risk of a costly error was to be eliminated. The AIM-7 Sparrow was capable of engaging targets at ranges well in excess of 12 miles, and at that distance the foolproof identification of a target without some form of visual enhancement was virtually impossible. The Phantom entered full RAF service in the air-defence role without any aid to visual identification, although US variants had carried an electro-optical device for this purpose for some time. The British variant was eventually fitted with air-to-air IFF, radar warning sensors and a telescope system.

Principally, the RAF's air-defence system had to guard against attacks by a new generation of fast Soviet aircraft armed with long-range missiles, and this generated a requirement for an interceptor capable of spending lengthy periods on patrol on the axis of the potential air threat, a long way from its home bases. At the beginning of the 1970s the Lightning was reaching the end of its useful life and its systems left a lot to be desired, while the Phantom, although expected to fulfil the air-defence role adequately, would need to be phased out in favour of a more advanced weapons system in the late 1980s.

In 1971, therefore, the UK Ministry of Defence (MoD) issued Air Staff Target 395, which called for a minimum-change, minimum-cost but effective interceptor to replace the Lightning and the F.4 Phantom in the air defence of the UK. Its primary armament was to be the British Aerospace Dynamics XJ521 Sky Flash medium-range, air-to-air missile, and the primary sensor a Marconi Avionics pulse-Doppler radar. The result was the Air Defence Variant (ADV) of the Panavia Tornado interdictor/strike (IDS) aircraft. The original Tornado ADV study envisaged four Sky Flash missiles under the wings, long-range tanks under the fuselage and a modified nose to accommodate the AI radar. Early aerodynamic trials, however, showed that with pylon-mounted missiles the ADV's performance fell short of requirements, giving little or no advantage over the Phantom it was intended to replace, even allowing for further engine developments. The answer was to carry the AAMs semi-submerged under the fuselage, giving a low-drag configuration. To accommodate the front pair of missiles some lengthening of the forward fuselage was necessary, but this produced an added bonus in that it increased internal fuel capacity by 10

This Panavia Tornado ADV (F.2) carries four Sky Flash, two Sidewinders and two long-range fuel tanks.

per cent. A further armament change involved the deletion of one of the ADV's two planned Mauser 27mm cannon, providing more space for the installation of avionics. The overall structural changes entailed stretching the fuselage by 53in (136cm) and giving the wing-root glove increased sweep, moving the centre of pressure forward to compensate for the resultant change of c.g. and to reduce wave drag.

Because of the minimum-change requirement, the only changes permitted to the Tornado IDS weapons system were those that would produce an effective air-defence aircraft at minimum cost. First of all, this involved the removal of all equipment not required for the air-defence role, including the Texas Instruments terrain-following/ground-mapping radar. The next stage was to identify equipment that only required modification for the air-defence role. This included the command stability-augmentation system (CSAS), which required inputs to reduce stick-pitch forces and increase roll rates for air combat. The result was a system common to both Tornado ADV and IDS, with the air-defence equipment added. This comprised the Marconi Avionics AI radar, with integrated Cossor IFF interrogator, a Singer-Kearfott secure datalink, a Marconi Space and Defence Systems radar homing-and-warning receiver, a Smiths Industries/Computing Devices missile-management system, and a new electronic head-down display in the front cockpit. All of this required considerable rewriting of the main computer software, and resulted in more changes than had originally been envisaged. Each step was approved separately by the MoD, which considered a number of alternatives, including the F-14 and F-15, before finally approving the whole ADV project in 1976.

The aircraft that eventually emerged was a long-range interceptor, with long on-CAP time, capable of engaging multiple targets in rapid succession, in all weathers and in complex electronic countermeasures (ECM) conditions. It was designed to operate with the UK Air Defence Ground Environment (UKADGE), airborne early warning (AEW) aircraft, tankers and air-defence ships, all linked in due course to a secure ECM-resistant data-and-voice command-and-control network. The problem of navigation at extreme range from fixed navigational systems was overcome by a highly accurate twin inertial platform, the Ferranti FIN1010, which provided the computer with accurate position data for steering to a large number of fixed or moving positions. This could be done automatically by use of the autopilot, allowing the crew to concentrate on the tactical information provided by the AI radar and datalink.

The intercept radar selected for the Tornado ADV was the Marconi (later GEC-Marconi) Avionics AI24 Foxhunter, development of which began in 1974. The essential requirement was that detection ranges should in no way be limited to target altitude. Look-down capability against low-level targets was the most demanding case, particularly when the interceptor itself was at low altitude. Severe and sophisticated electronic counter-measures also had to be overcome.

By the time the first Tornado ADV was ready to fly, late in 1979, the external stores fit had also undergone changes. The four Sky Flash AAMs were now joined by four AIM-9L Sidewinders on underwing stations, and the capacity of each drop tank was increased from 1,500 litres to 2,250 litres to extend unrefuelled range and time on CAP.

Three Tornado ADV prototypes were built. All were powered by the Turbo-Union RB.199 Mk 103 turbofan, which was also to power the initial production batch of Tornado F.2s for the RAF. These aircraft also featured manually controlled wing sweep, which would be automatic on later production aircraft. The first development Tornado ADV, A01, was a single-stick aircraft assigned to handling, performance and general systems evaluation. Early in 1982, to demonstrate that the ADV could fulfil its CAP requirements in all respects, this aircraft flew a CAP of 2hrs 20min over the North Sea, involving a flight of 325nm (602km) to the CAP area and a similar return flight. The aircraft was climbed out of Warton, Lancashire, and cruised at high altitude over the North Sea, then descended to medium altitude to take up a CAP racetrack pattern. On arriving back at base the aircraft loitered in the local area for 15min at low level before landing with more than 5 per cent internal fuel remaining after a total flight time of 4hrs 13min.

This was a very promising indication of the ADV's capability. So were the armament trials, carried out by A02 in the same year. Sky Flash firings were carried out from Mach 0.9 into the supersonic envelope, while Mauser gun-firing trials covered the subsonic flight envelope above 200kt (370km/h) from zero g to the angle-of-attack limit, and up to 30,000ft (9,150m). By the end of 1982 A03 had done most of the necessary radar and weapons-system-integration flight trials, and pre-production radar flight trials were scheduled to start in the near future, although it was now apparent that deliveries of the operational AI24 were going to be alarmingly late.

Despite problems with the AI radar there was nothing wrong with the aircraft and its other systems, and orders for the RAF now stood at 165, to be delivered in three batches. Pilots of 'A' Squadron of the Aeroplane and Armament Experimental Establishment (A&AEE) at Boscombe Down, who evaluated it, were very enthusiastic about all aspects except the radar, which failed to meet its specification in no fewer than fifty-two areas.

The problems with the Foxhunter were still far from resolved when the first Tornado F.2s were delivered to 229 Operational Conversion Unit (OCU) at RAF Con-

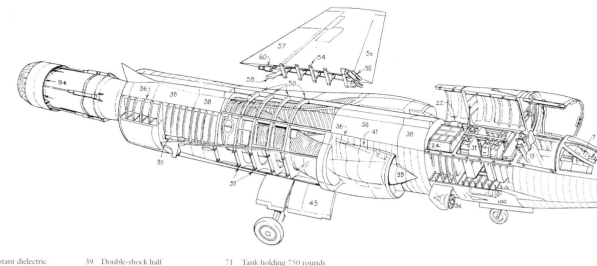

1. Erosion-resistant dielectric nose, rail mounted for access
2. Nose mounting runners
3. Packaged ASC-14 fire-control unit
4. Radar cooling air supply
5. Cooling air outlet
6. Battle camera
7. Radar gunsight
8. One-piece casting below windscreen
9. Retracting shroud
10. Radar scope
11. Angle-of-attack vane
12. Rear-view mirror
13. Downward-ejecting seat
14. Servicing and escape hatch
15. Radar aerial
16. Steerable nose undercarriage
17. Mechanical door linkage
18. Taxiing lamps
19. Air exit louvres
20. Gun blast tube
21. Six-barrel T.171-E3 gun (20mm)
22. Ammunition feed chute
23. Ammunition compartment
24. Ammunition tank
25. Case ejection chute
26. Gun drive motor
27. Recoil shock mountings
28. Floor to electronics and ammunition compartments
29. Supply and circuit-breaker box
30. Common shock-mounted electronics racking
31. 'Jeep-can' electronics, cooled through rack supply
32. Flush aerial
33. Access to tank booster pump
34. Ram-driven emergency hydraulic pump and alternator
35. Bottom longerons
36. Top longerons
37. Central keel member
38. Stressed access panels along decking

39. Double-shock half centre-body
40. Boundary-layer bleed on 39
41. Space for boundary layer inboard of intake
42. Precision-cast intake lip
43. Drape-type fuel cell
44. Stressed floor to aft-fuselage tank bay
45. Pre-closing main-undercarriage doors
46. Liquid spring unit
47. Door linkage
48. Main retraction jacks
49. Wheel-pivoting linkage
50. Wing carry-through frames
51. Wing pick-up points
52. Machined leading edge (R=0.016in)
53. Machined trailing edge
54. Wing root forged brackets
55. Continuous machined skin, root to tip
56. Hinged leading edge
57. Plain flap with blowing
58. Bleed air duct for flap-blowing
59. Leading-edge actuator
60. Flap actuator
61. Grouped aileron actuators (10)
62. Stores pylon
63. Tip tank (200 USgal)
64. GAR-8 (Sidewinder) air-to-air missile
65. Infrared seeker head
66. Control servo section
67. Norris-Thermador or Hunter Douglas motor tube
68. Tracking flares
69. Pod containing T.171-E3 gun
70. Linkless ammunition feed

71. Tank holding 750 rounds
72. Generator access panel
73. Generators (Red Bank division of Bendix)
74. Generator cooling-air feed
75. Chemically milled duct
76. Inner wall of starboard duct
77. Low-speed auxiliary intake doors
78. Hamilton Standard pneumatic starter (60hp)
79. Variable-stator actuator
80. Hydraulic group on engine-bay door
81. Filters
82. Accumulators
83. Charging points
84. Forward portion of ventral fin
85. Airbrake ram
86. Fuselage break-joint
87. Attachment-bolt access flaps
88. Engine mounting
89. Afterburner fuel gallery
90. Navigation light
91. Braking parachute door
92. Afterburner
93. Hydraulic nozzle actuators
94. Ejector air ducts
95. Tailplane actuator group
96. Tailplane horn
97. Tailplane hinge
98. Single skin, tip to toe
99. Autostabiliser tab
100. Air-conditioning bay

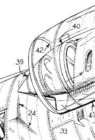

Lockheed F-104A Starfighter

(see page 165)

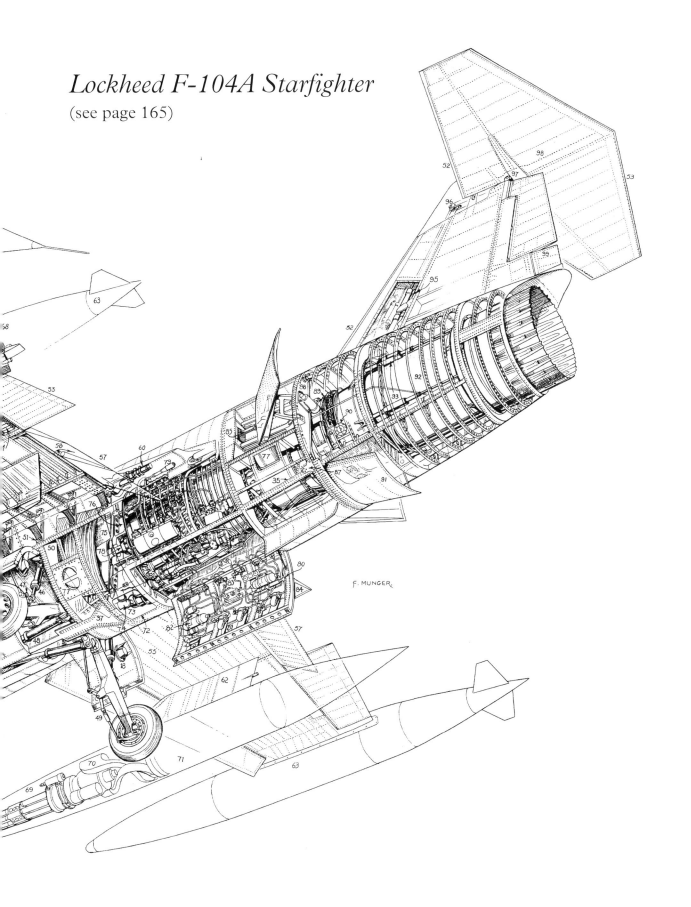

F. MUNGER

A Tornado F.3 of 229 Operational Conversion Unit, RAF.

ingsby, Lincolnshire, in November 1984. The first eighteen aircraft were all powered by Mk 103 engines; aircraft after that had the more powerful Mk 104, which combined a 360mm reheat extension with a Lucas Aerospace digital electronic engine-control unit (DECU). These later aircraft, designated Tornado F.3 (the definitive production version of the design) also featured the full armament of four Sky Flash and four AIM-9Ls, automatic wing sweep, and automanoeuvre devices, with the slats and flaps deploying as a function of angle of attack and wing sweep.

It was not until 1986 that the first modified AI24 Foxhunter radars were delivered for installation in the OCU aircraft, the necessary modifications having cost an additional £250 million. The first squadron, No 29, was formed at RAF Coningsby in May 1987 and declared operational at the end of November. The aircraft eventually equipped seven squadrons in addition to 229 OCU (which became 56 Reserve Squadron on 1 July 1992).

The Tornado F.3 opened up a whole range of tactical possibilities for No 11 Group RAF, the air-defence group responsible for its operations. Its excellent take-off and landing characteristics mean that the aircraft can, if necessary, deploy to small airfields or even sections of motorway, together with its auxiliary power unit and datalink. All the crew needs to do is remain on

cockpit alert, monitoring tactical developments on the multifunction displays via the datalink, and wait for the order to scramble. Long before combat is joined, pilot and navigator will have an accurate appraisal of the tactical situation.

Normal air-defence operations with the Tornado F.3 involve what is known as a 'heavy combat fit', which means four Sky Flash, four Sidewinders and no external tanks. The CAP fit with the two tanks is reserved specifically for long-range sorties. A good example of what the F.3 can achieve without the long-range tanks was given on 10 September 1988, when two aircraft of 5 Squadron were scrambled from RAF Coningsby to intercept a pair of Tupolev Tu-95 *Bear*-D maritime radar reconnaissance aircraft over the Norwegian Sea. A VC10 tanker was scrambled from RAF Leuchars to rendezvous with the Tornados, which carried out the intercept successfully.

The Tornado F.3 is, first and foremost, a missile platform. The aircraft's AI24 radar uses a technique known as frequency-modulated-interrupted continuous wave (FMICW), with which is integrated a Cossor IFF-3500 interrogator and a radar-signal processor to suppress ground clutter (one of the major sources of the problems associated with its protracted development). The radar's high pulse-repetition frequency (PRF) enables it to detect targets at an initial range of about 100nm

(185km), while FMICW allows the range of the target to be determined from the frequency change between transmission and reception.

As they are detected, the targets are stored in the central digital computer, which is the same as that in the Tornado IDS variant. Since the radar continues to scan normally, the targets are unaware that they are the subject of detailed analysis. The system rejects unwanted signals, leaving only real targets which then pass through the radar data processor before display to the aircraft's crew. While the radar keeps up a 'running commentary' on ranges, velocities and tracks of established targets, it continues to scan and report new plots. With the computer fully updated, the crew plan their approach to engage the maximum number of targets. Displays are duplicated in the front cockpit for the pilot, who steers to the engagement on his HUD. The symbology for Sky Flash, Sidewinder or gun attacks is very clear, and an important feature is the target indicator, which aids the pilot in an early visual sighting.

For a long-range interception the Sky Flash semiactive radar-homing AAM would be used. Developed from the AIM-7E Sparrow, this weapon features several improvements, including early discrimination between grouped targets, positive target-detection and tracking against ground radar clutter, ECM resistance, more accurate guidance resulting in reduced miss distance, better proximity fuzing and improved reliability. The original version required continuous-wave illumination by the launch aircraft's radar all the way to the target, but the latest version is fitted with a monopulse radar-homing head. It can engage targets at high altitude or down to 250ft (76m) in the face of heavy ECM and at stand-off ranges of more than 25nm (46km).

The Sky Flash launch sequence lasts less than a tenth of a second, the missile being driven down from its fuselage recess and through the flow fields around the aircraft by two gas-operated, long-stroke rams (developed by Frazer-Nash). The rams, which also stabilise the missile in roll and yaw during ejection, are then retracted to avoid adding post-launch drag. The system enables the F.3 to launch its missiles across the entire flight envelope. The Tornado F.3 is also compatible with the AIM-120 Advanced Medium Range AAM (AMRAAM).

For engagements at closer range the AIM-9L infrared-homing AAM Sidewinder would be used. To respond quickly to a close-in threat, the pilot can take control of the weapons systems by selecting the air-to-air override mode. This mode, optimised for visual combat, is controlled by two multifunction buttons mounted on the throttle. Pressing the buttons in sequence selects the close-combat radar mode and associated HUD displays, as well as the required weapons, without the pilot having to take his hands off the throttle or stick. A hand controller, located aft of the throttles, may be used to slew the radar scanner or missile homing heads if the automatic HUD scan pattern is insufficient to acquire the target. Once the target is in scan, lock-on is automatic. The AIM-132 Advanced Short Range AAM (ASRAAM) is also integrated on the F.3.

Although it is not a fighter in the strictest sense of the word, the Tornado F.3 gives an excellent account of itself in combat with other contemporary aircraft, including the F-16 Fighting Falcon. With its wings swept at 45° the Tornado can hold its own in a turning fight with most combat aircraft of its generation. The aircraft's spin-prevention and incidence-limiting system (SPILS) provides carefree handling, and stick forces are about 30 per cent lighter than those of the Tornado GR.1. Another useful feature is that the pilot can bang the throttles open and shut without penalty. The F.3 is capable of Mach 2.2 at high level, and more than 800kt (1,482km/h) at low level; in both cases, fuel consumption is surprisingly low. A 'clean' F.3 can fly for one hour at 420kt (778km/h), low level, and still have sufficient fuel for half an hour's flying.

Electronic support for the defensive fighter

No modern fighter, whether designed for air superiority over the battlefield or for long-range interception, can function successfully without being fully integrated with airborne and ground-based electronic surveillance systems. Today's ground-based systems combine a centralised command structure with a decentralised sensor network that is secure, survivable and capable of functioning even after sustaining substantial damage. They are based on advanced portable ground radars, enabling sensors to be deployed almost anywhere, and telecommunications technology providing a network of lines and exchanges that would continue to route both voice and data transmissions along any path so long as some sort of physical connection remains.

The Improved UK Air Defence Ground Environment (IUKADGE) is typical of such a system. It involves three different types of new-generation radar, operating in two wavebands. There are two General Electric GE592 and four GEC/Marconi Martello 23cm radars, operating in the L-band, and six Plessey/ITT 10cm radars operating in the S-band. All are three-dimensional radars capable of measuring target range, bearing and height. Each radar is deployed in a convoy of about fifteen vehicles to a presurveyed but unmarked site indistinguishable from the surrounding countryside. The radar head is located remotely from its associated reporting post, and is protected by decoys intended to confuse anti-radar missiles. The overlapping L- and S-band coverage also reduces the risk of enemy jamming. As an extra insurance, an electronic counter-countermeasures officer forms part of the reporting post (RP) trailer crew, his function being to assist the radar in overcoming any jamming problems.

Associated with four of the twelve RPs are hardened Command and Reporting Posts (CRPs) with local tracking and fighter-control capability. These provide backup facilities for the Command and Reporting Centres (CRCs), which under normal circumstances are responsible for tracking and interceptor control, and are the nerve centres of the UK air-defence system.

The process of building up a picture of a possible air threat begins with the first receipt of radar plots (target positions) and strobes (the bearings of enemy jammers). This information is fed into the air-defence system via a narrow-band datalink. At the CRC the plots are combined with those of other radars for multi-radar target tracking; these active tracks are then combined with passive tracks derived from jamming strobes. Tracks from AEW and interceptor aircraft are also introduced, together with those from other CRCs, and track-to-track correlation is carried out to produce the local picture. Then the recognition process begins, an automatic interface with the principal air traffic control centre ensuring instant access to all currently filed civil flight plans.

With the threat revealed, the fighter controllers can now marshal and direct their forces. Sea tracks are introduced into the system to produce the final recognised air-sea picture; this mutual exchange of information between elements ensures that all centres share the same constantly updated picture of the UK Air Defence Region, so that even if an element is lost, the big picture

will remain intact. In addition, the CRCs interface with the NATO Air Defence Ground Environment (NADGE) and France's STRIDA II air-defence systems for target data exchange.

Another key element in the air-defence system is the AEW aircraft, and in this respect the NATO requirement is filled by the Boeing E-3 Sentry. The E-3, originally known as the EC-137, stemmed from a NATO requirement for an early warning aircraft equipped with radar systems capable of extending the low-altitude radar view of Warsaw Pact territory by as much as 150 miles, thereby filling the existing gaps in low-altitude coverage left by ground-based radars, and providing a major advance in early warning protection. The aircraft's role was summed up by General John S Pustay, Director of the USAF Airborne Warning and Command System (AWACS) Task Force, speaking in 1976, a year before the first E-3As entered USAF service:

The E-3A would not only be able to track enemy formations as they approach the border; it would also make very difficult the deceptive forward assembly of large numbers of aircraft. Through routine surveillance ... we could monitor typical aircraft activity patterns throughout East Germany and the western portions of Czechoslovakia and Poland. We could then determine changes in patterns which may be threatening – not only an obvious infusion of attack aircraft at forward bases, but also

Two Tornado F.3s of No 5 Squadron from Coningsby accompany a Boeing Sentry AEW Mk 1 AWACS of No 8 Squadron, based at RAF Waddington.

more subtle activities such as the movement of support and transport aircraft out of the forward zone to clear ramp and hangar space to an unusual degree. Acting on such changes in pattern, or whenever our intelligence suggests a need for more concentrated surveillance, we could deploy more E-3As and fly continuous orbits to provide uninterrupted surveillance.

Although the perceived threat from the East has receded over the horizon, if it has not vanished entirely, the core of the E-3's role today remains the detection of an air threat. Its primary function in the Gulf War was to detect the movement of Iraqi aircraft and to direct Allied fighters to the point where a successful interception could be made. It has been used extensively for surveillance of the former Yugoslavia (Operation 'Deny Flight'), providing intelligence of aircraft, helicopter and missile-battery movements that might present a threat to UN peacekeeping forces. In this context it has worked closely with USAF F-15s and F-16s, RAF Tornado F.3s, and French Air Force Mirage 2000s.

At the heart of the E-3's systems is its Westinghouse surveillance radar, which can track targets more than 300nm (550km) away while the E-3 orbits at 30,000ft (9,000m). The 30ft (9.15m)-diameter radome turns at six revolutions per minute when the equipment is active, and has various operating modes depending on the task in hand. The standard E-3A's radar was later modified to track ships, and other modifications included the fitting of a faster central computer with expanded memory, together with improved communications equipment. This included the Joint Tactical Information Distribution System (JTIDS), which ensures an unbroken transmission of data if main communications links are disrupted and gives fighter and attack crews an unprecedented picture of the air battle. Fighters equipped with the system include the F-15 and Tornado F.3. The E-3 Sentry fulfils the AWACS role with the USAF, the RAF and NATO, and with the French Air Force.

Air-combat training
Superiority in air combat is not necessarily guaranteed by having superior equipment. This was apparent following the unification of Germany, when the Luftwaffe vetted a number of East German MiG-29 pilots, and found them to be seriously below NATO standards in terms of training and performance in the air.

NATO fighter squadrons based in Europe send detachments periodically to the NATO Air Combat Manoeuvring Instrumentation Range (ACMI) at Decci-mommanu, in Sardinia, which became operational in 1979 under the auspices of the USAF in Europe (USAFE) for the combat training of NATO fast-jet fighter pilots. 'Decci' is one of twelve similar ranges throughout the world, these facilities providing fighter

pilots with the opportunity for aggressive fighter combat in a realistic scenario without requiring special targets, live missiles, or, more importantly, such an exercise leading to the possible accidental loss of a pilot or an aircraft.

The range itself is a 30nm (60km) circle over the sea about 50nm (93km) off the west coast of Sardinia, with a base height of 5,000ft (1,525m) and a ceiling of 50,000ft (15,250m). Any aircraft straying from the circle, unless transitting to or from the range, can be recalled to base by the local coastal radar at Mirto. This applies particularly to the adjacent northwest area outside the range, where there is a civilian air route.

The ACMI consists of four principal interfaced elements. The first is an Airborne Instrumentation Subsystem (AIS), a pylon-attached transponder pod with locking and connection points identical to those of the AIM-9 Sidewinder and linked to the aircraft's electrical, avionic and weapons systems. The AIS pod communicates directly with equipment in four 35-ton (35.56-tonne) buoys – the Tracking and Communications Subsystem (TCS) – moored at sea beneath the range, one in the centre and the others around the circumference. Two additional land-based monitoring units located on mountains to the north and south of Decci complete the remote part of the TCS.

The information is passed to the land-based TCS master station situated some 4,000ft (1,220m) up a mountain north of Decci, and from there is fed by microwave to the Computer and Computation Subsystem (CCS) at Decci. This processes the data received from each aircraft: altitude, speed, bearing, angle of attack, and what types of missile are programmed into it. It also calculates the range and simulated track of a missile in relation to the dynamic track of its selected target.

From the CCS computers the data is passed to two large graphical VDU screen displays above a console manned by the Range Training Officer (RTO); these can be watched by an audience of about twenty. It is the responsibility of the RTOs to monitor the exercise, to

An Airborne Instrumentation Subsystem pod carried by a Royal Navy Sea Harrier.

vector the pilots towards the opposition (saving time and simulating ground radar control) and to have radio contact with their own pilots. Not only can the audience see the aircraft in plan view, but the image can be rotated through 90° to give an elevation. Furthermore, a second screen, normally used for an alphanumeric display of the aircraft data, can be used to show a graphical cockpit view of any combatant.

A typical range sortie starts two hours before take-off with a briefing of all participating aircrew, which might involve two USAF F-15 pilots and two RAF Tornado F.3 crews. Individual element briefs then follow, where tactics for the day are discussed. Ten minutes before on-range time, the computer is programmed for the mission with details of aircraft, weapons fits and limits. Once the aircraft are in position, and the computer has locked on to their AIS pods, the fight starts. A two-versus-two combat is usual, as this gives the best training value. While a combat is in progress, those gathered before the monitoring screens can hear the radio chatter between the opponents, a strange mixture of twenty-first-century terminology and Battle of Britain jargon. A two-versus-one situation, for example, might sound something like this:

> **Ground controller:** 'Bogey [suspected hostile aircraft] thirty degrees at eighteen miles.'
> **Lead aircraft:** 'Heading 340 degrees, seventeen miles.'
> **Wingman:** 'Visual. Contact twenty degrees right of nose.'
> **Lead aircraft:** 'On nose, six miles.'
> **Wingman:** 'On nose, two and a half.'
> **Lead aircraft:** 'Tally ho!'
> **Wingman:** 'Where is he?'
> **Lead aircraft:** 'Passing ... in a left-hand turn.'
> **Wingman:** 'Do you have a visual?'
> **Lead aircraft:** 'Continue left turn and look a couple of thousand feet below the sun.'
> **Wingman:** 'Going hard left – got a visual.'
> **Lead aircraft:** 'Fox Two.'
> **Bogey:** 'OK ... Good shot.'

A 'Fox Two' is a simulated heat-seeking missile launch, 'Fox One' is a radar-guided missile launch, and 'Fox Three' is a gun engagement.

When an aircraft is 'killed', a coffin-shaped outline appears around it and its pilot is vectored out of the fight by his RTO for 45sec, at which point he is free to return and the coffin is removed. During this period the computer will not recognise, and therefore not record, any missile launch or gun firing from the killed aircraft. The length of combat time over the range is strictly controlled to 20min slots for the aircraft using the facility. At the end of their slot the pilots return and debrief, using a video recording of the combat at the Display and Debrief Subsystem. They can freeze a frame or play back to identify mistakes, lost opportunities and incidents during the range slot to get a clear and complete overall picture of the combat.

Which enemy?

Although exercises such as that described above help to keep the modern fighter pilot and interceptor crew honed to a fine degree of skill, they were devised during the Cold War, when objectives were clearly defined. Then, the fighter's mission was to defend its territorial airspace, or the airspace of a recognised alliance such as NATO or the Warsaw Pact. Today the mission has changed radically. Although the integrity of national airspace remains vitally important, the fighters of one or other of the former major power blocs may be called upon to operate anywhere in the world, sometimes in concert with each other, sometimes not, in support of a UN resolution. Pilots may find themselves locked in combat with aircraft and weapon systems built in their own countries and sold to Third World powers, flown by opposing pilots trained by the same system as themselves.

Instability and the proliferation of weapon exports make the prediction of potential threats almost impossible. Not only do such threats exist, however; they are likely to increase as Third World nations, with their ability to buy 'off-the-shelf' components for ground-launched cruise missiles and access to the science necessary to build up a stockpile of nuclear, chemical and biological warheads, acquire a substantial military capability. The day of the air-defence fighter is far from over.

9
Airlift Operations
Keith Chapman

On 2 August 1990, Iraqi tanks thundered into Kuwait, crushing all resistance and threatening Western access to the Gulf oilfields. This brutal invasion triggered widespread condemnation and provoked an immediate response by a coalition of Allies acting under the authority of the United Nations. Within a few days, Operation 'Desert Shield' had been launched. Its initial objective was to thwart any Iraqi attempt to invade Saudi Arabia, and to demonstrate to the regime in Baghdad that the Allies were resolved to use force, if all else failed, to dislodge the Iraqi army from Kuwait. Agreeing and declaring these aims was one thing, but implementation was quite another.

One of many formidable problems facing the Alliance was the distance over which troops and equipment would have to be deployed. This posed particular difficulties for the Americans, who, from the outset, recognised that they would have to shoulder the lion's share of any international action against Saddam Hussein. The Gulf was 8,000 miles (12,800km) by air from the East Coast of the USA, and some troops would have to be deployed from the West Coast, which was a daunting 11,500 miles (18,400km) from the Gulf by air. Although the Suez Canal was expected to remain open to Allied shipping, the distance by sea was 10,350 miles (16,560km) from the East Coast and 12,650 miles (20,240km) from the West Coast. This meant that even the fastest logistic ships, sailing from East Coast ports, would take at least two weeks to reach the Gulf. Speed being of the essence, and with relatively little US equipment pre-positioned in the region, it was obvious that only a major airlift could insert sufficient forces in time to deter an Iraqi invasion of Saudi Arabia, thought to be next on Saddam Hussein's list of objectives.

Prudently, the USA had prepared for such an eventuality. The Cold War was coming to an end and the USA, together with her NATO allies, was reviewing her strategy to reflect the changing threat. A corollary of the sharp reduction in US forces stationed in Europe was an increased reliance on strategic lift, both for reinforcement within the NATO area and for intervention in regional conflicts elsewhere. Against this changing geopolitical background the USA had recognised the vital importance of maintaining a substantial airlift capability for the rapid projection of forces to deter, counter or defeat aggression wherever it might threaten Western interests. Such contingency planning (plus recent measures to improve the co-ordination and inte-gration of military transport assets under a new and unified command headquarters, United States Transportation Command (USTRANSCOM)) meant that the USA was well placed to react effectively to the Iraqi action. The remarkable contribution of airlift to the ensuing deployment is described in the inset below.

Although new lessons were learned from what turned out to be one of the largest and most successful airlifts ever mounted, the real significance of this operation lay in its emphatic confirmation of existing principles. This point was well summarised by General John Shalikashvili, Chairman of the US Joint Chiefs of Staff, who wrote:

> Strategic mobility, the capability to transport military forces rapidly across intercontinental distances into an operational theatre, lies at the heart of US military strategy. Nowhere has the importance of strategic mobility been more evident than in Operation 'Desert Shield'/'Desert Storm'. It was strategic mobility which enabled the USA and her Allies to assemble an overwhelming military force to defeat Iraq and free Kuwait.

Growing importance of airlift operations since 1945
The Allied victory in the Gulf War would have been far more difficult without the major airlift which preceded it. Yet that operation, impressive as it was, was only one of several such airlifts mounted during the past fifty years.

The first large-scale air transport operation of the postwar era began in June 1948, when the USSR imposed a total blockade on all surface access to the British, French and US sectors of Berlin. Determined that the enclave (which contained two million German citizens as well as the Allied garrisons) should not be starved into submission, the three Allies reacted by launching an emergency airlift. A task of such magnitude had never previously been attempted, and the chances of success must have seemed remote. However, the Allies surprised all concerned, including the Soviet leadership, with the effectiveness of their response. Using the combined air transport assets of the USAF and the RAF, plus a modest contribution from French military and British commercial sources, the Allies successfully ran a round-the-clock and virtually all-weather operation between various mounting bases west of the Iron Curtain and the three receiving airfields inside West Berlin. Although the aircraft employed were much less capable and reliable than modern airlifters, the Allies collectively delivered a staggering 2,325,800 short tons

Operations 'Desert Shield' and 'Desert Storm'
7 August 1990 to 10 March 1991

The US airlift for Operations 'Desert Shield' and 'Desert Storm' was run by Military Airlift Command (MAC) under the direction of its superior headquarters, USTRANSCOM. When deployment began, on 7 August 1990, the strategic airlift fleet at MAC's disposal comprised 110 Lockheed C-5 Galaxies and 234 C-141 Starlifters.

On 17 August, recognising that even assets on this scale would be insufficient for the task, USTRANSCOM activated Stage One of the Civil Reserve Air Fleet (CRAF) agreement. This was a long-standing arrangement between the US Department of Defense and a number of commercial airlines, whereby the latter had agreed to provide aircraft in time of tension or war in return for military business in peacetime. Activation of this agreement yielded thirty-two passenger aircraft and thirty-six cargo aircraft, a total of sixty-eight drawn from sixteen airlines. Added to its force of 344 military transports, these additional civilian resources increased MAC's overall strategic assets to 412 aircraft. As the operation progressed, further airlift was provided by up to twenty KC-10 tanker/transports of the US Air Force's Strategic Air Command (SAC), though there were periods when some or all of these aircraft were unavailable to MAC because of prior commitments in support of deploying fighters.

During 8–26 August MAC carried the 82nd Airborne Division from the USA to Saudi Arabia on 244 C-141, 100 C-5 and 40 CRAF flights. In addition it airlifted the 101st Airborne Division into the operational area on sixty-two C-141, fifty-five C-5 and twenty-nine CRAF missions between 17 August and 25 September, as well as the 1st Marine Expeditionary Brigade on 33 C-141, 117 C-5 and 20 CRAF missions between 25 August and 22 September. Once these deployments were completed the tempo eased, allowing aircraft to resume scheduled maintenance and giving their crews a well-earned rest.

The respite was brief. Following President Bush's decision on 8 November to commit additional forces, including two heavy armoured divisions from Germany, the airlift intensified still further, building to a peak of 127 missions (one arrival every 11 minutes) on D-Day, 17 January 1991, the day when 'Desert Storm' was launched.

According to official US statistics, USTRANSCOM moved more personnel and equipment to the Gulf during the first three weeks of 'Desert Shield' than were moved into theatre during the first three months of the Korean War. MAC's contribution to this deployment was notable not only in terms of missions flown and payloads carried, but also for its wider military implications. By demonstrating that credible air and ground forces could be rapidly airlifted at short notice over vast distances, together with much of the logistic support to sustain them, MAC (and its Allied equivalents in France, the UK and elsewhere) was directly instrumental in deterring Saddam Hussein from invading Saudi Arabia.

of food, coal and other supplies during the 463 days from 26 June 1948 to 30 September 1949.

The Berlin Airlift ended when the Soviet authorities, realising that their bluff had been called, reopened the surface logistic routes. The operation cost aircrew lives and aircraft, but saved the occupants of the beleaguered city from starvation or worse. Equally important, it was a powerful demonstration of Western resolve in the face of Soviet intimidation. As such, it confirmed that air transport forces could be used to apply political as well as military pressure.

Airlift's contribution to force projection
The outcome of the Berlin Airlift was a powerful incentive to both the leading and lesser powers to maintain strong air transport forces. The contribution which such assets could make was underlined by the steady improvement in the capabilities of airlifters coming off the various aerospace production lines in the postwar decades. Range, speed, payload capacity and reliability all improved immeasurably, further enhancing the

potential of military air transport for force projection. Political and military leaders alike came to realise that the quickest and sometimes the only way of bringing pressure to bear was to deploy forces by air. Conversely, without airlift, circumstances were likely to arise – particularly at the strategic level, but also in some tactical scenarios – in which force could not be exerted within an acceptable time-frame.

This does not mean that units can deploy expeditiously only if they are flown to their area of operations. In certain situations – where, for example, the distance involved is only a few hundred miles – it might be almost as quick and certainly more cost-effective to deploy units by road, rail, sea or a combination of all three where such methods are practicable. Furthermore, airlift cannot compete in terms of payload with the huge capacity of an efficient rail system or a fleet of cargo ships. In practice, the strategic mobility on which effective force projection depends derives from a combination of airlift, sealift, overland logistics and, where feasible, pre-positioning of equipment in the anticipated area of operations.

Preparing to load a helicopter on to a C-5B Galaxy of US Military Airlift Command.

Nevertheless, the fact remains that in many situations, especially where speed of response is critical, airlift will assume an overriding importance. For example, a fighter squadron cannot operate away from its home base without ground crew, specialist equipment, weapons and fuel. Apart from the latter, all of this logistic support will normally have to be airlifted to the forward operating base if the inherent speed and flexibility of the fighter aircraft is not to be jeopardised. Depending on aircraft performance, distance, availability of staging airfields and overflight clearances, air-combat units may be unable to be deployed unless air-to-air refuelling (AAR) is available *en route*. The tanker/transport aircraft specifically designed to perform the AAR and airlift roles simultaneously have proved extremely effective in supporting such deployments. The most notable example of a tanker/airlifter currently in frontline service is the McDonnell Douglas KC-10 Extender, operated by SAC. This aircraft is examined in detail later in this chapter.

Strategic airlift operations

As already noted, airlift has an especially crucial role to play in the exertion of military pressure over intercontinental distances. However, strategic airlift operations are not undertaken solely in the context of power projection, but are often conducted for other purposes, such as the support of overseas garrisons, deployment exercises and humanitarian relief. Many examples of

The McDonnell Douglas KC-10 Extender was designed to perform AAR and airlift missions simultaneously.

THE MODERN WAR MACHINE

the latter have occurred in recent years, including the international airlift into Sarajevo during July 1992–January 1996. The Sarajevo airlift is covered in more detail at the end of this section.

Airlifters destined for the strategic role must meet a wide range of exacting criteria. Ideally, they should be capable of:

Carrying outsize items (e.g. self-propelled artillery, armoured fighting vehicles and small helicopters).

Carrying a flexible mix of personnel and cargo.

Long-range operations (at least 3,450 miles (5,520km) with maximum payload) with the capability to extend range/increase payload by AAR.

High cruising speed (at least Mach 0.75).

Rapid on-load and off-load, with large cargo doors and integral ramps.

Operations from austere airfields at forward locations.

Air-dropping (for contingency strategic/tactical missions).

The need for such versatility poses formidable challenges to the aerospace industry. With its design driven by the above criteria, a modern strategic airlifter will usually feature a high wing fitted with lift-enhancing devices, an elevated tail, a low-slung fuselage and rugged landing gear (a combination of suspension, wheels and tyres) able to withstand severe stresses during landing and take-off. These parameters permit the provision of a

spacious cargo hold with access via large rear (and sometimes front) doors and integral ramps. Few manufacturers have produced strategic airlifters, mainly because few states other than the USA and former USSR have ever been able to justify their need or high cost. Apart from these two countries, only the People's Republic of China and the UK have operated significant numbers of strategic transports in recent years, and then only on a minuscule scale compared with the current fleet of over 300 such aircraft in the USAF inventory.

The USA has also led the way in terms of quality, with aircraft such as the C-141, C-5, KC-10 and C-17. Immediately before its political demise the former Soviet Union could field some 360 strategic airlifters, but few of these stood comparison with the generally superior machines produced by US manufacturers. Arguably the only exceptions were the Ilyushin Il-76 (with a similar performance to that of the C-141) and the mighty Antonov An-124.

An-124 *Condor*

When the An-124 (dubbed *Condor* by NATO) made its public debut at the Paris air show in 1985 it was immediately hailed as the world's largest aircraft, surpassing even the huge C-5. Although by no means the sole criterion by which such aircraft should be judged, size definitely does matter in the case of airlifters! Hence it is interesting to compare the dimensions of the An-124 and C-5.

As the data in Table 1 confirm, the An-124 has greater wingspan and a taller fin than the C-5, but the American aircraft is 21ft (6.4m) longer than its Ukrainian rival. Hence the C-5's cargo hold is over 2ft (0.6m) longer than that of the An-124, an advantage which

Table 1: Comparison of Antonov An-124 and Lockheed C-5 Galaxy

	An-124	C-5B
Length	226ft 8.5in (69.1m)	247ft 9.5in (75.53m)
Height	69ft 2in (21.08m)	65ft 1in (19.84m)
Wingspan	240ft 6in (73.3m)	222ft 8.5in (67.88m)
Length of cargo hold (excluding ramp)	119ft 9in (36.5m)	121ft 1.5in (36.982m)
Length of cargo hold (including ramp)	142ft 7in (43.45m)	144ft 7in (43.38m)
Maximum height of hold	14ft 5in (4.4m)	13ft 6in (4.11m)
Maximum width of hold	21ft 11in (6.68m)	19ft (5.79m)
Maximum fuel capacity	468,151lb (212,350kg)	332,500lb (149,625kg)
Empty weight	385,800lb (175,000kg)	374,000lb (169.643kg)
Maximum payload	330,693lb (150,000kg)	261,000lb (118,390kg)
Maximum take-off weight	892,871lb (405,000kg)	837,000lb (379,657kg)
Range with maximum payload	2,796 miles (4,500km)	3,435 miles (5,525km)

The Antonov An-124-100, currently the world's largest aircraft, in the livery of Heavylift-Volga Dnepr.

Despite its generally larger dimensions and its greater payload and fuel capacities, the An-124's empty weight is only 4,990kg (11,000lb) greater than that of the C-5. This is the result of skilful design based on the use of immensely strong but relatively light materials including titanium alloy (used to construct the cargo hold floor), glassfibre reinforced plastic (GRP) and carbonfibre composites (CFC). Although GRP and CFCs are not used in the primary airframe or control surfaces, they are incorporated as widely as possible elsewhere. Altogether, it is estimated that the GRP and CFC components are 1,815kg (4,000lb) lighter than if they had been constructed from metal.

Like the C-5, the An-124 has two decks, the lower serving as the cargo hold. A kneeling undercarriage system allows the aircraft to be tilted for loading or unloading through either the nose visor or rear doors. Integral ramps are fitted at both front and rear. The upper deck is divided at the wing into two sections, the rear cabin providing seats for eighty-eight passengers. The forward section consists of the flight-deck, galley and rest area for a second crew.

C-5 Galaxy

Although it is slightly smaller overall than the An-124, the C-5 is nevertheless a goliath among airlifters. Despite having entered service in 1970 (fifteen years earlier than the An-124), the C-5 has several advantages over its rival. Not least among these is its ability to refuel in the air. There are two variants of the Galaxy, the C-5A and C-5B, both in service exclusively with the USAF. Eighty-one C-5As were acquired during 1970–3, and fifty C-5Bs during 1985–9. When 'Desert Shield' began on 7 August 1990, MAC could call upon sixty C-5As and fifty C-5Bs.

increases to more than 24ft (7.3m) if the loading capacity of the C-5's rear ramp is included. Cargo cannot be carried on the rear ramp of the An-124. Nonetheless, thanks to its higher and wider hold, the An-124 has a greater volumetric capacity and can carry significantly more payload, being able to lift 31,635kg (69,693lb) more than the C-5. Whether this can be fully exploited is uncertain, for airlifters have a tendency to 'bulk out' before reaching their weightlifting limit. Normally, the latter can be fully utilised only when particularly dense loads, such as pallets of ammunition, are carried.

A Lockheed C-5A Galaxy of the US Military Airlift Command.

While it can carry up to 345 troops, the C-5 is employed primarily as a freighter. With its integral ramps, kneeling landing gear and forward and rear doors which open to expose the full width and height of the cargo hold, the aircraft can be speedily loaded and unloaded. Vehicles can drive right through the hold, loading at the rear and then, on arrival, unloading at the front once the nose visor is raised and front ramp extended. With aircraft that lack this drive-through capability, vehicles must either be reversed into the hold during loading if a speedy off-load is required, or be driven on board normally and then reversed out at the destination. Both methods are laborious and operationally undesirable, but they are the only options unless there is access to the hold at each end.

The load-bearing strength of its cargo deck and full-width access to its roomy hold enable the C-5 to carry a variety of outsize loads. For example, it can accommodate two M-1 main battle tanks, eight armoured personnel carriers or six UH-60A helicopters. This allows the C-5 to carry virtually every item in the US Army's inventory of combat equipment. The upper-deck configuration is similar to that of the An-124: a passenger cabin to the rear with seventy-five seats and a forward section containing the flight-deck, rest facilities for a second crew and seats for a further eight passengers.

KC-10 Extender

A derivative of the McDonnell Douglas DC-10 airliner, the KC-10 is an advanced tanker/airlifter specifically designed for the global force-projection role. In service with SAC, its primary mission is to provide AAR during the long-range deployment and redeployment of combat aircraft, while simultaneously carrying their support personnel and equipment. The KC-10 can also be used to provide AAR for strategic airlifters such as the C-5, C-17 and indeed other KC-10s in order to increase their range and/or payload and reduce their reliance on staging airfields and overflight clearances. Additionally, as a versatile airlifter in its own right, the KC-10 is sometimes used to augment the regular strategic transport fleet.

In 1979 a squadron of twelve F-15s, 115 tons of support equipment and 209 personnel were deployed from the USA to Saudi Arabia. The deployment took only two days but required sixteen KC-135 tankers, three C-141s, two C-5s and the use of staging airfields in the Azores and Spain. Had KC-10s been available, only six would have been needed to accomplish this entire logistic task. No other aircraft would have been required, and there would have been no need for staging bases. Moreover, the deployment would have taken only one day and there would have been an overall saving of 600,000 gallons of fuel.

C-141B Starlifter

Like the C-5, the C-141 was manufactured by Lockheed and acquired only by the USAF. Although the Starlifter is much thinner and shorter than the wide-bodied Galaxy, the two types clearly share a common pedigree, each featuring the distinctive T-tail, wings swept to 25° and four turbofan engines mounted on pylons beneath the wings. The Starlifter was built between 1963 and 1967, entering service as the C-141A. The USAF received 284, effectively doubling MAC's cargo capacity at a time when the Vietnam War was exerting tremendous pressure on strategic airlift.

Soon after it entered front-line service the C-141 was found to suffer from a serious drawback, namely an

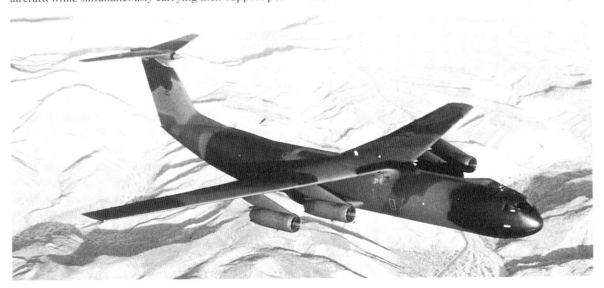

A C-141B Starlifter of the USAF.

imbalance between its volumetric capacity and its payload capacity in terms of weight. Except where the cargo carried was especially dense, the sheer bulk of many loads tended to fill the hold before the maximum payload weight was reached: the phenomenon of 'bulking out' mentioned earlier. The solution was to stretch the aircraft. Recognising the operational benefits and cost-effectiveness of such a modification, the USAF awarded Lockheed a contract to stretch 270 C-141As from 145ft (44.2m) to 168ft 3 1/2in (51.29m) and simultaneously to equip each aircraft to receive fuel in flight. This programme, completed in 1982, increased the aircraft's volumetric capacity by 25 per cent, enabling it to carry thirteen instead of ten standard pallets. Put another way, the stretch programme gave MAC the equivalent of seventy new aircraft without any significant reduction in performance or the need for any more aircrew or maintenance personnel. The modified Starlifter was designated C-141B.

Although it cannot operate into short or unpaved airfields, the C-141B remains a versatile aircraft which can perform a wide variety of missions. Designed for easy loading via the rear doors, the passenger/cargo compartment can accommodate twelve pallets on the main floor and a further pallet on the ramp. The hold can be quickly reconfigured to carry up to 208 passengers or 168 paratroops. Another feature of the Starlifter's versatility is its ability to air-drop both troops and equipment. Special equipment is needed for this role, but it can be quickly installed. Cargo to be air-dropped, usually

rigged on platforms, is despatched through the rear doors; paratroops exit through two doors on either side of the rear fuselage. In practice, the C-141B is seldom used in the air-drop role because such operations usually take place in tactical scenarios to which the Lockheed C-130 is better suited.

At the beginning of 'Desert Shield' in August 1990, MAC could call upon a fleet of 234 C-141Bs. These formed the backbone of the Gulf airlift, completing 8,536 missions in 216 days and delivering 159,462 tons of cargo, or 30 per cent of the total freight airlifted during the operation.

C-17 Globemaster III

Intended as a replacement for the Starlifter, the C-17 Globemaster entered operational service with the USAF in January 1995. By the end of 1998 some 40 aircraft had been delivered, building to a total of 120 when the final C-17 is handed over in 2004. Built by McDonnell Douglas (now part of Boeing), the C-17 is a high-wing, four-engined, T-tailed aircraft with a rear loading ramp. In terms of external dimensions it is slightly larger than the C-141B, but its maximum payload (170,400lb (77,292kg)) is approximately twice that of the Starlifter. With a payload of 160,000lb (72,575kg) the C-17 can take off from a 7,600ft (2,316m) runway, fly 2,760 miles (4,442km) and then land at an austere airfield on a runway of only 3,000ft (914m). The ferry range of the C-17, which can refuel in flight, is 5,400 miles (8,690km). It has externally blown flaps which allow a steep, slow, final

A USAF C-141B air-drops equipment.

A Boeing C-17 Globemaster III of the USAF approaches to land on a steel-matted runway in a US desert warfare training area in California.

approach with low landing speeds for good short-field performance. These features owe as much to exacting criteria laid down by the USAF at the concept stage as they do to skilful aeronautical design and engineering.

The net result is an airlifter of unequalled versatility which can deliver huge payloads over intercontinental ranges directly into small airfields. Put another way, the C-17 can carry Galaxy-type loads into Hercules-sized strips. Moreover, when it reaches those small fields, its manoeuvrability on the ground, including its small turning circle and ability to reverse fully loaded up a 2° gra-

dient, means that it can get into and out of tight parking areas, as well as turn around on narrow runways. The extent to which the C-17 can be employed in both strategic and tactical roles is highlighted in Table 2, where its capabilities can be seen to compare favourably with those of the Galaxy, a typical commercial freighter and the Hercules.

As Table 2 indicates, another of the C-17's attributes is its ability to air-drop troops and outsize loads. While there have been relatively few air-drop operations of any size since 1945, the capability to deploy a force by parachute

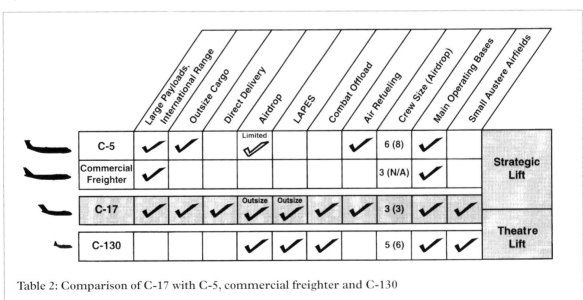

	Large Payloads, International Range	Outsize Cargo	Direct Delivery	Airdrop	LAPES	Combat Offload	Air Refueling	Crew Size (Airdrop)	Main Operating Bases	Small Austere Airfields	
C-5	✓	✓	Limited ✓			✓		6 (8)	✓		**Strategic Lift**
Commercial Freighter	✓							3 (N/A)	✓		
C-17	✓	✓	✓	Outsize ✓	Outsize ✓	✓	✓	3 (3)	✓	✓	**Theatre Lift**
C-130				✓	✓	✓		5 (6)	✓	✓	

Table 2: Comparison of C-17 with C-5, commercial freighter and C-130

remains a valuable military option. Indeed, there are some missions in both war and peacetime where an air-drop operation may be the best, if not the only way to achieve success. Examples include the use of special forces to seize key facilities or destroy enemy command, control and communications systems; the use of paratroops to seize and secure a point of entry (such as an airfield, port or beach-head) for follow-up forces; and humanitarian relief operations in inaccessible areas.

A few general points about air-drop procedures should be noted. Paratroops are usually despatched in simultaneous 'sticks' from doors on either side of the rear fuselage. Speeds and heights vary with aircraft type and national preferences, but troops are normally dropped from about 800ft (245m). Special forces usually jump from the ramp at high altitude (up to 20,000ft, 6,100m) where the need for oxygen apparatus adds to their already bulky equipment, requiring a larger exit than the conventional parachute door. Cargo is dropped at lower altitudes than troops, working on the principle that the lower the drop height, the greater the accuracy. Armoured vehicles rigged on platforms are usually released at about 500ft (150m) but, when extreme accuracy is required, loads can be delivered at ultra-low level using techniques such as the Low Altitude Parachute Extraction System (LAPES) referred to in the table opposite. This is a demanding but effective method of delivering heavy loads with great precision either on to airfields (where it would be impossible or imprudent to land) or on to any suitable flat terrain. The aircraft, with landing gear down in case of momentary contact with the ground, flies at a height of 5–10ft (1.5–3m) at about 140mph (220km/h). At a predesignated spot a crew member releases the extraction parachutes. Three seconds (or 600ft (180m) of ground travel) later, the load leaves the aircraft and comes to rest some 750ft (230m) beyond the point where the parachutes were activated. In trials, the C-17 has dropped single loads of up to 60,000lb (27,216kg) using LAPES.

Another notable feature of the C-17 is its advanced digital avionics, enabling the flight-deck to be managed by two pilots and obviating the need for the navigator and flight engineer required on previous generations of airlifters. The cockpit incorporates several features not previously available on military transports. These include HUDs for each pilot, allowing more precise control during steep approaches and other manoeuvres where attention must be focused outside rather than inside the cockpit, and four large multi-function electronic displays. As the first military transport with an all-digital fly-by-wire control system, the C-17 is equipped with control sticks (instead of yokes) for more precise control and to allow a better view of the flight instruments.

A USAF Lockheed C-130 Hercules uses a low-altitude parachute extraction system (LAPES) to make a pinpoint air-drop.

Meticulous attention to detail has gone into the design of the cargo compartment, which is equipped for single-loadmaster operation in all roles. With a dedicated station in the hold, the loadmaster has effective control of all cargo procedures and can reconfigure the aircraft from one mission (e.g. eighteen pallets of freight) to another (102 passengers) in less than an hour. Such self-sufficiency is invaluable when operating into austere airfields with restricted parking space and limited support facilities. On aggregate the C-17 is a remarkable and revolutionary airlifter which, with its flexibility, maintainability and all-round performance, is certain to have a profound impact upon the concept of strategic mobility and air-logistic operations. Some indication of its merits, *vis-à-vis* older airlifters, can be gained from the diagrams below.

Tactical airlift operations

As inferred above, the advent of the C-17 has further blurred the distinction between strategic and tactical airlift operations. When a nominally strategic aircraft such as the C-141 or C-17 undertakes a long-range mission terminating in a low-level phase and air-drop, this can be viewed as either a strategic task with a tactical dimension or vice versa. To a lesser extent, similar ambiguity exists with tactical airlifters such as the Lockheed C-130 Hercules, which have a quasi-strategic capability. Only a few states – those with international responsibilities or pretensions, and a military budget to match – operate a strategic airlift force, whereas large numbers of states, recognising the contribution that airlift can make within theatre, maintain at least some semblance of tactical transport capability. Exploiting the classical attributes of

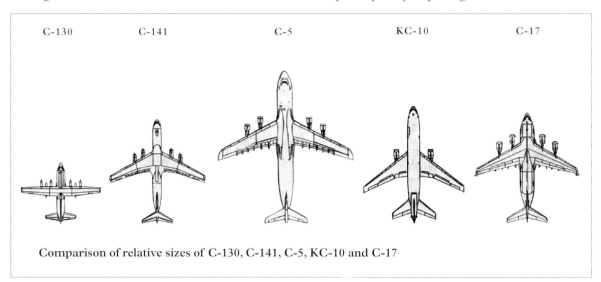

Comparison of relative sizes of C-130, C-141, C-5, KC-10 and C-17

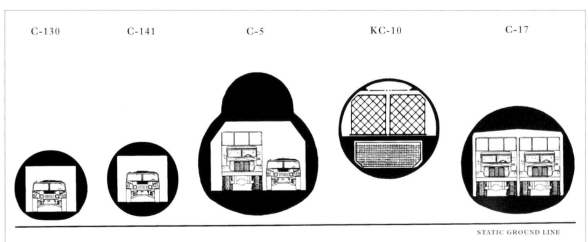

STATIC GROUND LINE

Comparison of cargo holds (cross-section) of C-130, C-141, C-5, KC-10 and C-17

Sarajevo Airlift, July 1992 to January 1996

The international airlift of food, medicine and other supplies into the besieged city of Sarajevo, capital of war-torn Bosnia, began on 3 July 1992. When it ended, 1,281 days later, on 9 January 1996, it had saved many thousands of lives and had, in the process, become the longest-running humanitarian airlift in history.

The Sarajevo operation was of much longer duration than the Berlin Airlift of 1948–9, but carried considerably less cargo: a total of 160,000 tons (162,568 tonnes) compared with the 2,325,800 tons (2,363,129 tonnes) flown into West Berlin. This was because Sarajevo was essentially a low-intensity operation with few aircraft committed at any one time, unlike the Berlin Airlift, which operated virtually non-stop, with aircraft arriving every five minutes, day and night. Furthermore, only one airfield was available in the Bosnian capital, and it was frequently under attack from artillery, mortars and snipers. There was also a constant danger in the air, especially in the vicinity of Sarajevo during descent, approach and departure. Although pilots adopted special procedures to minimise the risk, every mission was exposed to the possibility of hostile action. Many air transport aircraft were hit by ground fire, the worst incident occurring on 3 September 1992, when an Italian Air Force Aeritalia G.222 (a twin-turboprop airlifter) was shot down by a surface-to-air missile while inbound to Sarajevo some 17 miles (27km) west of the airfield. Tragically, all four crew members were killed.

Thereafter, it became mandatory for all aircraft engaged in the airlift to be equipped with some form of self-defence system such as sensors to warn of radar illumination, chaff to confuse hostile radar, and flare dispensers to decoy incoming infrared-seeking missiles. Despite such measures, every flight into Sarajevo continued to face a real if unpredictable threat.

A USAF C-17 launches decoy flares during a trial to test the effectiveness of its self-defence system. Similar defence measures were employed by aircraft taking part in the Sarajevo airlift.

An Aeritalia G.222 of 46 Air Brigade, Italian Air Force. One of these aircraft was shot down by a surface-to-air missile on 3 September 1992 while approaching Sarajevo.

197

air power, tactical airlifters can operate with speed and flexibility in support of ground forces, enabling the field commander to employ his resources to optimum effect. Aircraft such as the C-130, on which this section will now focus, can perform all tactical missions from air-dropping to aeromedical evacuation.

Not all tactical airlifters share this versatility, but there are certain basic features which such aircraft should possess. These include rugged construction and heavy-duty landing gear; short take-off and landing (STOL) capability on both paved and unpaved airfields; a good range-to-payload ratio, with a radius of action of 1,500 miles (2,400km) with maximum payload; air-drop capability; and all-weather capability. These requirements generally lead to a design which incorporates a high wing with a low-slung fuselage. Such an arrangement not only protects the engines and flaps from debris on unpaved surfaces, but also maximises the cross-section and hence the volumetric capacity of the cargo hold. This basic configuration is usually complemented by an upswept tail which permits the provision of rear doors and a ramp, the latter being necessary for air-dropping equipment and special forces, as well as for easy handling of cargo. As well as having the necessary space and access/egress for the load, the aircraft must also be equipped with high-lift and slow-flying devices which, with robust landing gear, are essential for STOL or semi-STOL operations. Such

A close-up of the nose of an RAF C-130H, showing its in-flight refuelling probe.

requirements have produced a generation of tactical airlifters (US, Soviet, British, German, Italian, etc.) which all tend to be variations on a basic theme. However, one aircraft above all others has dominated this category for the past forty years: the C-130 Hercules.

Built by Lockheed Martin, the C-130 is universally acknowledged as the most effective tactical airlifter yet built. Its primary mission is to deliver cargo or personnel in theatre, by air-landing or air-dropping, operating if necessary from short, unpaved fields. Since the type entered service with the USAF in 1957, more than 2,100 military C-130s and commercial derivatives have been produced for operators in more than sixty countries. Indeed, the Hercules has enjoyed a longer uninterrupted production run than any other US military transport. Naturally the C-130 of the late 1990s bears little resemblance to its forebears of forty years ago. Throughout this period the Hercules has been under continuous development, partly in response to changing military requirements, and partly as the manufacturer has incorporated new technology.

As the aircraft evolved, new marques were introduced. In 1959 the C-130A gave way to the C-130B, which in turn was replaced in 1962 by the C-130E, itself quickly superseded by the C-130H in 1964. Many improvements were introduced over the years, enabling the aircraft to carry more payload over a greater distance and enhancing its maintainability. In the early 1990s Lockheed Martin unveiled the latest version, the C-130J. The first customer for this model was the RAF, which ordered twenty-five in 1994. At least fifteen of this batch will be the C-130J-30, a longer variant in which the fuselage is stretched by 15ft (4.57m). Depending on the type of cargo, mission and configuration, this extra length increases the payload by 30–50 per cent. The C-130J is radically different from the C-130H. With uprated engines producing 29 per cent more take-off thrust, it climbs faster and cruises at a higher level and speed. A 15 per cent improvement in fuel efficiency gives the C-130J a range of 3,260 miles (5,250km) with a 40,000lb (18,144kg) payload. This represents an increase in range of 45 per cent compared with the C-130H. The C-130J can also take off and land in shorter distances than earlier models. Other enhancements include:

Advanced digital avionics, including multifunctional electronic displays, fully integrated navigation systems with dual GPS/INS, and mission-planning computers for more accurate air-drops. This allows the aircraft to be flown by a crew of two pilots, dispensing with the navigator and flight engineer needed on earlier models.

A HUD for each pilot, to assist accurate flying in the low-level or other tactical environment. The cockpit is compatible with night-vision equipment.

A simplified fuel system, with provision for the addition of an AAR receiver probe and/or equipment to enable the aircraft to operate as a tanker.

An extensive built-in diagnostics system to warn of technical malfunctions.

Provision of a cargo control station in the hold for operation by the sole loadmaster.

Another advanced feature of the C-130J, and one which makes its appearance conspicuously different from previous versions, is its six-bladed propeller. Constructed from composite materials, each propeller weighs 15 per cent less than the four-bladed equivalent on the C-130H. At first glance, the C-130J's curved propellers look rather odd and unnatural, but by twisting the blades and increasing their number to six the designer has added 18 per cent more thrust for a given power setting. Consequently, the C-130J can climb to 20,000ft (6,100m) in just 14 minutes, compared with the 22 minutes needed by the C-130H. Moreover, the propellers' improved aerodynamic efficiency means that the engines burn less fuel and run more quietly.

In the conventional air-landing role the C-130J can carry a wide variety of loads. Permutations include ninety-two passengers, or seventy-four stretcher (litter) patients plus two attendants, or sixteen one-ton containers, or two Rapier missile batteries plus sixty missiles. In the air-drop role it can deliver sixty-four paratroops, or sixteen one-ton containers, or two medium-sized plat-forms. The longer C-130J-30 can carry 128 passengers, or ninety-seven stretcher patients plus four attendants in the air-landing role. In air-drop mode it can deliver ninety-two paratroops. Although these loads are virtually the same as those carried by the C-130H and C-130H-30 (the stretched version of the earlier model), the C-130J flies higher, faster and farther than any previous Hercules. It also offers appreciable manpower savings, thanks to a 50 per cent improvement in maintainability and the reduction from five to three aircrew.

Logistic helicopter operations

While fixed-wing aircraft such as the C-17 and C-130 can deliver large payloads into forward airstrips, there are many logistic tasks in and around the operational area which they cannot perform. After troops and equipment have flown into an airhead, most need to be redeployed further forward, where they will subsequently have to be regularly resupplied. They may also have to redeploy. Depending on such factors as distance, terrain and the prevailing threat, some of these tasks will be feasible by surface transport. However, there will usually be a number of logistic missions in both the forward and rear areas which can be undertaken only by the logistic helicopter, thanks to its combination of agility and manoeuvrability.

Airmobile operations

One of the primary roles of logistic helicopters is the rapid movement of troops, weapons and supplies as directed by the field commander. Within this general framework of

In the foreground, a C-130J of the USAF; note the curvature of its six-bladed propellers. In the background, an EC-130E of 193rd Special Operations Wing, the unit responsible for all US airborne psychological warfare missions; note the special antennae on its fin.

missions the airmobile operation is the most important. In essence, the airmobile concept is based on the use of helicopters to confer enhanced tactical mobility by enabling a field commander to move his units around the battlefield as expeditiously as possible in reaction to the changing situation. Airmobile operations are therefore integral to the land battle, with a vital part to play in wresting the initiative from the enemy. Such operations may include:

Deployment of troops to attack the enemy from the flank or rear.

Leapfrogging fresh troops to maintain the momentum of an advance.

The deployment of reserves to reinforce success or oppose a counterattack.

Casualty evacuation.

Infiltration behind enemy lines. Using clandestine techniques and operating under cover of darkness, logistic helicopters are ideal for the insertion and recovery of reconnaissance patrols, including special forces. Personnel can be infiltrated by parachute, abseiling, jumping from the low hover, or air-landing.

Assaults and raids. Such operations take many forms. For example, it might be necessary to seize an airstrip or destroy a fuel dump. The logistic helicopter is often the preferred vehicle for such missions, but the risks can be high. Suppose that a bridge needs to be captured intact, before it can be destroyed by its defenders. The assault force commander may consider mounting a *coup de main*, the term for an operation which aims to surprise and defeat the enemy by a sudden, decisive blow. However, the dangers inherent in a 'vertical envelopment' operation – a heliborne assault directly on to a defended position – are considerable both for the helicopters and for the troops on board. The commander will need to consider most carefully whether the benefits will be outweighed by the possibility of heavy losses. A striking example of a raid that went tragically wrong is outlined on the opposite page.

Cargo configuration of logistic helicopters

Cargo can be carried internally or underslung beneath the fuselage, usually in nets, from one or more hooks. These hooks are anchored to strong-points, the main hook directly beneath the rotor head at the helicopter's c.g. The choice between internal and external mode is decided jointly by the ground and air unit commanders after considering the following factors:

Size and shape of load

Low-density loads tend not to 'fly' very well when underslung. Such cargo is best carried internally. Conversely, high-density loads such as crates of ammunition are comparatively

stable when rigged externally. This is important, as the weight of very dense items might exceed the floor-loading limits in the hold, whereas hooks are usually stressed to carry maximum payload.

Excessively bulky loads might not fit inside even the largest helicopters. In many cases such loads can be carried externally, albeit at the expense of speed or range.

Type of load

Wheeled vehicles can be easily loaded and unloaded, but other freight can be difficult to handle unless it is palletised and the cabin floor fitted with a roller conveyor system. Hazardous items, such as fuel bladders or ammunition, are usually best underslung.

Time and distance

Cargo for delivery by helicopter must be carefully prepared and weighed. External loads may take longer to prepare than internal freight, but most helicopters can pick up and set down an external load in only one or two minutes, whereas the handling of internal cargo can take much longer. When the time factor is critical, such considerations may be overriding.

Distance may also be a deciding factor. Drag and instability induced by underslung loads combine to lower a helicopter's transit speed, increase its fuel burn and hence reduce its range.

An underslung load carried beneath a US Army UH-60A Black Hawk.

The operation to rescue hostages from Iran, April 1980

The failed attempt in April 1980 to rescue fifty-three Americans being held hostage in the US Embassy in Tehran is a graphic example of the risks inherent in mounting an assault or raid with helicopters. Units from all four US Services, including special forces personnel, were assigned to this operation. Airlift and logistic support were provided by six C-130s and eight Sikorsky RH-53D Sea Stallion helicopters.

The first phase of the rescue, scheduled for the evening of 24 April 1980, called for the C-130s to fly the assault troops, interpreters, equipment, and fuel for the helicopters from Masirah Island, off the coast of Oman, to a remote airstrip in the Iranian desert, a distance of 690 miles (1,110km). This airstrip, designated 'Desert One', was 300 miles (480km) south of Tehran. There, the C-130s were to rendezvous with eight Sea Stallions launched from the carrier USS *Nimitz* on station in the Gulf. The raiding party would then transfer to the helicopters and, under cover of darkness, fly on to 'Desert Two', an isolated location in the mountains some 57 miles (92km) from Tehran. The helicopters would then move to a nearby site, where they would remain concealed during the following day and evening. After nightfall on 25 April the assault teams would be driven from 'Desert Two' to Tehran in trucks, and at 2300hrs would storm the compound where the hostages were being held.

Raiders and hostages were to be extracted by the Sea Stallions using an adjacent open area, with two AC-130H gunships (Hercules adapted to carry weapons capable of considerable firepower) orbiting overhead to provide support. The helicopters would then recover to a third desert airfield 40 miles (64km) south of Tehran which, secured by eighty rangers, would receive two C-141 Starlifters assigned to evacuate the hostages, casualties and all other surviving personnel. The Sea Stallions were to have been abandoned (and destroyed) at this location.

The C-130s duly arrived at 'Desert One' on schedule, but the Sea Stallions did not. Soon after crossing the Iranian coast on their low-level transit of 575 miles (925km) from *Nimitz* to 'Desert One', the eight helicopters, flying in loose formation, encountered a severe and extensive sandstorm which had not been forecast at their pre-mission weather briefing. One Sea Stallion experienced a serious malfunction, causing the pilot to doubt whether he could safely penetrate the murky conditions ahead. Reluctantly, he decided to return to *Nimitz*, but could not inform anyone of his decision because radio silence had been imposed to preserve security. As ill luck would have it, the helicopter which turned back was carrying hydraulic maintenance equipment for the whole formation. Shortly after this a warning caption illuminated in the cockpit of another Sea Stallion, indicating imminent failure of a rotor blade. The pilot immediately landed, again maintaining radio silence, but he and his crew were picked up by the pilot of another Sea Stallion which had fortuitously witnessed the forced landing. When the depleted force of six helicopters finally assembled at 'Desert One', much later than planned owing to the bad weather and technical problems, another Sea Stallion was found to have a major hydraulics failure, but could not be repaired because the equipment in question was now back on the carrier. This reduced the available helicopters to only five, one less than the minimum number of six considered essential for the next phase of the operation.

At this point, with dawn only an hour or two away, the mission commander decided to abort. The 130 Army Green Berets, Rangers, drivers and Iranian translators would be flown out by C-130, and the Sea Stallions would return empty to *Nimitz* after refuelling from the Hercules tankers. However, while positioning his aircraft in a low hover alongside one of the Hercules tankers, the pilot of a Sea Stallion became disorientated in the darkness and dust cloud kicked up by his rotors and collided with a C-130. Both aircraft ignited in a huge fireball and eight men were killed.

This tragic event prompted another change of plan, the mission commander now deciding to abandon the remaining helicopters and evacuate all personnel by C-130. Everyone then flew out, leaving behind an assortment of weapons, communications equipment, maps and five intact Sea Stallions. All were supposed to be destroyed shortly afterwards by US fighter-bombers, but President Carter had second thoughts and decided not to authorise this strike.

This ill-fated attempt to rescue hostages, involving the loss of eight lives, seven Sea Stallions, one Hercules and a great deal of presidential credibility, is a telling example of what can go wrong when a mission depends, *inter alia*, on deep penetration of hostile territory by helicopter. While it is beyond the scope of this brief account to analyse the diverse reasons for failure, author Paul Ryan, who has examined this episode in great depth, contends that the plan was fatally flawed because it called for the raiding force to spend nearly forty-eight hours inside enemy territory. It thereby contravened the golden rule for covert operations: 'get in fast and get out fast'.

Cargo must usually be carried internally if the mission requires the aircraft to operate over its maximum radius of action.

Cargo handling

A major advantage of the underslung mode is that loads can often be delivered exactly where they are needed. For example, ammunition can be set down immediately alongside the artillery. On the other hand, helicopters carrying heavy internal cargo not only require landing areas which are relatively firm and level, but may also need special equipment to handle non-wheeled freight. Dependence on such equipment, often in short supply in forward areas, can be a serious disadvantage.

Freedom of manoeuvre

As indicated above, helicopters carrying external cargo must fly at reduced speeds. Moreover, the inherent instability of large underslung loads may render an aircraft difficult to handle, particularly at night, in cloud, or in poor visibility. Aircraft with underslung loads must also fly higher, further reducing their tactical freedom of manoeuvre *vis-à-vis* helicopters with internal cargo which can employ nap-of-the-Earth tactics to avoid detection. On the other hand, if a helicopter with an underslung load is attacked or suffers a serious malfunction, the pilot may be able to jettison the load immediately by activating a quick-release device, instantly reducing the aircraft's weight and increasing manoeuvrability. This option of shedding cargo instantaneously is denied to the pilot of a helicopter with an internal load.

It is beyond the scope of this chapter to mention, let alone compare, the many types of logistic helicopters in service around the world. Suffice it to say that, just as with fixed-wing airlifters, some helicopters are much more capable than others. With that in mind, this section concludes with a brief look at two of the most successful examples.

UH-60A Black Hawk

Manufactured by Sikorsky, the UH-60A first flew in 1974. Four years later it entered operational service with the US Army, by far the largest operator of these aircraft, with more than 900 still in the front-line inventory. The UH-60A is an extremely versatile multi-purpose helicopter. In its primary role, that of battlefield-mobility vehicle, it can carry fourteen fully equipped troops, or a 105mm howitzer on the cargo hook plus the gun's five-man crew and fifty shells in the cabin. Alternatively, it can evacuate casualties, move equipment and supplies, perform reconnaissance tasks and act as an airborne command post. Moreover, the Black Hawk is itself airportable. One can be carried in a C-130H, two in a C-141B and six in a C-5B. Therefore a unit of UH-60As can be rapidly deployed over strategic distances and start operations in a distant theatre within much the same timescale as the troops they are assigned to support.

The UH-60A can also be fitted with an External Stores Support System (ESSS), comprising two remov-

A US Army UH-60A Black Hawk operating in the aeromedical role.

able pylons on each side of the fuselage on which ancillary fuel tanks or various special pods can be mounted. In battlefield scenarios or on operations in which some measure of self-defence is deemed prudent, guns, missiles and ECM pods can be carried on the ESSS. However, the UH-60A is not an attack helicopter, and a balance must always be struck between the weight of any weapons and that of the payload, if the aircraft's capacity to move the latter is not to suffer. Nevertheless, the ESSS makes the UH-60A ideal for clandestine missions behind enemy lines with small teams of special forces. With such tasks in mind, it is designed to be fully compatible with night-vision devices, allowing it to operate at low level into unlit landing sites.

CH-47D Chinook

Produced by Boeing Helicopters, the CH-47D Chinook is the latest version of a distinguished family of aircraft which first entered operational service as the CH-47A in 1962. This was followed by the CH-47B in 1967, the CH-47C in 1968 and the CH-47D in 1984. The principal customer for all of these variants was the US Army, but many have also been exported in both military and civilian configurations. More than 600 Chinooks are currently in use around the world, and the production line is still open.

The Chinook is a twin-engined helicopter designed for the airlift of troops, weapons and cargo by day or night in visual and instrument flight conditions. Aerodynamic lift is produced by two fully articulated, counter-rotating rotors, each of which has three blades made from composite materials. The CH-47D bears little resemblance to earlier variants beyond sharing a similar silhouette. During the Vietnam War the performance of the CH-47A was degraded by the combination of high ambient temperatures and high operating altitudes, which reduced the power of its gas-turbine engines. Equipped with more-powerful engines which permit a maximum take-off weight of 50,000lb (22,680kg), the CH-47D can carry more than twice the payload of the CH-47A. Other improvements introduced over the years include better electrical and hydraulic systems, the provision of triple cargo hooks, and an advanced cockpit featuring digital avionics and compatibility with night-vision equipment. The result is a rugged workhorse with much better performance, reliability and maintainability than earlier versions.

While its primary mission is airmobile operations, the CH-47D can perform a wide range of logistic tasks on and around the battlefield. For example, it can be used for long-range special forces missions, its cabin being

A US Army CH-47D Chinook delivers an underslung cargo.

large enough to accommodate an extra fuel tank as well as twenty troops and their equipment. For everyday purposes it can carry forty-four personnel in basic seating, but more than twice that number sitting on the floor when operational necessity dictates. In the aeromedical role, twenty-four stretcher patients plus two attendants can be carried.

The Chinook owes much of its success to its tandem-rotor system. Torque created by single-rotor helicopters must be counteracted by a tail rotor, sometimes to the detriment of performance, but the Chinook's counter-rotating rotors cancel out each other's torque. The tandem-rotor system also improves handling precision in the hover and 'broadens' the c.g., permitting greater flexibility in the positioning of loads. One benefit is that exceptionally long items can, if necessary, be carried with the ramp open. The tandem-rotor design also permits the entire length of the fuselage to be used for payload; no space is wasted on an empty tailboom. For such a compact helicopter, the CH-47D (which at 51ft (15.5m) is only 1ft (0.3m) longer than the UH-60A) has a spacious cargo compartment. Using the built-in winch, cargo can be quickly loaded via the full-width rear ramp. The fixed quadricycle landing gear lends stability during loading and unloading, enabling the aircraft to operate from slopes of up to 20°. The central of its three hooks can carry 26,000lb (11,794kg), while the forward and aft hooks each have a capacity of 17,000lb (7,711kg). The ability to carry such weights externally is operationally advantageous because urgently needed weapons and equipment, such as howitzers and bulldozers, can be moved intact, without needing to be dismantled before flight or reassembled after delivery. Another important benefit of the triple-hook system is that outsize cargo can be carried in a more stable configuration and hence faster. The Chinook normally flies at 132mph (213km/h) when carrying a large load secured to all three hooks, but is limited to about 57mph (92km/h) when flying with the same load on a single hook.

Conclusion

During the second half of the twentieth century, airlift operations have come to occupy a pivotal role in the exertion of military power, whether at the strategic, tactical or battlefield level. Such an assertion does not mean, however, that airlift is the only important factor in the projection/logistics equation. As emphasised above, sealift and pre-positioning are equally crucial to the concept of strategic mobility. Similarly, within a theatre of operations, road and rail systems (if available) are an essential complement to whatever tactical airlift can be provided. In any case, for all its flexibility, there are limits to what airlift can achieve, owing to such factors as aircraft performance, availability of AAR and location of suitable airfields. Nevertheless, the fundamental importance of both fixed- and rotary-wing airlift to the deployment of forces cannot be overstated.

In the contemporary international arena, where crises and conflicts are liable to arise with little or no warning, speed of reaction is paramount. Airlift not only possesses sharp reflexes and long reach, but also confers these very same attributes upon the forces which are airlifted. Thus a nation's (or an alliance's) political and military credibility has come to depend increasingly on the extent to which its forces can be deployed by air to deter, counter or extinguish any hostile action. With the advent of ever-more-capable aircraft, such as the C-17 Globemaster, airlift operations have an assured and central role for the foreseeable future.

Bibliography

Bakse, C et al, *Airlift Tanker – History of US Airlift and Tanker Forces* (Turner Publishing, Paducah, Kentucky, USA, 1995).

Chapman, K, *Military Air Transport Operations* (Brassey's (UK), London, 1989).

Matthews, J K and Holt, C J, *So Many, So Much, So Far, So Fast: The Strategic Deployment for Operations Desert Storm and Desert Shield* (Office of the Chairman, US Joint Chiefs of Staff, Washington DC).

Ryan, P B, *The Iranian Rescue Mission: Why it Failed* (Naval Institute Press, Annapolis, Maryland, USA, 1985).

Skorupa, J A, *Self-Protective Measures to Enhance Airlift Operations in Hostile Environments* (Air University Press, Maxwell Air Force Base, Alabama, USA, 1989).

The greatest advantage in warfare is knowing where the enemy is, what equipment he has, what he is doing, and what his potential for mischief is. Two world wars saw the photo-reconnaissance mission grow in importance, with aircraft fitted with cameras aligned vertically and/or obliquely. Meanwhile, as radar and communications played an increasing part, the monitoring of electronic emissions (ELINT) emerged as yet another form of intelligence gathering.

The reverse side of the ELINT coin was that electronic intelligence had to be denied to the enemy. The sequence then became detect, identify and counter. Electronic countermeasures (ECM) have been with us ever since 1940, under the blanket heading of electronic warfare (EW). This is a support function rather than reconnaissance, but it is too closely entwined with ELINT to be easily separated. Another support function to emerge has been airborne early warning (AEW).

Maritime reconnaissance, or more properly surveillance, is a vital part of the war at sea, and is generally flown at medium level. The requirements are long endurance and a good loiter time, as well as anti-surface-vessel (ASV) radar to aid detection.

Photographic reconnaissance

The essential aim of any reconnaissance mission is to ensure the safe and timely arrival of information. Avoiding interception is paramount. For the photographic mission this is done either by flying very high and/or very fast, in an aircraft lightened by the omission of all non-essential equipment, including armament, and powered by a high-altitude-rated engine, or by very low and fast 'agricultural' flying to keep the aircraft below the radar horizon. The first option reduces the time-span between detection and interception; the second gives the defenders little or no advance warning of its presence.

Tactical reconnaissance 1945–55

The potential of the turbojet made most shorter-range (i.e. tactical) piston-engined aircraft obsolescent overnight. But the jet priority was for offensive aircraft; the reconnaissance mission had to wait until jet fighters and bombers became available for conversion or adaptation. Over the next few years RAF Spitfires and Mosquitoes, and USAAF (USAF from 1948) Mustangs, soldiered on in the photo-reconnaissance role.

The advent of the turbojet gave fighter designers a new-found freedom in selecting configurations, even though technically it posed new problems. Ideally, the turbojet needed an unobstructed flow of air to the compressor face to avoid duct choking and disturbed airflow, and a short tailpipe to avoid thrust losses. The simplest way of avoiding these problems was to mount the engine(s) in such a way that both inlet and efflux ducts were as short as possible. Two first-generation jet fighters adapted for the photo-reconnaissance mission used the minimum-inlet, minimum-exhaust configuration, and both were twin-engined, although their layouts differed greatly. These were the British Gloster Meteor FR.9 and PR.10, and the American McDonnell F2H-2P Banshee.

The Meteor started to replace the Spitfire from July 1950. Of orthodox layout, it was powered by Rolls-Royce Derwent centrifugal-flow turbojets mounted outboard in the wings. The FR.9 (fighter/reconnaissance) was used for the low-altitude mission. It retained its four-cannon armament, and carried a single camera which was remotely controlled by the pilot to look through ports in the side or front of the nose. The PR.10, unarmed and optimised for the high-altitude mission, had a wingspan of 43ft (13.1m) compared with the 37ft 2in (11.2m) of the FR.9. In addition to the remotely controlled nose camera, it carried vertical cameras mounted aft in the fuselage. Still-air range was 690 miles (1,100km) at low level for the FR.9, and 1,400 miles (2,240km) at altitude for the PR.10.

The Banshee, by contrast, was powered by two small axial-flow Westinghouse J34 turbojets located in the wing roots. This had the advantage of minimising the effects of asymmetric thrust with one engine out, at the expense of structural complexity and weight and difficulty of access for maintenance. As with the Meteor, the Banshee carried cameras in a lengthened nose. It saw limited action over Korea with Marine Fighter Wing 1.

In single-engined, propeller-driven fighters the cameras had to be housed in the fuselage behind the pilot. This was not ideal, but with the nose full of engine it was the only place. Single-engined jets were not so constrained. Their engines could be mounted amidships in the fuselage, more or less on the c.g., allowing the cockpit to be moved forward, improving forward vision. If side or wing-root intakes were used, it also left the nose free for armament or cameras.

The F2H-2P was preceded into action over Korea by two single-engined jets: the USAF Lockheed RF-80C Shooting Star and the USN Grumman F9F-2P Panther. The Shooting Star was a Second World War design,

Grumman's F9F Panther was a stalwart of US Navy reconnaissance in the Korean War. Seen here with camera ports clearly visible is an F9F-5P.

but had been too late to see action in that conflict. Side intakes left the nose free for cameras, which displaced the guns of the fighter variant, while drop tanks were carried beneath the wingtips to extend the range. The RF-80C was badly outclassed by the Soviet-built and flown MiG-15, and in action it was often escorted by F-86 Sabres. Of 1947 vintage, the Panther was rather faster and had a better ceiling than the RF-80. A carrier fighter, its centrifugal-flow turbojet was fed by wing-root inlets, and the tailpipe was terminated to exhaust beneath the high-set empennage. Unlike the RF-80 it carried fixed wingtip tanks. Two photo-reconnaissance Panther variants served in Korea: the F9F-2P from March 1952, and the F9F-5P towards the close of hostilities. The latter was fitted with a more powerful turbojet, was 2ft (0.6m) longer, had a taller vertical tail, increased internal fuel capacity and a camera installation of one K-17 and a Trimetrogon vertical/oblique fan.

The quest for greater performance resulted in a radical redesign of the F9F. A 35° swept wing was just a start. To maintain the control qualities needed by a carrier aircraft, it was given more than 40 per cent more wing area, coupled with leading-edge slats and huge trailing-edge flaps, with spoilers replacing the ailerons. The tip tanks were discarded, and internal fuel capacity was increased to compensate. This radically altered machine was renamed Cougar. Two photo-reconnaissance Cougars entered service: the F9F-6P and the F9F-8P. This final variant had yet another large increase in wing area, but its main difference was an enlarged and drooped nose which housed two Trimetrogon fans in tandem and a forward-looking oblique camera.

Meanwhile, the USAF needed a replacement for the elderly Shooting Star. The chosen aircraft was the Republic F-84F Thunderstreak, a swept-wing rehash of the 1940s Thunderjet, designed around a large axial-flow turbojet. It was an odd choice, because the F-84F had a nose inlet, which precluded a camera bay. This was overcome by fitting a solid nose, holding up to six cameras, which necessitated wing-root intakes. These caused pressure losses, but maximum speed was still an acceptable 510mph (820km/hr). With external tanks, still-air range was a remarkable 2,200 miles (3,520km). The RF-84F Thunderflash was the most important Western tactical reconnaissance machine of the 1950s and early 1960s.

A final postscript to the Thunderflash story was the FICON (fighter conveyor). This was an attempt to combine strategic range with tactical versatility by carrying modified RF-84Ks semi-submerged in the bomb bays of modified B-36 bombers, from where they were launched and recovered on trapezes. An alternative scheme was Tom-Tom, in which pairs of RF-84Fs were hooked on to the wingtips of a B-36. Trials established that both techniques were extremely hazardous, and they were quickly terminated.

Deep penetration

Deep-penetration reconnaissance missions called for greater range than tactical jets could supply, so light jet bombers were pressed into service. Three nations took this route. The USSR, as it then was, converted the Ilyushin Il-28 twin-jet bomber, which first flew on 8 August 1948, to carry cameras. The USAF did the same with the North American B-45 Tornado, which first

With an enlarged nose, and swept wing and tail surfaces, the Panther became the Cougar. This is the F9F-8P, the last in the series.

Although speed was sacrificed when wing-root intakes were adopted to allow cameras to be housed in its nose, the Republic RF-84F Thunderflash was the West's leading tactical reconnaissance aircraft in the 1950s.

207

flew on 17 March 1947. This aircraft was a four-engined bomber with paired turbojets outboard in the wings. As the RB-45C it carried photoflash bombs for night missions, and could be given extended range by inflight refuelling. The latest of the three was the RAF's English Electric Canberra, first flown on 13 May 1949. Twin-engined, this aircraft was unusual in having an exceptionally broad-chord wing, which gave it an operational ceiling far higher than the other two.

The Tornado saw action over Korea, but its performance maxima of Mach 0.72 at 38,000ft made it vulnerable in daylight to high-performance MiG-15 interceptors. Fighter escort was seldom available, and it was soon used mainly at night. Little is known about the operational usage of the Il-28R, but both Tornado and Canberra were used for overflights of the Soviet Union during the 1950s.

At that time the world was preparing for nuclear war. The nuclear bombs were to be carried by hundreds of bombers, flying singly. In daylight their losses would have been horrendous, so they planned to attack at night or in bad weather, finding their targets with ground-mapping radar. The difficulty was target recognition, for at the time it was impossible to forecast how a target

would appear on the radar screen. The solution was to make a series of overflights, during which the radar pictures of potential targets would be photographed for future use. The aircraft selected were RB-45Cs, but they were flown by RAF crews from Sculthorpe in England, using inflight refuelling both out- and inbound. Only two missions, of three sorties each, were flown, and all aircraft returned safely. As a bonus, the Y (listening) Service monitored the Soviet defences, giving the West valuable insights into their capabilities.

Little information is available on even riskier daylight penetrations by RAF Canberras, believed to have taken place in 1953/54. The main object of their attentions was the Soviet missile research base at Kapustin Yar, on the Volga. Soviet fighters made several attempts to intercept, but were defeated by the sheer altitude of the Canberras, which was approaching 60,000ft (18,300m).

The USAF also operated the Canberra in the reconnaissance role, as the Martin RB-57A and RB-57E. The quest for greater altitude capability led to the RB-57D, with extended-span wings, from 1956. The final variant was the RB-57F, with almost twice the wingspan and more than double the wing area of the original machine, and two supplementary engines. This

The B-45 Tornado's 'greenhouse' nose was replaced by a rather inelegant proboscis when it was turned into the RB-45C.

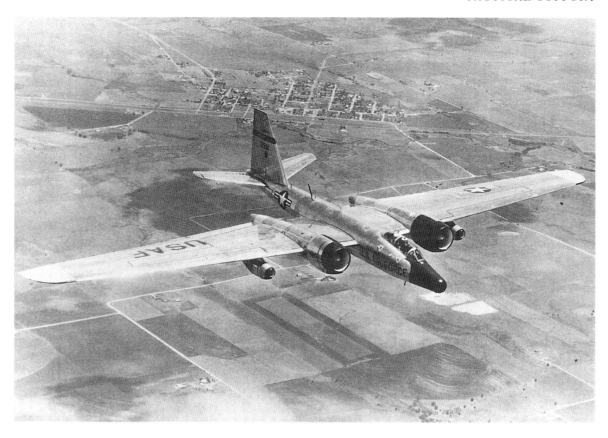

The ultimate reconnaissance development of Martin's B-57 Canberra derivative was the RB-57F, which had the power of its two Pratt & Whitney TF33-P-11 turbofans supplemented by a pair of J60-P-9 turbojets in underwing pods.

carried the monster 66in (167.6cm) focal length HIAC-1 camera for oblique photography, the first camera with programmable computer logic for automatic stepping, focusing and image-motion compensation. Resolution was just 22in (56cm) at 46 miles (74km) range. Although they had an endurance of ten hours, both the D and F models suffered structural weakness in the wings, which limited their usage.

Ever higher

As the Cold War worsened, the need for deep-penetration reconnaissance intensified. At the same time the advent of surface-to-air missiles made it increasingly risky. Extreme altitude appeared to be the best defence, and Lockheed designed its notorious U-2, which first flew on 1 August 1955.

Optimised for very high flight, the U-2 was essentially a high-powered glider with very-high-aspect-ratio wings, able to sustain altitudes up to 75,000ft (23,000m) and with a range exceeding 4,600 miles (7,350km). The cockpit was pressurised, but as a backup the pilot wore a bulky and uncomfortable pressure suit. Flight at operational altitudes was wryly known as 'coffin corner', as

only a narrow margin separated the critical Mach number from the stall. As a weight-saving measure, structural limits were set low, giving little margin of safety if an out-of-control situation developed, while landing on the tandem main undercarriage was also tricky. Consequently U-2 pilots had to have above-average flying skills. One interesting navigational aid was an optical drift sight mounted high on the panel, which allowed the pilot to see the terrain directly below.

The first U-2 overflight took place on 4 July 1956. Starting from Wiesbaden in Germany, the aircraft went east to Moscow and then north to Leningrad before returning to base. More followed, interspersed with 'stand-off' missions, in which intelligence was gleaned without crossing the frontier. Other bases used were Bödo in Norway, Incirlik in Turkey, Peshawar in Pakistan and Atsugi in Japan. For nearly four years the Russians were impotent against these intruders, and when, on 1 May 1960, they finally succeeded in downing one near Sverdlovsk, luck seems to have played a part. Be that as it may, overflights of the Soviet Union then ceased, although China, North Vietnam and the Middle Eastern hot spots were kept under surveillance for many years.

For several years Lockheed's U-2 was able to defeat air defences by ultra-high flight. For this it used a very-high-aspect-ratio wing and a powerful engine. This is a U-2R.

The U-2 is known to have carried at least fourteen different types of camera, but increasingly it was fitted with electronic systems and detectors. As weight increased, performance suffered, despite the substitution of the more powerful J75 turbojet for the J57. The solution was the U-2R, a larger and slightly heavier machine, the altitude performance of which was improved by wing of greater span and area. This expanded the 'coffin corner' margin, easing high-altitude handling. Provision was also made for large wing pods. First flown on 28 August 1967, the U-2R remains in service more than thirty years later.

Ever faster

The most famous reconnaissance platform of all is the Lockheed SR-71, commonly known as the Blackbird. First flown in December 1964, it could reach Mach 3.5 (making it the fastest aeroplane ever to enter service), sustain flight at 85,000ft (26,000m), and exceed 17,250 miles (27,600km) with inflight refuelling. Moreover, it led the field in stealth technology.

The SR-71 did not come about by accident. Although SAMs spelt the end of overflights of the USSR by U-2s, the deep-penetration mission was still vital. To survive Soviet fighters and SAM defences, extreme speed and stealth were now required in addition to high altitude, and these demands pushed the state of the art pretty hard. For example, the aircraft needed large fuel tankage for deep penetration using

afterburners all the way, and space for the cameras and other sensors. Pratt & Whitney developed the J58 turbo-ramjet, which used highly specialised JP-7 fuel, and this in turn demanded specialised tankers. The airframe had to be able to soak at high temperatures for long periods, and other requirements were a low-drag wing able to provide sufficient lift in the attenuated air at operational altitudes, and a low radar cross-section to delay detection. The SR-71 met all these demands.

It took the form of a large tailless delta, with the turbo-ramjets mounted outboard in the wings to avoid the worst of the shock wave from the nose at trisonic speeds. Twin fins located atop the rear of the engine nacelles were canted inwards, partly for aerodynamic reasons and partly to reduce radar returns. Wing-body blending, coupled with chines running the entire length of the forebody, also helped to reduce the radar signature. Beneath the black 'iron ball', radar-absorbing paint finish, most of the structure was made of titanium, then a rare and hard-to-work material, but able to withstand the kinetic heating of flight at Mach 3. Like the U-2, the SR-71 was structurally limited to save weight.

The aircraft started life as the A-12, a slightly smaller but almost identical single-seater, first flown on 26 April 1962. Various shortcomings were quickly apparent, and the SR-71 was ordered barely eight months later, eventually completely eclipsing its predecessor.

The USAF Fact Sheet credits the SR-71 with the ability to scan more than 100,000 square miles

The outlandish lines of the SR-71 Blackbird originated in the need to combine trisonic speed, ultra-high altitude capability and stealth. It was arguably the most successful reconnaissance aircraft of all time.

(259,000km²) of the Earth's surface per hour from above 80,000ft (24,400m). This is an impressive achievement, but it surely puts a premium on intelligence analysts!

Operationally, the SR-71's deeds were equally impressive. Where there was trouble there also was the Blackbird, gathering intelligence for its country and monitoring the situation. From the Barents Sea to Libya, from Egypt to China, the SR-71 has peered down from on high. Although SAMs have been launched and MiG-25s scrambled against it, they proved to no avail. Then, in 1990, the SR-71 was retired, only for a couple of the aircraft to be reactivated several years later. After three decades, the Blackbird was still a credible reconnaissance platform.

Tactical supersonics

Both the U-2 and the SR-71 were strategic reconnaissance vehicles, but the need for tactical reconnaissance persisted. Reconnaissance variants of the majority of the world's supersonic fighters were developed: the French Dassault Mirage IIIR and F1CR, the Swedish Saab SF/SH37 Viggen and the American Chance Vought RF-8 Crusader and North American RAH-5 Vigilante among them. Others carried reconnaissance pods. But high-speed flight at low level was an uncomfortable

business owing to gust response; what was needed for flight at high speed and low level was small wing area and high wing loading.

An American aircraft which met this requirement was the McDonnell F-101 Voodoo. Designed as a long-range escort fighter, powered by two afterburning Pratt & Whitney J57 turbojets and with a wing loading of 132lb/ft² (644.5kg/m²) at maximum weight, it was a natural for the

Many tactical fighters were modified for reconnaissance, such as this Mirage F1CR of France's Armée de l'Air. Its relatively small and highly loaded wing gives a smoother ride at low level than the delta-winged Mirage III.

The Phantom was the most versatile aircraft of its era, and inevitably it was adapted for reconnaissance. This is an RF-4C of the 10th Tactical Reconnaissance Wing, USAFE.

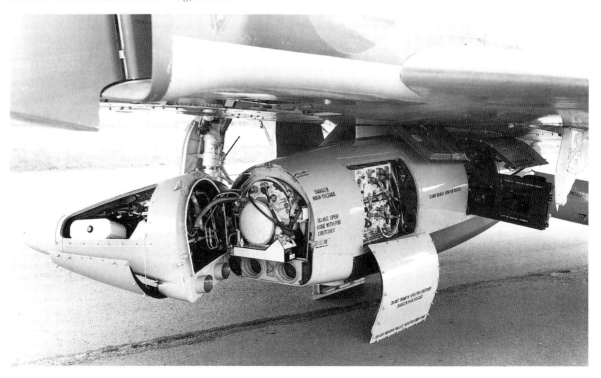

A close-up of an EMI reconnaissance pod on an RF-4 Phantom.

photo-reconnaissance mission. The RF-101A, with a modified nose containing five cameras, first flew in May 1956. With a range of 1,550 miles (2,480km) it carried out overflights of China from Taiwan from 1958, and was the main USAF photographic platform in Vietnam until November 1970, for pre-strike reconnaissance and post-strike damage assessment.

The first RF-4C Phantoms arrived in Vietnam late in 1965. A year later they were given sideways-looking air-borne radar (SLAR), which at 30,000ft (9,000m) gave cover out to 35 miles (56km) of the flight path at night. Photoflash was all very well, but it was soon dubbed 'MiG Magnet'. The RF-101s usually flew singly, as did the RF-4Cs at night, but in daylight RF-4Cs generally flew in pairs. Photographic Phantoms were still in service in the Gulf War, though by then they were equipped with infrared linescan (IRLS) and real-time data transmission. There was one tremendous advantage to IRLS; it could detect where an aircraft had been on the ground by the heat signature left by its engines. A few reconnaissance Phantoms remained in service in 1998.

For many years, affordability has been the criterion for many air forces. The Northrop F-5 was developed from the T-38 supersonic trainer of 1959 vintage, as an austere light fighter. In 1972 it was upgraded as the F-5E Tiger II, and shortly after that a reconnaissance version emerged, the Tigereye. A reconfigured nose holds interchangeable pallets, one for panoramic cameras and an IRLS, and the other for long-range oblique photography.

Most Soviet tactical aircraft have reconnaissance variants, but one is of particular interest. This is the MiG-25R, adapted from the *Foxbat* high-speed, high-altitude interceptor and fitted with cameras or SLAR. With a maximum speed of Mach 2.83 and a ceiling of

68,800ft (21,000m), the MiG-25 was almost uninterceptable. Between October 1971 and March 1972 MiG-25Rs based at Cairo overflew most of Israel. One actually reached Mach 3.2 over Sinai, but barely limped back to base after wrecking its engines by overspeeding.

Electronic reconnaissance

Active and passive electronic reconnaissance (ER) has long been the source of much valuable intelligence. Active ER uses airborne radar for ground-mapping (of which the RB-45 sorties described earlier were a classic example), and to detect hostile surface assets. However, as air-defence systems improved, overflights were not possible. They were avoided by using SLAR, which enabled a radar picture to be built up from an aircraft flying parallel to the frontier under surveillance. Initially interpretation was a problem, but as computer technology improved this became less so. The later introduction of synthetic-aperture radar (SAR), in which the forward speed of the aircraft is used to give a high-resolution image of quite small objects, was a great advance.

By far the greater part of ER was passive, listening to and analysing foreign emissions. Airborne detectors were of great value in this field, as from 30,000ft (9,000m) the straight-line horizon was over 230 miles (370km) away, enabling them to pick up the shorter wavelengths from great distances. Another advantage was mobility. Aircraft can avoid operating in areas of magnetic interference, or in radar blind spots, and they are not vulnerable fixed targets. Moreover, by moving a set distance on a straight course they can locate a particular emitter by combining direction-finding with triangulation.

Passive ER has distinct branches, the main one of which is signals intelligence (SIGINT). This is defined

The Northrop F-5 series was developed as austere, affordable fighters. The obvious next step was to modify the nose to produce the RF-5E Tigereye.

as the detection, identification, classification and analysis of electronic emissions from hostile or potentially hostile sources. Factors such as signal strength, emitter location, waveband, operating methods and pulse-repetition frequency reveal a great deal about the type of emitter and its probable purpose, and a pattern can gradually be built up. SIGINT itself has two branches: communications intelligence (COMINT) and electronic intelligence (ELINT). COMINT consists of gathering technical and intelligence information derived from communications, other than the intended recipient, while ELINT concerns the gathering of technical and intelligence information from man-made emitters other than those used for communications.

The distinctions are not absolutely clear-cut. For example, telemetry intelligence (TELINT) is the interception, processing and analysis of telemetry signals by a third party, whereas telemetry is the provision of real-time information during flight or rocket testing. By definition, TELINT should be part of ELINT, but its extreme specialisation sets it apart.

Finally there is radiation intelligence (RINT), or the gathering of intelligence derived from the collection and analysis of non-information-bearing elements extracted from electromagnetic energy unintentionally emitted by foreign equipment and systems, of which radar sidelobes are a good example. On the other hand, RINT specifically excludes emanations arising from nuclear explosions.

Electronic reconnaissance is a vast subject, and invariably it overlaps with more orthodox photo- and maritime-reconnaissance (MR) missions and also ECM, which comes under the general heading of electronic warfare (EW). A tremendous variety of aircraft have flown electronic missions, types generally being chosen to suit specific scenarios.

The primary requirement was long range/endurance, combined with the capacity to accommodate large banks of bulky electronic sensors and their specialist operators. This virtually dictated a large, multi-engined, multi-crew aircraft, although there were exceptions. In the main, passive ER was a stand-off mission, flown outside the territorial airspace of the target nation. Speed was therefore not essential in most cases, although again there were exceptions. During the 1950s the USAF and USN lost almost fifty aircraft to fighter attack, most of them multi-engined reconnaissance types.

The first generation of long-range reconnaissance aircraft consisted mainly of converted Second World War bombers, such as the Boeing RB-29. However, one very interesting machine entered service with the US Navy in 1950. This was the Martin Mercator. Conceived as a long-range minelayer, it was powered by two huge Pratt & Whitney Wasp Major piston engines and two Allison J33 turbojets. For endurance it cruised on the Wasp Majors at 200mph (320km/hr), but the jets

enabled it to wind up to 390mph (625km/hr). The fourteen-man crew contained seven electronics specialists. Several of the nineteen Mercators to enter service were attacked by communist fighters, and at least one was lost to this cause. The remaining aircraft were retired in 1960, by which time only seven were left.

Large mixed-power aircraft were not exclusive to the USN. Convair's huge B-36D strategic bomber was powered by six piston and four jet engines, the jets being used on take-off and to give a dash speed of some 400mph (640km/hr) over the target, combined with a ceiling of 40,000ft (12,000m). The first reconnaissance variant, the RB-36D, first flew on 18 December 1949. It carried a fourteen-camera package weighing 1.5 tonnes, including a massive 48in (122cm) focal-length model, supplemented by eighty flash bombs for night photography, plus ECM gear in the rear bay. Including specialists, the crew sometimes numbered as many as twenty-two. In all, more than 130 RB-36s were delivered.

The RB-36 was replaced by the Boeing B-47 six-jet swept-wing bomber, a considerable number of which were converted to the reconnaissance role. With a cruising speed of 550mph (880km/hr) at altitude, the B-47 was difficult to intercept, and about 300 were converted to RB-47 or EB-47 configuration. One function of the EB-47 was to tease the defenders into trying to intercept, thereby enabling their radar and ground control to be monitored and assessed. Usually the speed of the RB-47 kept it out of trouble, but not always. On 1 July 1960 an RB-47 was shot down into the Barents Sea by a Soviet MiG-19.

An interesting variant was the EB-47E(TT), of which only three were built. In addition to the ELINT suite they carried TELINT equipment. When the Soviet ballistic-missile programme was at its height, the aircraft flew at maximum altitude to catch the Soviet telemetry signals, from which the state of the art could be deduced. Launches were monitored by aircraft flying from Incirlik in Turkey, while splashdowns in the Pacific were observed by Hawaiian-based machines. Following this, they recorded details of the manned Soviet space flights before retiring in 1967.

The Soviet Union had exactly the same ER needs as the West, and followed a similar pattern in choosing a strategic bomber and equipping it for electronic missions. The Tupolev Tu-20/142, given the reporting name *Bear* by NATO, first flew in 1954. It was powered (unusually) by four large Kuznetsov turboprops, which were largely responsible for its enormous range of 7,800 miles (12,480km). Its swept wing allowed it to attain a maximum dash speed of 575mph (920km/hr), remarkable for a propeller-driven aircraft. Such a performance made it ideal for maritime reconnaissance, and later models were given an increasing amount of ELINT kit, although

With bulges and aerials almost everywhere, the Tupolev Tu-20 Bear *flew both maritime- and electronic-reconnaissance missions. The combination of swept wings and turboprop engines is most unusual.*

unlike most of its Western counterparts the *Bear* continued to carry offensive weaponry, notably anti-ship missiles. Its best-known function is as a 'Zombie', probing Western air defences, noting radar and communications emissions and checking the speed of reaction of the fighters which arrive to escort it off the premises.

Space for black boxes and their operators was at a premium in adapted bombers, and accommodating them in a bomb-bay pod, as in the EB-47, was at best a compromise. Far more accommodation and a better working environment were needed. Civilian airliners could more easily meet these requirements.

The swept-wing Boeing 707 of 1954 vintage spawned a whole family of military variants: transports, tankers and AWACS, as well as ELINT aircraft. The latter first appeared in 1961 as the EC and RC-135, and updating with new equipment coupled with codenames such as Rivet Joint and Combat Sent has been an almost continuous process, the only external difference between subtypes being the various bulges and aerial 'farms'. Crew numbers vary, but average about twenty-one, of whom sixteen are specialists. Four Pratt & Whitney TF33 turbofans give a cruising speed of 560mph (900km/hr), a ceiling of more than 40,000ft (12,000m) and an operational radius of 2,670 miles (4,280km). A few RC-135s remain in service in 1998.

The Soviet Union followed a similar pattern to that of the USA in using converted bombers, notably the Tupolev Tu-16 *Badger* and the Myasischyev Mya-4 *Bison* for ER, before switching to an airframe designed for civilian use. This was the Ilyushin Il-20 *Coot*-A. First identified by the West in 1978, *Coot*-A is a straight-wing design powered by four Ivchenko Al-20M turboprops. Distinguishable from the Il-18 transport by an enormous ventral fairing and cheek bulges on the forward fuselage, it carries a crew of twenty-five for 4,034 miles (6,450km) at a cruising speed of 390mph (624km/hr).

The final SIGINT type which must be mentioned is the Lockheed EC/RC-130 Hercules. Powered by four Allison T56 turboprops, the Hercules first emerged as a transport in 1954, but has since been adapted for almost every mission under the sun. The ER variant first came to public notice in 1958, when one was shot down over Armenia by Soviet fighters. As the RC-135 carries out the main SIGINT tasks, the Hercules tends to be more specialised. Some are stand-off jammers, while others are equipped to beam radio and TV signals into the homes of the target nation, as was done during the operation against Haiti a few years ago. Then there is the Senior Scout, which uses a clip-on aerial and antenna array plus a mission crew capsule in the cargo hold to convert a Hercules into a SIGINT platform in just twelve hours.

Electronic countermeasures

Electronics have played an ever-increasing part in warfare, and particularly in air war. Detection, command and control, weapon-aiming and guidance, terrain-following and avoidance, and even navigation have all become heavily dependent on electronics. As these have increased in importance, so has the effort devoted to defeating them.

During the Second World War specialised ECM aircraft were used to form barrier screens against detection radars, while others, equipped to jam ground-to-air communications, accompanied the bomber stream to the target. At the end of the war the esoteric art of ECM fell into abeyance, only to be hurriedly resurrected when fighting broke out in Korea a few years later.

For many years airborne ECM took two forms: bombers carried their own low-powered, non-directional jammers, or they were supported by ER aircraft operating in a stand-off role. At first this was good enough; in fact, in the days when it was believed that the next war would be an all-out nuclear exchange, there was little choice. Only when it became apparent that future wars would be conventional and tactical was it realised that dedicated ECM aircraft should support the raiders over hostile territory. The reason for this was that, like all electronic emissions, the strength of jamming decays rapidly with distance, and with stand-off ECM aircraft it was ineffective. The attackers could be fitted with ECM pods, but these were low-powered, non-directional and generally limited. By the time of the Vietnam War they had to counter high-powered ground detection, SAM guidance and fighter air interception radars, all on different wavelengths.

What was needed was a tactical aircraft that was sufficiently fast and agile to survive for extended periods over hostile territory while carrying the equipment for the job. Ancient Douglas EF-10B Skyknights of the USMC became available from April 1965, and flew jamming missions in support of attacks on SAM sites, but they were not really up the task. Rather better was the Douglas EB-66C Destroyer, a USAF development of the USN Skywarrior. A version of a fast twin-jet light bomber, it provided close-range, stand-off jam-

The Douglas EF-10B Skyknight was the first aircraft to fly electronic escort missions over Vietnam, but its poor performance made it very vulnerable to interception.

With two EWO positions spliced into the forward fuselage, a battery of jamming pods beneath the wings and a tailful of aerials, the EA-6B Prowler made a very effective EW machine.

ming cover. Several were lost in 1965–6, but they were still active in the war in 1972, finally being withdrawn from service in 1974.

Jamming support was also needed by the USN carriers. A truly dedicated EW machine, the Grumman EA-6B Prowler, derived from the A-6 Intruder all-weather attack aircraft, arrived on Yankee Station in June 1972, replacing the EA-6A, which was configured more for ELINT than for ECM. A subsonic, twin-engined machine, the EA-6B differs from its predecessor in having two extra seats for electronic warfare officers (EWOs), and the ALQ-99F jamming system, carried externally in five ram-air-turbine-powered pods, each of which cover seven frequency bands. In addition, it can carry four anti-radiation missiles for defence suppression, plus two Sidewinder AAMs for self-defence. The EA-6B performed superbly in the Gulf War; it has also operated over Bosnia and will remain in service for some time yet.

Much later in concept is the Lockheed EF-111A Raven. Derived from the F-111 variable-sweep strike bomber, the Raven carries the same ALQ-99 EW suite as Prowler, housed in its bomb bay. It is, however, far more automated, as only one EWO is carried to operate it. Externally, the EF-111A differs from strike variants in having a large pod atop the fin and a ventral 'canoe' fairing. Powered by two Pratt & Whitney TF30 after-burning turbofans, it is easily supersonic. The Raven also gave sterling service in the Gulf War.

The Russian equivalents of the these last two aircraft were the Yakovlev Yak-28PP *Brewer*-E and the Sukhoi Su-24MP *Fencer*-F. First deployed in 1970, the *Brewer*-E was a twin-engined, swept-wing derivative of a light bomber. With a two-man crew in tandem, *Brewer*-E carried its ECM suite, which was believed to give 360° coverage, in a pod in what had been the bomb bay. It was replaced by *Fencer*-F in 1992.

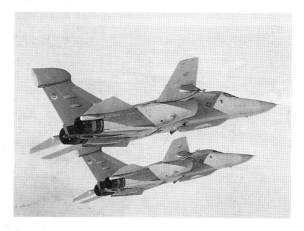

The General Dynamics EF-111 Raven carried the same ECM suite as the Prowler, but it was located in the bomb bay and automated for one-man operation. Much faster than the Prowler, and better suited to the high-speed, low-level mission, the Raven had better survivability.

Twin-engined, with variable-sweep wings, *Fencer*-F is the Russian equivalent of the F-111, including side-by-side seating for the two-man crew. It cannot, however, match the payload/range performance of the American machine, nor its maximum speed at altitude. It is extremely doubtful whether its ECM suite even remotely approaches the capability of ALQ-99.

AEW/AWACS

Airborne early warning has two advantages. Not only does it lift a search radar to an altitude from which the horizon is more than 230 miles (370km) away, but it confers mobility, allowing the carrier aircraft to patrol where it is most needed. Add sophisticated electronics, secure communications and fighter controllers, and it becomes an airborne warning-and-control system. But it took many years to reach this stage.

The first halfway-capable AEW aircraft was the Lockheed EC-121 Warning Star, which used the airframe of the four-engined Constellation airliner. It carried two radars: the APS-20 search radar with a rotating antenna ventrally, coupled with a height-finding radar in a dorsal radome. Warning Star entered service in 1953 and was first used as a radar picket off the Atlantic and Pacific coasts, for which its endurance of twenty hours was well-suited. During their long service life EC-121s underwent several upgrades, and many served in Viet-

nam, monitoring Vietnamese MiG activity and acting as communications relay aircraft.

The RAF entered the AEW field much later, primarily because the ground-based radar system was deemed adequate when the main threat was the high-altitude bomber. When, about 1970, the threat changed to low level, AEW was needed. The most affordable and quickest solution was to convert Avro Shackleton MR.2s by fitting them with APS-20 radars taken from redundant Fleet Air Arm (FAA) Fairey Gannets. Powered by four Rolls-Royce piston engines, the Shackleton had an endurance of twenty-four hours. It entered service in 1973 and was finally phased out in 1991.

AEW at sea

Carrier groups needed AEW aircraft small enough to operate from ships at sea. The first major type to be used in the role, by both the US Navy and the FAA, was the single-engined Douglas Skyraider. Originally a single-seater dive and torpedo bomber, the Skyraider was fitted with an APS-20 radar in a ventral radome, with the cockpit and fuselage modified to carry two extra crewmen. These changes caused stability problems, and the vertical tail surfaces were enlarged to overcome this. AEW Skyraiders were supplanted in USN service from 1958 by the Grumman E-1B Tracer, and in FAA in 1960 by the Fairey Gannet AEW.3.

Grumman's E-2C Hawkeye set a fashion in AEW aircraft with its 'mushroom' rotating radome. Originally intended for carrier use, it is in land-based service with several air forces.

Designed for the anti-submarine role, the Gannet was powered by the unique Armstrong-Siddeley Double Mamba turboprop, which combined twin-engined safety with single-engined drag, and enabled half of the engine to be shut down in flight to extend patrol time. To convert the basic machine to AEW configuration, the fuselage was completely redesigned with a ventral radome housing APS-20, a new crew station with side-by-side seating in the mid-section, an enlarged vertical tail, and shortened jet pipes. Endurance was increased to between five and six hours. The Gannet AEW.3 became operational on 1 February 1960, and retired eighteen years later, when the last British fleet carrier was decommissioned.

By contrast, the US Navy selected a carrier-compatible transport for conversion to the AEW mission: the Grumman C-1 Trader. Named the Tracer, this was a conventional machine, powered by two wing-mounted Wright piston engines. The search radar chosen was the APS-82, the scanner of which was mounted above the fuselage in a huge fixed radome of flattened teardrop shape. This blanketed the vertical tail surface, so the empennage was modified to have twin fins and rudders outboard. The radome also required the wings to fold sideways, instead of upwards as in Trader. Two specialist operators were seated behind the pilot. Tracer entered service in 1958 and was phased out after the end of the Vietnam War.

Grumman's E-2 Hawkeye, first flown in 1960, is unique in being the only AEW aircraft specifically designed for the mission. Variants have played an active role in the conflicts in Vietnam, the Middle East, and the Gulf, and serve with several air forces worldwide. Although bearing a superficial resemblance to the E-1, the Hawkeye differs in many ways. It is powered by Allison turboprops, the circular radome rotates with the scanner, and it has a multi-fin tail. The cabin is pressurised, providing a 'shirtsleeve' working environment. At an economical cruising speed of 230mph (370km/hr) the latest E-2C model can remain on station at its service ceiling of 37,000ft (11,280m), 230 miles (370km) from the carrier, for five and a half hours.

Updated nearly four decades ago, the Hawkeye's capabilities are now phenomenal. With only three mission specialists, the system is highly automated. It can track more than 2,000 contacts, and control up to forty interceptions simultaneously. Not all of this is down to the radar, the range of which is typically 230 miles (370km). It has a passive detection system which can pick up tactical aircraft at twice the range of the radar. Even small targets such as cruise missiles can be detected at 145 miles (230km). Displays are colour- and touch-sensitive, and overland look-down is now in the same class as that of the larger and more expensive E-3 Sentry.

At the top of the AEW range is the Boeing E-3 Sentry AWACS, based on the Boeing 707 airframe with four Pratt & Whitney turbofans. Operationally, the Sentry is a little more capable than the Hawkeye. Endurance is six hours on station at 1,000 miles (1,600km) from base, and it is considerably faster, which aids escape from attack. Up to 2,400 tracks can be monitored at one time, while seventeen mission specialists allow a greater degree of fighter controlling. Sentry is used by the USAF, RAF, NATO, Saudi Arabia, and France's Armée de l'Air.

Top of the range in the AEW/AWACS field is the Boeing E-3 Sentry, but while it outperforms all competitors, very few nations can afford it.

A change from the dorsal-radome configuration is evident in the Phalcon, which combines a large nose radome with phased-array radars in cheek positions.

Another interesting machine is the Phalcon, also based on the Boeing 707. Its Israeli designers have eschewed the classic dorsal mushroom radome for banks of solid-state, phased-array radars. First seen in public at Le Bourget in 1993, Phalcon combines AWACS with SIGINT. Externally it has a bulbous nose radome, two flat panels on either side of the forward fuselage and a fourth fairing under the tail. The advantage is stated as being that Phalcon's phased arrays can detect targets far faster than the rotating antenna of the Sentry. It is also reportedly much cheaper than the American aircraft.

Airborne early warning is one area in which the Russians have fallen far behind the West. The Soviet's first true aircraft of this type was the Ilyushin Il-76 *Mainstay*, which is believed to have achieved initial operational capability in 1988. Reliability is not high, and its weight is such that full fuel load cannot be used. Its crew is believed to total fifteen, including eleven specialists.

'Full-up' AEW is very costly, but there have been many attempts to market an affordable platform. One of the best of these is the Saab 340 Erieye, a twin-engined 'bizjet' carrying a fixed dorsal phased-array antenna with electronic scanning. Range performance against $5m^2$ ($54ft^2$) targets is stated to be about 210 miles (340km), and endurance is six hours on station 115 miles (180km) from base.

The Royal Navy's 'Harrier Carriers' are far too small for use by non-STOVL fixed-wing aircraft, yet the need

for AEW remains. The answer is the Westland Sea King AEW.2A helicopter, which carries its Searchwater radar in an inflatable 'shopping basket'. The Sea King can manage four hours on station at 115-mile radius at 10,000ft (3,050m), from where the radar horizon is 150 miles (240km). The Russians have also experimented with heliborne AEW radar.

Lighter-than-air AEW platforms have inherent advantages. They can remain on station for extended periods, up to thirty days if refuelled at sea, and are relatively cheap. Under evaluation by the USA is the Westinghouse Sentinel 5000, while experiments are made to produce a low-observable gondola, and the LASS tethered aerostat is currently used for monitoring border infringements by drug smugglers and illegal immigrants.

Battlefield reconnaissance

Battlefield reconnaissance was for many years the province of the fast-mover tactical jet, supplemented by light observation machines, but neither was entirely satisfactory. The fast jet needed a fixed base, which was necessarily far behind the battle area, slowing reaction time, while the lightplane simply lacked capability.

For the US Army the gap was filled by the Grumman OV-1 Mohawk, a two-seater powered by two Lycoming T53 turboprops, which combined a reasonable turn of speed with exceptional agility and the ability to operate from short forward airstrips while carrying a full comple-

The E-8 J-Stars gave a new dimension to battlefield surveillance and control when it made its debut during the Gulf War. From this angle, the 40ft (12m)-long canoe fairing shows up well, as does the aerial 'farm'.

ment of sensors. First flown in April 1959, the Mohawk was built in several variants, with cameras, infrared sensors or SLAR in a pod. It was widely used in Vietnam.

Top of the battlefield reconnaissance range is the E-8 J-Stars, which turned in such a remarkable performance during the Gulf War and currently monitors events in Bosnia. The airframe is that of the ubiquitous Boeing 707, with an advanced SAR radar carried in a 40ft (12m)-long ventral canoe fairing, coupled with real-time secure datalink communications. This allows it to stand-off 150 miles (240km) away and still see events on the ground with remarkable clarity. The SAR discrimination is so good that it can even tell the difference between wheeled and tracked vehicles, provided they are

Seen here is the French army's heliborne Orchidée battlefield surveillance radar system, mounted on a Super Puma helicopter. Like J-Stars, it made its combat debut during the Gulf War.

moving. Eighteen operators monitor consoles for different functions. However, few nations can afford J-Stars or its equivalent, and several low-cost systems have been proposed. These include ASTOR for the British Army, and Orchidée, a French heliborne system.

Maritime reconnaissance

The needs of maritime reconnaissance vary according to whether the aircraft is land- or carrier-based. The one common factor is that it must be able to remain on station for extended periods. Anti-submarine aircraft need to carry a load of active or passive sonobuoys, as well as mines, depth charges or homing torpedoes, while anti-shipping aircraft must be able to provide targeting information to friendly submarines or surface vessels. Alternatively, they need to carry anti-ship missiles. Land-based aircraft frequently take a long while to reach the patrol area, so they need a high cruising speed for transit.

Of the land-based types, the Russian *Bear* has been mentioned elsewhere. The West has three main MR types in service. The French Dassault Atlantique is powered by two turboprops, the Lockheed Orion by four turboprops, and the BAe Nimrod has four Spey turbofans. There can be no doubt that all can fly the mission satisfactorily, but the advantage lies with the Nimrod, which can reach the patrol area much faster, before shutting down two engines for economical loitering.

Unmanned aerial vehicles

The hazards of the reconnaissance mission have led to the development of unmanned aerial vehicles (UAVs), optimised for the task. These can be made very small, little bigger than model aeroplanes; with VTOL capability, to operate from small ships at sea; or very stealthy and therefore survivable. The main advantage is that very expensive aircrew are not put at risk. They also tend to be affordable.

UAVs can carry a variety of sensors. AEW, battlefield reconnaissance, ELINT and standard photography, are all within their remit, as are chemical and nuclear warfare reconnaissance. Equipped with TV cameras, they can provide their operators with a real-time picture of the battlefield, as in the Gulf War, when several dozen misguided Iraqis tried to surrender to one. Most are driven by small piston engines, although the smaller ones are powered by electric batteries. The larger models are turbine-driven. Most way out is the peanut-shaped Canadair CL-227 Sentinel, with twin rotors projecting from its waist. Sikorsky's Cypher is much like a flying saucer, with a shroud surrounding its rotors. Most mysterious of all is Lockheed's Dark Star, a saucer-shaped aircraft with wings of very high aspect ratio. Powered by a Williams FJ44 turbofan, Dark Star is designed to loiter for eight hours more than 500 miles (800km) from base, at an altitude exceeding 45,000ft (14,000m), and has a cruising speed of more than 290mph (460km/hr). It will carry SAR or an electro-optical sensor.

The British Aerospace Nimrod MR.2 is powered by four Spey turbofans which give it high speed to the patrol area. Once there, two engines are shut down to save fuel and extend time on station.

11
Future Military Aircraft
Robert Jackson

In the mid-1980s the designs of combat aircraft to replace existing ones for service in the twenty-first century were clearly defined. Vast sums of money were earmarked for the development of these new and advanced aircraft, which fell into three principal categories: supersonic V/STOL, agile multi-role and advanced technology (stealth). The first category undoubtedly had its attractions, and at first sight the operational requirement for a supersonic V/STOL aircraft seemed apparent to the planners of the 1980s, faced with the prospect of an ongoing Cold War increasingly dominated by advanced technology. Yet there were doubts about the validity of the supersonic V/STOL concept.

It seems natural to assume that if a combat aircraft is faster than others of its type it is therefore better and more effective. This is not necessarily true, as events in the 1982 Falklands conflict proved. At low level, supersonic capability can rarely be used to advantage, and success depends primarily on the quality of the pilot, his aircraft weapons systems and his ordnance. In the Falklands, the Sea Harrier/Sidewinder combination proved the best in combat across all three categories.

In low-level air combat a supersonic aircraft requires reheat to extricate itself from a disadvantage. But then, paradoxically, it is immediately more at risk because of its increased infrared (IR) signature and combat fuel usage. At similar performance levels, reheat fuel flow is two or three times that of a 'dry' engine. The protagonist who breaks off a close combat owing to concern about his low fuel state, and uses reheat to get away, is inviting a hostile AAM. Broadly, supersonic speed can be effective only at high altitude, in the specialised interceptor role. In low-level combat, or in ground-attack operations, a supersonic capability can often hinder rather than help. Although it can aid penetration of, and escape from, the target area (albeit with a major penalty in fuel consumption), it is of little help over the target itself; target acquisition and attack at speeds in excess of 12 miles/min present problems.

Relative to subsonic V/STOL fighters such as the Harrier, supersonic V/STOL capability allows earlier interception of hostile aircraft (an important asset as the ranges of stand-off missiles increase), and also offers a better chance of intercepting and destroying such missiles once they have been launched. The same principle applies when intercepting a hostile aircraft on a ground-attack mission. Rapid reaction, which is already a major factor in the Harrier's operational success story, would

be backed up by the ability to intercept the target aircraft before it was able to reach its weapons-release point.

Supersonic and subsonic aircraft are distinguished in current thinking by the use of reheated and unreheated engines respectively. But if a reheated engine is married to a subsonic airframe the result is a comparatively lightweight aircraft which has a significantly better performance at low level than a supersonic aircraft with the same powerplant. The weight saving includes avionics and general systems, but is mainly due to the use of thicker aerofoil sections in the wing and tail unit; this permits more fuel to be carried in the wing and therefore less in the fuselage, which can then be shortened. An aircraft of this type would be considerably cheaper than current supersonic designs and so could be available in greater numbers, offering much-improved operational flexibility.

Supersonic capability is essential for a modern radar-equipped fighter/interceptor in air-to-air combat. However, an active radar emits a signal which is clearly undesirable in a low-level ground-attack role, as it advertises the aircraft's presence, as well as its speed, direction and distance from the target, enabling hostile ground defences to be prepared. Apart from this, the radar would also occupy the prime nose area, which is better employed for the installation of the laser-ranging or FLIR systems required for a fully effective ground-attack mission. Furthermore, the ground-attack mission calls for high penetration speed with reheat off, a high g capability and a good view from the cockpit, together with advanced self-defence systems.

An ideal mix would be a majority of high-performance subsonic V/STOL aircraft, covered by a minority of supersonic interceptors. Many current combat aircraft are supersonic, multirole and have a very-short-take-off capability. None, however, can recover vertically, which would be essential for true invulnerability to anti-airfield counterattacks. Configurations for supersonic V/STOL designs have varied over the years, and it is worth remembering that the prototype of a supersonic V/STOL strike aircraft, the Hawker Siddeley P.1154, was well advanced in construction when the project was cancelled in 1965. Its cancellation led directly to the development of the P.1127 (RAF), which first flew eighteen months later and was the progenitor of today's substantial Harrier family.

Although the P.1154 was cancelled, a later, similar supersonic configuration was studied in 1973 for the US Navy. Designated AV-16S, this project was the

Detail design of the prototype Hawker Siddeley P.1154 supersonic V/STOL aircraft was well advanced when the project was cancelled in 1965.

product of a joint programme between Hawker Siddeley Aviation and McDonnell Douglas, and stemmed from a US Navy requirement for a supersonic deck-launched aircraft capable of VTOL intercept missions as well as large-radius subsonic strike against surface targets. The AV-16S's engine was to have been a large-diameter Rolls-Royce Pegasus 15 with plenum chamber burning (PCB, a new type of exhaust boost system). Perfor-mance was initially aimed at a Mach 1.7 capability, with a Mach 1.9 potential. Although the wing was larger than that of the P.1154, and the main undercarriage units were relocated in pods on the wing trailing edge, the design was still recognisable as a Harrier derivative. However, the programme never moved beyond the Phase One study stage owing to the predicted develop-ment costs versus the available budgets in the US Navy. Even a complementary subsonic project, the AV-16A, was seen as needing almost $1 billion for research, development and testing. There was little chance at that time that the USN could be persuaded to spend that kind of money on a weapons system just for the Marine Corps. However, the loss of the AV-16 programme led to the development, in 1975–6, of the Harrier II, an air-craft that will continue to provide a viable strike system in the twenty-first century.

There is no doubt that the concept of the supersonic V/STOL aircraft is valid. What is doubtful is whether the continued development of such an aircraft can be justified, in view of the enormous cost involved. In fact, escalating research-and-development (R&D) costs, and a drastic alteration in the perceived threat resulting from the breakup of the former Soviet Union, are factors that have also greatly influenced R&D work on every future combat-aircraft project, often leading to major delays in production programmes. Nowhere is this more true than in the case of the European Fighter Aircraft (EFA).

In October 1981 the RAF's Operational Require-ments Branch began planning for a next-generation fighter to replace the F-4 Phantom in the air-defence role and the Jaguar in the offensive-support role. The need crystallised in Air Staff Requirement (Air) 414, which specified a short-range, highly agile air-defence/offensive-support aircraft. The European Fight-er Aircraft programme was the project that met this requirement. An outline staff target for a common European fighter aircraft was issued in December 1983 by the air chiefs of staff of France, West Germany, Italy, Spain and the UK. The initial feasibility study was completed in July 1984, but France withdrew from the project a year later. A definitive European Staff Requirement (Development), giving operational requirements in greater detail, was issued in September 1987, and the main contracts for the development of engines and weapons systems were signed in November 1988.

To prove the necessary technology for EFA, a contract was awarded to British Aerospace in May 1983 for the development of an agile demonstrator aircraft (not a prototype) under the heading Experimental Aircraft Programme (EAP). The cost was to be shared between the partner companies of the EFA consortium and the UK Ministry of Defence (MoD). The EAP demonstrator flew for the first time on 8 August 1986, only three years after the programme was conceived. Powered by two Rolls-Royce RB.199 Mk 104D engines, it was the most advanced aircraft ever produced in Britain. A single-seat delta canard, its design emphasis was on air-combat performance, which in practice means a combination of high turn rates and high specific excess power, the measure of a fighter's ability to regain speed or altitude after a manoeuvre. The EAP demonstrator was, in fact, a superb blueprint for the fighter that was originally intended to form much of NATO's front line, and project the Alliance's air forces into the twenty-first century, providing the means to counter any foreseeable air threat.

The task of Eurofighter, as EFA ultimately became known, is to fight effectively throughout the combat spectrum, from engagements beyond visual range down to close-in combat. The technologies that enable it to do this are so advanced, and in some cases so unique, that the role of the EAP aircraft was vital to the Eurofighter project as a whole.

The end of the Cold War led, in 1992, to a reappraisal of the whole programme, with Germany in particular demanding substantial cost reductions. Several 'low-cost' configurations were examined, but only two turned out to be cheaper than the original EFA, and both were inferior to the MiG-29 and Su-27. Finally, in December 1992, the project was relaunched as Eurofighter 2000, the planned in-service entry having now been delayed by three years.

The Eurofighter 2000 development programme is managed by the NATO Eurofighter and Tornado Management Agency (NETMA) on behalf of the four-nation partnership comprising Alenia of Italy, British Aerospace, CASA of Spain and Deutsche Aerospace, acting together. The consortium is responsible for managing the complete weapons system with the exception of the engines.

In the air-defence role, as soon as a hostile aircraft is detected beyond visual range, Eurofighter must accelerate from its CAP loiter as quickly as possible in order to give its medium-range, fire-and-forget missiles maximum launch energy, fire as soon as it is within range, and then manoeuvre hard without losing energy to force incoming enemy missiles into making violent course corrections near the end of their flight, thereby reducing their chances of scoring hits. This phase of the engagement, therefore, requires high acceleration and good supersonic manoeuvrability.

The next phase, close-in combat, requires maximum usable lift and a high thrust-to-weight ratio, so that energy lost in turns can be quickly regained. In this respect Eurofighter uses all-aspect, short-range weaponry, the engagement starting with fast head-on attacks and then breaking down into a turning fight, with pilots manoeuvring hard to acquire good firing positions quickly. The weapons chosen for Eurofighter are the Hughes AIM-120 AMRAAM as the primary weapon, with the AIM-132 ASRAAM as the secondary. The aircraft also has a built-in gun armament.

Eurofighter is designed to be a 'pilot's aeroplane', with emphasis on the best possible all-round visibility and comfort during high-g manoeuvres. One major asset is the pilot's head-mounted sight, which avoids the need to pull tight turns to achieve missile lock-on and consequently reduces the risk of g-induced loss of consciousness (G-loc). Pilots also have the advantage of a new, fast-reacting g-suit. These innovations mean that there is no need to rake Eurofighter's ejection seat at more than the conventional 18° angle, which is good from the visibility

The EAP fitted with pressure transducers for measuring aerodynamic load.

EAP with its spine-mounted airbrake extended.

The first prototype Eurofighter 2000.

point of view. It also means that a centrally positioned control column can be retained. Aircraft with highly raked seats, such as the F-16, need a sidestick. The cockpit features colour, head-down multi-function displays and a wide-angle holographic HUD. Direct-voice input (DVI) controls such items as radio channel changes and map displays, but not safety-critical systems such as undercarriage operation or weapon-firing. The cockpit area is relatively lightly armoured, providing protection against light-to-medium calibre AAA; the heavy armour is reserved for the critical systems, the thinking being that it is more important to provide the pilot with additional defensive electronics than extra armour plate.

One of the most advanced and ambitious Eurofighter systems is the defensive avionics subsystem (DASS), which was designed to cope with the multiple and mass threats that would have been a major feature of a war on NATO's central front. The system combines and correlates outputs from Eurofighter's radar-warning receiver, laser detectors and other sensors, and then automatically triggers the best combination of active and passive defences while warning the pilot of the threat priority.

To engage targets, particularly in the vital beyond-visual-range battle, the aircraft is equipped with the Euroradar ECR90 multi-mode pulse-Doppler radar.

This is a development of GEC Ferranti's Blue Vixen radar, which is fitted in the British Aerospace Sea Harrier FRS.2. The ECR90 is designed to minimise pilot workload; radar tracks are presented constantly, analysed, allocated priority or deleted by track-management software. A third-generation coherent radar, the ECR90 benefits from a considerable increase in processing power, and has all-aspect detection capability in look-up and look-down modes. It also has covert features to reduce the risk of detection by enemy radar-warning receivers. Its full capability is classified, but it is thought to be able to engage at least ten targets simultaneously.

As a result of the reduction of the air threat to Western Europe, Germany expressed a desire to incorporate off-the-shelf avionics, including the less-expensive Hughes APG-65 radar, which was already in operation, to downgrade the standard of defensive aids and to make other deletions in order to effect a cost saving of up to 30 per cent. In 1996, however, these suggested downgrades were abandoned.

Eurofighter is powered by two EJ200 high-performance turbofan engines developing 13,500lb st (60kN) dry and 20,000lb st (90kN) with reheat. The first two Eurofighter prototypes flew in 1994, followed by several more. The original customer requirement was 250 each for the UK and Germany, 165 for Italy and 100 for Spain. The last-named country announced a firm requirement for 87 in January 1994, while Germany and Italy revised their respective needs to 180 and 121, the German order to include at least 40 of the fighter-bomber version. The UK's order was for 232, with options on a further 65. Deliveries to the air forces of all four countries were scheduled to begin in 2001.

Eurofighter has an intended service life of thirty years, or 6,000 hours. It has an integrated structural-monitoring system, the first in any combat aircraft, which calculates structural fatigue at twenty positions on the airframe sixteen times per second during flight. Operational turn-round by a six-man ground crew takes only twenty-five minutes, and four engineers can carry out an engine change in forty-five minutes.

Although Eurofighter is optimised for the air-superiority role, a comprehensive air-to-surface attack capability is incorporated in the basic design. Eurofighter is able to carry out close air support, counter-air, interdiction and anti-ship operations; it will also have a reconnaissance capability. Typically, the aircraft has a lo-lo combat radius of 350nm (648km) and a hi-lo-hi combat radius of 750nm (1,390km). Eurofighter has a maximum speed of Mach 2.0, depending on altitude.

Eurofighter's principal contender for foreign orders in the twenty-first century is the Dassault Rafale (Squall),

the development of which came about as a result of France's withdrawal from the EFA project, mainly because of a squabble over design leadership. Rafale A, as the technology demonstrator is known, flew for the first time on 4 July 1986. Powered by two SNECMA M88-2 augmented turbofans, each rated at 19,950lb st (48.7kN) dry and 16,400lb st (72.9kN) with reheat, Rafale is a single-seat aircraft with a compound-sweep delta wing, an all-moving canard, a single fin and semi-vented intakes. It incorporates digital fly-by-wire, relaxed stability and an electronic cockpit with voice command. A wide use of composites and aluminium-lithium has resulted in a 7–8 per cent weight saving.

In the strike role Rafale can carry one Aérospatiale ASMP stand-off nuclear bomb; in the interception role armament is up to eight AAMs with either active or infrared-homing; and in the air-to-ground role, a typical load is sixteen 500lb (227kg) bombs, two AAMs and two external fuel tanks. The aircraft is compatible with the full NATO arsenal of air-to-air and air-to-ground weaponry. Built-in armament comprises one 30mm DEFA cannon in the side of the starboard engine duct. The aircraft has a maximum level speed of Mach 2.0 at altitude and 864mph (1,390km/h) at low level.

France, which plans to have 140 Rafales in air force service by 2015 (the naval version, Rafale M, will equip France's aircraft carriers), sees the aircraft as vital to the

The first British-assembled EF2000, ZH588, on test from Warton.

The Dassault Rafale A undergoes early engine ground runs in April 1986, before its first flight.

The Rafale A technology demonstrator made its maiden flight in July 1986.

Five development Rafales over Istres in January 1994. From furthest to nearest they are: Rafale A, C01, B01 (air force), M01 and M02 (navy).

defence of her territory, particularly in view of rising hostility towards Europe in the governments of some Arab nations on the other side of the Mediterranean. The aircraft's low-level penetration combat radius with twelve 250kg (550lb) bombs, four AAMs and three external fuel tanks is 570nm (1,055km).

The demise of the Cold War also had an effect on America's multirole combat aircraft for the twenty-first century, the Lockheed-Martin F-22 Raptor, a far different aircraft from either Eurofighter or Rafale. The F-22's development history is in effect a catalogue of the problems, both technological and financial, that can beset an advanced system of this kind.

In the late 1970s the USAF identified a requirement for 750 examples of an Advanced Tactical Fighter (ATF) to replace the F-15 Eagle. The goal was to produce a tactical aircraft that would remain viable for at least the first quarter of the twenty-first century; one that would have a range 50–100 per cent greater than that of the F-15, be capable of short take-off and landing on damaged airfields, and be able to engage multiple targets at once, beyond visual range. It had to incorporate stealth technology and supercruise (supersonic cruise without afterburning) and, operated by a single pilot, it had to be able to survive in an environment filled with people, both in the air and on the ground, whose sole purpose was to destroy it.

To test the concepts that would eventually be combined in the ATF, the USAF initiated a series of parallel research programmes. The first was the YF-16 control-configured vehicle (CCV), which flew in 1976–7 and demonstrated the decoupled control of aircraft flight path and attitude; in other words the machine could skid sideways, turn without banking, climb or descend without changing its attitude, and point its nose left or right or up or down without changing its flight path.

A second research programme involved HiMAT, a highly manoeuvrable, remotely piloted research aircraft built by Rockwell. First flown in July 1979, HiMAT was a scale model of an ATF design, and was required to demonstrate the manoeuvring performance of such an aircraft, which would need to be capable of a sustained 8g turn at 30,000ft (9,150m) and Mach 0.9. The test vehicle, which weighed 3,400lb (1,540kg) and was 20ft (6m) long, was carried into the air on a pylon under the wing of a B-52 and launched at Mach 0.7 at an altitude of between 40,000 and 45,000ft (12,200–13,720m), landing at Edwards Air Force Base at the end of an hour-long sortie. The whole operation, from launch to landing, was under the control of a ground-based pilot who sat in front of a console containing a full set of flight controls and instruments. Inputs were telemetered from the ground-based computer, which was programmed with the flight characteristics and simulated control system of the aircraft, to the primary on-board processor which drove the digital fly-by-wire control system. Data telemetered from the aircraft included input for the flight instruments, sampled fifty-five times a second; accelerations, pitch, roll and yaw rates and angle of attack and sideslip, which were sampled 220 times a second. This high data-sampling rate was designed to give the ground controller instantaneous feel of the aircraft's control system, necessary in the handling of precision manoeuvres.

Backup control on every HiMAT flight was provided by a TF-104 chase aircraft, whose pilot could exercise limited authority through the test vehicle's autopilot. If the control system was switched from normal to backup, the autopilot took over and HiMAT executed a programmed recovery manoeuvre, returning to level flight. The vehicle then entered a constant-speed, constant-altitude orbit, maintaining a 35° bank. The TF-104 pilot then took over, using discrete signals to control throttle, left or right turn, climb or dive, orbit or exit orbit, and normal or landing flight mode. The approach to land was controlled by the ground pilot with the aid of a TV camera mounted in HiMAT's cockpit position, and the touchdown, on steel landing skids, was made at the relatively high speed of 220kt (408km/h).

Grumman's forward-swept X-29, one the test vehicles involved in the ATF programme, flew for the first time in December 1984.

Other test vehicles involved in the ATF programme included the Gruman X-29, which first flew in December 1984 and was designed to investigate forward-sweep technology, and an F-111 fitted with a mission-adaptive wing (MAW) – in other words, a wing capable of reconfiguring itself automatically to mission requirements. Flight-testing of all of these experimental aircraft came under the umbrella of the USAF's Advanced Fighter Technology Integration (AFTI) programme.

In September 1983, while the AFTI programme was well under way, the USAF awarded ATF concept-definition-study contracts to six American aerospace companies, and two of these, Lockheed and Northrop, were selected to build demonstrator prototypes of their respective proposals. Each produced two prototypes, the Lockheed YF-22 and Northrop YF-23, and all four aircraft flew in 1990. Two different powerplants, the Pratt & Whitney YF119 and the General Electric YF120, were evaluated, and in April 1991 it was announced that the F-22 and F119 was the winning combination. The F119 advanced-technology engine, two of which power the F-22, develops 35,000lb st (155kN) and is fitted with two-dimensional convergent/divergent exhaust nozzles with thrust-vectoring for enhanced performance and manoeuvrability.

The McDonnell Douglas YF-23, seen here over Edwards Air Force Base, was the other contender for the ATF requirement.

230

Lockheed's contender for the ATF contract was the YF-22.

An airborne study of Lockheed's YF-22. The aircraft costs twice as much per unit as Eurofighter.

The F-22 combines many stealth features. Its air-to-air weapons, for example, are stored internally, three internal bays housing Sidewinders, four AIM-120As or six AMRAAMs. Following an assessment of the aircraft's combat role in 1993, it was decided to add a ground-attack capability, and the internal weapons bay can also accommodate 1,000lb (454kg) GBU-32 precision-guided missiles. Designed for a high sortie rate, the F-22 has a turn-round time of less than twenty minutes, and its avionics are highly integrated to provide rapid reaction in air combat, much of its survivability depending on the pilot's ability to locate a target very early and kill it with a first shot.

The F-22 is a very expensive aircraft, and its development has been dogged by financial constraints. Although the initial requirement for 750 aircraft was reduced to 438 in a cost-saving exercise, the total procurement cost was estimated, in 1996, to be $87 billion, with flyaway cost per aircraft $92.6 million, around twice that of Eurofighter.

The F-22 was designed to meet a specific threat, which at that time was presented by large numbers of highly agile Soviet combat aircraft, its task being to engage them in their own airspace with beyond-visual-range weaponry. That threat was very real: the USAF's last fighter, the F-16, had entered service in 1979, and in the decade that followed the Soviets introduced no fewer than five fighter/attack types. The Su-24 *Fencer*, with its all-weather, low-altitude-penetration capability, greatly enhanced the Soviet ability to carry out deep strikes into NATO territory; the Su-25 *Frogfoot* ground-attack aircraft quickly proved itself to be an excellent close-support fighter in Afghanistan; the MiG-29 *Fulcrum* and the Su-27 *Flanker* were a match for NATO aircraft in the air-superiority role, as well as having a substantial ground-attack capability; and the MiG-31 *Foxhound*, developed to counter US bombers armed with cruise missiles, brought a new dimension to the Soviet air-defence system. The Soviets clearly had the

The second Lockheed YF-22 on the occasion of its roll-out at the manufacturer's Marietta plant on 10 February 1998.

Sukhoi's Su-37 incorporates three-dimensional vectoring nozzles to give extra agility.

ability to develop an aircraft in the F-22 class, and there were serious concerns that they would do so first.

Then came the breakup of the Soviet Union, with its attendant economic problems, and it soon became clear that, instead of developing new combat aircraft, the Russians were applying new technology to existing designs in order to make them viable into the next century. The trend was exemplified in the Sukhoi Su-37, a single-seat fighter and ground-attack aircraft developed from the Su-27/35 and incorporating three-dimensional vectoring nozzles to give it super-agility. For example, the Su-37 can pitch up rapidly beyond the vertical, perform a tight 360° somersault within its own length, and pull out to resume level flight with no height loss.

The Russians thus appear to have succeeded in producing aircraft that will perform much of the F-22's mission at a fraction of the cost. Some of them will be available on the world export market in the twenty-first century, probably at cut prices, creating a dangerous imbalance. They will be available to nations that hitherto could only afford small, relatively cheap multirole aircraft, of which the British Aerospace Hawk, in its several variants, is a good example. The Hawk serves with several air arms worldwide, and as the T-45 Goshawk is also used in the training role by the US Navy. In the strike role it can carry 7,000lb (3,173kg) of stores on six underwing stations. Armament options include air-to-air missiles such as Sidewinder and the French MATRA Magic, anti-shipping weapons such as Sea Eagle, and even torpedoes of the Sting Ray type. The Hawk Series 100 has enhanced ground-attack capability, featuring a hands-on-throttle-and-stick (HOTAS) weapons system comprising inertial nav/attack, a HUD-and-weapon-aiming computer system, a colour head-down display, a stores-management system, a radar altimeter, a radar-warning receiver and a chaff/flare dispenser, all linked by a digital databus. A laser rangefinder is an optional extra.

In 1984 British Aerospace announced the launching of the single-seat Hawk 200 strike fighter. The decision to develop this aircraft was taken in the light of the rapid escalation of costs associated with modern front-line aircraft and their growing complexity. A small subsonic aircraft with sophisticated avionics and heavy payload capability can effectively perform the same roles, but being less expensive it can be deployed in greater numbers, resulting in an increased target coverage.

Previous attempts to produce cost-effective small fighting aircraft had generally failed because, although they were inexpensive, they were unable to carry adequate loads over appropriate distances, and were too small to carry the sensors needed for night and all-weather operations. The single-seat Hawk represented a clear breakthrough in these fields, offering unique operational cost-effectiveness. Advanced aerodynamics and design layout permit a disposable fuel and ordnance load approaching 150 per cent of airframe weight, and its highly economical Turboméca Adour turbofan engine makes efficient use of fuel, giving the aircraft a substantial combat radius and an endurance of more than five hours.

The Hawk 200 retains a high degree of commonality with its predecessors, all the changes having been confined to the nose and cockpit fuselage section. The removal of the second seat enables the aircraft to carry two built-in high-velocity 25mm Aden guns, each with 100 rounds, leaving the fuselage station, which accommodates a single 30mm gun pod on other variants, free for additional ordnance, fuel or an ECM pod. Hawk 200 operators can choose from three options of forward-fuselage equipment to cover the full operational spectrum required by any air arm in any location throughout the world, whether for defence or strike, over land or sea, by day or night and in virtually any weather conditions.

For daytime operation the equipment package consists of a gyro-stabilised attack sight together with attitude-and-reference-heading system, or an inertial navigation system with a HUD, plus a weapon-aiming computer, digital databus and optional laser ranging. For night operation the aircraft is fitted with FLIR, converting low-light conditions to daytime standards and enabling accurate ground-attack and tactical-reconnaissance missions to be flown twenty-four hours a day, while for all-weather operation the package includes advanced multi-mode radar for target-acquisition and navigation.

The Hawk 200 can lift an exceptionally wide range of ordnance, including 2.7in (68mm) rockets, runway-denial and tactical-strike bombs, retarded and cluster bombs, air-to-air and air-to-surface missiles and a variety of external fuel tanks. In the airspace-denial role the aircraft is designed to loiter at 30,000ft (9,150m) with two AAMs and two external 860-litre (189gal) fuel tanks. It can remain on station for four hours at up to

A British Aerospace Hawk armed with Sidewinder air-to-air missiles.

A single-seat British Aerospace Hawk 200 armed with Sidewinders.

233

100nm (185km) from base, for two hours at 425nm (787km) and for one hour at 600nm (1,111km). Its maximum intercept radius is 770nm (1,427km).

In the close air-support role, lo-lo radius is 135nm (250km) with a 6,000lb (2,718kg) warload; in the interdiction role hi-lo-hi radius is 540nm (1,000km) with a 5,000lb (2,265kg) warload, and in the reconnaissance role the total range is 1,950nm (3,614km). Armed with two Sea Eagle ASMs in the anti-shipping role, Hawk 200 has a hi-hi radius of 800nm (1,482km), equipped with two 860-litre (189gal) fuel tanks, and the same tankage gives the aircraft a range of 2,200nm (4,077km) for ferrying or long-range deployment.

For a small nation, an aircraft like the Hawk may be all that is necessary to assure its self-defence for the foreseeable future. Such aircraft pack a powerful punch, and their small size increases their chances of survival in a hostile AAA and SAM environment. In the 1982 Falklands conflict, for example, it was an attack aircraft in the Hawk category, an Aermacchi MB339A, that sank the British frigate HMS *Ardent* with considerable loss of life.

Other nations, however, taking advantage of the worldwide instability caused by the disintegration of the massive communist bloc, may not be content with a mere defensive posture. In the Far East, China, despite an apparently growing *rapprochement* with the West, remains a perceived threat to the stability of the Pacific Basin. Not only is she armed with modern Russian types such as the Su-27, but also her ambitions are backed up by a powerful nuclear capability. In the mid-1970s, with no sign of a manned strategic bomber under development to replace the Tu-16, it was becoming clear that the Chinese were placing their eggs in the strategic-missile basket. In 1978 the US Department of Defense stated:

> The Chinese now have a limited but credible capability for nuclear strikes around the periphery of the PRC [People's Republic of China]. Their capacity to produce fissionable materials is expanding.... During 1977, Chinese air-to-surface missile and related programmes apparently expanded. In addition, there have been nuclear-weapon tests. This activity suggests a continuing emphasis by the Chinese on developing strategic missile and space systems. The PRC has made a substantial investment in research, developmental testing and production facilities for both liquid- and solid-propellant missile systems. Although the Chinese have not yet tested a solid-propellant ballistic missile, they continue to expand their solid-propellant rocket-motor facilities. They will probably develop solid-propellant ballistic missile systems.

At the time this statement was made, China had already deployed three liquid-fuel missile systems. The first, the CSS-1 MRBM, was deployed in the late 1960s and was capable of reaching targets in the eastern USSR; it was based on the Soviet SS-2. The CSS-2, developed from the SS-4 (both Soviet missile types had been supplied to China in very small numbers before the Sino-Soviet split), was deployed soon afterwards, about sixty rounds going into service; its Chinese designation was *Dong Feng* 3. Its successor, the CSS-3 (*Dong Feng* 4) was a limited-range (4,000-mile) ICBM and was armed with a 2-megaton warhead; no more than eight rounds were deployed.

The first really viable Chinese ICBM was the CSS-4 (*Dong Feng* 5), which has a range of over 6,000 miles and carries a 5-megaton warhead. A small force of five rounds was deployed in 1983, and the weapon was later armed with an MRV warhead system. It was followed by the CSS-5, which is based on the Long March satellite-launch vehicle and carries a payload of up to ten MRVs.

The deployment of these vulnerable land-based missile systems was an interim measure, the main emphasis being on the development of submarine-launched ballistic missiles (SLBMs). Design of a Chinese SLBM system began in the late 1960s, and the first such weapon, the CSS-N-2, was tested on a locally assembled, Soviet-designed, *Golf*-class conventionally powered submarine in the early 1980s. The definitive Chinese SLBM is the CSS-N-4 *Julang* (Great Wave) 1, a two-stage solid-propellant weapon which was deployed on six new-construction nuclear-missile submarines, each boat carrying fourteen rounds. China therefore entered the 1990s with a considerable nuclear-attack capability, and has demonstrated her offensive power in live missile launches from submarines exercising in the western Pacific.

Apart from assuring the continued national integrity of Taiwan through the deployment of modern air-superiority aircraft, therefore, the main twenty-first-century requirement in the Pacific will be the provision of adequate maritime patrol and surveillance resources. These already exist in the form of the Lockheed Martin P-3 Orion, which serves with Australia, Japan and South Korea as well as with the US Navy. As a weapons platform the Orion has a good deal of life remaining, and is yet another good example of an elderly design which has proved capable of continual upgrading.

In the more distant future, the maritime-surveillance role may be undertaken by long-endurance unmanned aircraft using solar power. Prototypes of such an aircraft were under test in the USA in the late 1990s; operational versions would cruise 12½ miles (20km) above the Earth, where winds are relatively light, and would be powered by solar-driven electric motors. The craft would store enough energy during the day to keep them aloft at night. In fact, they might never have to land.

Sensors on board such aircraft would be able to survey huge tracts of ocean, taking photographs at far higher resolution than equipment on satellites. Unlike satellites, they would also be able to circle areas of interest, passing a continual stream of information to ground stations and directing hunter-killer aircraft to the spot. Developed versions might even carry their own anti-submarine weaponry.

It is highly likely that, before too many years have passed, remotely piloted vehicles (RPVs) will be at the forefront of the air-combat arena. There is already a vast library of experience behind the development of such vehicles, which were first used to test weapons systems and to train gunners. Their next application was as reconnaissance systems; for example, Teledyne Ryan Firebee RPVs, launched by C-130 Hercules, were used in the Vietnam War to overfly heavily defended targets in the North, and drones were extensively employed by Israeli forces in operations in the Lebanon. Battlefield reconnaissance drones were also used in the Gulf War.

The Teledyne Ryan Model 147 (AQM-34) flew more than 3,400 operational sorties during the Vietnam War. This one has thirteen missions chalked up. Overall recovery rate exceeded 80 per cent.

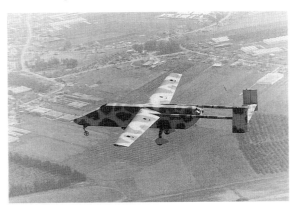

Israel Aircraft Industries' third-generation Searcher has been deployed since the early 1990s on surveillance over Israel's northern borders with Lebanon and Syria.

Reconnaissance drones, with their array of sensors, are already capable of operating at night, in bad weather and in all battlefield environments. Drones have been developed to destroy tanks and radar stations, and there is no technological reason why they should not ultimately perform all the tasks currently in the domain of manned combat aircraft. Because they carry no pilot, RPVs can be made very small and can be subjected to accelerations and forces that would be totally unacceptable to a human being. Moreover, their small size gives them a relatively small radar cross-section, which can be further reduced by incorporating 'stealth' materials in their structure.

Because there is no need for the costly systems that are necessary to defend a pilot, RPVs are relatively cheap. Assuming that in an air attack across an air-defence system there would be an attrition rate of 20 per cent, if 500 aircraft made three sorties, 244 would be lost. Assuming a unit cost of $40 million, the loss in monetary terms would be $9,760 million. It does not need agile arithmetic to work out that this amount of money would buy 976 advanced combat RPVs costing $10 million dollars each.

All of this still lies in the future, and in the meantime the agile combat aircraft will rule tomorrow's skies. Its weaponry continues to get smarter. Apart from smart missiles, scientists are developing smart bullets – barrel-launched adaptive munitions (BLAMS) – that will follow the twists and turns of a target after they have left the barrel of a gun. Each bullet has a nose that can swivel, changing the angle it makes with the airflow. At supersonic speed, very small angles generate huge amounts of lift, so angling the nose towards the target causes the bullet to veer in that direction. The nose of the 'smart' bullet is connected to the body by a number of rods or tendons,

The General Atomics RQ-1A Predator was used for surveillance overflights of Bosnia in the mid-1990s. It equips the USAF's first dedicated UAV unit, the 11th Reconnaissance Squadron, and carries a combined electro-optical infrared sensor and a synthetic-aperture radar for near real-time intelligence imagery.

which change length when a voltage is applied to them. Increasing the length of a rod on one side of the bullet, while shortening its opposite number, changes the angle of the nose by up to a tenth of a degree in any direction.

Simple actuators of this kind are ideal for bullets because they can withstand the huge forces generated during firing, being able to survive accelerations of more than 17,000g. They are also able to expand and contract hundreds of times a second, an important factor because a spinning bullet travels at several times the speed of sound and any control mechanism must be able to act quickly to compensate. It has been demonstrated in windtunnel tests that the actuators can produce good control of a round travelling at more than Mach 3.0.

Much of the work on BLAMS has concentrated on large-calibre (20mm or 30mm) ammunition, the accuracy of which drops off significantly with distance because of the effect of the wind on the round and the fact that it follows a parabolic trajectory. The only way a hit can be guaranteed is to use a multi-barrel gun with a high rate of fire, literally filling the sky with fire. On the other hand, BLAMS generate lift and so overcome the combined effects of wind and gravity, giving them at least twice the range of conventional rounds.

To guide the smart bullets to their target, the latter would be 'painted' with a laser beam and the bullets equipped with a sensor, stressed to withstand the massive acceleration involved and the size of a microchip, that would home in on the objective, just like a smart bomb. BLAMS rounds would not be cheap, but they would be cost-effective in that only a few, instead of hundreds, would be expended before a target was destroyed.

Munitions such as these will be vital to future air combat. It was once suggested that, by the middle of the next century, the entire gross national product of a country like the USA would not be sufficient to develop a new combat aircraft, but that was before computer technology absorbed much of the strain, and the cost, of R&D. Through computer simulation, the world's major defence research agencies are currently studying the designs of agile aircraft for the year 2050, a generation beyond the F-22, Eurofighter and Rafale. Such aircraft will be able to manoeuvre closely around one another in situations where missiles will be of little use, and the gun will be all-important. The pilot who has the ability to outmanoeuvre the other in close-in combat, and the means of delivering a killing blow, will win. The pilots who fought over Flanders in 1917 knew that, too.

12
Postwar Naval Aviation
Norman Friedman

For the Western navies, naval aviation at the end of the Second World War was a mixture of triumph and disaster. The triumph was the proof that aircraft carriers could not only destroy enemy fleets, but that they could also deal with enemy land-based air forces on equal terms. At the war's end both the US Navy (USN) and the Royal Navy (RN) possessed carrier forces far more powerful than those they had had at its outset. In both navies, moreover, it was generally accepted that carriers should form the core of the future fleet.

Yet it was by no means clear that the carriers would survive for long. The war ended with the dropping of the two atomic bombs on Japan. In 1945 the only aircraft capable of delivering these very heavy weapons were the land-based Boeing B-29s operated by the US Army Air Force, which in 1947 became the US Air Force (USAF). From a technical point of view, it was by no means clear that existing carriers could be modified to operate aircraft capable of lifting the requisite weights. From a political point of view, the nascent USAF hoped to justify itself as the sole means of nuclear attack. In Britain, the RAF clearly had similar ideas. By the late 1940s, however, it was clear that atomic bombs were not powerful enough to destroy an enemy country completely. But with the advent of H-bombs in the early 1950s the situation seemed quite different.

The navies and the air forces had diametrically opposed views of the nature of modern war against a land power, the Soviet Union. It was widely agreed during the 1940s that the Western powers could not match the sheer size of the Soviet army. As the West began to rearm from 1948 onwards, the question was always how to deal with a possible Soviet thrust to the West. Also, the struggle with the Soviets encompassed political and economic dimensions. Thus the US budget had to support not only a military build-up, but also the Marshall Plan for the recovery of the Western European economies, military aid to the countries of the new NATO alliance, and other programmes.

The problem was that each of the nation's three Services badly needed new weapons reflecting the lessons and the developments of the war. The US Army would have liked to assemble a force powerful enough to stop the Soviets, but by 1948 it had to admit that this was impossible, given existing fiscal limits. The badly exhausted Western Europeans could not do much better. The Army's dilemma was that, once NATO was formed in April 1949, the new European Allies would not cheerfully accept any sort of surrender in the face of a Soviet advance. Yet it was by no means clear how a weak Allied army could stand and fight.

The USAF argued that a quick series of nuclear attacks could knock out the Soviets. From its point of view, the most important role of naval and ground forces would be to maintain the bases from which its heavy bombers would fly. Initially it hoped to attack from both the UK and the Middle East, but under budgetary pressure it retreated towards the UK alone.

The USN argued for a radically different strategy. It doubted that atomic bombs alone could bring down the Soviet Union, and pressed instead for a flanking strategy, in which the Navy's mobility would make it possible to attack the lines of communication of the advancing Soviet army. Carriers, particularly in the Mediterranean, were the key to this idea. Not only could they hit the Soviet supply lines, they could also support amphibious landings in the Soviets' rear.

In 1949 and 1950 the US defence budget was far too limited to pay for both an atomic offensive and powerful carrier forces. The Navy's bid for postwar nuclear participation was a new and very large carrier, USS *United States*. In 1948 the USN hoped to build four such ships and to modernise many existing *Midway*- and *Essex*-class carriers to operate its new jet fighters. It would eventually form four four-ship carrier task forces, each built around a *United States*-class vessel. The ship was ordered after the USN secured agreement, at the 1948 Key West Conference, that it could share nuclear responsibility with the new USAF. As it turned out, the USAF reneged on this agreement. It saw in the 1948–9 budget squeeze an opportunity to kill off its naval rival. In April 1949, with the budget in crisis, the new Secretary of Defense, Louis Johnson, cancelled the big carrier.

The USN was outraged, not least because it believed that the carrier (and its postwar future) had already been approved, and that the USAF had acted treacherously in inciting Johnson, its friend. The ongoing strategic debate within the government became public, in the 'revolt of the Admirals'. Johnson himself was charged with corruption: he had, it was said, favoured the USAF because he had a personal interest in its Convair B-36 superbomber, which the Navy alleged was being bought with money originally earmarked for the supercarrier. In fact the money freed by cancellation went into the modernisation of existing *Essex*-class carriers, and the Navy was permitted to continue work on carrier-based nuclear bombers. However, as the budget continued to contract, further carriers were laid up.

The Truman administration was painfully aware that its strategy was risky. As long as the USA had a nuclear monopoly it could hope that its relatively inexpensive bomber force could balance the growing Soviet army. Once Stalin had the bomb, the US bombers clearly no longer sufficed. Several within the US government warned that the military budget would have to grow enormously. The government hesitated, fearing fiscal disaster.

In June 1950 the North Koreans demonstrated that the nay-sayers had been right. With Stalin's approval they invaded South Korea, and within a few weeks most of the airstrips in the South had been overrun. USAF aircraft based in Japan provided some support, but their bases were far from the battle. Fortunately a carrier, USS *Kearsage*, was in the Western Pacific when the North Koreans attacked. Her aircraft proved invaluable. So did aircraft from a British light fleet carrier in the Far East. The outbreak of war in Korea proved that the Soviets could no longer be restrained. The US military budget was quadrupled. Now there was enough money to pay for new carriers and a much larger active carrier force. By the end of 1952 the USN was operating twelve attack carriers and building a new ship, USS *Forrestal*, nearly as large as the cancelled *United States*.

When Dwight D Eisenhower became president in 1953 he, like Truman before Korea, badly wanted to restrain US spending. Unlike Truman he had substantial forces, the fruits of the Korean War build-up. He reasoned that the Soviets would be deterred from any major war, since they could win neither at the nuclear nor the non-nuclear level. He proclaimed a new policy, the 'New Look', in which the USA would rely on mobile forces armed with tactical nuclear weapons to deal with local crises, depending on 'massive retaliation' to preclude major Soviet or Chinese attacks. The carrier-based Navy was the natural mobile force; until 1958 Eisenhower bought a big carrier each year.

From 1961 onwards, US policy favoured an ability to fight limited wars, and the carrier's future seemed assured. The RN's situation was not as happy. Several times during the postwar period the RAF tried to eliminate British naval aviation, on the grounds that air power should be 'unified'. As it was, the RAF retained control of British land-based maritime patrol aircraft. These aircraft were affected, as were their USN counterparts, by the general shrinkage of base rights at the end of the Cold War. The RN has a small carrier force; ships are built in batches, run for a few decades, and then must be replaced on what amounts to a batch-by-batch basis. Replacement is always seen as a major capital investment. In fact, many aircraft programmes are much more expensive than entire carrier purchases, but governments tend to concentrate on unit prices for aircraft, on the theory that the programme can always be stopped before it gets out of hand.

This study of HMS Ark Royal *in the 1970s, following interim modification during 1967–70, shows the angled deck to advantage. Six Hawker Siddeley Buccaneer S.2s of 809 Squadron, Fleet Air Arm, are ranged forward, and six McDonnell Douglas Phantom FG.1s of 892 Squadron are lined up aft.*

The British jet carriers were completed (from hulls laid down in wartime) between 1952 and 1959; they were due for replacement in 1972–9. The programme for replacement was up for approval in 1965. Its sheer cost provoked a defence-funding crisis, and it died. The last British large-deck carrier, HMS *Ark Royal*, was retired in 1974, more or less as expected. By then there was interest in a new generation of small carriers, which were completed in the early 1980s. They are due for replacement by about 2010, which is why there was interest, in 1998, in what (if anything) is to replace them.

The USN escaped this sort of trouble because its carriers were built in a rolling programme. There was never a time, after 1949, when a US administration was faced with a choice between building a whole class of replacements and not having any useful carriers at all. That was partly because, after the Korean War, the Navy was always allocated twelve to sixteen active full-deck attack carriers (plus amphibious carriers), so their lives always overlapped.

Recent experience shows that carriers are valuable even when bases are in place, because they are not always available. That was dramatically demonstrated in 1990. After the Iraqi army seized Kuwait, the USA offered the Saudis help in the form of US forces. For a variety of reasons the

Saudis feared that the presence of US (i.e. non-Muslim) troops in their kingdom might prove destabilising. However, US carriers were sent in, in effect protecting Saudi Arabia despite that hesitation. With the carriers *en route* the Saudis could reasonably say that they had little choice in the matter, and they could welcome US land-based aircraft much more comfortably. Moreover, the carriers had on board not only aircraft but also weapons, spares and fuel: they were self-contained. Had the Iraqis attacked in the autumn of 1990, they would have mounted a defence. True, by that time there were numerous US and British aircraft on the scene, but they could not have flown more than a few sorties because their mass of weapons, spares and even jet fuel were not yet in place. When the US and British governments considered attacking Iraq in the spring of 1998 the Saudis were even more reluctant. Carriers still provided bases from which those aircraft could fly; and because they were sovereign territory they could fly at the behest of the US and British governments.

In 1945 it was not clear that carriers could operate the new jet aircraft. Unless they could be modified to do so they would be unable to face land-based air forces. Compared with piston-engined aircraft, jets accelerated much more slowly at take-off because their engines produced much less power at very low speeds (the opposite was true at high speeds). At the least, it might take the full length of a flight-deck to launch a single aeroplane. That would preclude the usual practice of assembling an entire strike before take-off.

Jets consumed far more fuel per flight hour and had far less endurance. Fuel consumption was a major issue because aviation gasoline was quite dangerous; it had to be stowed in special tanks, and hull capacity limited the size of such tanks. If jets needed similarly protected fuel, a carrier would be unable to operate its aircraft for very long. Jet power posed a particular problem for fighters. In 1945 there were two alternative approaches to fleet air defence. In one, fighters orbited on Combat Air Patrol (CAP) stations. As enemy aircraft approached they were assigned to targets by fighter controllers. CAP operation required considerable endurance. The alternative was deck-launched interception (DLI). Given sufficiently high performance, a fighter could be launched on warning, and could still reach attackers well clear of a carrier.

The first jet engines produced relatively little thrust, so airframes had to be very small to achieve high performance. As a consequence, aircraft such as the US McDonnell FH-1 Phantom had very limited endurance. To combine jet performance with useful endurance the USN bought a series of abortive hybrid fighters (piston/jet), epitomised by the Ryan FR-1 Fireball. By about 1945 jet-engine performance had improved to the point where an aeroplane could combine higher performance with greater fuel capacity for longer range. The USN bought two alternative subsonic jet fighters in numbers, the single-engine Grumman F9F Panther and the twin-engine McDonnell F2H Banshee. The Banshee was favoured, partly because it could increase its endurance further by shutting down one engine while on CAP. On the other hand, the Panther was simpler and much cheaper. The British equivalents to these aircraft were the Supermarine Attacker and the Hawker Sea Hawk.

The Supermarine Attacker, the first jet fighter to be standardised in first-line FAA squadrons, mated the wing of the piston-engined Spiteful to a new fuselage housing a Rolls-Royce Nene engine. Here, an Attacker F.1 of 803 Squadron takes a wire while landing on HMS Eagle *in the early 1950s. Note the batsman in the background.*

239

A total of ninety-five McDonnell F3H-2M Demons were supplied to the USN. In addition to its four 20mm cannon, this variant of the manufacturer's first swept-wing naval fighter was armed with four AIM-7C Sparrow III missiles, as seen here on aircraft 51-37037.

Deck crew huddle together between a pair of Supermarine Scimitar F.1s of 803 Squadron seconds before the aircraft are launched from the steam catapults of HMS Victorious *in the late 1950s. The Scimitar enjoyed the double distinction of being the FAA's first swept-wing single-seat fighter and the first capable of supersonic flight, albeit in a shallow dive.*

240

By about 1946 the existing straight-winged configuration had given about as much speed as it was likely to offer. The next step, then, was to change to a swept-wing arrangement which reduced transonic drag enough to make somewhat more-powerful engines worthwhile. The USN tried to exploit the additional power to combine useful endurance and high speed in a swept-wing fighter powered by a new-generation engine. That produced the McDonnell F3H Demon, which turned out to be underpowered. This aeroplane's failure led to a pair of interim solutions, a swept-wing version of the Panther (the Grumman F9F Cougar) and an adapted version of the USAF's F-86, the North American FJ-2/3 Fury. The British equivalents to these aircraft were the Supermarine Scimitar and the de Havilland D.H.110 Sea Vixen, both twin-engine fighters. The Scimitar became the first British naval nuclear strike aircraft, while the Sea Vixen became a two-seat all-weather interceptor.

To get really sparkling performance the new engines had to be allied to lightweight short-range airframes. The US versions were the radical tailless Chance-Vought F7U Cutlass and Douglas F4D Skyray, the latter being by far the more successful. The final development in this series was the supersonic Grumman F11F Tiger, one of the first applications of the 'area rule', with its 'Coke bottle' fuselage. None of these aircraft had the range to be an effective fleet fighter, since none could operate for long on a CAP station.

Then engine power improved again. Vought produced a long-endurance supersonic fighter, the F8U Crusader (later F-8). It used variable wing incidence to limit landing speed and CAP tactics were once again very practical. The Crusader in turn was superseded by a larger supersonic fighter, the massive McDonnell F4H Phantom (redesignated F-4 in 1962).

All of these aircraft required large-deck carriers with high-powered catapults. This posed a particular problem to the US Marine Corps (USMC), which had large numbers of fighters operating from carriers and also had exclusive use of several escort carriers for aircraft providing vital amphibious support. The relatively short decks of the escort carriers were perfectly adequate for the Marines' piston-engined Corsairs, but it was another story altogether when it came to jets.

The RN faced much the same problem. In 1945 it operated six fleet carriers and it was rapidly completing a series of light fleet carriers. Both types of ships had short flight-decks and hydraulic catapults and could not operate jets. In 1949 the RN adopted an ambitious programme under which all six fleet carriers would have been modernised, with steam catapults and side lifts. The process

Grumman's F11F Tiger, represented here by an experimental F11F-1F powered by a General Electric J-79-GE-3A which gave the type Mach 2 performance, was one of the first production aircraft to feature an area-ruled fuselage, waisted in the region of the wing to reduce wave drag.

With flames shooting from the afterburners of its two Westinghouse J46-WE-8A turbojets and its leading-edge slats extended, a Chance Vought F7U-3 Cutlass accelerates down the deck of the USS Hancock during steam-catapult tests in the mid-1950s. The Cutlass was one of the most unconventional designs to go into production.

Although the supersonic Convair YF2Y-1 Sea Dart was acclaimed as the fastest water-based aircraft in the world, a fatal accident marred the test programme and poor stability at take-off dashed any hopes of production. The experimental fighter took off from and alighted on water on retractable twin hydroskis.

The short flight-decks of the RN's immediate postwar carriers posed no problems for piston-engined aircraft such as this Hawker Sea Fury FB.11 of 801 Squadron, seen landing on HMS Glory *in the early 1950s, but jets needed significantly longer decks for their landing runs.*

The steam catapult, a British invention, provided the steady and sustained acceleration required to launch jet and turbo-prop aircraft from carriers. Here, a McDonnell Douglas Phantom FG.1 of 892 Squadron, FAA, makes its departure from HMS Ark Royal.

was very expensive, and only HMS *Victorious* was rebuilt. Its modernisation took seven years, partly because it had to be altered to take account of rapidly changing technology.

The RN did not consider its light fleet carriers worth modernising. For a time it appeared that the RN would use some of these ships for antisubmarine warfare, but that plan was dropped during the 1957 Defence Review. The RN was left with the larger carriers laid down during the Second World War, but not completed – and hence suitable for completion in drastically modified form. The last of these ships, HMS *Hermes*, was not retired until the 1980s. Several light fleet carriers were sold to friendly navies, some of whom discovered that the ships really could operate lightweight jets, most notably the US Douglas A-4 Skyhawk. In 1998 the sole survivor of this series in service was the Brazilian *Minas Gerais*, which is more than half a century old.

Until the advent of the Harrier, a carrier had to provide a catapult powerful enough to launch jets in minimum-wind conditions plus arrester gear with sufficient pull-out to recover the same aeroplanes. The key issues were aircraft weight and stalling speed, since the catapult had to impart enough energy to accelerate an aeroplane of a given weight beyond its stalling speed (for take-off), while the arresting gear had to absorb a similar amount of energy when the aeroplane landed. Taken together, the length of the catapult and the arrester gear pull-out determine a minimum flight-deck length.

It took about a decade to solve the problems of operating jets from carriers. A British engineer, Mitchell, had been working for some years on a direct-acting catapult to replace the old hydraulic type. In 1948 he completed work on a steam version, in which the aeroplane was connected to a piston running in a slotted cylinder. The key development was a sort of zipper which closed the slot behind the piston sufficiently to contain most of the steam. In the early 1950s the USN thankfully adopted Mitchell's invention, both in new and rebuilt carriers.

Recovering jet aircraft was more difficult. Jets complicated the situation in three ways. First, with limited endurance they had to be recovered much more quickly than their forebears; otherwise they would not have very much time in the air. Second, since they had no propellers, barrier wires would always ride up their noses and would usually kill their pilots. Third, since landing speeds were much higher, the rate of landing errors went up sharply. The 'batsman', or Landing Signal Officer (LSO), system imposed a time lag. First, the LSO himself had to judge what he was seeing; then he had to signal the pilot, who had to interpret the signal and react.

On the other hand, unlike a propeller-driven aeroplane, a jet could, in theory, land on its belly. The British found that such an aeroplane could land on a flexible flight-deck. The idea did not last because an undercarriageless naval aeroplane could not have operated from a land base. However, it left an important legacy. After it landed, the undercarriageless aeroplane had to be moved off the flexible deck by crane before it could be placed on a catapult. If the catapults were immediately forward of the flexible deck, the area between them and the deck was likely to become congested. The solution was to angle the flexible deck away from the catapults, to create an area in which the aircraft could be recovered. Although the flexible deck was abandoned, the angled deck helped solve the jet landing problem, as the landing area was pointed away from the parking area. If

A graphic illustration of the advantage of the angled deck, another British innovation. On 21 October 1961 Lt (jg) Kryway landed his ChanceVought F8U-1 Crusader hard on the USS Franklin D Roosevelt. *The aircraft lost its right main wheel and then caught fire and lost the arrester wire, going off the angled deck into the sea. Kryway ejected in his Martin-Baker F5 seat and escaped with minor injuries.Without the angled deck the stricken Crusader might have piled into parked aircraft and personnel.*

a pilot overshot he could simply run out over the front end of the landing area, apply maximum power, and go round again. When *Ark Royal* was being completed in the early 1950s the idea was incorporated, and quite soon was taken up by the USN.

The solution to the 'batsman' problem, again developed by the RN, was a mirror sight. The pilot would look into a mirror set alongside the landing area. What he saw would tell him whether he was on the appropriate glidepath or not. Because the time lag associated with the LSO was eliminated, the pilot could safely land at much higher speed.

As for the fuel issue, fortunately jet fuel did not form explosive vapours similar to those of gasoline. It could, therefore, be stowed in tanks without the elaborate protective arrangements needed for gasoline.

Two other wartime developments affected postwar naval aviation. One was German work on stand-off missiles, such as the Henschel Hs 293, and on guided bombs like the Fx-1400. The Soviets captured German missile technology and, in many cases, technologists. Surely they would deploy similar weapons. Even if they

did not develop missiles, once they had atomic bombs they could make stand-off attacks, flipping such weapons into naval formations from a distance. The Germans had used their guided bombs successfully both in the Bay of Biscay and in the Mediterranean, particularly at Salerno and Anzio.

Until the advent of Aegis in the 1980s, the US fleet lacked any very reliable anti-aircraft missile capable of dealing with heavy (saturation) raids by regiments of Soviet bombers. The bombers, moreover, could launch at increasingly greater ranges, hundreds of miles from their targets. By the 1970s, then, the fighters were often expected to concentrate not on the bombers (their natural targets) but on the incoming missiles, which were much more difficult targets.

The Soviets combined bombers and anti-ship missiles in another way as well. Many of their submarines and surface ships were armed with a big transonic missile which NATO called *Shaddock* (SS-N-3). The launch platforms could not detect their targets, which were well beyond their horizons. To solve this problem, some Tu-95 *Bear* bombers were fitted with big surface-search radars and datalinks down to the launch platforms, a system the Soviets called *Uspekh*. The missile sent its own radar picture down to the platform that fired it, and the two were matched. On this basis the missile could be locked on to a target far from its launcher. Conversely, if the *Bear* were shot down in time the missile attack could be frustrated.

It was essential to keep enemy bombers out of missile-launching range. During the Second World War it was standard practice to maintain a CAP orbiting at a range great enough to deal with bombers before they could attack. The advent of stand-off missiles increased the minimum range at which a CAP had to be maintained. With jets, the situation was complicated in that fighters had to have enough endurance to fly back and forth to the CAP range and to orbit for about ninety minutes with enough reserve fuel to fight. Air-to-air refuelling helped solve the problem. In any case, only a few fighters could be maintained on CAP stations.

Naturally the Soviets were well aware of the threat presented by US naval fighters and by radars on the ships. A typical anti-ship regiment of the 1980s consisted of two strike squadrons (nine to twelve aircraft each) and a support squadron (two to four *Badger*-H (Tu-16PP) chaff layers, one of two *Badger*-J (Tu-16 *Buket*) escort jammers, three to six *Badger* tankers). The chaff aircraft laid laid walls of chaff to hide approaching aircraft from search radars. The problem for the defence was expected to worsen when the Soviets replaced their subsonic *Badgers* with supersonic Tu-22Ms. As it happened, they found it difficult to develop an escort jammer version of the *Backfire*, so for years their attack formations could not fly supersonically; they had to slow down so that the *Badger* escorts could keep up. Only in 1992 did a jammer version of *Backfire* appear (Tu-22MP), and as of 1996 it had not yet entered service.

From the first, the bombers had radars, so they could attack at night and in bad weather. In the postwar world it was unlikely that very large numbers of carriers would ever operate together, so each carrier needed its own night/bad-weather capability. Nightfighters needed a combination of long endurance and reasonably good performance, in order to deal with the new jet bombers. During the war the US experience had been that, properly coached by a carrier's radar, a pilot could handle an interception without needing a separate radar operator. Thus early postwar USN all-weather fighters could be relatively compact versions of the single-seat Banshee and Demon. The exception, the massive Douglas F3D Skyknight, proved unsuited to carriers.

Jet bombers raised a further issue. To be effective, a fighter needed a margin of speed over the bomber. Postwar, bombers were about as fast as the fighters intended to intercept them. A carrier's radar could still coach a fighter into a collision-path attack from ahead, but that gave the fighter very little time to destroy the bomber. Without a considerable speed margin, pursuit attacks from behind were pointless. This problem led to a series of attempts to arm fighters with more lethal weapons, such as rockets. By the mid-1950s it was clear that only guided missiles could solve the problem. They offered an interesting possibility. If much of the performance of the overall weapons system had to go into the missile in any case, perhaps it would be better to abandon any attempt to give the fighter high performance. In that case, the fighter could achieve much longer endurance, loitering for hours in a CAP station far from the carrier.

Soviet bombers flew in regiments including eighteen to twenty-four missile carriers. A regimental attack might well be opposed by no more than two or four fighters on CAP duty. That posed a real problem: how could the fighters deal with so many targets? Sparrow, the main fleet air-defence weapon from about 1960, homed semi-actively. The fighter had to keep its radar trained on the target until the missile exploded; it could then switch to the next target. It seemed unlikely that any fighter would have time to deal with, say, four targets in sequence as the bombers passed the CAP area. By the late 1950s the USN badly wanted a much more capable missile system which could engage several bombers simultaneously. It became the current Phoenix. An F-14 equipped with Phoenix and the AWG-9 fire-control system can track an entire bomber regiment (twenty-four targets), firing its six missiles at six targets simultaneously, at ranges up to about 100 miles (160km). Thus, at least in theory, four F-14s on CAP stations can shoot down a bomber regiment.

To penetrate to their targets, carrier strike aircraft often need fighter support. That role cannot be filled by a stand-off aeroplane firing missiles from a great distance. Something with high performance is needed, or else the strike aircraft themselves need some sort of fighter performance. The problem is that the carrier's aircraft capacity is quite limited. United States policy was always to provide fighters with some bomb-carrying capacity, but clearly some types were optimised mainly for one role or the other.

There was also an important electronic issue. Fighter and bomber radars use quite different waveforms, because they look at very different targets. They also have very different fire-control requirements, because their weapons are very different. In an earlier analogue era, the fire-control equipment itself was very different, because it embodied the ballistics of the weapons. The effect of the advent of programmable computers is to move specialisation from hardware to software; the same computer can be programmed to fire anything at all. In the 1970s it became possible to do more: to use software to control the waveform a radar produced. Then the radar, too, could be made truly multi-purpose. Given this sort of electronics, an aeroplane could be built that was capable of optimum air-to-air *and* air-to-surface combat. That was particularly important for carriers, with their limited aircraft capacity.

The first such aeroplane was the McDonnell Douglas F/A-18 Hornet, now the standard USN fighter. Its dual capability was dramatically demonstrated during the Gulf War, when two F/A-18s assigned to bomb an Iraqi target were jumped by MiGs. In the past, fighter-bombers caught in such a situation would probably have jettisoned their bombs and run, but in this case the pilots flipped the switches to air-to-air mode and shot down the MiGs. They did not have to run, and their missiles offered enough performance that they did not have to get rid of their bombs. Then they proceeded to attack their targets as planned.

Another major Second World War development was the fast U-boat, initially the battery-powered Type XXI. With its snorkel and large battery a Type XXI could spend all its time submerged, showing only the very small radar target of its snorkel – and that only from time to time. Submerged, it was faster than most surface escorts – and also than the existing antisubmarine homing torpedo, Fido (Mk 24). However, even Type XXI was not nearly as fast as a modern fast carrier.

Given the carrier's speed advantage, any submarine, even a Type XXI, had to lie in wait roughly ahead of its target. During the Second World War it was generally enough to fly-off aircraft which could spot a submarine working into position on the surface. Now the same submarine might be approaching submerged. A carrier's security in attacking a land target would lie far more in having the largest possible area from which to launch a strike. Again, air-to-air refuelling could help.

On the other hand, convoys were not fast enough to evade these new submarines. They needed some way of sanitising the area through which they were expected to pass. Surface escorts were not likely to be enough. Instead, the convoy needed aircraft capable of seeding the area with sonobuoys and then attacking any submarines they detected. Specialised antisubmarine aircraft were developed, but initially equipment was so heavy that aircraft had to work in teams, one hunting and the other attacking. For example, the USN adapted a torpedo bomber designed during the war, the Grumman TB3F, as the Guardian (AF). The hunter version needed a radar which could distinguish a small snorkel amid the clutter of the sea. It turned out that the new airborne early warning radar, APS-20, could be adapted for this purpose. The same radar was placed aboard contemporary land-based antisubmarine aircraft, such as Lockheed Neptunes.

A snorkel is a very small radar target. An alternative sensor developed after the war was the 'sniffer' (Autolycus in British parlance), which automatically analysed chemicals it picked up in the air. It could recognise a snorkel exhaust, and in theory the exhaust left a trail the hunting aircraft could follow up to the snorkelling submarine. Sniffers were discarded largely because, as world shipping turned from steam to diesel, many merchant ships produced snorkel-like residues. The sniffer is interesting historically as one of the first attempts to develop a non-acoustic sensor for ASW aircraft, something they could use continuously instead of seeding it into the water or landing to dip it into the water. The only such sensor to have been particularly successful is magnetic anomaly detection (MAD), which senses the effect of the metallic submarine on the Earth's magnetic field.

A Dassault-Breguet 1150 Atlantic land-based maritime patrol and ASW aircraft of France's Aéronavale displays the tail-boom housing its magnetic anomaly detection (MAD) sensor.

About 1950 a solution suddenly became available. The US Woods Hole Oceanographic Institution pointed out that low-frequency sounds travelled extraordinary distances through the sea, and that submarines emitted characteristic low-frequency signatures. Bell Laboratories, which was concerned mainly with analysing human voices, discovered that the signatures contained discrete frequencies ('lines') which could be recognised against the noise of the sea. This technique was promptly named LOFAR (usually translated as low-frequency analysis and ranging, a largely meaningless cover name). Initially it was applied to large acoustic arrays planted in deep water (the SOSUS, or Sound Surveillance, system). Like wartime code-breaking, SOSUS could cue an antisubmarine aeroplane to a likely submarine location. It entered service in the late 1950s, and soon US arrays could 'see' out to the mid-Atlantic ridge. In the 1960s NATO added arrays on the other side of the Atlantic. Long-range underwater acoustic sensors were also emplaced in the Pacific and in the Mediterranean. Aircraft could exploit their outputs.

The first major post-1945 antisubmarine aeroplane, the P-2 Neptune, lacked the range for effective mid-ocean operation. To close the mid-ocean gap, therefore, the USN operated specialist antisubmarine carriers (CVS). It says much about the rate of aircraft development that they were conversions of Second World War *Essex*-class fleet carriers. With the advent of the Lockheed P-3 Orion in the 1960s, shore-based aircraft could fully cover the areas in which SOSUS could detect submarines; the CVS no longer seemed vital. By that time, however, the Soviets were deploying nuclear submarines. These craft were fast enough to intercept battle groups; speed no longer bought safety. Carrier groups had, therefore, to incorporate antisubmarine aircraft of their own. For example, in the 1950s the ideal carrier formation was three ships. In the late 1960s the ideal shifted to three attack carriers and an accompanying antisubmarine carrier with two kinds of antisubmarine aircraft: aeroplanes (S-2s) for distant coverage – e.g. to sanitise an area through which the group was to go – and helicopters for close-in defence. Dipping their sonars, the helicopters were expected to detect enemy submarines closing in for torpedo shots.

In the mid-1950s the British developed a somewhat less-ambitious alternative to SOSUS, Corsair, which never entered service. It had an interesting political twist. In the early 1950s the RAF had a monopoly over the emerging British nuclear deterrent. The RN's argument to retain its carrier force was based on the need to maintain sea communications in the face of a large Soviet submarine force. Given Corsair, land-based aircraft (which the RAF controlled) could, in theory, deal with the Soviet submarines. As it happened this challenge failed, partly due to a growing comprehension that Britain had to deal with challenges other than central war.

In the late 1950s LOFAR technology was applied to the sonobuoys dropped by antisubmarine aircraft, under the codename Jezebel. Initially it seemed that it would be effective only in detecting snorkelling submarines. Ironically, it turned out that Jezebel/LOFAR was much more effective against nuclear submarines. A snorkeller ran its diesel, its source of noise, only occasionally, whereas a nuclear submarine ran its own sources of noise, its turbo-generators and pumps, continuously, because otherwise its reactor would melt down. Silencing was possible, but it was extremely expensive, and it did not become a major problem for Western navies until the late 1970s.

The Soviets eventually discovered LOFAR for themselves, and in the 1970s they began to field their own version of Jezebel aboard aircraft such as '*Bear*-F' (Tu-142M). Conversely, they began to silence their submarines to frustrate Western LOFAR systems.

The postwar period also saw the rise of a very different kind of naval air power, associated with amphibious operations. The US Services' interpretation of Eisenhower's strategy was that they might well have to fight a tactical nuclear war. That had particular implications for the USMC. During the Second World War it had assembled enormous amphibious forces in the Pacific. Now it seemed that any such assemblage would make an ideal atomic target. The Marines' solution was to move troops ashore by helicopter. Helicopters were fast enough to allow the ships to be positioned well away from each other and from the beach. Indeed, the Marines could be landed behind the beachhead, a technique called 'vertical envelopment'.

Vertical envelopment offered advantages quite aside from its nuclear ones. Troops defending a beach usually face towards the sea, whence the threat is likely to come. Helicopters can take them from the rear. At the least, the presence of helicopters ought to force troops to divide their attention between beach and rear, thus weakening their effort in either direction. Once coast-defence missiles came into service in the 1960s, vertical envelopment offered the possibility of keeping vulnerable amphibious ships out of their range. In addition, a combination of helicopters (and, more recently, Bell/Boeing V-22s) and LCACs could land troops and their supplies and vehicles from well beyond the horizon as seen from the beach. An amphibious force offshore could threaten a very wide swathe of beach, and a defender might be unable to concentrate to meet that threat (or, for that matter, to decide just where to plant minefields). Because the LCAC could cross beaches too shallow for conventional landing craft, it widened the range of possible attack sites.

As it happened, the first to use vertical envelopment were the British, at Suez in 1956, when a makeshift helicopter force was placed on board a light fleet carrier. The attack was very successful; the RN converted a series of ships into what it called 'commando carriers'. Aircraft car-

A Westland Wessex helicopter picks up supplies from the commando carrier HMS Bulwark *in 1969. A BAe Harrier shares the deck with assorted military vehicles and landing craft.*

riers were well suited to conversion because their hangar decks could easily be fitted to take troops and vehicles. The USN built its own amphibious carriers while converting several obsolescent Second World War fleet carriers.

Through the 1950s the minimum size of nuclear weapons shrank dramatically. The bombs dropped on Japan weighed about 8,500lb (3,860kg), and it was generally agreed that to be an atomic bomber an aeroplane had to be able to carry a nominal 10,000lb (4,540kg) bomb. In 1946 the USN began work on just such an aircraft, which emerged as the North American AJ Savage. It could barely fit on board the largest carriers, but it provided a minimal delivery capacity. Until the AJ was ready, the Navy modified a few (normally land-based) P2V Neptune patrol bombers so that they could be launched from carriers with rocket assistance. They could not have been recovered on board the ships, so plans called for them to return and ditch in the sea.

The RN did not expect to operate nuclear bombers of its own, but British interests extended well beyond the likely range of atomic bombers based in the British Isles. In 1945 the RAF had planned some attacks in

Southeast Asia using Mosquitoes launched by carriers. In 1949 there was serious, if brief, consideration given to adapting British carriers to launch atomic-armed Canberras (which, like the Neptunes, would have had to land ashore or ditch on their return).

In 1950 it suddenly became clear that truly lightweight bombs could be built without any sacrifice in explosive power. The US Mk 7 was designed to be carried by USAF and USN fighters. At this time the Navy's most effective bomber was the propeller-driven Douglas AD (later A-1) Skyraider. With its very long range it could threaten much of the southern Soviet Union from carriers in the Mediterranean. The problem was that, approaching at low altitude to avoid radar, it might not be able to escape the blast of its own bomb. The USN therefore developed an unguided missile, Boar, which the A-1 could fire at the target.

Meanwhile, work continued on the Savage and on a jet successor, the Douglas A3D (later A-3) Skywarrior. In the late 1940s it had seemed that really long range, about 1,500 miles (2,400km), would require a carrier aeroplane far too large to fit on board existing ships. As it happened, however, Ed Heinemann of Douglas was able to accommodate both the big bomb and enough fuel on the A3D to achieve the requisite performance in a package which could fit on board existing ships (with steam catapults). Armed with Skywarriors, US carriers in the Norwegian Sea, the Mediterranean, and the Western Pacific could reach virtually anywhere in the Soviet Union. They could not deliver anything like the firepower offered by the USAF, but the Soviets knew where USAF bases were located, and they could arrange air defences accordingly. The existence of the carrier bombers ruined that calculation, and forced the Soviets to spread out their defences.

The Skywarrior was comparable in performance with contemporary subsonic USAF bombers such as the Boeing B-47 and B-52. In the mid-1950s much higher performance became possible. In 1955 the USN bought North American's supersonic NAGPAW (North American General Purpose Attack Weapon), which became the A3J (later A-5) Vigilante. To slim down its airframe it used a radical linear bomb bay; the bomb was stowed forward of spare fuel tanks, and was fired out of the rear end of the fuselage. The Vigilante also had inertial navigation (to avoid giving itself away by frequent use of radar), using perhaps the first US airborne digital computer. Unfortunately it entered service just as Polaris missiles provided a far more effective seabased nuclear force. Hence there was little point in solving its main teething problem, the aerodynamic quirk which caused the bomb to trail behind the aeroplane instead of separating as it should have. The supersonic Vigilante spent its time in service as the very effective RA-5 reconnaissance aeroplane.

The nuclear bombers exemplified a classic problem of carrier aviation. The ship can accommodate only so many aircraft, which must be combined into a tactically effective air wing or air group. Special-purpose aircraft demand their own maintenance crew and equipment – and spares. From 1945 the USN found itself operating an increasing variety of aircraft from its carriers. Periodically it tried to reduce that variety, in hopes of simplifying maintenance. Moreover, a carrier might be called upon to conduct a variety of missions. The more flexible the aircraft, the more flexible the air group.

By 1945 the USN was buying a new class of multipurpose attack aircraft, initially designated BTs (B for combined dive bomber and T for torpedo bomber), but soon redesignated attack bombers (A). The most successful was the Douglas AD Skyraider (later A-1).

At the same time, some carrier-based fighters were used mainly as fighter-bombers. In effect the fighter-bombers became light attack aircraft, the earlier attack aircraft (and the new ones) becoming medium attack aircraft. The new nuclear bombers, conceived from 1946, became heavy attackers.

Thus US carrier air groups became far more complex than they had been in, say, 1942. In place of three categories of aeroplanes (fighters, torpedo and dive bombers) by 1946 four or even five were in prospect: fighters (which might divide into long-endurance all-weather and interceptor types) and heavy, medium, and light attackers. Yet overall carrier capacity did not grow. Indeed, since many of the new aircraft were substantially larger than their predecessors, total numbers which an existing ship could accommodate began to fall. There was, to be sure, some overlap in types. Thus the McDonnell F2H Banshee was used as both an all-weather fighter and as a light bomber (in its F2H-2B version), but the two roles were not shared by the same aeroplanes.

Moreover, as time passed aircraft became more, not less, specialised. By 1950 it was clear that atomic bombs would soon be available in packages that fighters could carry. The fighter-bomber was suddenly much more important, because it was a potential short-range nuclear strike bomber. The Banshee and then the North American FJ-4 Fury were adapted to this role. Meanwhile, a specialised light nuclear attack aeroplane, the Douglas A4D (later A-4) Skyhawk, was being designed and built. It superseded the fighter-bombers. Ironically, it was sometimes used as a lightweight subsonic fighter.

Thus, by the late 1950s a US carrier accommodated interceptors, long-endurance all-weather fighters, and heavy (Savage or Skywarrior), medium (Skyraider), and light (Skyhawk) attack aircraft. The heavy attackers were sometimes used to extend the operating range of lighter aircraft by tanking. In 1954 the Bureau of Aeronautics proposed simplification: the interceptor and light (day) attack roles could be merged. Contrary to the study's recommendations, the Bureau decided to merge the all-weather and nuclear-delivery roles. The outcome was the outstanding McDonnell F4H Phantom. Given the power of its twin engines, it could lift a combination of fuel (for endurance) on CAP and weapons; yet it also achieved high performance. The US interceptor category was abandoned.

As it turned out, light day-attack bombers were still worthwhile, though in a rather different sense than had been imagined in the 1950s. By the 1960s US strategists were more interested in limited non-nuclear war. To deliver large bomb loads the USN needed the simplest possible bomber, without the fighter systems required for an F-4. The solution was the subsonic Vought A-7 Corsair II, which remained in service from the late 1960s through to the Gulf War.

The story of the medium bomber was even more convoluted. The Skyraider began its life as a simple (and relatively high-performance) bomber. It soon became obvious that, far more than a jet, it could penetrate enemy air defences at low altitude. It could also lift a heavy bomb load yet loiter longer than a jet. By the mid-

1950s it was valued partly as a nuclear bomber. The big strategic nuclear bombers were no longer as attractive as they had been, particularly since the new missiles could do much the same job more effectively. However, in the late 1950s nuclear attack itself was still very important to US strategists.

A 1956 study of future naval requirements suggested a new tactical bomber with STOL capability, so that the Marines could use it from short Third World airstrips. It became the Grumman A-6 Intruder (originally A2F; the STOL feature was dropped). The design concept was to carry all ordnance on underwing pylons. That limited the aeroplane to the minimum required to accommodate a sophisticated strike radar and the associated navigation and fire-control computer. Ironically, the aeroplane conceived as a nuclear bomber spent its career as an extremely effective all-weather non-nuclear attack aircraft. Intruders were used not only as strike aircraft, but also as tankers, extending the carrier's reach.

In another irony, in the 1980s the Intruder's ability to deliver nuclear attacks at very long range became a key feature of the US Maritime Strategy. The idea was to force the Soviet naval air arm to accept battle (and defeat) at the hands of F-14s, as the only naval weapon likely to destroy Soviet naval bombers equipped with stand-off missiles was the F-14. Unless the bombers were destroyed (preferably in the air, so that their crews were killed), they could probably wipe out much of the vital Allied shipping crossing the Atlantic in wartime. The threat of Intruder attacks against Soviet base area, particularly in the Arctic, from about 1,000 miles (1,600km) would, it was hoped, force the Soviets to make all-out attacks on the carriers from which these aircraft would be launched. The attacks would be made mainly by bombers, and the carriers' F-14s would be well placed to deal with them.

In Vietnam, carrier strike aircraft encountered very heavy radar-controlled air defences, and to operate effectively the aircraft needed escorts that could help jam the defenders' radars. The solution to this problem was a special version of the A-6, the EA-6B Prowler. In an extension of the Intruder concept, underwing pylons were used for jammer pods (and later for anti-radar missiles).

Kamikazes made a third category of aeroplane valuable: carrier-based airborne early warning aircraft. Initially they were airborne radars which could send their data directly to the carrier via a datalink. In effect, an AEW aeroplane was an additional radar for the ship, with a horizon extended well beyond what the ship could normally see. The first such aircraft were Grumman Avenger torpedo bombers, whose big APS-20 antennae were housed in belly radomes.

Ideally, the AEW aeroplane had to be something more. All the radar data the ship received was filtered and analysed in its Combat Information Center (CIC; Action Information Centre in British parlance). This information was handled manually. A manual CIC could handle only a limited number of targets at a time. Decentralisation was needed to deal with heavy attacks. That entailed placing a CIC, with its operators, on board the radar aeroplane. The initial solution was to use a Boeing B-17 bomber (redesignated PB-1W); attempts were also made to use the new land-based P2V Neptune patrol bomber. Eventually Lockheed Constellation airliners were adapted.

It took about a decade to solve the problem of building a sufficiently large carrier aeroplane to accommodate a CIC. The first in the USN was the Grumman E-1, a twin (piston)-engined aeroplane based on the contemporary S-2 carrier-based antisubmarine aircraft. By 1960 the USN was computerising its CICs; they could now handle more than 100 targets at a time. The corresponding computerised airborne CIC was the Grumman E-2 Hawkeye.

A Lockheed WV-3 of USN airborne early warning squadron VW-4, with prominent radomes above and below its fuselage, accompanied by a pair of McDonnell F2H-2P Banshees of light photographic squadron VFP-62 based at Jacksonville, Florida, en route to investigate hurricane conditions in the Caribbean in 1956.

Grumman's computerised airborne Combat Information Center, the E-2C Hawkeye, with its distinctive 24ft (7.3m)-diameter rotodome housing the stacked elements of its AN/APA-171 radar antennae, could automatically track 600 targets over land and water and direct friendly aircraft to intercept those identified as hostile.

These AEW aircraft also provided a picture of sea activity several hundred miles from a carrier. To a much greater extent than the USN, the postwar RN was concerned with anti-ship combat. For it, AEW was an essential complement to ship-based strike aircraft. For that matter, an AEW aeroplane can provide a strike group with timely warning of enemy air activity, and thus can be an valuable complement to the strike.

With smaller carriers, the RN could not afford anything like the variety of aircraft – or carriers – the USN had. In the 1950s it operated a mixture of fighters (mainly Sea Hawks and de Havilland Sea Venoms), turboprop strike aircraft (Westland Wyverns), early warning aircraft (US-supplied Avengers and then Skyraiders), and antisubmarine aircraft (adapted Firefly fighters, then specialised Fairey Gannets). There was never much hope of buying really large early warning aircraft, and the Gannets competed for scarce space with the fighters and attackers. Since it was clear that carrier size would always be limited, the RN became interested in moving some of the carrier functions to other kinds of ships. It became an enthusiastic operator of antisubmarine helicopters, which could fly from the 'County'-class missile destroyers introduced in the 1960s. It even went so far as to design a small carrier, which it called an Escort Cruiser, specifically to operate a carrier's complement of antisubmarine helicopters. Alternatively, the Escort Cruiser could carry troops and fly them off by helicopter, a tactic first tried at Suez in 1956.

As in the USN, aircraft development was lineal. During the 1960s the straight-wing day fighter-bombers gave way to swept-wing Scimitars; the Sea Venom night fighters gave way to Sea Vixens. The Wyvern was replaced by a very different kind of aeroplane, the all-weather Blackburn Buccaneer, designed to fly Intruder-style all-weather low-level strikes. To a much greater degree than the Intruder it was intended to attack enemy warships; the RN had to concede most land attacks to the RAF. A version of the Gannet took over the AEW role, and the antisubmarine Gannets were retired in favour of helicopters.

Also as in the USN, there was growing pressure to unify many of these types of aircraft. Moreover, by the mid-1960s the RN knew that it had to replace the last of its existing carriers. At the same time it was given responsibility for the national British nuclear deterrent, in the form of Polaris submarines. In 1963–5 the RN argued that carriers were needed for two reasons. First, without them Britain could not discharge her treaty obligations 'East of Suez', then being dramatised by the 'confrontation' with Indonesia over Malaysia. Second, as the Soviets deployed ballistic missiles air bases were likely to be less and less tenable, whereas a moving carrier might well escape attack.

These arguments would have doomed the RAF. The Polaris decision eliminated the rationale for Bomber Command, its mainstay after 1945 (the decision was made when the USA cancelled Skybolt, the missile

A Hawker Siddeley Buccaneer S.2 of 809 Squadron flying from HMS Hermes *in the late 1960s. As the aircraft was designed for the all-weather low-level strike role, its construction made extensive use of steel fittings and components machined from the solid to achieve the required fatigue strength.*

250

which would have been carried by the bombers). That left a tactical role in the East and in NATO. In the East, distances were such that land-based aircraft could not be effective; in NATO the Royal Navy opened the question of whether their airfields could possibly be secure. Little or nothing would have been left. The RAF counterattacked. The British government of the day was already nervous, given the very high cost of the required fleet of five replacement carriers. It needed rationales. The RAF provided them, including a notorious brief in which Australia was moved about 700 miles (1,120km) to bring possible operating areas within the range of aircraft based there. The replacement carrier was cancelled by the Labour government in 1966. The carrier force would be allowed to run down for the next few years as the existing ships wore out.

Reality soon set in. The Australian continent refused to move, so the RAF could not fulfil the 'East of Suez' commitment. It had to be abandoned. That left a variety of NATO commitments, including North Atlantic anti-submarine warfare and the support of Norway. The RN retained a commando carrier for the Norwegian role, and it also began to study the consequences of having no carrier. An early paper pointed out that the carrier was a vital surveillance platform and fleet guardian.

With the withdrawal of the British carriers, only the USA and France retained conventional aircraft carriers. The French had completed their first carrier in the 1920s, and the USN had encouraged the revival of French carrier aviation after 1945. Both the USA and Britain had provided small carriers, and then France had built two of her own in the 1950s. French naval aviation was extremely important during the Indo-China War (1946–54). Later, the French carriers were valued for their ability to project power (France retained important security relations with her ex-colonies in Africa) and also for their ability, in a major war, to make 'pre-strategic' attacks. France relied heavily on nuclear deterrence, and the theory was that warning shots (short of strategic attacks) might well end a war short of mutual devastation. To this end French Dassault Super Étendard strike aircraft were armed first with nuclear bombs and then with the ASMP supersonic cruise missile. The accompanying fighters were Crusaders bought from the USA. These carriers also operate Breguet Alizés, bought initially for antisubmarine warfare but now used for surface and low-altitude air search. The next-generation carrier, the nuclear-powered *Charles de Gaulle*, is eventually to operate a single type of tactical aircraft, the dual-purpose Dassault Rafale, alongside E-2C early warning aircraft.

A prototype Dassault Super Étendard single-seat attack aircraft displays its perforated underfuselage airbrakes as it lands on the French carrier Clemenceau *during carrier trials.*

251

A stern view of the Clemenceau *with a Dassault Rafale prototype on approach during trials. Parked on its deck are a Breguet Alizé low-altitude search aircraft and a Chance Vought Crusader, both dated and overdue for replacement.*

Without a carrier, the RN still needed helicopters for antisubmarine operations, and it soon fastened upon the earlier Escort Cruiser idea as a combination helicopter and commando ship. There was one new ingredient, the British Aerospace Harrier, which had been of little interest as long as the RN had had access to large flight-decks with big catapults and arrester gear. It was adapted to naval operations, with a dual-purpose (air-to-air and air-to-surface) radar. In this form it was a STOVL (short take-off/vertical landing) aircraft, since it used the flight-deck for a rolling take-off. It turned out that the Harrier could exploit a ramped ('ski jump') flight-deck, which gave it extra lift as it took off, to carry greater weights.

The idea of reviving British naval aviation by using the Harrier on board a small carrier was not greeted with universal enthusiasm. Money was limited; to build even a small carrier (cruiser) would cut resources for submarines and surface escorts. Moreover, the smaller the carrier the more expensive each aircraft spot, and the smaller the aircraft capacity per ton. Because British practice was to stow all aircraft in the hangar, the hangar determined aircraft capacity. When the new small carrier, HMS *Invincible*, was designed, its turbine uptakes and downtakes occupied considerable space on either side amidships, limiting her hangar to a dumbbell shape. Aeroplanes with fixed wings (Harriers) could not be stowed amidships.

The advent of the Sea Harrier had made it possible to operate more-or-less modern aircraft from ships less than a third the size of contemporary US carriers. However, small size limited the number of such aircraft, initially to only five Harriers per ship. The new carriers were supposed to operate very differently from their predecessors. Just as the Escort Cruiser had removed the helicopters from the carrier, the missile destroyers operating with the small carrier were intended to take over the fleet air-defence role, using their Sea Dart weapons. In theory, the RAF would help, using long-range fighters based in Scotland; but as early as 1977 exercises showed that this was unlikely. The problem is one of timing. No matter how alert the defences, an aircraft from a distant airfield is unlikely to arrive in time to deal with a sudden attack. At any rate, the new Sea Harrier was thought of more as a strike weapon than as an interceptor.

Thus, between about 1975 and 1980 the Sea Harrier was considered to be almost a manned missile used to strike at sea and shore targets. The very small air wing was justifiable if land attacks were likely to be mounted with nuclear weapons. For sea attack, the Sea Harrier was intended to deliver a powerful Sea Eagle missile. The real problem was how potential targets might be located. Given a very small number of aircraft, the last thing that might have been desirable would have been

British Aerospace Sea Harrier FRS.1s of 800 and 899 Squadron aboard Hermes, *with a pair of Westland Sea King HAS.5 antisubmarine helicopters of 826 Squadron for company.*

for them to use their radars to search. The radar radiation would have given them away; few if any would have survived to hit their targets.

Fortunately, the USN had a new anti-ship missile, Tomahawk, which it hoped would give its submarines and surface combatants a way of striking Soviet warships from well beyond their horizons. Its solution was to maintain a database of Soviet warship (and other) movements at ashore centres (Fleet Command Centres), transmitting the picture thus obtained to fleet units by means of a special satellite datalink. The RN became part of this programme; it built its own Fleet Command Centre at Northwood. Given data on expected Soviet ship positions, a Sea Harrier could be sent into the area of the target, then limit its search to that area.

The Harrier drastically lowered the cost of naval air power, at least at a minimum level. It was bought by the Indian, Italian, Spanish and Thai navies, in each case to equip a small carrier or carriers. It was also bought by the USMC, as a very handy means of bringing firepower to bear near a battlefield. Once the Marines were operating Harriers it was impossible for them to resist the temptation to place some aboard their large-deck amphibious ships, which previously had operated only helicopters. The Second World War organic air-support capability had been resurrected. This ability was exercised for the first time off Kuwait in 1991.

The USN did not, of course, escape from the 1970s unscathed. It lost its specialist ASW carriers (the CVS). These ships had been practicable to operate only because the Second World War programme had provided so many large carriers, which became surplus as postwar attack carriers were completed. As in the case of the RN, the USN had to face block obsolescence and the potential cost of block replacement. As early as 1963 it was clear that the CVSs would not be replaced. Their capability was important, but not sufficiently important to justify building several such ships. The solution, in the 1970s, was to move the antisubmarine aircraft on to the already crowded carriers. At the same time the ships were fitted with the necessary command centres, to become multipurpose carriers (CV rather than attack carriers, CVA). Initially the ASW aircraft added to the attack carriers were Grumman S-2 Trackers. As the only piston-engined aircraft aboard, they required that ships be fitted to carry dangerous aviation gasoline. Soon, however, they were retired in favour of the current Lockheed S-3 Viking, a jet. With the demise of the Soviet submarine threat, Vikings have been modified to improve their ability to attack surface ships. During the Gulf War they even led strike groups against land targets.

The ASW aircraft complicated carrier operations. An aircraft carrier runs its deck in a cycle, dominated by the endurance of the aircraft. The shorter the endurance, the more critical it is to recover aircraft in time. Fighters, for example, are expected to spend about sixty to ninety minutes on CAP stations; the distance from the carrier to the stations depends on their endurance. A carrier providing CAP to a fleet is almost constantly recovering and launching fighters. Because of their much longer endurance, antisubmarine aircraft follow a radically different cycle. Strikes are yet a different matter, with numerous aircraft being launched in quick succession, then returning together. Consequently, one carrier might provide day CAP, a second night CAP, a third antisubmarine protection, and a fourth would launch strikes.

Unfortunately it is very rare for four carriers to work together, simply because carriers are few and demands on them are many. From the mid-1950s onwards the USN's role was to deal with sudden crises all over the world. To do that the Navy maintained its carriers in forward areas, particularly the Mediterranean and the Far East. During the Cold War the Mediterranean carriers were responsible for quick air strikes against Soviet forces massing to invade Turkey, and also for attacks against the Black Sea Fleet bases in the Crimea. The Far East situation was more complicated, partly because the theatre was so much larger. Until the early 1970s, US strategists tried to cover both the Soviet Far East and China, so they had to maintain credible strike forces both north and south. The minimum in any one area was two carriers, to provide a spare deck in the event one was damaged or disabled by accident (which was not unusual). That meant two in the Mediterranean and three in the Far East (the third carrier could swing north or south).

To maintain one carrier on a distant station, the USN needed a total of three: one on station, one working up or returning to the USA, and one refitting. Thus to keep five carriers constantly forward-deployed took a total of fifteen ships, the Navy's ideal from about 1955 onwards. In a major war, ships returning or working-up would have been added. Thus the Atlantic ships would have formed the core of the NATO Strike Fleet, attacking the northern flank of any Soviet advance into Europe. A similar strike group would have formed in the Pacific.

These concepts began to break down during the 1970s. As the older carriers retired, the USN found itself with just twelve in active service. Fortunately, at the same time the hostility between the USA and China dissipated, so that it was no longer so important to cover two Far East stations simultaneously. At the end of the 1970s, however, a new problem arose with the fall of the Shah of Iran. The USA decided to maintain a presence in the Arabian Sea, which gave rise to an official directive that a carrier would constantly occupy a box from any part of which it could steam to deliver an air strike against a set target within a set short period of time. The Arabian Sea presence was extremely onerous, because a carrier was not considered on station even if it was a day out of the box. It took many more than three ships to keep one on station, given so strict a definition of presence.

Money was very tight after the end of the Vietnam War. In theory, the US carrier force should have been re-equipping with a new fighter, the Grumman F-14 Tomcat, replacing the F-4. The Tomcat had been developed mainly as an all-weather fleet air-defence aircraft, exploiting swing-wing technology to land slowly enough despite its very high maximum performance. Unfortunately it inherited the turbofan engine of the F-111, which drastically limited its performance. A planned F-14B, with a new engine, did not materialise (the designation was re-used later) because money was short; the Navy bought underpowered F-14As instead. Meanwhile, the USAF bought the large, expensive F-15. It seemed that, given tight funding, neither Service could afford sufficient numbers of fighters.

Some in the Department of Defense saw a way out: a low-cost lightweight fighter optimised for high performance. Ideally, both Services would buy the same aeroplane, to save more money by buying it in large numbers. To encourage innovation, the Defense Department held a fly-off, the final contestants being General Dynamics (with the single-engine F-16) and Northrop (with the twin-engine F-17). As it happened, the Navy refused to buy the single-engine fighter. It did not offer enough size (for a radar dish), endurance, reliability or growth potential. Instead McDonnell received a contract to redesign the F-17 for carrier operations, as the F-18. To save money, the same airframe would be used as a light bomber, the A-18, replacing the subsonic A-7. The result was not nearly as capable as an F-14, but it was much less expensive to buy and to operate. Hitherto, fighters and bombers had required different radars, because their sets did rather different jobs. By the late 1970s it was possible to build a radar controlled by computer software, and a computer system which could adapt itself to either air-to-air or air-to-surface combat; the same aeroplane could do both jobs. The F/A-18 Hornet was born. It could supplement the F-14 and it could replace the A-7.

Money for carrier aircraft was tight during the 1970s, partly because the carriers' role was under attack. In the aftermath of Vietnam, the new Chief of Naval Operations, Admiral Elmo Zumwalt, feared that the Navy would be cut drastically. To defend it he tried to fence off missions which were exclusively naval; sea control and power projection. A USA withdrawing upon itself after Vietnam was less than interested in power projection, so the carrier's future depended on its role in sea control. To many that meant antisubmarine warfare, hardly a large carrier's strong suit. Zumwalt was well aware of the threat presented by Soviet land-based bombers. He envisaged convoy operations, in which a big carrier would cover a convoy. The carriers would be split up. Within the Navy, however, Zumwalt's form of

analysis was widely seen as potentially disastrous. Carriers are the most multi-purpose units of a service that is valuable mainly because of its flexibility.

Zumwalt feared that, with the demise of the CVS, Soviet submarines might be able to operate far too freely on the world's oceans. He wanted some way of reviving CVS capability at an affordable price, and he hit upon the idea of building a series of small carriers which he called 'sea-control ships' (SCS), which would operate a mixture of antisubmarine helicopters and VTOL fighters. Innovative tactics would be used. For example, in a test conducted from an amphibious ship, a Harrier laid down a lane of sonobuoys which the ship and her convoy might steam. The buoys indicated any attempt by a submarine to enter the lane and threaten the ships. A helicopter maintained at readiness on board the ship could, in theory, intercept the submarine. As for air defence, airborne warning was to have been provided by an unmanned high-altitude airship which could track the carrier, to stay with the formation.

Zumwalt's sea-control ships were never built, but a modified version was built for the Spanish Navy, and a reduced version of that ship was later built for Thailand. Both operate a mix of helicopters and Sea Harrier fighter-bombers. For the USN the last gasp of the sea-control ship idea was the decision to build some sea-control features into the latest class of large amphibious carriers, the *Wasp*-class LHDs, which can operate USMC Harriers.

President Jimmy Carter took office in 1976, determined to mend fences with Third World countries. Power projection, the great role of the big carriers, seemed anathema. Carter refused to build a carrier during his term of office. He wanted the Navy to concentrate on the degree of sea control needed to ensure that Europe could be reinforced in wartime.

Matters began to change even before Carter left office early in 1981. In 1979, with the Shah's fall, it became painfully obvious that the USA had real interests in places in the Third World which only carrier aircraft could reach. At the same time the Pacific Fleet under Admiral Tom Hayward began to press for a more aggressive maritime strategy, in which carrier air strikes would be used to affect Soviet wartime strategy.

These ideas crystallised under Ronald Reagan and his Secretary of the Navy, John Lehman. The carriers were central. New technology made it possible for them to change their tactics. With the advent of a really effective anti-aircraft missile system – Aegis – carrier-based fighters were no longer needed to shoot down Soviet bomber-launched missiles fired at the fleet. Instead, they could concentrate on destroying the bombers, i.e. on seizing sea control by destroying the Soviet threat to that control. The new concept was called the Outer Air Battle. Ideally, fighters would no longer orbit on station, waiting for an attack. Instead they would wait on deck, to be launched

An unusual view of a McDonnell Douglas F/A-18 Hornet multi-mission fighter as it moves into position for a catapult launch. The cost of modern combat aircraft has made it necessary for them to be capable of performing a variety of roles.

toward the bombers, intercepting them as far out as possible, before they could fire their missiles. It became vital to detect the bombers as early as possible. To do that, the USN developed a Relocatable Over-the-Horizon Radar (ROTHR), which could be set up as needed (plans called for installations in the Aleutians and in northern Scotland). Land- or carrier-based electronic reconnaissance aircraft (mainly EP-3Es and ES-3s) might even be able to pick up the chatter of Soviet bomber crews getting ready to take off. Special fighter tactics with names like 'chainsaw' and 'grid logic' were developed.

The point of the Outer Air Battle was not simply to defend a carrier. It was to destroy the Soviet naval air arm, a major threat to free wartime use of the sea. The Soviets had to have some reason to throw their valuable bombers against well-defended carrier battle groups, and the carriers' attack aircraft were that reason. By the early 1980s the long-range strike bomber, the Intruder, was ageing. It had to be replaced. Secretary Lehman faced a dilemma. He knew that the new technology of stealth was very promising but also somewhat risky. McDonnell Douglas, which made the F/A-18, offered him a two-seat strike version, while Grumman offered an upgraded Intruder, the A-6F. Lehman saw the two-seat F/A-18 as only an interim step, which the advent of stealthy attack aircraft would make pointless. He chose to buy the upgraded A-6 to save enough money to pay for a stealthy successor, the A-12.

This gamble ended sadly. As the Cold War wound down in the late 1980s the very expensive US military aircraft programme was reviewed. Both the USAF and the USN were pursuing stealthy next-generation aircraft, the F-22 and the A-12, and it was already clear that both would be more expensive than expected. Unfortunately the A-12 proved more difficult to develop than had been imagined. Not only was it little-advanced at the time of review, but unfortunately it was described to Secretary of Defense Cheney as being on time and on cost. It was neither; the furious Secretary cancelled the programme. That the F-22 was already far more expensive proved irrelevant. A Navy attempt to buy a more modest next-generation strike aeroplane, the F/AX, also failed. Meanwhile, the A-6 upgrade had been killed to provide funds for the stealthy bombers.

As a result, by 1990 the USN had no successor strike aeroplane in its pipeline. Its only alternatives were to modify the existing F-14D (with new engines and much-improved avionics) as a strike bomber, or to grow the existing F/A-18. The F/A-18 was far less expensive, and it seemed to have more growth potential, so it was chosen. The resulting F/A-18E/F Super Hornet is about a quarter larger than its predecessor. It is far stealthier than an A-6, and it can carry a heavy load, but not to A-6 range. It can also replace the F-14 itself, carrying the AMRAAM air-to-air missile. An F/A-18 variant may also replace the EA-6B. Meanwhile, the A-6 follow-on requirement remains. It is to be filled by a new aeroplane, the Joint Strike Fighter (JSF), of which the USMC are to receive a STOVL version.

That leaves the two support aircraft, the E-2C and the S-3. The hope is that they can both be replaced by a common support aircraft which would be adapted to one role or the other (and possibly to the EA-6B role) largely by changing software and some palletised equipment. If this idea succeeds, then some time in the next century US carriers will be back where they were more than half a century ago, with only three distinct types of aeroplane on board.

One of the surprises of the Falklands conflict of 1982 was that surface-launched missiles could not destroy attacking enemy aircraft. Fighters, even the few Sea Harriers which the two British carriers could accommodate, were essential. The carriers had not been conceived with that sort of operation in mind. In particular, they lacked any means of detecting low-flying Argentinian aircraft; the last RN AEW aircraft had been given up nearly a decade earlier, with the large-deck carriers. After the conflict a solution was improvised: Sea King helicopters were fitted with special radars. Unfortunately helicopter endurance is limited, so the helicopters cannot provide anything like the round-the-clock coverage offered by, say, an E-2C on board a US large-deck carrier. The most important outcome of the war was a redefinition of the role of the Sea Harrier, emphasising its air-to-air capability. A modified version was developed with a new software-controlled dual-purpose radar (Blue Vixen), capable of guiding long-range AMRAAM air-to-air missiles. This version was designated Sea Harrier FA.2, i.e., Sea Harrier Fighter Attack Mk 2 rather than the initial FRS.1, for Fighter/Reconnaissance/Strike, and existing Sea Harriers were rebuilt to conform (new ones were also built).

As of 1998, then, the three main Western navies, those of the USA, Britain and France, all seem solidly committed to operating carriers well into the next century. Italy, Spain and Thailand have built STOVL carriers, and Brazil and India still operate old British light fleet carriers (in the Indian case, a much-enlarged version heavily rebuilt in the 1950s). Several countries, particularly China, seem poised to enter the carrier club some time in the next two decades.

That leaves the other side of the Cold War, the Soviet Union. Its experience was rather different than the West's. The Soviets had been interested in carriers, on and off, since well before the Second World War. In 1944 the Soviet naval staff was ordered to prepare a ten-year postwar programme based on wartime experience, and asked for several carriers. Stalin objected that they would be extremely expensive, and procurement was apparently deferred to the second postwar ten-year-plan period, which would have begun in 1954 or 1955.

However, there is tantalising evidence that heavy carrier bombers were ordered from Tupolev as early as 1950. One of them, the big turboprop Tu-91, actually flew. Some accounts say that it was shunted to land-based sea attack after Stalin's 1953 death killed off the projected carrier. On the other hand, at least two small carriers were apparently included in the 1956–60 Five Year Plan.

Khrushchev killed that programme in 1957, declaring that large surface ships were no more than missile targets. Apparently his navy was less convinced. In 1958 Khrushchev approved construction of two ASW cruisers. As the design progressed, countering US ballistic missile submarines became a primary Soviet naval role. A requirement was set that the ship be able to maintain two helicopters continuously airborne throughout her mission, i.e. that she accommodate eight. It resulted in a small semi-carrier, *Moskva*, which was completed in 1967.

Work had already begun on the design for a third ship, *Kiev*. *Moskva* was considered too small. The project was suspended in 1968 when aircraft designer Aleksandr Yakovlev proposed that it accommodate a combat version of his experimental Yak-36 VTOL aeroplane, which had just been publicly demonstrated. Given such aircraft, the ship might engage other ships and shore targets, and thus support amphibious operations. To back up the aircraft, it was given a battery of anti-ship missiles. The design began to grow. There were even versions equipped with catapults and MiG-23 fighters. Finally the design for what became the *Kiev* class was completed in December 1970. It was equipped with a combination of ASW helicopters and Yak-38 VTOL strike aircraft. Unlike the Harriers, Yak-38s could not make use of a ski-jump. They were intended primarily for surface attack, although they had limited air-to-air capability. Four *Kiev*-class carriers were built.

Although not altogether successful, the *Kievs* demonstrated what could be done with a carrier. The possibility of building a full carrier was debated through the 1970s; a design for a 75,000 to 80,000-ton (76,200 to 81,280-tonne) ship (with sixty to eighty-eight aircraft) was approved in 1973, only to be dropped. A formal decision to build two ships in 1978–85 was approved in April 1976, but then work stopped later in the year. Finally, a new design was approved in 1980. Attempts to obtain catapult technology having failed, the new carrier incorporated a ski-jump for its conventional fighters (MiG-29s and Su-27s). It was completed in December 1990 as *Admiral Flota Sovyetskogo Kuznetzov*. As the Soviet Union collapsed, a second ship, *Varyag*, was left incomplete at Nikolaev, in the Ukraine. A more ambitious project, the nuclear-powered *Ulyanovsk*, which would have had catapults, was cancelled in 1992 and broken up on the slip. At the time of writing the Russians are operating the *Kuznetzov* but are finding it difficult to pay for her maintenance. Of the six older carriers, all but the last (*Admiral Gorshkov*, a much-improved *Kiev*) have been sold for scrap, and the fate of the remaining one is unclear.

The mission of the fighter carrier was to protect Soviet naval forces, including strike bombers, from Western air attackers. Thus, had the Cold War turned hot, fighters from the ship might have been assigned to deal with F-14s heading north to the Outer Air Battle – or with P-3s and S-3s trying to sink Soviet attack submarines headed out into the North Atlantic.

Index